Ulrich Duchrow, Craig Nessan (Hg./Eds.)

Befreiung von Gewalt zum Leben in Frieden
Liberation from Violence for Life in Peace

Die Reformation radikalisieren
Radicalizing Reformation

herausgegeben von/edited by

Ulrich Duchrow
(Heidelberg)

Daniel Beros
(Buenos Aires)

Martin Hoffmann
(San José, Costa Rica/Nürnberg)

Hans G. Ulrich
(Erlangen)

Band/Volume 4

Befreiung von Gewalt zum Leben in Frieden

Liberation from Violence for Life in Peace

herausgegeben von/edited by

Ulrich Duchrow und / and Craig Nessan

LIT

Bibliografische Information der Deutschen Nationalbibliothek
Die Deutsche Nationalbibliothek verzeichnet diese Publikation in der
Deutschen Nationalbibliografie; detaillierte bibliografische Daten sind
im Internet über http://dnb.d-nb.de abrufbar.

ISBN 978-3-643-12974-1

© **LIT** VERLAG Dr. W. Hopf Berlin 2015
Verlagskontakt:
Fresnostr. 2   D-48159 Münster
Tel. +49 (0) 2 51-62 03 20   Fax +49 (0) 2 51-23 19 72
E-Mail: lit@lit-verlag.de   http://www.lit-verlag.de

Auslieferung:
Deutschland: LIT Verlag Fresnostr. 2, D-48159 Münster
Tel. +49 (0) 2 51-620 32 22, Fax +49 (0) 2 51-922 60 99, E-Mail: vertrieb@lit-verlag.de
Österreich: Medienlogistik Pichler-ÖBZ, E-Mail: mlo@medien-logistik.at
E-Books sind erhältlich unter www.litwebshop.de

INHALT

Einführung in die neue Reihe	11
Introduction to the New Series	19
Die Reformation radikalisieren – provoziert von Bibel und Krise 94 Thesen	26
Radicalizing Reformation – Provoked by the Bible and Today's Crises 94 Theses	49
Introduction	71
1. Summons to Repentance	72
2. Imperative of Global Economic Justice	73
3. Heeding the Cry of the Earth	73
4. Appeal for Radical Peacemaking	74
5. Need for Interreligious Reconciliation	75
6. Call for a New Reformation	76
Beyond Luther to ethical Reformation: Peasants, Anabaptists, Jews Craig L. Nessan	77
1. Religious Identity Politics Today: Abortion, Homosexuality, and the State of Israel	78
2. Religious Identity Politics in Luther: Peasants, Anabaptists, and Jews	80
2.1 Luther against the Peasants	80
2.2 Luther against the Anabaptists	85
2.3 Luther against the Jews	90
3. Fallacy in Luther's Ethical Theology	95
4. Reconstructing Luther's Two Strategies as Neighbor Politics, Beginning with the Least	99
Abstract	102
Prejudice and its Historical Application: A radical Hermeneutic of Luther's Treatment of the Turks (Muslims) and the Jews: Charles Amjad-Ali	105
1. Introduction: Re-examining Fundamental "Truths" of Europe	105
2. The Multi-Cultural and Multi-Religious Context of Europe	107
3. Christianity as a Western Religion, Luther's Vitriol against Jews and Muslims	110

4. From Rome to Constantinople (the New Rum) and the Founding
     of Christendom ... 113
  5. The Pervasive Fear of Islam and the Crusades ... 116
  6. The Turkish Threat and the Apocalyptic Visions ... 119
  7. Medieval Christendom's Approach to Islam and the Jews ... 121
  8. Luther's Seeming Contradictory Views of Islam and the Turks ... 126
  9. Contra-Catholic Crusade and Anabaptist Pacifism, Luther
     on Christian Vocation and the Two Kingdom Theory ... 130
  10. The Anachronism of Cuius Regio Eius Religio and the de facto
      Exclusion of the Other ... 134
  11. The Essentialization of Islam, from Judenfrage to Muslimfrage
      and the Turkish Minorities in Germany ... 135
  12. The Use of Hermeneutical Subtilitas (Intelligendi, Explicandi,
      and Applicandi): Towards the Role of the Other in Human History ... 139
  Abstract ... 142

DAS EVANGELIUM ALLER KREATUR.
THOMAS MÜNTZERS UND HANS HUTS BOTSCHAFT FÜR DIE HEUTIGE WELT
Jaime Adrián Prieto Valladares ... 143
  Einleitung ... 143
  1. „Geet hin in die Welt und predigent das Evangelion aller Creaturen"
     (Markus 16,15): Ordo Dei ... 146
  2. „Geet hin in die Welt und predigent das Evangelion aller Creaturen"
     (Markus 16,15): Pflanzen und Tieren, allem Erschaffenem
     im Himmel und auf der Erde ... 153
  3. „Geet hin in die Welt und predigent das Evangelion aller Creaturen"
     (Markus 16,15): in der Ehrfurcht Elisabeths, Marias, Rahabs,
     Ruths und Judiths ... 158
  4. „Geet hin in die Welt und predigent das Evangelion aller Creaturen"
     (Markus 16,15): Nationen, Kulturen und Religionen ... 166
  5. „Geet hin in die Welt und predigent das Evangelion aller Creaturen"
     (Markus 16,15): der „gemeine Mann" ... 176
  6. „Geet hin in die Welt und predigent das Evangelion aller Creaturen"
     (Markus 15,16): Taufe in Feuer, Wasser und Blut ... 184
  7. „Geet hin in die Welt und predigent das Evangelion aller Creaturen"
     (Markus 16,15): „Christusförmig" werden und der wahre Freund
     Christus (verus Amicus Cristus) ... 189

Inhalt

8. Schlussfolgerungen für die Welt von heute: „Geet hin in die Welt und predigent das Evangelion aller Creaturen" (Markus 16,15) 195
Abstract 200

THE RESPONSIBILITY OF CONVICTION: CHRISTIAN PACIFISM
Antonio González Fernández 202
  1. Responsibility and Conviction 202
  2. The "Just War" 204
  3. Analysis of Responsibility 209
  4. Responsible Conviction 211
  5. Universal Responsibility 214
  6. The Pacifism of Jesus 216
  7. Conclusion 221
Abstract 222

MIGRATIONS OF ENCHANTMENT IN THE RADICAL REFORMATION
THE UNDOING OF A MATERIAL AND NATURAL WORLD
Karl Koop 223
  1. Dialectical Patterns of Enchantment 225
  2. Anabaptists and the Sacred 231
  3. Retrieving other Imaginaries 239
Abstract 243

REFORMATION RADIKAL: „BUEN VIVIR" –
EIN BEITRAG AUS LATEINAMERIKA
Claudete Beise Ulrich 244
  Einleitung 244
  1. „Buen Vivir", Bem viver", „Gutes Leben" – Begriff und Konzept 246
  2. Buen Vivir – Prinzipien und Wissen 248
  3. Politische Bedeutung 252
  4. Buen Vivir: Widerstand, Visionen, Hoffnung und Gnade Gottes 254
Abstract 260

DIE PSALMEN ALS MANTEL DES MESSIAS
Klara Butting 262
  1. Spiritualität ist „in" 262
  2. Die Einheit Gottes 263
  3. Reformation heute – Umkehr zum Alten Testament 266
  4. Das Mysterium der Einheit 269

5. Der Körper des Messias ... 275
Abstract ... 279

MARTIN LUTHER'S CONCERN FOR THE COMMON PERSON
IMPLICATIONS FOR THE PROCESS OF ECONOMIC GLOBALIZATION
Santhosh J. Sahayadoss ... 280
  1. Globalization and Its Impact ... 281
    1. 1. Salient Features of Globalization ... 281
    1.2 Globalization and Poverty ... 284
    1.3 Globalization and Greed that Negates the Interest
        of the Common Person ... 288
  2. Foundations on which Luther's Concern for Society are Built ... 292
    2.1 Defending Luther against Criticisms and Establishing Luther's
        Concern for Society ... 292
    2.2 Justification by Faith as Basis for Social Concern ... 293
    2.3 Luther's Two Kingdom Concept: A Call for Involvement
        in Society ... 296
    2.4 Re-visiting Luther's Involvement in the Peasant's Revolt ... 300
  3. Relevance of Luther's Theology and Ethics
    for the Globalized World ... 304
    3.1 Luther's Concern for the Common Person Reflected
        in the Bible Translation Work ... 304
    3.2 Luther's Interest in the Welfare of the Poor ... 306
    3.3 Luther's Ethical Concern in Trade and Commerce
        against Greed ... 308
  Abstract ... 314

MARTIN LUTHER AND REFORMATION THEOLOGY:
AN EAST ASIAN PERSPECTIVE
Paul S. Chung ... 316
  1. Luther and God's Pain in Japanese Colonial Context ... 317
  2. God's Suffering in Solidarity with Minjung ... 319
  3. Martin Luther: The Triune God and the Church ... 321
  4. Hermeneutic of the Gospel and Interpretation ... 322
  5. Gospel in the Midst of Political Witness ... 325
  6. God and Economic Justice ... 327
  7. God's Universal Reign and Creatio Continua ... 330
  8. Mission: Invitation and Dialogue ... 332

9. Conclusion	334
Abstract	336

EINE KRITISCHE WEITERFÜHRUNG REFORMATORISCHER IMPULSE
DIETRICH BONHOEFFER UND DOROTHEE SÖLLE

Renate Wind	338
1. Luthers Rechtfertigungslehre im Licht der Bergpredigt. Bonhoeffers Kritik an der „billigen Gnade" in der „Nachfolge"	338
2. Die Forderung nach einer neuen Reformation. Dorothee Sölles befreiungstheologische Aktualisierung	346
Abstract	354
AUTHORS/AUTORINNEN UND AUTOREN	355

Einführung in die neue Reihe

„Die Reformation radikalisieren – Radicalizing Reformation"

Wie soll man 2017 die 500jährige Wiederkehr des Beginns der Reformation begehen? Viel ist in diesem Zusammenhang über den Charakter der „Jubiläen" 1817 und 1917 geschrieben worden. Es wird kritisiert, dass die Reformation jeweils instrumentalisiert wurde für die zeitgeschichtlichen Interessen (der nationalistischen Romantik und des deutschen Imperialismus). Es kann aber gar nicht anders sein, als dass man von brennenden Fragestellungen der eigenen Zeit ausgeht. Man muss dies nur ausdrücklich reflektieren und die eigene Perspektive offenlegen.

So hat sich eine internationale Arbeitsgemeinschaft von Theologinnen und Theologen gebildet, die sich die Frage stellt: Von welcher Perspektive aus ist es sinnvoll, heute auf die Reformation zu blicken? Wir haben uns entschieden, eine Doppelperspektive zu wählen, die im Titel unseres Projekts zum Ausdruck kommt: *„Die Reformation radikalisieren – provoziert von Bibel und Krise"*. Das heißt, wir gehen von der umfassenden Krise des Lebens heute aus und blicken darauf und auf die Reformation samt Wirkungsgeschichte aus der Perspektive heutiger sozialgeschichtlicher Bibellektüre, d.h. inhaltlich aus der Perspektive der *Befreiung zum Leben in gerechten Beziehungen*. Was heißt das im Einzelnen?

Welches ist der historische Ort, der heute unsere Perspektive bestimmt und bestimmen sollte? Aus der Situation in den verschiedenen Weltregionen ist evident, dass global Menschen und Erde in ihren Lebenschancen gefährdet sind, wenn die Zivilisation, die jetzt umfassend herrscht, so fortgeführt wird wie bisher. Daraus folgt die

1. notwendige Dimension der heutigen Frage nach der Reformation: Was bedeutet die Reformation und ihre Wirkungsgeschichte im Blick auf die globale Gefährdung von Menschheit und Erde – sowohl positiv wie negativ?

Wenn der Grund für die Gefährdung mit der herrschenden Zivilisation zu tun hat, so ist zu fragen, was das heißt. Mit Zivilisation sind nicht nur das politisch-ökonomische System und die herrschende Kultur einschließlich Wissenschaft, Technik und Kunst gemeint, sondern auch Lebens-, Denk- und Verhaltensweisen der Menschen. Das heißt der Begriff versucht, den umfassenden Charakter des Problems zu verdeutlichen. Auf der anderen Seite besteht hier sogleich ein terminologisches Dilemma. Zivilisation hat in den Ohren unterworfener Völker seit dem Hellenismus und dem Römischen Reich, vor allem aber in den letzten 500 Jahren des europäischen und später nordamerikanischen Kolonialismus einen üblen Klang, weil der Begriff selbst imperialen Charakter hat. Es ist schwierig, einen anderen Begriff für dieses umfassende Phänomen zu finden. Das Wort System ist zu eng, weil es nicht die mentalen, psychischen und Verhaltenselemente von Menschen umfasst. Wahrscheinlich muss man den Begriff Kultur verwenden, obwohl dieser eigentlich überwiegend positive Bedeutung hat. Aber er kann auch gleichzeitig negativ und positiv verwendet werden. Das heißt, er kann sowohl die herrschende Kultur bezeichnen, von der die Gefährdung ausgeht, wie auch (relativ) eigenständige Kulturen, aber auch Gegenkulturen. Daraus folgt die

2. notwendige Dimension der heutigen Frage nach der Reformation: Die Reformation darf nicht nur in ihrem kirchlichen Sinn thematisiert werden, sondern muss auf ihre Beziehung zur Kultur im Ganzen befragt werden.

Inhaltlich ist die herrschende Kultur hegemonial von Europa und Nordamerika bestimmt, also vom „Westen". Allerdings hat sie die „Eliten" in allen Erdteilen ergriffen, so dass sie nicht etwa geografisch abgegrenzt werden kann. Deshalb spricht man auch vom „globalen Norden". Diese herrschende Kultur ist die der „Moderne". Hier liegt nun eine direkte Verbindung zur Frage der Reformation vor. Denn diese fällt genau in den Zeitraum, in dem die Moderne beginnt. Wir leben am Ende der Moderne, weil diese sich als tödlich, ja selbstmörderisch für Menschheit und Erde erweist. Daraus folgt die

3. notwendige Dimension der heutigen Frage nach der Reformation: Wie verhält sich die Reformation zur Moderne an deren Beginn, und zwar positiv wie negativ? Was hat dies uns und speziell den in der Tradition der Reformation stehenden Kirchen zu sagen, die wir das Ende der Moderne erleben, weil sie das Leben selbst gefährdet?

Wie lässt sich die westliche Moderne charakterisieren? Zwei fundamentale Charakteristika, aus denen weitere folgen, sind die herrschende Rolle des Geldes in der Form zu akkumulierenden Kapitals und zweitens imperialer Expansionismus. Es ist aber freilich sofort hinzuzufügen, dass dies nicht rein strukturell zu verstehen ist, sondern es hat eine subjektive Seite. Es geht einher mit mentalen Charakteristika, nämlich Rationalität im Sinn kalkulierenden, berechnenden Denkens (männliche Zweck-Mittel-Rationalität). Dies wiederum findet seinen Ausdruck einerseits in einer bestimmten Art von Wissenschaft, Technik und bürokratischer Herrschaftsorganisation, andererseits in ego-zentriertem Individualismus. Alle diese Merkmale sind wiederum stark an patriarchale Strukturen und Vorstellungen gekoppelt. Wenn diese Charakteristika mitverantwortlich sind für die Gefährdung des Lebens in Gegenwart und Zukunft, so ist wiederum zu fragen, wie sich die Reformation und ihre Wirkungsgeschichte zu ihnen verhalten, und was dies uns zu sagen hat. Daraus folgt die

4. notwendige Dimension der heutigen Frage nach der Reformation: Wie verhält sich die reformatorische Tradition zum imperialen Kapitalismus und zur Zweck-Mittel-Rationalität in Wissenschaft, Technik und individualistischer kalkulierender Mentalität?

Die Moderne ist aber nicht nur gekennzeichnet durch die angedeuteten Charakteristika, sondern auch durch kritische und emanzipatorische Bewegungen. Um nur einige Beispiele zu nennen: Rousseau widerspricht der Ausbeutung und Vergewaltigung der Natur, Karl Marx der Ausbeutung der arbeitenden Menschen. Er trägt so zur entstehenden Arbeiterbewegung bei. Die Frauenbewegung erkämpft immer mehr Rechte usw. Das heißt die Moderne ist ambivalent. Daraus folgt die

5. notwendige Dimension der heutigen Frage nach der Reformation: Wie verhalten sich die Reformation und die sich ihr anschließenden Kirchen zu den Emanzipationsbewegungen der Moderne?

Eingeschlossen im europäischen Imperialismus ist der Eurozentrismus. Seit 1492 Columbus die Aggression der Europäer gegen die Bevölkerungen der Amerikas richtete, haben die Kolonisatoren auch Güter anderer Kulturen geplündert. Das beginnt indirekt schon früher. Zum Beispiel wird bei dem Rückgriff auf die antike griechische Kultur verschwiegen, dass diese ohne andere Kulturen, insbesondere die asiatischen und vorderasiatischen früheren Kulturen, undenkbar ist. Zunehmend wird auch der Beitrag der jüdischen und islamischen Kultur zur europäischen verdrängt, seit im gleichen Jahr 1492 die Reconquista Juden und Muslime aus Spanien vertrieb. Daraus folgt die

6. notwendige Dimension der heutigen Frage nach der Reformation: Wie verhalten sich die Reformation und die ihr folgenden Kirchen zur Integrität anderer Kulturen und Religionen? Ist unsere Perspektive konsequent postkolonial?

Nach welchen Kriterien aber stellen wir all diese Fragen? Das implizite Kriterium der bisherigen Argumentation ist: Leben in seiner geschenkten Vielfalt und Fülle. Denn angesichts der generellen Gefährdung des Lebens unter den herrschenden Verhältnissen muss die Ermöglichung von Leben in der Zukunft das fundamentalste Kriterium sein (vgl. Joh 10:10). Anders ausgedrückt: Wir urteilen mit der reproduktiven Vernunft (im Unterschied zur instrumentellen Zweck-Mittel-Rationalität der Moderne). Auch Luther beruft sich immer wieder auf das Kriterium der Vernunft, allerdings gebunden an die Heilige Schrift. Insbesondere alle Tradition beurteilt er nach dem Kriterium der Vernunft und der Bibel (sola scriptura). Dabei gibt er dem historischen Literalsinn der Texte hermeneutische Priorität. Genau an dieser Stelle hat die sozialgeschichtlich arbeitende Bibelexegese einen großen Reichtum an Einsichten gebracht. In der 1. unserer 94 Thesen drücken wir das so aus: „Biblisch gesehen ist die erste und eigentliche Tat Gottes Befreiung. Auch die messianische Befreiung im Neuen Testament ist nach dem Muster des Exodus gestaltet. Im *Römerbrief* geht es Paulus darum, dass Christus Befreiung von der ‚Schreckensherrschaft der Sünde' bringt (Röm 5,12-8,2). Wird Rechtfertigung dagegen nicht im Exodus-Muster verstanden, sondern wie weithin üblich in der Linie Augustin/Anselm von Canterbury auf (Ur-)Schuld und Vergebung reduziert, bedeutet das eine problematische Verengung mit erheblichen Verlusten gegenüber dem sozialen und politischen Reichtum der Bibel." Wenn man also Luthers eigenes Kriterium zugrunde legt, ist die reformatorische Tradition selbst nach dem Kriterium der Schriftgemäßheit zu beurteilen. Daraus folgt die

7. notwendige Dimension der heutigen Frage nach der Reformation: Wie sind die theologischen Positionen der Reformation und der ihr folgenden Kirchen unter dem doppelten Kriterium zu beurteilen – der Lebensförderlichkeit (reproduktiver Vernunft) und der Bibel in sozialgeschichtlicher Präzision, inhaltlich also unter dem Kriterium der Befreiung zur Gerechtigkeit.

Wenn man die Ergebnisse der sozialgeschichtlichen Bibelforschung zugrunde legt, kommt man nämlich zu dem Kanon im Kanon der biblischen Schriften: Gottes Gerechtigkeit, die Israel und aus dieser Wurzel hervorgehend Menschen aus allen Völkern zur Teilnahme an dieser Gerechtigkeit befreit. Das Ziel ist shalom, umfassender Friede in gelingenden Beziehungen. In dieser historischen Dynamik tritt Gott als Mitleidende den Opfern von Ungerechtigkeit und Gewalt an die Seite und inspiriert sie mit transformativem Geist, um sie selbst zu Subjekten neuer Gemeinschaften zu machen. Dies ist nicht zu verstehen als dogmatisch-begriffliche Quintessenz, sondern als der Horizont, in dem die konfliktreichen Texte der Großen biblischen Erzählung zu lesen sind. In diesem Horizont kann es angesichts der lebensbedrohenden gegenwärtigen Krise nur um tägliche Umkehr gehen – genau in dem Sinn, den Luther in der ersten der 95 Thesen von Jesus übernimmt: „Gottes gerechte Welt ist nahe – Kehrt um!" Daraus folgt die

8. notwendige Dimension der heutigen Frage nach der Reformation: Hat die Reformation und haben Kirchen in der reformatorischen Tradition bis heute an Gottes Befreiungshandeln zur Gerechtigkeit teilgenommen, und lässt sich aus dieser Tradition heute noch schöpfen, wenn es darum geht, zu einer neuen Kultur des Lebens in gerechten Beziehungen umzukehren?

Aus diesen Erwägungen heraus haben wir unser Projekt also genannt: *„Die Reformation radikalisieren – provoziert von Bibel und Krise"*. Das bedeutet: Wir fragen nach der Reformation nicht aus historischen Gründen, sondern bewusst im Kontext der lebensgefährlichen Krise, in der sich Menschheit und Erde befinden. Und wir fragen nach der Wurzel der Reformation, die sie selbst als Heilige Schrift angibt (darum „Die Reformation radikalisieren", also an die Wurzel gehen).

Bei dieser Art von Fragestellung haben wir eine interessante Entdeckung gemacht. Die Kultur der Moderne, die durch Kapitalismus, Kolonialismus und kalkulierenden Individualismus gekennzeichnet ist, hat ihre Vorgeschichte in den Entwicklungen des Alten Orient (von China bis zum Mittelmeer) genau in der Zeit seit dem 8. Jh. v.u.Z., in denen der Großteil der biblischen Schriften entstanden ist. Der Philosoph Jaspers nennt diese Geschichtsepoche die Achsenzeit, weil dort alle bis heute wirksamen Philosophien und Weltreligionen entstanden sind. Was er nicht beachtet, ist allerdings die sozialgeschichtliche Beobachtung, dass gerade in dieser Zeit die frühe Geldwirtschaft entsteht und sich mit den Imperien verbindet. Der Höhepunkt dieser frühen Entwicklung sind die hellenistischen Reiche und das Imperium Romanum – letzteres der Kontext der messianischen Schriften des Neuen Testaments. Das heißt, die biblischen Schriften beziehen sich explizit kritisch auf die Mechanismen der Geldwirtschaft und die Verbindung mit imperialer Politik und Verhaltensweisen, deren neue Stufe im Frühkapitalismus Luther erlebte und deren Klimax wir heute im imperialen Finanzkapitalismus erfahren. Somit ist über die Kontextanalyse ein hermeneutischer Zusammenhang zwischen Bibel, Reformation und gegenwärtiger Krise auszumachen, den es im einzelnen zu bearbeiten gilt.

Genau dies ist der Sinn der zweisprachigen *Publikationsreihe unter dem Titel „Reformation radikal"*, die mit fünf Bänden in der ersten Hälfte des Jahres 2015 eröffnet wird. Sie zielt auf die interdisziplinäre Zusammenarbeit zwischen sozialgeschichtlicher Bibelexegese, Reformationsgeschichte und kritisch systematischer Theologie angesichts der epochalen Krise, in der wir uns befinden. Die folgenden Publikationen enthalten auch 94 Thesen, die die Kapitel der fünf ersten Bände zuspitzen.

Band 1: Befreiung zur Gerechtigkeit

Hier geht es um das Herzstück der Reformation: Rechtfertigung – Gesetz – Evangelium. Zentral ist dabei die kritische Perspektive der neuen Paulusdeutung gegen die individualistische Auslegung, die Gottes Gerechtigkeit und Befreiung auf das westliche Ich umdeutet und den kalkulatorischen Kapitalismus vorbereitet; gegen die Identifikation des tötenden Gesetzes mit der Tora statt mit dem Gesetz des römischen Imperiums; gegen die schroffe Entgegensetzung von Gesetz und Evangelium, die die Loslösung des NT vom AT bewirkt und Antijudaismus und Antisemitismus hervorruft.

Band 2: Befreiung vom Mammon

Diese Fragestellung verbindet Bibel, Reformation und heutige Krise: das Geld in religiöser, politisch-ökonomischer und mentaler Perspektive. Im AT und NT wirkt die imperiale Herrschaft des Geldes als strukturelle Sünde, die alle zu Mittäterinnen und Mittätern macht. Gottes Befreiung vollzieht sich wesentlich über die Bildung torageleiteter und neuer messianischer Gemeinschaften, die Solidarität statt egozentrischen Individualismus praktizieren. Dem entspricht Luthers Verwerfung des käuflichen Heils ebenso wie seine systemische Kritik des Individualismus und des Frühkapitalismus.

Band 3: Politik und Ökonomie der Befreiung

Luther übt systemische Kritik am Frühkapitalismus. Er durchschaut den religiösen Charakter des Kapitalismus auf der Basis des 1. Gebots. Seine Schriften zum Handel und Wucher (Finanzsystem) sind zwar im Protestantismus am Rande wirksam geblieben (wie z.b. bei Winstanley im 17.Jh.), aber insgesamt sind die lutherischen Kirchen dieser kritischen Perspektive nicht gefolgt. Erst in jüngster Zeit sind die Potenziale der Position Luthers für die Kritik am Neoliberalismus und für eine politische Ethik der Parteinahme und der Versöhnung wiederentdeckt worden.

Band 4: Befreiung von Gewalt zum Leben in Frieden

Das lateinamerikanische Buen Vivir kann als Kriterium einer neuen Kultur des Lebens gelten. Danach sind viele Fehlentwicklungen in und nach der Reformation aufzuarbeiten: Die Wiedergewinnung der politischen Lektüre der Bibel und der materiellen Naturbasis als Medium des Glaubens und des Kircheseins; die Überwindung der gewalttätigen „religiösen Identitätspolitik" Luthers gegenüber Bauern, Täufern, Juden und Muslimen; eine postkoloniale Perspektive auf Luther; der Durchbruch zu aktiver Gewaltfreiheit – eine „neue Reformation" im Sinn Bonhoeffers und Sölles.

Band 5: Kirche – befreit zu Widerstand und Transformation

Das Kreuz ist ein Zeichen des Bösen, des Trosts für alle, die gefoltert werden und leiden, ein Zeichen der Hoffnung und der Befreiung. Jesus Christus nimmt die sozio-politischen, kulturellen und wirtschaftlichen Bedingungen derer auf sich, die ihrer Rechte beraubt werden. Die Kirche muss ihren Bestand aufs Spiel setzen, indem sie mit den und für die Armen lebt. In der Sünde leben wir getrennt, durch den Geist werden wir wieder miteinander verbunden. Der Geist wirkt frei in den Menschen und in der Welt, darum auch in nichtchristlichen Religionen. Statt sich nur auf die einzelnen Individuen zu konzentrieren, gehört es zum Wesen der Kirche, einen gemeinschaftlichen Ansatz für Widerstand und Transformation zu entwickeln.

Dies sind in Kürze die ersten Versuche, den Ansatz „Die Reformation radikalisieren – provoziert von Bibel und Krise" in konkrete Forschungen umzusetzen. Wir rechnen damit, dass diese Fragestellung so fruchtbar ist, dass weitere Veröffentlichungen folgen werden. Leider können wir die Bände aus finanziellen Gründen nicht vollständig in gleichzeitig Englisch und Deutsch vorlegen. Allerdings werden wir die vorhandenen Übersetzungen zunehmend auf unsere Website stellen: www.radicalizing-reformation.com. Dort werden auch solche Originale veröffentlicht, die ursprünglich in Portugiesisch oder Spanisch geschrieben wurden.

Wir danken herzlich allen Institutionen, die unser Projekt bisher finanziell unterstützt haben: Ökumenischer Rat der Kirchen (ETE), Evangelisches Missionswerk (EMW), Brot für die Welt, Evangelische Kirche in Deutschland (EKD), die Evangelischen Landeskirchen in Baden, Hannover, Mitteldeutschland und Westfalen.

Daniel Beros, Ulrich Duchrow, Martin Hoffmann, Hans G. Ulrich

INTRODUCTION TO THE NEW SERIES "RADICALIZING REFORMATION"

How shall we deal with the quincentenary of the Reformation in 2017? There has been much discussion about the character of the "celebrations" in 1817 and 1917. People criticize that in each of these cases the Reformation was manipulated in service of powerful contemporary interests (e.g. Romantic nationalism or German imperialism). However, there is no other way than to start with the burning issues of one's own time. The key challenge is to reflect upon the issues and put one's own position clearly on the table.

With this understanding an international group of theologians has come together to ask the question: From which angle does it make sense to look at the Reformation today? We have decided to choose a double perspective as the title of our project reveals: *"Radicalizing Reformation – Provoked by the Bible and Today's Crises"*. This means we start from the multiple crises of life today and look at them together with the Reformation, including its impact on history, from the perspective of socio-historic Bible research, i. e. from the material perspective of *liberation for life in just relationships*. What does this mean in detail?

What is the historical place, or locus, which should shape our perspective? Looking at the situation in the different regions of the world we clearly see that the life of human beings and the Earth is threatened, if the dominant civilization continues as it is. From this follows the

1st *necessary dimension of today's perspective on the Reformation: What does the Reformation and its historical impact mean in view of the global threat to humanity and the Earth – both positively and negatively.*

If the cause of this threat has to do with the dominant civilization we have to ask what this means. The term civilization does not only refer to the system of political economy and science, technology and the arts but also people's way of living, thinking and behaving. So the term tries to indicate the all-embracing character of the problem. At the same time we have a terminological dilemma here. The word civilization has had a bad connotation in the ears of oppressed peoples since Hellenism and the Roman Empire, even more so in the last 500 years of European and later US colonialism because the term itself has an imperial character. It is difficult to find another concept for this all-encompassing phenomenon. The word system is too narrow, because it does not reflect the mental, psychological and practical elements of human behavior. Probably the only fitting term is *culture* although it has a predominantly positive meaning. Yet it has the capacity of expressing both positive and negative connotations, i.e. it can mean both the dominant culture, the source of the danger, and also (relatively) independent cultures and even counter-cultures. From this follows the

2nd necessary dimension of today's perspective on the Reformation: The Reformation must not be discussed in terms of its ecclesial meaning only but also in its relation to culture as a whole.

In terms of content and character Europe and North America, i.e. the "West", have been the hegemonic powers shaping the dominant culture. However, it has reached the "elites" in all parts of the earth so there is no way to limit it geographically. This is why we speak of the "global North". The dominant culture is what we call "modernity". With this term we have a direct connection to the age of the Reformation, because it is that period in which modernity began. We live at the end of modernity because it is turning out to be death-bound, indeed, suicidal for humanity and the earth. From this follows the

3rd necessary dimension of today's perspective on the Reformation: How does the Reformation relate to modernity at its beginning – positively and negatively? What does this say to us and our churches in the tradition of the Reformation as we experience the end of modernity because it is endangering life on earth?

How can we characterize western modernity? There are two fundamental features: first, the dominant role of money in the form of capital which has to be accumulated at all costs and, second, imperial expansionism. However, we have to immediately add that this is not just a structural phenomenon, it has a subjective side. It is accompanied by mental characteristics, namely rationality in the sense of calculating thinking (male means-end rationality). This, on the one hand, is expressed in a certain kind of science, technology and bureaucratic organization of dominion, on the other hand in egocentric individualism. All these features are again linked to patriarchal structures and conceptions. If all these characteristics are co-responsible for endangering life today and in the future we have to ask how the Reformation and its historical impact relate to them and what this has to say to us. From this follows the

4th necessary dimension of today's perspective on the Reformation: How does the tradition of the Reformation relate to imperial capitalism and to the male means-end rationality in science, technology and individualistic calculating mentality?

Modernity is not only characterized by the above mentioned features, but also through critical and emancipatory movements. To mention only a few of them: Rousseau resists the exploitation and rape of nature, Karl Marx the exploitation of working people. He contributes greatly to the emergent labor movement. Women's movements struggle for and achieve more and more rights. This means that modernity is ambivalent. From this follows the

5th necessary dimension of today's perspective on the Reformation: How do the Reformation and the churches following from it relate to the emancipatory movements of modernity?

Eurocentrism is part and parcel of European imperialism. Beginning 1492 when Columbus started Europe's violent aggression against the indigenous people of the Americas the colonizers also looted the goods of other cultures. Indirectly this even starts earlier when the Renaissance draws upon Greek culture without mentioning that this is unthinkable without the other cultures from Asia. Since the Reconquista expelled Jews and Muslims from Spain in 1492 also the contribution of Jewish and Muslim culture to the European one has been neglected more and more. From this follows the

6th necessary dimension of today's perspective on the Reformation: How do the Reformation and the churches following from it relate to the integrity of other cultures and Religions? Is our perspective consistently post-colonial?

According to which criteria do we raise these questions? The implicit yardstick of the argument so far is *life in its fullness as a gift*. In view of the general danger for life under the dominant circumstances the most fundamental criterion must be: giving life in fullness the possibility to flourish even in the future (cf. John 10:10). In other words: we judge according to reproductive reason (in contrast to the means-end-rationality of modernity). Luther also claims to follow reason, yet linked to the Holy Scriptures. In fact, he judges all traditions according to the criteria of reason and scripture (sola scriptura). In doing so he gives hermeneutical priority to the historical, literal meaning of the texts. I n this respect, socio-historical Bible research has brought a great wealth of insights. In the 1st of our 94 Theses we put it this way: "From the perspective of the Bible, liberation is the first and foremost act of God. The messianic liberation in the New Testament also is shaped according to the model of the Exodus. In his letter to the Romans the Apostle Paul maintains that Christ brings liberation from the 'terrorizing domination of sin' (Rom 5:12-8:2). By contrast, when justification is not understood according to the pattern of the Exodus but reduced only to individual guilt and forgiveness (as in Augustine and Anselm of Canterbury), it is seriously cut off from the wide social and political richness of the Bible." So if we base our deliberations on Luther's own criterion, Scriptures, the tradition of the Reformation itself has to be judged according to the yardstick of whether it follows the Bible. From this follows the

7th necessary dimension of today's perspective on the Reformation: How can we understand and judge the theological positions of the Reformation and the resultant churches on the double criteria: 1. are they life-enhancing, 2. do they follow the Bible in socio-historic precision, which means in terms of content, do they contribute to liberation for justice?

The reason for this argument is the following: If we take the insights of socio-historical Bible research seriously, we arrive at the canon within the canon, which is God's justice/righteousness liberating Ancient Israel in the first place and then, out of this root, people of all nations towards this justice. The goal is shalom – an all-embracing peace in succeeding relationships. Within this historical dynamic God sides compassionately with the victims of injustice and violence, inspiring them with the transformative spirit to become the subjects of building new communities. This is not to be understood as dogmatic conceptual abstract, but as the context in which we can reread the conflicting texts of the Great Biblical Narrative. In this context the key challenge in view of the life-threatening crisis is to turn around every day (metanoia) – exactly in the sense of Jesus call "God's just world is near – turn around", quoted in the first of Luther's 95 theses. From this follows the

8th necessary dimension of today's perspective on the Reformation: Did the Reformation and the churches following from it participate in God's liberating actions towards justice to this day? Can we still today build on this tradition when we have to turn around towards developing a new culture of life in just relationships?

On the basis of these considerations we call our project *"Radicalizing Reformation – provoked by the Bible and Today's Crises"*. This means: We are not looking at the Reformation for historic reasons, but consciously in the context of the life-threatening crisis of humanity and earth. And we look at the root of the Reformation which itself defines this as being the Holy Scriptures (this is why we say "Radicalizing Reformation" – going back to the root=radix in Latin).

On the basis of this approach we made an interesting discovery. The culture of modernity, characterized by capitalism, colonialism and calculating individualism has its pre-history in developments of the Ancient Orient (from China to the Mediterranean) – precisely in that period starting in the 8th century BCE in which most of the biblical texts were written. The philosopher Karl Jaspers called this historical period the Axial Age because it saw the shaping of all world religions and philosophies that have influenced our thinking and feeling until today. What he does not realize, however, is the socio-historical observation that this was precisely the time when the early money economy emerged and linked up with empires. The climax of these early developments is the Hellenistic and Roman Empires – the latter being the context of the Messianic Scriptures of the New Testament. This means that the Bible explicitly confronts the mechanisms of the money economy and its linkage with imperial politics and behavior, booming again in Luther's time with early capitalism and finding its climax today with imperial financial capitalism. So via a context analysis we have a direct hermeneutical connection between the Bible, Reformation and today's crises, which can be elaborated in detail.

This is the objective of the bilingual book series titled *"Radicalizing Reformation"* starting with five volumes published in the first part of 2015. Our starting point is the general crisis of life today. We look at this crisis and the Reformation, including its impact on modernity, from the perspective of contextual Bible research, i.e. from the perspective of *liberation for life in just relationships*. According to Luther, all traditions have to be judged on the basis of Scripture. The following publications contain 94 theses which were distilled from the material of the 5 volumes.

Volume 1: Liberation towards Justice

Here we are dealing with the centerpiece of the Reformation: justification – law – gospel. Key is the new interpretation of Paul – against an individualistic understanding, reducing God's justice and liberation to the western Ego, thus preparing the way for calculating capitalism; against the identification of the Torah with the "killing law" instead of with the law of the Roman Empire; against the sharp antithesis of law and gospel leading to the separation of the New and Old Testament, to anti-Judaism and anti-Semitism.

Volume 2: Liberation from Mammon

This issue connects the Bible, Reformation and today's crisis: money in religious, political, economic and mental perspective. In the Old and New Testaments the imperial rule of money is understood as structural sin, making all people into co-perpetrators. God's liberation happens as the formation of Torah led to new messianic communities, which practice solidarity instead of egocentric individualism. This corresponds to Luther's rejection of purchasable salvation and his systemic critique of individualism and early capitalism.

Volume 3: Politics and Economy of Liberation

Luther systemically criticizes early capitalism. He is aware of the religious character of capitalism on the basis of the first commandment. His writings on trade and usury (finance) only marginally affected later Protestantism (e.g. Winstanley in the 17th century) but mainline Lutheranism did not follow this critical line. The potential of Luther's position for the theological critique of neoliberalism and for a political ethics of partisanship and reconciliation were rediscovered only recently.

Volume 4: Liberation from Violence for Living in Peace

The Latin American term, buen vivir, serves as a marker for a new, life-affirming culture. This approach can assist us in overcoming several misdirections generated through the Reformation – reclaiming a political interpretation of the Bible, affirmation of the materiality of the natural world as the foundation for faith and ecclesial existence, and overcoming the violent, "religious identity" policy of Luther against peasants, Anabaptists, Muslims, and Jews. This volume calls for a post-colonial reading of Luther and a radical turn toward active non-violent engagement. The authors advocate a "new Reformation" in the trajectory of Bonhoeffer and Soelle.

Volume 5: Church – Liberated for Resistance and Transformation

The cross is a sign of evil, of consolation for all those tortured and suffering, a sign of hope, of liberation. Christ takes on the socio-political, cultural and economic conditions of those who have been deprived of their rights. The church needs to risk its sustainability by being with and for the poor. Whereas in sin we are disconnected, through the Spirit we are re-connected. The Spirit works freely in people and the world, therefore also in other religions besides Christianity. Rather than being only focused on the person or individual, resistance and transformation should have a more communal *ecclesial* focus.

In short, these are the first attempts to implement the approach *"Radicalizing Reformation – Provoked by the Bible and Today's Crises"* in the form of specific research. We think that this way of asking questions will prove to be creative so that more publications will follow. We regret that due to financial reasons we are not in a position to publish the volumes fully in both English and German. However, we shall put the existing translations on our website: www.radicalizing-reformation.com. Here you shall also find some Spanish and Portugese originals.

We sincerely thank all institutions which have supported our project financially: World Council of Churches (WCC), Protestant Mission Service in Germany (EMW), Brot für die Welt, Protestant Church in Germany (EKD), the Protestant churches in Baden, Hannover, Mitteldeutschland and Westfalen.

Daniel Beros, Ulrich Duchrow, Martin Hoffmann, Hans G. Ulrich

Die Reformation radikalisieren – provoziert von Bibel und Krise

94 Thesen

"Ruft eine Befreiung aus im Land" (Lev 25,10)

Martin Luther begann seine 95 Thesen von 1517 mit der Umkehrforderung Jesu: "Kehrt um, die gerechte Welt Gottes ist nahe". Fünfhundert Jahre später leben wir in einer Zeit, die wie das biblische "Jobel-Jahr" („Erlassjahr", Lev/3. Mose 25) ebenfalls Umkehr und eine Veränderung hin zu gerechteren Verhältnissen anmahnt. Das sagen wir heute nicht im Gegensatz zur römisch-katholischen Kirche und den vielen in ihr verwurzelten Befreiungsbewegungen, sondern im Gegensatz zu den Strukturen des Imperiums, die gegenwärtig herrschen. Nur im Hören auf das Wort vom Kreuz (1 Kor 1,18) und das Seufzen der misshandelten Kreatur (Röm 8:22), nur wenn wir unsere Ohren öffnen für den Schrei der Opfer an der Unterseite unserer hyper-kapitalistischen Weltordnung kann das Reformationsjubiläum zum befreienden "Jubel-Jahr" werden. Christliche Selbstgerechtigkeit, die dieses System stützt, ist der reformatorischen Rechtfertigung aus Glauben entgegengesetzt. Rechtfertigung wird nur gelebt in umfassender Solidarität.

Wir sind Theologinnen und Theologen – vorwiegend lutherische, aber auch reformierte, mennonitische, anglikanische und methodistische –, die sich zu einem noch andauernden Projekt zusammengefunden haben, um die biblischen Wurzeln und gegenwärtigen Herausforderungen reformatorischen Denkens neu zu bedenken. Die ungezügelte Zerstörung menschlichen wie nicht-menschlichen Lebens in einer vom totalitären Diktat des Geldes und der Gier, des Marktes und der Ausbeutung regierten Welt erfordert eine radikale Rückbesinnung auf die biblische Weisung, wie sie auch am Beginn der Reformation stand. Das herrschende Wirtschaftssystem, gestützt durch imperiale politische Machtapparate, betreibt den Ausverkauf der Erde, des Menschen und der Zukunft unserer Kinder. Sowohl unsere Kirchen und Gemeinden als auch einzelne Christen und Christinnen haben sich vielerorts eingerichtet im gesellschaftlichen status quo und ihre kritisch-prophetische Kraft des Protestes, des Widerstandes und der Transformation verloren. Gottes Gerechtigkeit aus Gnade ist abgetrennt von sozialer Gerechtigkeit und wie „dummes Salz" nicht mehr zu gebrauchen (Mt 5:13). Es gibt Irrwege reformatorischer Theologie, von denen wir umkehren müssen – mit Luther, aber auch gegen Luther. Reformation kann auch heute wieder neu zum Kairos der Transformation werden.

Die folgenden Thesen reflektieren unterschiedliche geographische und politische Kontexte sowie ein breites Spektrum reformatorischer Traditionen. Zu ihrer Begründung veröffentlichen wir Forschungsergebnisse in fünf Bänden. Nicht in allen Punkten waren wir uns alle einig, aber gemeinsam und gerade in dieser Vielstimmigkeit und Vielförmigkeit wollen wir aufrufen zur Auseinandersetzung mit diesen Problemen – und zur Umkehr. Die gegenwärtige Krise, mit der wir in allen Lebensbereichen und bis in den letzten Winkel unserer Erde konfrontiert sind, ist eine Chance zur Einsicht in die barbarischen und (selbst)zerstörenden herrschenden Kräfte und trägt den Hoffnungskeim des Neubeginns zu einer neuen Kultur des Lebens in sich.

„Zur Befreiung hat uns der Messias befreit" (Gal 5,1)

1. Biblisch gesehen ist die erste und eigentliche Tat Gottes Befreiung. Auch die messianische Befreiung im Neuen Testament ist nach dem Muster des Exodus gestaltet. Im *Römerbrief* geht es Paulus darum, dass Christus Befreiung von der „Schreckensherrschaft der Sünde" im Kontext des Römischen Reiches bringt (Röm 5,12-8,2). Wird Rechtfertigung dagegen nicht im Exodus-Muster verstanden, sondern wie weithin üblich in der Linie Augustin/Anselm von Canterbury auf (Ur-)Schuld und Vergebung reduziert, bedeutet das eine problematische Verengung mit erheblichen Verlusten gegenüber dem sozialen und politischen Reichtum der Bibel.

2. Paulus analysiert die Sündenmacht, die im Römischen Reich alle Menschen gefangen hält. Die zentralen Aussagen über die Sünde (*hamartia*) haben alle einen gemeinsamen Nenner: dass sie in Herrschaftsbeziehungen (nur sehr selten in Kategorien der individuellen Schuld und des sündigen Tuns) gedacht sind. Paulus denkt, wenn er von Sünde spricht, vor allem an ihre umfassende Schreckensherrschaft. Seine zentrale Vorstellung ist: Die Sünde herrscht über alle Menschen wie über Sklaven und macht sie so zu MittäterInnen im imperialen System.

3. Paulus spricht vom Beginn eines umfassenden Herrschaftswechsels. Seine Hoffnung richtet sich auf Gottes endgültiges Eingreifen, das für ihn mit Jesu Auferstehung bereits begonnen hat. Paulus verfolgt keine politischen Ziele. Andererseits hat aber der Glaube an die Herrschaft Christi und die Hoffnung auf den endgültigen Herrschaftswechsel sehr tiefgreifende politische Konsequenzen. Hier wird geglaubt, dass Christus allein der Herr (kyrios) ist, dass seine Befreiung die ganze Welt, alle Menschen, den ganzen Menschen betrifft.

4. Der Glaube führt dazu, dass die Glaubenden in ihrem gemeinschaftlichen Leben und in ihrem Leben mit anderen sehr konkret schon als befreite Menschen zu leben versuchen. Die Gemeinschaft der Glaubenden versteht sich als Anfang eines neuen Lebens für alle. Dieser Bezug auf die Befreiung aus einer realen totalitären Lebenswirklichkeit wie im Römischen Reich ist für Menschen, die unter der Herrschaft der Finanz- und Gewaltmärkte leben, hilfreicher als die traditionelle Generalisierung der Sünde als Erbsünde.

„Ihr könnt nicht Gott dienen und dem Mammon" (Mt 6,24)

5. Mindestens zwei Milliarden Menschen sind verarmt unter der Herrschaft des Geldes. Diese ist der heutige Ausdruck des Mammon und damit die zentrale Herausforderung des Glaubens.

    Geld ist inzwischen nicht einfach das von den Zentralbanken gedruckte Bargeld in der Tasche, sondern Geschäftsbanken haben das Recht, über Kredite grenzenlos mehr zinsbelastetes Schuldgeld zu schöpfen. Schon Luther nennt Mammon den allgemeinsten Gott auf Erden (Großer Katechismus zum 1. Gebot).

6. Diese Herrschaft des Geldes und der theologische Widerstand dagegen entwickeln sich historisch mit der Ausweitung der auf Geld und Privateigentum beruhenden Wirt-

schaft – von der Monetarisierung des Wirtschaftslebens in der Zeit der Propheten über den Handels- und Wucherkapitalismus der Zeit Luthers bis zum modernen Industrie- und Finanzkapitalismus. Der inzwischen globalisierte Kapitalismus der Moderne ist seit der Reformationszeit mit der europäischen Ausbeutung, Kolonisierung und den Völkermorden in Afrika, Asien und den Amerikas verbunden.

7. *„Das Land darf nicht unwiderruflich verkauft werden, denn mir gehört das Land, und ihr seid Fremde und Leute mit Bleiberecht bei mir" (Lev 25,23).* Eigentum ist also nur für den Gebrauch zum Leben gedacht. Im Gegensatz dazu macht der Kapitalismus das Privateigentum absolut und beginnt deshalb mit der Einzäunung gemeinsamen Landes und aller natürlichen Ressourcen. Das setzt sich heute u.a. in der Privatisierung (Patentierung) des genetischen Gemeinguts der Menschheit, des Landes (land grabbing), des Wassers, der Luft usw. fort.

8. Der antike und moderne Individualismus beginnt mit dem Eindringen von Geld und Privateigentum in das tägliche Leben.
Für die meisten Menschen in der globalisierten kapitalistischen Welt ist Individualismus selbstverständlich. Für Luther gibt es Menschsein als neutrales, beobachtendes und kalkulierendes Individuum nicht. Entweder ist ein Mensch von Gott bestimmt – dann lebt dieser Mensch mitfühlend und gerecht von den Anderen her und zwar von den „Geringsten" (Mt 25,31ff.) zuerst. Oder ein Mensch ist von der Macht der Sünde bestimmt – dann lebt dieser Mensch in sich selbst verkrümmt, ich-bezogen, die anderen Kreaturen zerstörend.

9. Die von Kapitalakkumulation getriebene Wirtschaft erzwingt grenzenloses Wachstum. Dieses Wachstum gefährdet das gesamte Leben auf unserem Planeten. Menschen sind von Gott geschaffen mit dem Auftrag, *„den Garten zu bebauen und bewahren"* (Gen 2,15). Luther zitiert zu Beginn seiner 95 Thesen Jesu Ruf zur Umkehr: "Da unser Herr und Meister Jesus Christus spricht: 'Tut Buße' usw. (Mt 4,17), hat er gewollt, dass das ganze Leben der Gläubigen Buße sein soll." Das bedeutet für heute, dass wir täglich persönlich und gesellschaftlich aus der zerstörenden Geldherrschaft aussteigen und – vertrauend auf die befreiende Gerechtigkeit Gottes – mitfühlend und solidarisch in gerechten Beziehungen mit den anderen Menschen und Kreaturen leben.

10. Nach der Schrift gehören wir Menschen zu einem Leib mit vielen Gliedern, die einander dienen (1 Kor 12). Nach der kapitalistischen Logik und Praxis besteht dagegen unser Menschsein in Konkurrenz und Wettbewerb. Nach Luther werden wir als Mitarbeiterinnen und Mitarbeiter Gottes geschaffen, erhalten und erneuert, um uns kooperativ in Wirtschaft, Politik und Kirche für Gerechtigkeit und Frieden zu engagieren (Von der Unfreiwilligkeit des freien Willens). Damit ist Luther nach ersten Anläufen im Mittelalter in den Armutsbewegungen, bei den Waldensern, Wiclif und Hus derjenige, der auf biblischer Basis die seit dem 8. Jh. v.u.Z. aufkommende egozentrische, kalkulierende Geldzivilisation fundamental in Frage stellt.

11. Die wirtschaftliche Individualisierung spiegelt sich religiös in der Individualisierung des Heils. Die Bibel und Luther sprechen dagegen von befreiten Personen in gerechten Beziehungen.

    Seit dem Mittelalter gibt es spiritualisierende Strömungen, die immer noch stark in unseren Kirchen sind. Jede rein individualistische Lektüre und Predigt biblischer Texte unterstützt willentlich oder unwillentlich die moderne kapitalistische Zivilisation.

12. Nach Jesus ist gerecht, wer Schulden vergibt, also wer das Gesetz der Schuldenrückzahlung um des Lebens der Verschuldeten willen verletzt (Mt 6,12). Nach Paulus macht die Sündenmacht (zu seiner Zeit verkörpert in der strukturellen Sünde der römischen Gierökonomie und totalitären imperialen Macht) das Gesetz zu einem Instrument des Todes (Röm 7,7ff.). Er sieht die Alternative im Aufbau solidarischer Gemeinschaften aus Juden und Griechen im Geist des vom Imperium gekreuzigten Messias, der die von Rom zu Feinden gemachten Menschen mit Gott und untereinander versöhnt.

13. Die Mehrheit der Kirchenväter interpretiert den Tod Jesu am Kreuz u.a. so, dass der Teufel ein illegitimes Lösegeld für die Befreiung der Menschen erpresst, weil er niemals Schulden erlässt. Christus entlarvt dies und befreit uns. Anselm von Canterbury (1033-1109) kehrt diesen Ansatz in seiner sog. Satisfaktionslehre um. Nach ihm steht das Gesetz der Schuldenrückzahlung über Gott. Darum muss Gott seinen Sohn opfern, um ein Guthaben zu erwirtschaften, das die Menschen anzapfen können, um ihre unbezahlbaren Schulden gegenüber Gott abzuzahlen. Damit legt Anselm nicht nur den Grund für die mittelalterliche Bußpraxis des

Schuldengeschäfts, mit deren Verwerfung durch Luther die Reformation beginnt, sondern auch für den Kapitalismus, der das Gesetz der Schuldenrückzahlung im Rahmen des Marktes absolut setzt.

14. Luther kehrt zur biblischen Wahrheit zurück, dass Gott Schulden umsonst vergibt und aus dem Vertrauen darauf die Solidarität mit den Nächsten erwächst. Konkret: wenn jemand in Not ist, reagieren Christinnen und Christen mit Geben, zinslosem Leihen und Schenken. Auch soll die Obrigkeit in den Markt intervenieren, wenn das Gemeinwohl gefährdet ist. Die kapitalistische Moderne hingegen – und auf ihrem Höhepunkt der Neoliberalismus – setzt den Markt absolut und die Intervention des Staates wird nur zugunsten der Kapitalakkumulation eingesetzt. Dem müssen Kirchengemeinschaften in der Nachfolge Jesu auf der Basis der Bibel und der Reformation Widerstand entgegensetzen.

15. *Der Geist Gottes bestätigt nach der Pfingstgeschichte kulturelle sprachliche Verschiedenheit* (Apg 2). In der westlichen Christenheit seit dem 4. Jh. wurde die Bibel nur in Latein gelesen. Wiclif und die späteren Reformatoren entdecken die Vielfalt wieder, indem sie die Schrift den Völkern in ihrer eigenen Sprache zu Gehör bringen. Neoliberaler Kapitalismus erzwingt erneut Uniformierung: Menschen werden konsumierende Individuen, Landwirtschaft wird zu Agrobusiness, der regionale Verkauf von Gütern weicht transnationalen Ketten und die regionale Produktion der Export-Monokultur.

16. *Die Bibel begründet eine politische „Ökonomie des Genug für" alle durch Teilhabe an den geschenkten gemeinsamen Gütern* (Ex 16). Alle Reformatoren sind sich einig in der Orientierung der Wirtschaft am Gemeinwohl und an den konkreten Bedürfnissen der Nächsten. Luther entwickelt dabei eine Interpretation des Kreuzes, die die Menschlichkeit vom Rande her bestimmt – von den Armen, den Schwachen und den Leidenden her. Heute rufen wir nicht zu einer Restauration des „Realsozialismus" auf, der manche ähnlich zerstörerische Konsequenzen wie der Kapitalismus hatte. Vielmehr geht es um eine trans-moderne Wirtschaft, die auf Gottes Gaben, den Gemeingütern aufbaut und Produktion und Verteilung aller Güter und Dienstleistungen für die Grundversorgung öffentlich demokratisch und ökologisch steuert.

17. *Die Heilige Schrift bestätigt, dass alle Menschen als Mann und Frau nach dem Bilde Gottes und darum mit gleicher Würde geschaffen worden*

sind (Gen 1,26-28). Das Buch der Richter und andere Texte der Tora zeigen, dass dieser Ansatz in Formen einer solidarischen Gesellschaft umgesetzt wurde. Diese Tradition wurde auch im Urchristentum aufgenommen (Apg 2 und 4). Stimmen der radikalen Reformation greifen auf diese Texte zurück und versuchen, nicht nur politische, sondern auch ökonomische Demokratie zu leben.

18. Luthers Lehre von der gnädigen Rechtfertigung durch Vertrauen allein auf Christus (Röm 5,1) ist eine legitime und befreiende Interpretation der Schrift inmitten der Unterdrückungen spätmittelalterlicher Frömmigkeit und entgegen der aufkommenden, auf Zinswucher aufbauenden Geldwirtschaft. Vergebung der Sünde (und der Schulden) umsonst, Befreiung von teuflischer Macht und die Verheißung dauernden Lebens bedeutete in diesem Kontext nicht nur geistliche Freiheit, sondern Befreiung zur Versöhnung mit und Verantwortung für die Mitmenschen (Von der Freiheit eines Christenmenschen).

19. Obwohl die Rechtfertigung aus Gnade auch für Luther die Gleichheit der Menschen vor Gott zum Ausdruck bringt, versagt seine Reformation darin, dies auch sozial und ökonomisch umzusetzen. So konnte es auch dazu kommen, dass das spätere Luthertum soziale und ökonomische Ungleichheit sogar in eine gottgegebene Ordnung umwandeln konnte. Dies gipfelt in der Behauptung einer Eigengesetzlichkeit des Marktes oder des Staates, was nicht nur die Bibel, sondern auch Luther direkt kritisierte.

20. *Nach der Schrift werden Menschen nach Gnade und nicht nach ihrer Leistung beurteilt* (Mt 20). Dem Leistungsmythos muss das Bedürfnisprinzip entgegensetzt werden, das die genaue Entsprechung zur Glaubensgerechtigkeit darstellt. Die sozialethische Konsequenz, die gezogen werden muss, ist eine Kritik der heutigen Arbeitswelt, die von dieser Leistungsideologie und ihren negativen sozialen und psychologischen Folgen beherrscht ist.

21. Luthers Lehre von den zwei Reichen und Regimenten wurde in der späteren Wirkungsgeschichte weitgehend zur Rechtfertigung des Quietismus und des Untertanengehorsams (nach Röm 13,1) missbraucht. Sie muss deshalb neu interpretiert werden als Ruf zu politischer Wachsamkeit und zum Engagement der Christinnen und Christen, damit sie ihre öffentliche Verantwortung für die „Nächsten" wahrnehmen, indem sie sich für Gerechtigkeit, Frieden und die Befreiung der Schöpfung einsetzen.

22. „Passt euch nicht den Strukturen dieser Weltordnung an..." (Röm 12,2) Angesichts ihrer Wirkungen auf die einfachen Leute seiner Zeit sagt Luther ein klares „Nein" zu Struktur und Handlungsweisen der Bank- und Handelsgesellschaften: „Sollen die Gesellschaften bleiben, so muss Recht und Redlichkeit untergehen. Soll Recht und Redlichkeit bleiben, so müssen die Gesellschaften untergehen" (WA 15, 312). Da heute der dreifache Zwang zum wirtschaftlichen Wachstum, zur Geldvermehrung und zur Privatisierung unseren Planeten in den Tod stürzt, helfen letztlich keine sozialen Abfederungen, sondern nur eine langfristige Überwindung des neoliberal-kapitalistischen Systems. Speziell ist eine neue Geld- und Eigentumsordnung nötig und möglich, die sich am Gemeinwohl orientiert und öffentlich-demokratisch verantwortet wird.

23. „Selig sind, die hungern und dürsten nach Gerechtigkeit, denn sie sollen satt werden". (Mt 5) Konkret kann dies im lokalen und regionalen Bereich beginnen. Hier haben auch Kirchen und Gemeinden große Möglichkeiten, z.b. Mitwirkung an dezentraler kommunaler alternativer Energieversorgung. Im Makrobereich können sich Kirchen mit sozialen Bewegungen verbinden, um schrittweise institutionelle Veränderungen zu unterstützen. „Wenn wir uns auf Politiker verlassen, erreichen wir zu wenig und zu spät. Wenn wir es allein versuchen, erreichen wir zu wenig. Wenn wir aber zusammenarbeiten, kann es gerade ausreichen, und das zur rechten Zeit" (Transition Town Movement).

„Von der Kreuzigung zu erzählen... lässt Gottes Macht Wirklichkeit werden" (1.Kor 1,18)

24. In vielen Kirchen und ihrer Verkündigung wird seit dem Mittelalter (Anselm von Canterbury) der Kreuzestod Jesu als Opferung des Gottessohnes verstanden, die die notwendige Sühne für unsere Sünden leistet. Diese Interpretation macht aus Gott einen sadistischen, Leid zufügenden Herrscher. Dies ist ein theologischer Irrtum. Gott erlöst von Gewalt, nicht durch Gewalt.

25. Das Kreuz war das Hinrichtungsinstrument des römischen Imperiums, insbesondere für Rebellen und entlaufene Sklaven, dem abertausende unschuldige Menschen zum Opfer seiner öffentlichen Machtentfaltung gefallen sind. Das Bild eines Gekreuzigten mit der Gasmaske oder einer

gekreuzigten Frau und die Darstellung eines gekreuzigten Campesino erinnern daran, dass bis heute viele Menschen auf vielfältige Weise den herrschenden Mächten zum Opfer fallen, und der gekreuzigte Jesus mit ihnen allen zutiefst verbunden ist.

26. Nach biblischen Traditionen bewirkt das Martyrium der Gerechten Vergebung für die Sünden des Volkes (4 Makk 17,21f.) und der unschuldige Tod des Gottesknechtes macht die Vielen gerecht (Jes 53,11f.). Das gibt dem Kreuzestod ganz neue Dimensionen.

27. Die Begegnung mit dem auferweckten Jesus lässt das Kreuz in ganz neuem Licht erscheinen (Lk 24) – im Licht des Gottes, „der die Toten lebendig macht und das Nichtseiende ins Dasein ruft" (Röm 4,17).

28. Von der Auferweckung her wird Jesus in die alten Klagegebete traumatisierter Menschen („*Mein Gott, warum hast du mich verlassen?*" Ps 22,2; Mk 16,34) und deren umfassende Hoffnung (*"Essen werden die Armen und satt werden!"* Ps 22,26) so eingeschrieben, dass auch wir einbezogen sind.

29. Eine Theologie des Kreuzes kann die frühere schändliche Bildvermischung zwischen Kreuz und Kreuzzug in der Geschichte des Kolonialismus überwinden. So kann die Theologie des Kreuzes wieder zu einer Theologie des Lebens (der Auferstehung) werden – im Licht von Gottes

Solidarität mit dem unterdrückten Volk (*minjung*), wirtschaftlicher Gerechtigkeit für alle und der Unversehrtheit des Lebensgewebes.

30. So erweist die Auferweckung den Kreuzestod als das Gericht über die Mächte der Gewalt, als den radikalsten Vollzug von Gottes unbedingter Solidarität mit allen leidenden Geschöpfen und als Ausdruck von Gottes Treue und Gerechtigkeit gegenüber seinem Volk, allen Völkern und seiner Schöpfung.

31. Glaube im biblischen Sinne ist Umkehr. Zu Jesu Bußruf erklärt Luther: „Es bezieht sich nicht nur auf eine innere Buße, ja eine solche wäre gar keine, wenn sie nicht nach außen mancherlei Werke zur Abtötung des Fleisches (d.h. egozentrischen Handelns) bewirkte." Einerseits sind wir so herausgefordert, in einen Prozess der Wahrheit und Versöhnung im Blick auf die Irrtümer der Reformation einzutreten. Andererseits können wir, indem wir Gottes Gerechtigkeit unbedingt für uns gelten lassen, uns zum Tun des Gerechten in diese Befreiungsgeschichte einbeziehen lassen. „Nur der Glaubende ist gehorsam, und nur der Gehorsame glaubt" (Bonhoeffer).

32. Luthers Rechtfertigungstheologie muss in verschiedenen Zeiten und Orten ausgeweitet und erneuert werden, insbesondere im Licht von Luthers Begriff des Evangeliums als der lebendigen Stimme Gottes. Die reformatorische Lehre von der Rechtfertigung muss aus der Einkapselung in den westlichen possessiven Individualismus und politischen Quietismus ausbrechen, indem sie die Menschen von all dem befreit, was sie Götzen unterwirft: Privilegien nach Art und Geschlecht, nach Volkszugehörigkeit, Religion, Nationalität und Klasse. Rechtfertigung muss wiederentdeckt werden als der Ausdruck für Gottes tiefes Mitleiden für alle im Tod Jesu. Dadurch wird dann unsere öffentliche Verantwortung für politische und wirtschaftliche Gerechtigkeit und für die Anerkennung „der Anderen" verstärkt.

„Seht, Neues kam zur Welt" (2 Kor 5,17)

33. Beim christlichen Evangelium geht es tatsächlich um die Versöhnung zwischen Gott und Menschheit und der Menschen untereinander. Aber wenn es dem Evangelium nicht gelingt, die ganze Schöpfung zu versöhnen, ist es nicht das Evangelium, die frohe Botschaft (2 Kor 5,18).

34. Die reformatorische Erkenntnis, dass wir durch das Vertrauen auf Gottes Gnade gerettet werden, sollte die Erkenntnis einschließen, dass Gott in der gesamten Schöpfung gegenwärtig ist und auf deren Schrei hört (Röm 8,18-23).

35. Sicher war es im 16. Jahrhundert ein Fortschritt, wenn die Reformatoren die äußerlichen und materiellen Formen des Gottesdienstes kritisierten. Einige gingen aber zu weit darin, jeden Begriff des Sakramentalen zu verwerfen, indem sie im aufkommenden Bildersturm alle materielle Kultur abstreiften. Dabei haben sie übersehen, dass alles Leben von Gott durchdrungen ist und dass die Welt als ganze eine sakramentale Realität ist.

36. Die reformatorische Erkenntnis, dass wir durch Gnade im Glauben gerettet sind, sollte auch Gottes gnädige Gegenwart in der ganzen Schöpfung bekräftigen. Gottes Gemeinschaft mit der Welt in Jesus Christus bedeutet, dass auch wir in die Gemeinschaft mit der Welt gerufen sind – ein diesseitiger Glaube wird dann verwirklicht, wenn wir an Gottes Mission zur Erneuerung der Schöpfung teilnehmen.

37. Mutter Erde wird gegenwärtig gekreuzigt und muss Auferstehung erfahren (Röm 8,18-22). Das ist zentral wichtig für uns Menschen, die Tiere, Pflanzen, Luft, Wasser und Erde. Wir sind Menschen nicht, weil wir konsumieren, sondern weil wir in Verbindung mit der Schöpfung leben und für ihr und unser Wohlsein sorgen müssen.

38. „Das Evangelium aller Kreatur" (Mk 16,15 nach Luthers Übersetzung), Gottes gute Nachricht für die ganze Schöpfung und Gottes Gebote (Ps 119) werden abgebrochen, wenn Menschen, geschaffen nach Gottes Bild, diese Ordnung durch Ungerechtigkeit zerstören (Röm 1,18-20).

39. Das Evangelium fordert uns heraus, die Schöpfung als Gottes Garten zu bewahren. Dies erfordert sowohl eine klare persönliche Entscheidung wie auch eine neue wirtschaftliche, soziale und ökologische Politik für das Wohlergehen der ganzen Schöpfung und aller Völker auf dem Erdball.

40. „Leben im Überfluss" (Joh 10,10) bricht mit den herkömmlichen Konzepten wirtschaftlicher Entwicklung: Es richtet sich zentral auf die Beziehung zur Schöpfung, auf die hin sich die menschliche Gemeinschaft orientieren muss. „Leben im Überfluss" zielt nicht auf Mehr-haben, nicht

auf Akkumulation und Wachstum, sondern auf die Balance aller Beziehungen.

41. Alle Menschen und die gesamte Natur haben das Recht und Bedürfnis nach „Brot und Rosen". Menschen und Natur haben einen Hunger nach Brot und Schönheit. Es ist eine unvollendete Aufgabe reformatorischer Theologie, das Recht auf Leben in Fülle für die ganze Schöpfung zu proklamieren und dafür zu kämpfen.

42. Die Erde gibt allen Kreaturen Leben (Gen 1,24). Was die Natur hervorbringt, ist eine Gabe Gottes, für die wir Sorge tragen müssen. Das ist Ausdruck unserer Dankbarkeit und unserer Berufung als Menschen Gottes (Psalm 104).

43. Leben im Überfluss bedeutet nicht Konsumismus, sondern die Verbundenheit mit der ganzen Natur. Menschen und menschliche Industrie sind nicht das Endziel der Schöpfung: der Höhepunkt in Gottes Schöpfung zielt darauf, dass wir in der Anbetung und in gegenseitigen Beziehungen zur Ruhe kommen (Gen 2,2).

44. Das Evangelium ruft uns, die Schöpfung als Gottes Garten dadurch zu bewahren und zu erneuern (Jes 65,17; 2. Petrus 3,13), dass wir einen bescheidenen persönlichen Lebensstil annehmen und mit anderen Menschen verschiedener Kulturen und Religionen zusammenarbeiten, um eine lebensförderliche Politik für die Wirtschaft, das soziale Zusammenleben und die Mitwelt durchzusetzen.

45. Was "Schöpfung" bedeutet, ist eng verbunden mit dem Leben künftiger Generationen. Theologien waren durchweg bestimmt von dem Personsein von Erwachsenen und nicht dem Personsein von Kindern. Es geht aber immer um Menschen in Gottes Geschichte. Dies gilt auch für Kinder und muss deshalb im Blick auf ihre gefährdete Zukunft ernst genommen werden.

46. Kinderrechte schützen Kinder vor Verletzung, Unterdrückung und Ausbeutung. Zugleich aber kommt es darauf an, Kinder mit all dem gelten zu lassen, was sie können und sind, und mit allem, was sie nicht können und nicht sind. In diesem Sinn müssen sie für die Theologie um ihrer Zukunft willen – aus ihrem Objektsein befreit – Subjekte werden.

„Selig sind die Frieden praktizieren" ... (Mt 5,9)

47. Der Schrei der Opfer ist zu hören, der Schrei derer, die Gewalt erfahren haben – hier besonders der Schrei der Opfer in den gewaltsamen Kämpfen um die Reformation: der Schrei der Bauern, der Täufer (Mennoniten), Juden und Muslime. Zu hören ist der Schrei derer, die heute Gewalt leiden – der Schrei der Opfer von häuslicher Gewalt, ökonomischer Ausbeutung, Verletzung von Menschenrechten, Ungerechtigkeit gegen die Schöpfung, Imperialismus und Krieg.

48. Zu rufen ist nach Umkehr zur Friedenspraxis (Jes 2,2-4). Friedenspraxis ist dort gegeben, wo Menschen Gottes Praxis und all der gewaltfreien Praxis folgen, wie sie Jesus ausübt. Mit solcher Friedenspraxis beginnt Gottes Reich, beginnt Gottes Frieden (Shalom; Jes 11,6-9).

Illustration von Jan Luyken im "Märtyrerspiegel": Dirk Willems rettet seinen Verfolger, der ihn dann dem Scheiterhaufen übergibt (aus: http:// de.wikipedia.org/wiki/ Dirk_ Willems)

49. Das Phänomen der Gewalt ist sichtbar überall, wo der Friedenspraxis widerstanden wird und wo sie verhindert wird – durch soziale, politische, ökonomische oder auch direkt staatliche Gewalt, deren Opfer zum Himmel nach Hilfe schreien.

50. Gewalt ist überall und in vielen Formen (strukturelle Gewalt, technische Gewalt, militärische Gewalt, Aktionsgewalt) präsent. Die Allgegenwart von Gewalt wird sichtbar auch in vielen besonders resistenten Praktiken – wie der Fixierung von Feinden und vor allem Sündenböcken (Apg 7,54-60).

51. Für alle Formen von Gewalt sind Gründe und Ursachen zu finden. Gewalt ist aber immer eine Folge von vorausgegangener Gewalt. Gewalt ist immer schon Gegengewalt.

52. Es gibt keinen Weg der Begründung oder der Legitimation von Gewalt. Gewalt ist immer illegitim. Es gibt keine rechtmäßige Gewalt, das heißt es gibt keine Gewalt, die durch Recht letztgültig begründet werden kann. Es gibt keinen gerechten Krieg und es gibt keinen gerechtfertigten Krieg. Luther, Zwingli und Calvin akzeptierten nur begrenzte Gewalt zur Minimierung größerer Gewalt. Aber selbst diese Logik ist angesichts moderner Massenvernichtungsmittel anachronistisch geworden. Gewalt kann niemals Mittel für irgendein Ziel sein; denn Gott hat alle Dinge mit sich selber versöhnt (Kol 1,19-20).

53. Die Durchsetzung von Recht kann nicht auf Gewalt beruhen. Wo Menschen Gewalt erleiden, sind sie mit Mitteln der Friedenspraxis zu schützen. In der Zeit der Reformation wurde begonnen, den Einsatz von Gewalt als ausschließlich 'obrigkeitlich' gebundene kriegerische oder polizeiliche Gewalt und ausschließlich als Schutz des Nächsten vor Gewalt zu bestimmen. Diese radikale Begrenzung ist weitgehend verdrängt worden. Diese äußerst begrenzte Gewalt ist dort, wo sie gebraucht werden muss, nicht einfach als notwendig gegeben zu verstehen, sondern als mahnendes Zeichen einer gebrochenen Welt.

54. Auch Rechtssetzung beruht auf Gewalt – das ist die äußerste Gewalt, die aber keine weitere Gewalt legitimiert, sondern das Tun des Gerechten fordert (Mt 5,38-42). Rechtssysteme müssen daraufhin beurteilt werden, ob sie Gerechtigkeit gewährleisten und so Frieden begründen.

55. Frieden praktizieren heißt, ohne Gewalt zu leben, zu reden und zu handeln. Frieden zu praktizieren heißt, das zu tun, worin sich Frieden vollzieht: Gerechtigkeit tun, hören, vergeben, teilen, verschenken, heilen, lindern, helfen – all dies als Widerstandsarbeit gegen Gewalt (Mt 5,3-11). Dies alles ist Gottesdienst (Rö 12,1-2) – Gottesdienst ist Friedenspraxis.

56. Frieden zu praktizieren gilt es auch im Reden – keine rhetorische Gewalt auszuüben, zu bezeugen, nicht zu überzeugen (Mt 5,33-37).

57. Frieden praktizieren heißt, darauf zu setzen, dass das Zusammenleben aller – die politische Gemeinschaft – einzig von den Praktiken des Friedens getragen ist. Frieden praktizieren heißt so, einer Überzeugung zu

folgen, die im Sinne der Verantwortung realistisch ist – weil nur durch Friedenspraxis Frieden in der Welt präsent wird (Mt 5,43-48).

Einer trage des anderen Last und erfüllet so die Tora Christi" (Gal 6,2)

58. Am Ursprung der Reformation liegt Luthers Wiederentdeckung von Gottes Gerechtigkeit als schöpferischer und erneuernder Macht in den Schriften des Paulus. In seiner Lehre von der Rechtfertigung fasst Luther diese Gerechtigkeit als barmherzige Zuwendung Gottes, selbst zum Gottlosen (sola gratia), und als Vertrauen auf die Treue Gottes im Glauben (sola fide) an Christus (solus Christus).

59. Die Gerechtigkeit Gottes führt Paulus zur visionären Einsicht, dass „in Christus" die Gegensätze und Hierarchien der „gegenwärtigen bösen Weltordnung" (Gal 1,4) außer Kraft gesetzt sind. "Wir" sind nicht das, was uns von den anderen abgrenzt, sondern mit ihnen verbindet. Die menschlichen Gegensätze von Nation, Religion, Geschlecht, Klasse, die das Selbst als Feind und Rivalen des anderen konstituieren, werden in der Taufe "abgelegt" wie alte Kleider. Eine neue Praxis des Einswerdens durch Miteinander und Füreinander bringt eine neue Form des Menschseins und der Welt hervor. (Gal 6,2.15) *„Hier ist nicht mehr Jude noch Grieche, nicht Sklave noch Freier, nicht männlich und weiblich, sondern Ihr seid alle eins in Christus"* (Gal 3,28). Damit sind Gottes Gerechtigkeit, die Rechtfertigung des Menschen und menschliche Gerechtigkeit untrennbar miteinander verbunden.

60. Ein außerordentlich problematischer und nicht-paulinischer Aspekt reformatorischer Rechtfertigungstheologie und ihrer späteren Auslegung im Protestantismus ist ihr Begriff des „Gesetzes". Luther setzt „Gerechtigkeit aus dem Gesetz" auf programmatische Weise der „Gerechtigkeit oder Rechtfertigung aus Glauben" entgegen und versteht diese Antithese als unversöhnliche Antithese von Judentum und Christentum.

61. Diese folgenschwere Polarisierung gründet in seiner Auslegung des Galaterbriefs. Zu Unrecht setzt Luther hier das von Paulus kritisierte Gesetz mit der Tora gleich. Die zentrale Kontroverse des Galaterbriefes um die Notwendigkeit des jüdischen Rituals der Beschneidung für die nicht-jüdischen Christusgläubigen wird als Zurückweisung "des" Judentums und seines Gesetzes verstanden. Wie neuere Forschung gezeigt hat, war je-

doch der eigentliche Widerpart im Streit des Paulus mit seinen galatischen Gegnern nicht die jüdische Tora, sondern das Gesetz und die Ordnung des Römischen Imperiums. Dieses setzte sowohl für Juden als auch Heiden bestimmte Konformitätsregeln. Das paulinische Modell einer solidarischen Gemeinschaft von Juden und Nicht-Juden „in Christus" kollidiert in erster Linie mit diesen imperialen Ordnungsvorstellungen und Sozialisationsmustern, nicht zuletzt im Rahmen der römischen Kaiserreligion.

62. Die Reformation setzte weiterhin Judentum mit dem Römischen Katholizismus gleich und verurteilte beide als „Gesetzesreligionen", die Rechtfertigung durch „Gesetzeswerke" erlangen wollen. Das polare Muster von „Werke oder Gnade und Glaube", „Evangelium oder Gesetz", angewandt auf konkrete Personen, hatte eine verhängnisvolle Folgegeschichte in seiner weiteren Auslegung: Es wurde nicht nur antijudaistisch und anti-römisch katholisch gelesen, sondern auch gegen „Schwärmer", Täufer, Muslime und andere „Häretiker" gewendet, oft mit tödlichen Konsequenzen.

63. Bis in die Gegenwart fallen befreiungstheologische, feministische und soziale Bewegungen oft dem Verdikt der „Werkgerechtigkeit" oder „Gesetzlichkeit" anheim, das ihnen den rechten Glauben abspricht. Rechtfertigungstheologie wird gegen innerweltliche Gerechtigkeit gewendet.

64. Damit ist die protestantische Tradition in ihrem Kern kompromittiert durch eine Identitätsbildung in Abgrenzung vom "anderen", die der radikalen paulinischen Solidarität eines Miteinanders über alle Grenzziehungen hinweg zuwiderläuft. Angesichts der gegenwärtigen Weltkrise ist es ein kategorischer Imperativ, dass sich protestantische Rechtfertigungstheologie neu auf die Gerechtigkeit Gottes besinnt und zu ihrem schriftgemäßen Wurzeln zurückkehrt.

65. Das Negativurteil über Judentum und Gesetz trug maßgeblich auch zu einer grundsätzlichen Abwertung des gesamten Alten Testaments bei. Die trinitarische Formel von Vater, Sohn und Heiligem Geist als gemeinsames Zeugnis aller christlichen Kirchen bezeugt die unauflösliche Verbindung zwischen den beiden Teilen des biblischen Kanons. Die Einheit der beiden Testamente zurückzugewinnen, ist eine weitere grundlegende Aufgabe reformatorischer Theologie heute.

66. Der Messias Jesus von Nazareth ist die Einladung an alle Völker, an der Zukunft teilzuhaben, die Israel verheißen ist: eine gerechte und gleiche Gesellschaft im Geiste der Tora. Die christliche Kirche ersetzt Israel nicht, das Alte Israel ist die Wurzel der Kirche. „Nicht du trägst die Wurzel, sondern die Wurzel trägt dich" (Röm 11,18).

67. Der Messias Jesus kündigt das nahe Reich Gottes, seine gerechte Welt, an (Mt 4,17). Im Horizont dieser Hoffnung legt der Messias Jesus die Tora Israels für die Gegenwart aus (Mt 5-7). Kriterien der Auslegung sind die Alleinverehrung Gottes und die Liebe zum Nächsten/zur Nächsten, insbesondere zu den Armen und Entrechteten (Mk 12,28-34; Mt 25,31ff). Gerade ihr Ergehen entscheidet darüber, wie die Tora ausgelegt werden soll. So wird die Tora, von der nicht das kleinste Gebot aufgehoben wird, zur Wegweisung für die messianischen Gemeinschaften (Mt 5,17-20; 28,19-20; vgl. auch Röm 3,31). Jesu Aufforderung sich an seiner Toraauslegung auszurichten, zielt darauf ab, die Tora immer wieder neu in der Hoffnung auf Gottes kommendes Reich auszulegen und mit Leben zu erfüllen.

68. Im Römerbrief hören wir den Schrei von Menschen, die in der imperialen Ordnung gefangen sind, die ein Leben nach der Richtschnur der Tora unmöglich macht. Sünde ist nicht einfach eine abstrakte menschliche Verfasstheit, sondern materialisiert sich in konkreten sozialen Gegebenheiten. Imperiale Herrschaftsstrukturen verkörpern für Paulus die Macht der Sünde, die die Menschen unausweichlich in die Übertretung der leben-schöpfenden Thoragesetze treibt und sie zu Komplizen der Kräfte des Todes und der Selbst-Zerstörung macht (Röm 7,24).

69. Die paulinische Rechtfertigung durch Glauben und aus Gnade schließt darum die doppelte Befreiung sowohl der Menschen als auch der Tora von der Macht der Sünde ein. Die messianischen Gemeinden schaffen einen Raum, wo jüdische und nicht-jüdische Menschen „in Christus" die Tora als Gesetz des Lebens erfüllen können durch die Liebe zueinander – und auch gegenüber ihren Feinden (Röm 8,2; 12,1-21; 13,8-10).

70. Die Gesetzeskritik des Paulus und auch der Reformation ist nicht gegen gesellschaftliche Rechtsordnungen als solche gerichtet (*usus civilis legis*). Recht und Gesetz sind notwendig, um menschliche Gesellschaft zu erhalten. Die Kritik richtet sich ausschließlich gegen die Instrumentalisierung des Gesetzes im Interesse der Starken und gegen die Schwachen,

wie sie bereits von den Propheten angeklagt wird. Das Gesetz ist für den Menschen da, nicht der Mensch für das Gesetz, wie sowohl Jesus als auch die Rabbinen erklärten. (Mk 2,27; Babylonischer Talmud, Traktat Eruvin 41b). Menschliche Gesetzgebung muss immer wieder kritisch hinterfragt und verändert werden, um in konkreten Kontexten das Recht der Opfer zu vertreten anstatt die Ungerechtigkeit der herrschenden Ordnung juristisch abzudecken.

71. Ein besonderes Problem stellt in diesem Zusammenhang Luthers Identifikation der Zehn Gebote (Dekalog) mit dem Naturrecht dar (Mose als „der Juden Sachsenspiegel"). Dadurch verwischt er die Besonderheit der Tora als alternatives Recht, das in entscheidenden Punkten von den Gesetzeswerken ihrer Umwelt abweicht – etwa im Blick auf die Sabbatgesetzgebung, den Schuldenerlass, das Verbot der Akkumulation durch Gier (zehntes Gebot). Diese kritische Stoßrichtung geht verloren, wenn die Tora gleichgesetzt wird mit jedwedem positiven Recht wie etwa dem das private Eigentum verabsolutierenden Römischen Recht.

72. Vor allem aber lässt Luther in seinem Kleinen Katechismus die politisch konkrete Einleitung des Dekalogs fallen: „Ich bin Adonaj, deine Gottheit, weil ich dich aus Ägypten, dem Haus der Sklavenarbeit, befreit habe." (Ex 20,2; Deut 5,6) Luther weitet ferner das Gebot des Elterngehorsams auf Autoritätsgehorsam als solchen aus. Diese beiden symptomatischen Veränderungen der Schriftgrundlage in Luthers einflussreichstem Katechismus zeigen bereits an, wie das Luthertum anfällig werden konnte für Untertanengehorsam und Anpassung gegenüber jedweder etablierten Rechts- oder Unrechtsordnung, statt dem Gott der Befreiung zu vertrauen (sola fide) und für die Entrechteten einzutreten.

73. Wenn die herrschende Ordnung keine Gerechtigkeit übt und sich gegenüber den Nöten der einfachen Menschen, besonders der Geringsten (Mt, 25,34-40), gleichgültig verhält und auf diese Weise Götzendienst übt und seinen Bürgerinnen und Bürgern eine unannehmbare Lebensweise aufzwingt, dann sollen Christenmenschen einer solchen üblen Regierung nicht nur den Gehorsam verweigern, sondern aktiv Widerstand leisten.

74. Innerhalb imperialer Strukturen ist die Orientierung an den befreienden biblischen Wegweisungen Widerstand gegen die tödlichen Logiken und Gesetze gewalttätiger und versklavender Macht. Um einen solchen Widerstand leisten zu können, muss eine umfassende Kenntnis der befrei-

enden Traditionen der Tora sowohl im Alten als auch Neuen Testament wiedergewonnen werden, die weithin verlorengegangen ist. Wie in der Reformation brauchen wir eine neue „Erweckung" zu eingreifender Bibelarbeit in unseren Gemeinden, die sowohl den Einzelnen als auch die sozialen und ökonomischen Probleme unserer Gegenwart kritisch und befreiend anspricht. Zum Beispiel gehören biblisch gesehen Schuldenerlass und göttliche Schuldvergebung untrennbar zusammen (Mt 6,12). Heutige Christinnen und Christen sollen die Möglichkeit bekommen, gerade das Alte Testament, die Hebräische Bibel, als einen reichhaltigen Schatz für ihre Lebensgestaltung und für ethische Urteilsbildung kennenzulernen.

75. Nachfolger und Nachfolgerinnen Jesu haben den Wunsch, sich in Gottes Geheimnisse in Gemeinschaft mit den heiligen Texten, die auch in anderen Religionen offenbart sind, zu vertiefen. Diese Freude erfahren sie, wenn sie in gemeinsamer Anstrengung zusammen mit Juden, Muslimen, Buddhisten, Hindus und allen anderen Kulturen in Afrika, Nord- und Lateinamerika, der Karibik, Asiens, des Mittleren Ostens, des Pazifiks und Europas (Jes 49,6) sich für den Aufbau einer besseren Welt einsetzen und dabei den Dialog stärken. Das Evangelium widerspricht jeglicher kulturellen, religiösen und militärischen Invasion.

76. Eine postkoloniale Interpretation der Reformationstheologie fördert ein Projekt der Inkulturation, um zu unterstreichen, dass interreligiöser Dialog ein prophetischer Dialog sein muss. Damit macht sie einen Neuanfang mit der Kritik an solchen Formen von Reformationstheologie, die der Kolonisierung dienen, oder deren Gelehrsamkeit für den Dienst der Mächtigen missbraucht wird.

„Der Geist weht, wo er will" (Joh 3,8)

77. Im Geist der aus der Reformation hervorgegangenen Kirche müssen wir heute auf den Schrei von Menschen rund um den Erdball hören, die wahrnehmen, dass die Kirchen ihre Leiden, Unterdrückung und kulturelle Situation übersehen und ausklammern (Mt 25,31ff.) und dadurch die Spaltungen in Kirche und Gesellschaft eher vertiefen statt zu heilen.

78. Die reformatorischen Bewegungen verstanden Kirche nicht so sehr als Institution, sondern als das getaufte Volk Gottes, das sich in örtlichen Gemeinschaften versammelt. Kirche als Gemeinschaft in der Nachfolge

Christi ist der heilige Ort, an dem das universale Wort Gottes gehört und die Sakramente gefeiert werden, und dies in verschiedenen Sprachen, Traditionen und Bekenntnissen. Ihr Auftrag ist, zur Heilung der Welt beizutragen (tikkun olam).

79. Das Priestertum aller Glaubenden war ein radikaler Schrei, die mächtigste Institution jener Zeit, die römische Kirche, zu demokratisieren. Heute muss dies übersetzt werden in einen revolutionären Ruf nach universalen Bürgerrechten und gerechter Verteilung der Produkte menschlicher Arbeit.

80. Im 16. Jahrhundert wurde die Kirche reformiert. Aber schon bald verwickelten sich Kirchen in der reformatorischen Tradition in Strukturen und Praktiken, die patriarchalisch und hierarchisch waren und in die Gefangenschaft von mächtigen wirtschaftlichen und politischen Interessen gerieten. Ihre Verfolgung der Täufer, Juden und Muslime war nicht nur beklagenswert, sondern unverzeihlich! Selbst hierfür Buße zu tun, ist nicht genug. Wir müssen uns vom Geist Gottes dazu antreiben lassen, insgesamt von solchen konstantinischen Formen der Kirche Abschied zu nehmen. Es geht darum, sich zur Gestaltung einer Kirche inspirieren zu lassen, in der angefangen von den gesellschaftlich Ausgeschlossenen alle mitbestimmen können und Grenzen überschritten werden, zu einer Kirche, die wirklich katholisch ist, das heißt, die alle einschließt – über die Grenzen von Religionen, Volkszugehörigkeit, Kontinenten und Eigeninteressen hinweg.

81. Nachfolge Christi geht Hand in Hand mit Kontemplation, geistlichen Übungen, Erleuchtung und die Einstimmung in den Willen Gottes. Wenn wir Gottes Stimme in der Ehrfurcht der Rahab (Josua 2) oder der Ehrfurcht von Maria und Elisabeth (Lk 1) hören und dem Geist Gottes erlauben, bis in die Tiefen unseres Seins zu fließen, sind wir auf dem Weg der Nachfolge Christi. Die Frauen der Bibel und die Frauen der radikalen Reformation zeigen uns den Weg der Nachfolge, der Mystik, des Zeugnisses und des Martyriums.

82. Die Geistkraft Gottes handelt frei und weht, wo sie will, um die Kirche ständig zu erneuern. Sie ist niemandes Eigentum und kann nicht von institutionellen Interessen oder Lehrdefinitionen gefangengehalten werden.

83. Der Geist bewirkt Erneuerung und Veränderung sowohl in der Kirche wie auch in der Gesellschaft. Zusätzlich zur Verwandlung von Personen ermächtigt er auch die Glaubenden, sich Seite an Seite mit Menschen anderer Religionen, Ideologien und sozialer Bewegungen zu engagieren und Leiden zu erdulden, die aus solchem Engagement für Liebe, Solidarität und Gerechtigkeit folgen.

84. Als Luther das Kreuz zum Zeichen der Kirche erklärte, setzte er damit einen Maßstab für die Kirche, an der sie zu messen ist: Um Kirche zu sein, muss sie sich verwundbar machen dadurch, dass sie an der Seite der Armen steht und für sie eintritt, dass sie ihren sozialen und politischen Status aufs Spiel setzt, indem sie öffentlich gegen ungerechte Strukturen und politische Praktiken protestiert.

85. Statt sich auf individuelle Frömmigkeit zu konzentrieren, muss sie gemeinschaftlich kirchlich das Schwergewicht auf Widerstand und gesellschaftliche Veränderung legen. Andernfalls werden sich die Ungerechtigkeiten weiterhin frei ausbreiten können und unsere grundlegenden Beziehungen zu Gott, uns selbst, unseren Nächsten und zur gesamten Schöpfung pervertieren. Durch Tätigkeiten wie Predigen, Lehren, Feiern, Fürsorge, Gemeinschaftsaufbau und -organisation zusammen mit anderen kann die Kirche helfen, Sünde, Abhängigkeit und Blindheit entgegenzutreten, die es dem Imperium in seinen verschiedenen Facetten möglich machen zu herrschen.

86. Durch die Kraft des inspirierenden und verbindenden Geistes werden die, die untereinander sehr verschieden sind, in eine Körperschaft, eine „neue Schöpfung" verwandelt. Der Geist erneuert und verwandelt nicht nur, sondern bringt Menschen zusammen in der Einheit des Leibes Christi. Er kann deshalb nicht dazu benutzt werden, weitere Kirchenspaltungen zu rechtfertigen. Eine sich reformierende Kirche muss deshalb mit sich selbst versöhnt sein und intensiv daran arbeiten, die Spaltungen zwischen Ost und West, zwischen Römischen Katholiken und Protestanten und zwischen den verschiedenen reformatorischen Kirchen zu überwinden, damit alle an einem Abendmahlstisch zusammenkommen können.

87. Eine sich reformierende Kirche wird ständig verändert durch das, was sie von anderen theologischen Traditionen und Kulturen empfängt. Luther betonte, dass der Geist an das Wort Gottes gebunden ist. Damit kritisierte er alle, die behaupteten, sie hätten besondere Offenbarungen unabhängig

von den biblischen Schriften empfangen. Das darf nicht fälschlich so interpretiert werden, als ob dem Geist Grenzen gesetzt würden und er nicht frei unter und in den Menschen wirken könne – einschließlich solcher aus anderen Traditionen oder Religionen, ja sogar einschließlich der gesamten Schöpfung (Röm 8).

88. Luthers Kritik an den sog. Schwärmern kann nicht auf unsere Zeit als allgemeine Kritik an den Pfingstkirchen übertragen werden. Natürlich müssen wir „Wohlstandstheologien" auf der Basis einer Theologie des Kreuzes kritisieren. Gleichzeitig müssen wir aber das Wirken des Geistes in den Pfingstbewegungen achtsam wahrnehmen, wie er Gemeinschaft aufbaut, an den Rand gedrückte Personen rettet und wie er die Würde von Menschen wiederherstellt, die unter Armut, Krankheit, Sucht und Erwerbslosigkeit leiden.

89. Die Wiederentdeckung und Neulektüre biblischer Traditionen auf der Grundlage sozialer Analyse aus der Perspektive der an den Rand Gedrängten und das kontextuelle und interkulturelle Lesen der Bibel in vielen Situationen der ganzen Welt ist ein wichtiges Zeichen der Hoffnung, dass die befreiende Weise der Reformation, die Bibel zu verstehen, heute in vielen Kirchen am Werk ist.

90. Der Reformation war es zentral wichtig, dass alle Menschen Zugang zu Bildung haben und dass die Bibel kontextuell neu gelesen werden muss in Bezug auf die jeweilige Situation. Als sich die aus der Reformation entspringenden Kirchen in der ganzen Welt ausbreiteten, wurde und wird dieser Ansatz keineswegs immer durchgehalten. Stattdessen finden wir weitverbreitet eine individualistische Frömmigkeit, die sich an mächtige Interessen anpasst und so illusionäres Bewusstsein fördert, und religiöser Fundamentalismus nimmt sogar zu.

91. Deshalb ist die Wiedergewinnung biblischer Theologie und kritischer theologischer Ausbildung (und Bildung im Allgemeinen) zentral für den Fortgang der Reformation und Erneuerung in der weltweiten Christenheit im 21. Jahrhundert.

92. Selig sind, die sich nicht an die herrschenden Systeme anpassen, sondern dagegen aufstehen, wie Gott bis heute von den Strukturen dieser Welt ans Kreuz geschlagen wird (Röm 12,2), und die zusammen mit anderen

eine neue Welt mit Gerechtigkeit und Frieden in menschlichen Gemeinschaften bauen.

93. Wir brauchen eine „neue Reformation". Jetzt wie damals können Leute leicht fromm sein. Aber diese Frömmigkeit drückt sich oft in unangemessenen Formen aus, weil Kirchen oft von der realen Situation, in der Menschen leben, entfremdet sind. Wie seinerzeit Luther brauchen wir eine Erneuerung der Sprache, eine Rückkehr zur befreienden Botschaft des Evangeliums.

94. Bonhoeffers Vorschlag einer in der Welt engagierten Christenheit, welche eine neue Sprache für das alte Evangelium entdeckt, muss übersetzt werden als „Beten und Tun des Gerechten unter den Menschen" (Bonhoeffer). Alle kirchliche Rede muss von diesem Gebet und diesem Tun her neu eingeübt werden. Genau darauf insistiert Befreiungstheologie, indem sie auf der Untrennbarkeit von Orthopraxis und Orthodoxie besteht.

„Die Reformation radikalisieren – provoziert von Bibel und Krise" ist für Kirchen und Theologie keine beliebige Option, sondern notwendig. Luther selbst machte die Schrift in ihrem historischen Wortsinn zum Kriterium aller Tradition. Die kontextuelle Auslegung der Bibel hat diesen Sinn kritisch-prophetisch geschärft. Und Luther übte systemische Kritik schon am Beginn der kapitalistischen Moderne – Wie sollten wir am Ende dieser immer mörderischeren und selbstmörderischen Menschheitsphase und ihrer Krise nicht neu auf unsere Glaubensquellen hören und mit anderen gemeinsam „dem Rad in die Speichen fallen"? Lasst uns gemeinsam mit andren auf dem Weg der Gerechtigkeit und des Friedens gehen.

Halle, 7. August, 2014 *Die Unterschriften der AutorInnen und UnterstützerInnen sind unter die englische Fassung gesetzt, siehe S. 69-70.*

Radicalizing Reformation – Provoked by the Bible and Today's Crises

94 Theses

"You shall proclaim liberation throughout the land" (Lev. 25:10).

Martin Luther began his *95 Theses* of 1517 with Jesus' call for repentance as a change of mind and direction: "Return, the just world of God has come near!" Five hundred years later is also a time that brings to mind the biblical "Jubilee Year" (Lev 25), calling for repentance and conversion toward a more just society. For us today, this is not in opposition to the Catholic Church and the many liberation movements rooted there, but in opposition to the realities of empire that rule. As we hear the testimony of the cross (1 Cor 1:18) and the groaning of the abused creation (Rom 8:22) and as we actively hear the cries of those victimized by our world (dis-)order driven by hyper-capitalism – only then can we turn this Reformation commemoration into a liberating jubilee. Christian self-righteousness, supporting the dominating system, is in contradiction to faith-righteousness as proclaimed by the Reformation. This must be lived out through just, all-inclusive solidarity.

We are theologians – predominantly Lutheran but also Reformed, Methodist, Anglican, and Mennonite – from different parts of the world, who are involved in an ongoing project of reconsidering the biblical roots and contemporary challenges facing Reformation theology today. The rampant destruction of human and non-human life in a world ruled by the totalitarian dictatorship of money and greed, market and exploitation requires a radical re-orientation towards the biblical message, which also marked the beginning of the Reformation. The dominant economic system and its imperial structures and policies have put the earth, human communities, and the future of our children up for sale. Our churches, congregations, and individual Christians have often become complacent and complicit with the established *status quo* and have lost their critical-prophetic power to protest, resist, and change what is occurring. God's justification by grace has been detached from social justice and thus serves as "useless salt" (Mt 5:13). Because the Reformation legacy has gone astray, we must at the same time return to some of Luther's thought and legacy, as well as standing decidedly against other things he said and did, if this is to become a *kairoitic* time of transformation today.

The following theses grow out of different traditions and understandings among the reforming movements, as well as from different geographical and political contexts. We have developed these theses from research, published in five volumes. We may not agree on every point, but out of this very diversity and pluriformity, we together call for serious debate on what is asserted here – and we also call for "turning around" and repentance (*metanoia*). The present moment of crisis that we currently face across the globe on all levels is a time to recognize the predatory and destructive forces inherent in what is dominating our world today, in order to re-orient ourselves in hope towards a new culture of life.

"For liberation the Messiah has liberated us" (Gal 5:1)

1. From the perspective of the Bible, liberation is first and foremost the act of God. The messianic liberation in the New Testament also is shaped according to the model of the Exodus. In his letter to the Romans the Apostle Paul maintains that Christ brings liberation from the "terrorizing domination of sin" in the context of the Roman Empire (Rom 5:12-8:2). By contrast, when justification is not understood according to the pattern of the Exodus but reduced only to individual guilt and forgiveness (as in Augustine and Anselm of Canterbury), it is seriously cut off from the wide social and political richness of the biblical context.

2. Paul analyzes the domination of sin, which, in the Roman Empire of his time, holds all people captive. The central passages about sin (*hamartia*) have a common denominator: they are to be understood in terms of relationships of domination, only very seldom in categories of individual guilt and sins. When Paul speaks about sin, he is referring especially to its all-embracing terrorizing domination. His overall idea is that sin rules over all human beings as a master over slaves and thus makes them collaborators in the imperial system and laws.

3. Paul speaks about the beginning of an all-encompassing change of rule. He directs his hope towards God's final intervention, which for him has already begun with Jesus' resurrection. Although Paul has no direct polit-

ical goals, his faith in Christ's rule and the hope for a final change of rule has deep political implications. He believes that Christ alone is Lord (*Kyrios*) and that liberation in Christ affects the whole creation, all people, and the whole human being.

4. Faith leads the faithful to live as liberated people, both in their faith community and in their common life with others. This is the beginning of a new life. This claim for liberation from totalitarian reality, such as under the Roman Empire, is more trenchant and empowering for all who live today under the domination of financial and violent markets than are traditional generalizations about sin.

"You cannot serve both God and Mammon" (Mt 6:24)

5. At least two billion people exist in extreme poverty under the present rule of money. The rule of capital is today's expression of Mammon, and thus the central challenge of faith. Today, money is not simply issued by the central banks or cash in your pocket, but commercial banks have the right to create money through unlimited loans that create debt with high interest. Already in the 16th century Luther called Mammon "the most common god on earth" (*Large Catechism*, Explanation of the First Commandment).

6. This rule of money together with theological opposition to it developed historically with the expansion of an economy based on money and private ownership – from the monetization of the economy in the time of the Prophets; through the early capitalism of Luther's time, based on trade and usury; to modern forms of industrial and financial capitalism. Since the time of the Reformation, the contemporary globalized capitalism of modernity has been manifest in

European exploitation, colonization, and genocide in Africa, Asia, and the Americas.

7. *"The land shall not be sold in perpetuity, for the land is mine; with me you are but migrant laborers and tenants"* (Lev 25:23). In Scripture, property is intended for the furthering of life for all (use value). By contrast, capitalism makes private property absolute and encloses common land and resources. This continues today in widespread land grabs (for example, in Africa and Latin America), in the privatization of the genetic commons of humanity (through patents), and through the privatization of land, water, air, and so forth.

8. Both ancient and modern individualism begins with the infiltration of money and private property into daily life. For most people in the globalized capitalist world, individualism is self-evident. For Luther, by contrast, there is no such thing as a neutral, observing, and calculating individual. Either people are determined by God – in which case they live compassionately and righteously in relation to others, above all toward those considered the "least" (Mt 5:31ff.) – or they allow themselves to be determined by the power of sin, living distorted, self-centered lives that destroy other creatures.

9. The capitalist economy drives unlimited growth which endangers all life on our planet. Human beings are created by God with the mission "to serve (*abad*) and keep the garden" (Gen 2:15). Luther begins the *95 Theses* by quoting Jesus' call to repentance: "When our Lord and Master Jesus Christ said, 'Repent' (Mt 4:17), he willed the entire life of believers to be one of repentance" (*95 Theses*, 1). Today this means that, personally and collectively, we seek to break free from the destructive rule of money. By trusting instead in the liberating righteousness of God, we are empowered to live in compassion and solidarity with other humans and the rest of creation.

10. According to Scripture, human beings form one body with many members, who serve one another (1 Cor 12). But according to the logic and practice of advanced capitalism, we are driven by competition. According to Luther, we are created, sustained, and empowered to work with God and others for the sake of justice and peace in the economy, in the political order, and in the church (*On the Bondage of the Will*). Here Luther follows the Waldensians, Wycliffe, and Hus.

11. Economic individualization is reflected in the religious individualization of salvation. By contrast, both the Bible and Luther speak of free persons in just relationships. From the Middle Ages on, there have been spiritualizing tendencies that are still strong in our churches. Reading and preaching on biblical texts individualistically implicitly or explicitly supports capitalist-based assumptions today.

12. *According to Jesus, that person is just who forgives debts for the sake of those indebted, rather than abiding by rules of debt repayment (Mt 6:12).* According to Paul the power of sin (as embodied in Roman law, a greed economy, and imperial rule) makes the law into an instrument of death. He proposes building alternative communities of Jews and Greeks who live in solidarity in the spirit of the Messiah who was crucified by the Empire. Those whom Rome had made enemies of each other are reconciled with God and with each other.

13. The Church Fathers interpreted the death of Jesus on the Cross in terms of a ransom theory. Anselm of Canterbury (1033-1109) turns this upside down in his satisfaction theory. According to him the law of debt-repayment stands higher than God. This is why God must sacrifice his son in order to establish a storehouse of merits, which people can draw on in order to pay off their debts. This not only lays the ground for the medieval penitential system, which Luther rejects, but also for capitalism's law of debt repayment.

14. Luther returns to the biblical truth that God forgives with no exceptions, and out of this forgiveness grows the trust that grounds solidarity with the neighbor. Thus, if someone is in need, Christians respond with interest-free lending and giving. It follows that the government should also intervene in the market when public welfare is endangered. Today, however, capitalism makes the market absolute and favors government intervention only for the interest of capital accumulation. Drawing inspiration from Scripture and the Reformation, faith communities must resist!

15. *The Spirit of God affirms cultural and linguistic diversity in the story of Pentecost (Acts 2).* From the fourth century until the Reformation, the Bible was read only in Latin. Wycliffe and the later Reformers opened up diversity again by allowing people to hear Scripture in their own language. This diversity is once again challenged by the homogenizing force of the global market, which turns all humans into consuming indi-

viduals, agriculture into agribusiness, regional selling of goods into transnational chains, and local and regional products into export-driven monocultures.

16. *The Bible establishes a political economy of "enough for all" based on the sharing of what is given for the common good of all (Exodus 16).* The reformers were unanimous in believing that the economy should serve the common good and the specific needs of the neighbor. In our time, we are not calling for a return to the historical forms of socialism that have had some effects as destructive as capitalism, but instead call for forms of economic life that build on God's gifts, protect the commons, and produce and distribute goods and services in ways that are both democratic and ecologically sensitive.

17. *Scripture affirms that all human beings, female and male, are created in the image of God and thus equal in worth (Gen 1:26-28).* In the book of Judges, as well as in Torah texts, this affirmation led to the formation of communities of solidarity. This tradition was taken up in early Christianity (Acts 2 and 4). Voices in the radical Reformation appealed to these texts and sought to establish not only political but also economic democracy.

18. Luther's teaching on justification by grace through faith in Christ alone (Rom 5:1) is a legitimate and liberating interpretation of Scripture within the oppressions of late medieval piety and against emergent money lending-for-interest economy. Forgiveness of sins by grace, deliverance from the power of the devil, and the promise of eternal life in this context meant not only spiritual freedom but freedom for reconciliation with and ethical responsibility to the neighbor (*Freedom of a Christian*).

19. While for Luther, justification by grace alone expressed this understanding of equality, the Reformation failed to make this concrete socially and economically. In fact, later Lutheranism even turned social and economic inequality into a hierarchical God-given order! This culminated in asserting the autonomy of the market and/or the state, which both Scripture and Luther explicitly critique.

20. *According to Scripture, people are justified by grace and not by their performance (Mt 20).* The performance myth, according to which people are judged by their merit, or by getting what they deserve, must be set

over against the principle of need, which is the equivalent of the righteousness of faith. The social and ethical consequences that follow from this constitute a critique of today's work world, which is dominated by this performance ideology and the negative effects that result.

21. While Luther's teaching about the two kingdoms has been used to justify political quietism and passive obedience to the state (Rom 13:1), this teaching needs to be reinterpreted as a call to political vigilance and activism by Christians to live out their public responsibility to the neighbor in advocating for peace, justice, and the integrity of the creation.

22. *"Do not be conformed to the structures of this world order but be transformed by the renewing of your mind..." (Rom 12:2).* Because of their effect on the common people of his day, Luther said a clear "No!" to the structure and practices of the bank and trading companies of his time: "Nothing good can come of them. If the companies are to survive, justice and honesty must perish. If justice and honesty are to survive, the companies must perish" (*WA* 15, 312). Today the forces of economic growth, monetary expansion, and privatization threaten planetary death. In this regard, tinkering with the social system will not help. A long-term alternative to the neoliberal capitalist system is needed. Many examples show that a new monetary and property order, oriented towards the common good and publicly responsible, is not only necessary but possible.

23. *"Blessed are those who hunger and thirst after righteousness, for they shall be satisfied" (Mt 5:6).* The new order can take root in any local area. Church communities can participate in decentralized local energy supplies and connect with social movements with slogans such as: "If we leave it to the politicians, it will be too little too late. If we try and do it ourselves, it will be too little. If we work together, however, it may be just enough, just in time" (Transition Town Movement).

"The message of the cross...is the power of God" (1 Cor 1:18)

24. Since the Middle Ages, many churches and theologians have understand Jesus' death as God's "sacrificing his son" in order to save human beings. This interpretation turns God into a sadistic ruler who produces suffering. However, God saves from violence, not through violence.

25. The cross was the Roman Empire's instrument to execute rebels and fugitive slaves. Many innocent people became victims of this public demonstration of power. The picture of the Crucified One with a gasmask, of a crucified girl or woman, and the painting of a crucified *campesino* remind us of those many people who in our day continue to be killed by the dominant powers. The crucified Jesus is deeply connected to them.

26. According to biblical tradition, the martyrdom of the just effects forgiveness of the sins for the people (4 Maccabees 17:21) and the innocent death of the servant of God makes the many just (Is 53:11f.), which opens up new meanings of Jesus' death on the cross.

27. The encounter with the risen Christ sheds new light on the cross (Luke 24). God gives life to the dead and calls into existence the things that do not exist (Rom 4:17).

28. In the light of the resurrection, Jesus is written into the lamentations of traumatized people, giving them hope ("My God, why have you forsaken me?" – Ps 22:2; Mk 16:34; "The poor shall eat and be satisfied" – Ps 22:26).

29. Theology of the cross can overcome a previous tainting imagery between the cross and crusade in the colonial time. This refers to a refurbishing of the theology of the cross for the theology of life (resurrection) seen in light of God's solidarity with the *minjung*, economic justice for all, and integrity of the ecological web of life.

30. So the resurrection proves to be judgment against the powers of violence, the most radical implementation of God's unconditional solidarity with all suffering creatures and an expression of God's faithfulness and justice toward all people and creation.

31. Biblically understood, faith is repentance. Luther declared: "Yet it does not mean solely inner repentance; such inner repentance is worthless unless it produces various outward acts of repentance" (*95 Theses*, 3). On the one side, we are called to a process of truth and reconciliation about the ethical failings of the Reformation. On the other side, accepting God's justice for us, we allow ourselves to be drawn into this history of liberation by doing justice: "Only the believers obey, and only the obedient believe" (Bonhoeffer).

32. Luther's theology of justification needs to be extended and renewed in different times and places, especially in light of Luther's congenial notion of the Gospel as the living voice of God. The Reformation teaching of justification should break through its encapsulation within Western possessive individualism and political quietism, liberating human beings from all the idolatrous assumptions, upon which we base our lives: the privileges of species, sex, gender, ethnicity, religion, nationality, and class. Justification should be reclaimed as a way of expressing God's deep compassion in the death of Jesus Christ for all, reinforcing our public responsibility for the political realm, economic justice, and recognition of the Other.

"See, everything has become new" (2 Cor 5:17)

33. The Christian gospel is indeed about reconciliation between God and humanity, and about reconciliation between human beings. But if "gospel" does not succeed in reconciling the whole of creation, it is not the gospel (2 Co 5:18).

34. The Reformation's recognition that we are saved through faith by God's grace should also be a recognition that God's gracious presence is in all creation, responding to its cries (Rom 8:18-23).

35. While many gains were achieved in the sixteenth century era when the Reformers criticized the worship of material reality, they went too far when they rejected all notion of the sacramental by stripping away at ma-

terial culture in a surge of iconoclasm. Here they failed to recognize that all of life is divinely infused and that the whole world is a sacramental reality.

36. The Reformation's recognition that by grace we are saved through faith should also affirm that God's gracious presence is in all of creation. God's communion with the world in Jesus Christ means that as followers of Christ we too are called into communion with the world – a this-worldly faith that is made real when we join in God's mission for the renewal of all creation.

37. Mother Earth is being crucified and has to experience resurrection (Rom 8:22). This is very important for our life as human beings, animals, plants, air, water, and earth. We are human beings not because we consume, but because we need to live connected to creation, caring for her and for our life.

38. "The Gospel of all creatures" (Mark 16:15, according to Luther's translation), the good news of God to the entire creation (Psalm 119), is interrupted, if human beings, made in God's image, destroy this order by exercising injustice (Rom 1:18-20).

39. The Gospel challenges us to preserve the creation as God's garden through a righteous personal stance and through new economic, social, and ecological politics for the welfare of the entire creation and all peoples of the world.

40. "Life in fullness" (John 10:10) breaks with previous concepts of economic development: it focuses on our inextricable relation to creation, to which the human community must be oriented. Life in fullness does not aim at "having more," as in accumulation and growth, but in living toward balance in all relationships.

41. All human beings and the whole of nature have a right to and a need for "bread and roses." Human beings and nature have a hunger for bread and beauty. An unfinished task of Reformation theology is to fight for and proclaim the right for life in fullness for the whole creation.

42. The Earth gives life to all creatures (Gen 1:24). What nature brings forth is a gift from God, of which we should take good care as an expression of our gratitude and calling as disciples (Ps 104).

43. Life in fullness does not mean consumerism but being connected to the whole of nature. Human beings and human industry are not the final purpose of creation: God's final act in creation is to bring us to Sabbath rest in worship and in relationships (Gen 2:2).

44. The gospel challenges us to preserve and renew creation as God's garden (Gen 2:15; Isaiah 65:17; 2 Peter 3:13) by adopting a modest personal lifestyle and collaborating with people of different cultures and religions in the world to implement life-affirming economic, social, and environmental policies.

45. The question of creation is closely related to the life of future generations. Theology has consistently been informed by adult personhood and not by childhood. Instead human beings are to be understood as determined by God's story with them. This is particularly true for children and must be taken seriously by theology in view of their endangered future.

46. Children's rights necessitate protecting children against violations, oppression, and exploitation. It is, however, equally important to appreciate children in all their capabilities and weaknesses, in their unique characteristics and their imperfections as with any adult human being. For theology children must be liberated from objectification and become subjects for the sake of their own future.

"Blessed are the peacemakers" (Matthew 5:9)

47. Hear the cries of those who have suffered violence, especially those made victims by followers of the Reformation – such as peasants, Anabaptists (Mennonites), Jews, Muslims! Hear the cries of those suffering violence today – whether through domestic abuse, economic exploitation, violations of human rights, injustice against creation, state imperialism, and ongoing wars!

48. We call for conversion to the praxis of peacemaking (Isaiah 2:2-4). The way of peacemaking, as embodied by Jesus, joins God's nonviolent praxis with the cause of all those who practice nonviolence. Nonviolent praxis is a sign of God's reign of shalom (Isaiah 11:6-9).

Illustration of Jan Luyken in "Märtyrerspiegel": Dirk Willems rescues his persecutor, who had handed him over to the ash heap. (from:http:// de.wikipedia.org/wiki/ Dirk Willems)

49. The phenomenon of violence becomes evident wherever there is resistance to the practice of peacemaking, especially in social, political, economic, or state violence where many victims cry out to heaven for God's help.

50. Violence is widespread and present in many forms – structural violence, technological violence, military violence, physical and psychological violence of every kind. The universality of violence becomes evident in the endemic practice of identifying others as "enemies," especially in making others into scapegoats (Acts 7:54-60).

51. Although reasons and analyses of the cause of violence can be given, all violence is in reaction to previous forms of violence.

52. It is not possible to justify or legitimize violence; it is always illegitimate. There is no "measured" violence, no "just" war," no "justifiable" war. Luther, Zwingli and Calvin only tolerated limited violence for minimizing greater violence. However, even this logic is anachronistic in face of modern weapons of mass destruction. Violence can never serve as a means for attaining any goal, for God has reconciled all things to Godself (Colossians 1:19-20).

53. Enforcing the law cannot rest upon violence. Wherever humans suffer violence, they are to be protected by practices of peacemaking. In the time of the Reformation the exercise of violence began exclusively as warfare and police violence on the part of the "authorities," determined exclusively as a protection of the neighbor from violence. This radical

limitation has been largely suppressed. This extremely limited use of violence, where it must be employed, is never to be understood as a matter of course but always as a warning sign of our broken world.

54. Legal systems are established on the basis of violence, a kind of foundational violence. This violence, however, legitimizes no further violence but rather calls for righteous action (Mt 5:38-42). Legal systems must be judged against the yardstick of bringing peace through justice.

55. Practicing peace means living, speaking, and acting without violence. Practicing peace means doing that which promotes peace – doing justice, listening, forgiving, sharing, giving, healing, being merciful, helping – all of these as works of resistance to violence (Mt 5:3-11). All of this is worship (Rom 12:1-2); worship is practicing peace.

56. Practicing peace also entails how one speaks, exercising no rhetorical violence (Mt 5:33-37). The gospel is inherently nonviolent – promising, inviting, witnessing – never forcing.

57. Practicing peace means being dedicated to the common life of all in a political community that is uniquely characterized by peaceful practices. Practicing peace means following the consequences of this conviction, being realistic with regard to one's own responsibility, because only by doing so will peace prevail in the world (Mt 5:43-48).

"Bear one another's burdens, and in this way you will fulfill the Torah of Christ" (Gal 6:2)

58. The Reformation originates with Luther's rediscovery of God's justice as creative and renewing power, as spelled out in the letters of Paul. In his doctrine of justification, Luther interprets this justice as God's merciful care even for the ungodly (*sola gratia*), and as trust in the faithfulness of God (*sola fide*) in Christ (*solus Christus*).

59. For Paul, the justice of God implies the visionary insight, that "in Christ" the polarities and hierarchies of this "present evil world order" (Gal 1:4) have been overcome. "We" are not what segregates us from the "others" but what interconnects us with them. The human divisions of nation, religion, gender, and class, which constitute the "self" as enemy and rival of the "other," are removed in baptism "like old garments." A new praxis

of becoming "one" through mutuality and solidarity creates a new form of being human – and a new world (Gal 6:2.15). "There is no longer Jew or Greek, there is no longer slave or free, there is no longer male and female; for all of you are one in the Messiah Jesus" (Gal 3:28). God's justice, the justification of the human being, and human justice are all inseparably connected.

60. One of the most troublesome and non-Pauline aspects of justification theology (as it was framed by the Reformation and subsequently interpreted by Protestantism) is the concept of "law." Luther regularly juxtaposes "justice/righteousness through the law" with "justice/righteousness through faith" and understands this antithesis as the irreconcilable polarity of Judaism against Christianity.

61. This fateful polarization emerges from Luther's interpretation of Paul's letter to the Galatians. Luther falsely identifies the law that Paul criticizes with the Jewish Torah. The core controversy of Galatians about the non-necessity of the Jewish ritual of circumcision for the Christ believers is thus understood as a rejection of Judaism as such. As recent scholarship has shown, however, the primary target in Paul's struggle with his Galatian opponents was not Jewish Torah, but the law and order of the Roman Empire. It prescribed certain rules of conformity for both Jews and Gentiles. The Pauline community model of solidarity between Jews and Non-Jews "in Christ" clashes in the first place with these imperial settings and social norms, not the least within the framework of Roman emperor religion.

62. The Reformation furthermore identified Judaism with Roman Catholicism, labeling both as "legalistic religions" that achieve "justice/righteousness through works of the law." The polarity of "works versus grace/faith" and "gospel versus law," applied to concrete people, has had a disastrous impact throughout the history of interpretation. It was not only read in an anti-Jewish and anti-Catholic manner but also turned against "enthusiasts", Anabaptists, Muslims, and other "heretics", often with deadly consequences.

63. Up to this day liberation theologies, feminist theologies, and social movements are often accused of "work righteousness" or "legalism" and thus denied legitimacy as expressions of proper faith. Justification theology and this-worldly justice are played off against each other.

64. Against this backdrop, the Protestant tradition at its core is compromised by defining its identity against the "other" – the one who acts, believes, lives, or thinks differently – rather than in line with Paul's radical solidarity with one another across boundaries and segregations. In light of the present world crisis, it is an urgent imperative that Protestant justification theology re-think the justice of God and return to its biblical roots.

65. The negative classification of Judaism and law also has become a major factor in the fundamental downgrading of the whole Old Testament. The trinitarian formula of "Father, Son, and Holy Spirit" as common witness of all Christian churches testifies to the indissoluble bond between the two parts of the scriptural canon. Regaining the unity of both Testaments is an essential task for doing theology in the legacy of the Reformation today.

66. The Messiah Jesus of Nazareth is the invitation to all peoples to participate in the future that has been promised to Israel: a just and equal society inspired by the Torah. The Christian church is not the replacement of Israel. Israel is the root of the church: "You do not support the root, the root supports you" (Rom 11:18).

67. The Messiah Jesus proclaims the kingdom of God, God's just world, coming near (Mt 4:17). In the horizon of this hope, Jesus interprets the Torah of Israel in the context of his time (Mt 5-7). The criteria of his interpretation are the exclusive worship of God and the love of the neighbor, especially to the poor and the disinherited (Mk 12:28-34). The situation of "the least" (Mt 25:31-46) determines how the Torah has to be interpreted. So the Torah, of which not the tiniest commandment is canceled, becomes the orientation for the messianic communities (Mt 5:17-20; 28:19-20; see also Rom 3:31). Jesus' call to his disciples to orient themselves according to his interpretation of the Torah aims at continuously reinterpreting and revitalizing the Torah in the hope of God's coming kingdom.

68. In Paul's letter to the Romans, we hear the cry of people who find themselves caught in the imperial system that makes it impossible to live according to the norms of Torah. Sin is not just an abstract human condition but materializes in concrete social circumstances. For Paul, imperial power structures embody the power of sin that inevitably turns people in-

to transgressors of the life-giving laws of Torah and makes them complicit with the forces of death and self-destruction (Rom 7:24).

69. Paul's justification by grace through faith thus implies a twofold liberation of both human beings and of Torah from the power of sin. The messianic communities establish a space where Jews and non-Jews "in Christ" can fulfill the Torah as law of life through love of one another – even of enemies (Rom 8:2; 12:1-21; 13:8-10).

70. The critical stance against the law in Paul and the Reformation is not directed against the legal order of societies as such (*usus civilis legis*). Legal rules and law are necessary in order to sustain human societies. The critique is directed exclusively against abusing the law on behalf of the strong against the weak, a practice already critiqued by the Prophets. The law is made for the people, not the people for the law, as both Jesus and the rabbis maintained (Mk 2:27; Babylonian Talmud, *Trakt. Eruvin* 41b). Human legislation must always be examined critically and continuously adjusted in order to defend justice for the victims instead of "legally" covering up the injustice of the dominant order.

71. Luther's reference to the Ten Commandments simply as "natural law" (Moses as "the Jews' *Sachsenspiegel*") poses a specific challenge. It eclipses the specificity of Torah as an alternative law that at decisive points moves away from the exploitative legislation of its environment – such as with regard to Sabbath laws, forgiveness of debt, or the prohibition against accumulation through greed (Tenth Commandment). This critical edge vanishes as Torah is simply identified with existing legal codes, like the Roman law, that absolutize private property.

72. Above all, in his *Small Catechism* Luther dropped the politically concrete preamble of the Decalogue: "I am the Lord your God who brought you out of the land of Egypt, out of the house of slavery" (Ex 20:2; Deut 5:6). Luther also extended the command to honor one's parents to honor authorities as such. These two symptomatic changes of the scriptural base in Luther's most influential catechism are indicative for how Lutheranism became prone to obedience and subservience towards any established order, including severely unjust ones, instead of being faithful to the God of liberation (*sola fide*) and standing in solidarity with the downtrodden.

73. When the established order lacks righteous action and remains indifferent to the concerns of the common people, especially to the least (Mt 25:31-40), revealing its idolatries and imposing an unacceptable way of life, Christians should not only disobey but also resist such evil authorities.

74. Within imperial structures, the liberating biblical instructions orient us to resist the death-bound logic and laws of violent, enslaving powers. This requires regaining an in-depth appreciation of the liberating traditions of both the Old and New Testaments. As in the time of the Reformation, we need a new "revival" of cutting-edge Bible study in our congregations that engages not only individuals but also the current social and economic problems in critical and liberating ways. For example, forgiveness of debt and God's forgiveness of guilt belong inseparably together biblically (Mt 6:12). Christians today should be empowered to get to know specifically the Old Testament, the Hebrew Bible, as a rich treasure for daily life and ethical judgements.

75. Disciples of Jesus Christ advocate a desire to understand the mystery of God in community with the sacred texts of divine revelation also in other religions and joy in strengthening the dialogue in their common efforts of constructing a better world together with Jews, Muslims, Hindus, Buddhists, and every other religion and culture from Africa, North America, Latin America, the Caribbean, Asia, the Pacific, the Middle East and Europe (Isaiah 49:6). The Gospel contradicts every form of cultural, religious, and military invasion.

76. A postcolonial reading of Reformation theology advances a project of enculturation, in order to underpin inter-religious dialogue as prophetic dialogue, adopting a new departure in the critique of colonization by Reformation theology or misuse of its scholarship in the service of the powerful.

"The Spirit blows where it wills" (John 3:8)

77. In the spirit of the church that emerged out of the Reformation, it is crucial that we listen today to the cries of people around the world, who feel that the church does not see but overlooks and excludes their suffering,

oppression, and cultural realities today (Mt 25:31ff.). Our ignorance and avoidance deepen rather than heal the divisions in church and society.

78. The Reformation movements understood the church not so much as an institution, but as the baptized people of God gathered in local communities. The church as community in the discipleship of Jesus is the holy space in which the universal Word of God is listened to and the sacraments celebrated in many different voices, traditions, and confessions for the sake of the mending of the world (*tikkun olam*).

79. The priesthood of all believers was a radical cry for democratizing the most powerful institution of that day, the Roman Church. Today it must be translated as a revolutionary call for universal citizenship and equitable distribution of the products of human labor.

80. In the 16th century the church was reformed, but it soon became enmeshed again with structures and practices that are patriarchal, hierarchical, and captive to powerful economic and political interests. Its persecution of Jews, Anabaptists, and Muslims was deplorable! In addition to repenting for such, the Spirit of God impels movement away from such Constantinian expressions of church into more participatory, boundary-crossing embodiments of church that are truly catholic, inclusive of all, and collaborative across boundaries of religion, ethnicity, geography, and self-interest.

81. Discipleship in Christ requires a stance of contemplation, spiritual cleansing, enlightenment, and surrender to the will of God. If we hear the voice of God with the fear of Rahab (Joshua 2) or the fear of Mary and Elisabeth (Luke 1), and allow the flood of God's Spirit into the depths of our being, thereby we undertake the path of discipleship in Christ. The women in the Bible and the women of the Radical Reformation demonstrate for us the way of discipleship, mysticism, witness, and martyrdom.

82. The Spirit of God acts freely, blowing when and where the Spirit so desires, continually renewing the Church. It cannot be a property of anyone, nor kept captive by institutional interests or doctrinal definitions.

83. The Spirit brings about renewal and change both in church and society. In addition to transforming individual persons, the Spirit also enables believers to struggle alongside those of other religions, ideologies, and so-

cial movements, and to endure suffering caused by this commitment to love, solidarity, and justice.

84. When Luther called the cross a mark or sign of the church, he was establishing a criterion: to be the church, the church needs to become vulnerable by being with and for the poor and to risk its social or political status by publicly protesting against unjust structures and policies.

85. Rather than only being focused on individuals, the church must venture a critical communal ecclesial focus for resistance and transformation. Otherwise, injustices continue to have free reign, distorting our most basic relationships to God, ourselves, one another, and the whole of creation. Through practices such as preaching, teaching, celebrating, caring, community-formation, and organizing with others, the church can help counter the sin, bondage, and blindness that enable domination by the many facets of empire to prevail.

86. Through the power of the indwelling and connecting Spirit, those who are most different from one another are transformed into one body or a "new creation" (1 Cor 12:12; 2 Cor 5:17). While fostering renewal and change, the Spirit also draws people together into the unity of the body of Christ, which cannot be used to justify further church divisions. A reforming church must be reconciled with itself and endeavor to overcome divisions between East and West, between Catholics and Protestants, and between the various Reformation churches, in order that all may come to celebrate at the Lord's Table together.

87. A reforming church continually is being transformed by what it receives from other theological traditions and cultures. In emphasizing how the Spirit is linked to the Word, Luther was criticizing anyone claiming to have received special revelations by the Spirit apart from what is revealed in Scripture. This must not be misinterpreted as limiting the Spirit's free work in people, including those of other traditions or religions, as well as in the rest of creation (Rom 8:22-23).

88. Luther's critique of the enthusiasts cannot be transferred to our times as a generalized critique of Pentecostalism. While "theologies of prosperity" must be criticized on the basis of a theology of the cross, we must be attentive to the work of the Spirit within Pentecostal movements for building up community, rescuing people from marginalization, and restoring

the dignity of people who suffer under poverty, disease, addictions, and unemployment.

89. The rediscovery and re-reading of biblical traditions from the perspective of the marginalized on the basis of social analysis, the contextual and intercultural reading of the Bible in many different contexts throughout the world, is an important sign of hope that the liberating hermeneutics of the Reformation traditions are active in many churches today.

90. At the heart of the Reformation was universal access to education, together with a critical re-reading of the Bible in relation to contextual situations of the day. As churches rooted in the Reformation have spread throughout the world, this approach to the Bible often does not prevail. Instead, individualistic spiritualities and religious fundamentalisms, which collude with powerful interests and which perpetuate illusions, are on the increase.

91. Recovering the crucial role of biblical theology and critical theological education (together with education in general) is key to the ongoing reformation and renewal needed within global Christianity in the 21st century.

92. Blessed are those who do not fit into the systems of this world, but who stand in protest of God's continued crucifixion in the schemes of this world (Rom 12: 2) and who cooperate with others in building a new world with justice and peace in human communities!

93. We are in need of a "New Reformation!" Now as then, people can easily be pious. However, they find inadequate forms of expression in the churches, because the churches are alienated from the realities of the actual world in which people live. As with Martin Luther, we need a renewal of language and a return to the liberating message of the Gospel.

94. Bonhoeffer's proposal of a worldly engaged Christianity, which would discover a new language for the old Gospel, must be translated as: "Prayer and action of the righteous among people". All church talk "must be born anew from this prayer and this action" and be taken up in liberation theology's insistence on the inseparableness of orthopraxis and orthodoxy.

"Radicalizing Reformation – Provoked by the Bible and Today's Crises" is not an option but an imperative for church and theology today. Luther himself made Scripture the criterion for all tradition. Contextual interpretations of the Bible have sharpened this hermeneutic critically and prophetically. Living at the onset of modern capitalism, Luther engaged in systemic critique. Living at the end of this murderous and suicidal period of human history, we must listen anew to the sources of our faith and join others in "putting a spoke in the wheel of the car, when the driver is drunk." Let us continue together with others on that pilgrimage of justice and peace!

Halle, 7 August 2014

Prof. Dr. Walter Altmann/Brazil, Prof. Dr. Charles Amjad-Ali/Pakistan/USA, Dr. Claudete Beise Ulrich/Brazil/Germany, Prof. Dr. Daniel Beros, Argentina, Prof. Dr. Karen Bloomquist/USA, Leonardo Boff, Prof. emer. for Theology and Ethics/Petrópolis, Prof. Dr. Klara Butting/Germany, Prof. Dr. Paul Chung/Korea/USA, Prof. Dr. Frank Crüsemann/Germany, Marlene Crüsemann/Germany, Dr. Silfredo Dalferth/Brazil/Germany, Prof. Dr. Wanda Deifelt/USA, Prof. Dr. Martin Dreher/Brazil, Prof. Dr. Ulrich Duchrow/Germany, Prof. Dr. Enrique Dussel/Mexico, Prof. Dr. Fernando Enns/Germany, Prof. Dr. Antonio González Fernández/Spain, Prof. Dr. Timothy Gorringe/UK, Prof. Dr. Peter Heltzel/USA, Prof. Dr. Franz Hinkelammert/Costa Rica, Dr. Martin Hoffmann/Germany/Costa Rica, Prof. Dr. Claudia Janssen/Germany, Prof. Dr. Carsten Jochum-Bortfeld/Germany, Prof. Dr. Brigitte Kahl/USA, Prof. Dr. Rainer Kessler/Germany, Prof. Dr. Karl Koop/Canada, Prof. Dr. Maake J Masango/South Africa, Prof. Cynthia D. Moe-Lobeda, Ph.D./USA, Dr. Kenneth Mtata/Zimbabwe/Geneva, Prof. Dr. Craig L. Nessan/USA, Prof. Dr. Axel Noack/University Halle-Wittenberg, Prof. Dr. Jaime Prieto/Costa Rica, Dr. Edelbert Richter/Germany, Prof. Dr. Santhosh J. Sahayadoss/Indien, Prof Dr. Dr. h.c. Luise Schottroff/Germany, Prof. Dr. Sturla Stalsett/Norway, Prof. Dr. Marisa Strizzi/Argentina, Prof. Dr. Samuel Torvend/USA, Prof. Dr. Hans G. Ulrich/Germany, Prof. Dr. Karin Ulrich/Germany, Lic. Ton Veerkamp/Germany, Dr. Dietrich Werner/Germany, Prof. Dr. Vitor Westhelle/Brazil, Prof. Dr. Renate Wind/Germany, Prof. Dr. Lauri Wirth/Brazil

Supporters (By January 1, 2015):

Anna Marie Aagaard, prof. emerita, University of Aarhus/Denmark, Prof. Dr. Evangeline Anderson-Rajkumar/India, The Rev. Norbert Arntz/Germany, Prof. Dr. Sigurd Bergmann/Schweden, Prof. Dr. Gregory Baum/Canada, Prof. Dr. Ulrich Becker/Germany, Dr. Dick Boer/Netherlands, Prof. Dr. Allan Boesak/South Africa/USA, Prof. emer. Dr. Pamela K Brubaker/USA, Prof. Dr. Nancy Cardoso/Brazil, Bishop Duleep de Chickera, Sri Lanka, Prof. Dr. John B. Cobb, Jr./USA, The Rev. Dr. Norma Cook Everist/USA, The Rev. Dr. Lisa

E. Dahill/USA, The Rev. Dr. Susan E. Davies/USA, The Rev Dr. Moiseraele Prince Dibeela/Botswana, Dr. Gabriele Dietrich/India, Dr. Beat Dietschy/Switzerland, Prof. Jacob J. Erikson/USA, Dr. Christopher Ferguson, General Secretary of the World Communion of Reformed Churches/Canada/Germany, The Rev. Dr. Jerry Folk/USA, Dr. Hartmut Futterlieb/Germany, Dr. Wolfgang Gern/Germany, Prof. The Rev. Dr. Arnfríður Guðmundsdóttir, Iceland, Rev. The Rev. Dr. Anna Karin Hammar, Sweden, Prof. Dr. Cees J. Hamelink/Netherlands, Prof. Dr. John Hiemstra/Canada, The Rev. Dr. George S Johnson/USA, The Rev. Dr. Kristin Johnston Largen/USA, Jonas Adelin Jørgensen, Secretary General, Danish Mission Council, Rev. Dr Jooseop Keum/Korea/Geneva, Rev Dr Sivin Kit/Malaysia, Dr. René Krüger/Argentina, Dr. Gerhard Liedke/Germany, Carter Lindberg, Professor Emeritus/USA, Prof. Dr. Dr. Peter Lodberg/Denmark, The Rev. Dr. David Lull/USA, Man Hei Yip, Ph.D. Candidate/U.S.A./Hong Kong, The Rev. Dr. Jim Martin-Schramm/USA, Dr. Daniel F. and Dr. Jean B. Martensen/USA, Esther Menn, Ph.D./USA, Dr. Rogate Mshana/Tansania, Ched Myers, PhD, Bartimaeus Cooperative Ministries/USA, Prof. Dr. Harry Noormann/Germany, Prof. Dr. Park Seong-Won/Korea, The Rev. Dr. Richard J. Perry, Jr./USA, Prof. Dr. Winston Persuad/U.S.A./Guyana, Dr. Praveen PS. Perumalla/India, The Rev. Dr. Vincenzo Petracca/Germany, Prof. Raymond Pickett/USA, The Rev. Dr. Shanta Premawardhana/USA, The Rev. Melinda Quivik, PhD/USA, Prof. J. Paul Rajashekar, U.S.A./India, Rev. Christopher Rajkumar/India, Prof. Dr. Larry Rasmussen/USA, Prof. Dr. David Rhoads/USA, Prof. Dr. Joerg Rieger/USA, Dr. Martin Robra/Germany/Geneva, Terra Rowe, Ph.D. Candidate/USA, Prof. Dr. Barbara Rossing/USA, The Rev. Robert Saler, Ph.D./USA, Violaine and Dr. Julio de Santa Ana/Uruguay/Geneva, The Rev. Dr. H. Paul Santmire/USA, Prof. Dr. Thomas H. Schattauer/USA, Prof. Dr. Franz Segbers/Germany, Dr. Jiří Silný/Czech Republic, Prof. Dr. Lilia Solano/Columbia, Prof. Mary M. Solberg/USA, Prof. Dr. Kirsi Stjerna/USA, Prof. Dr. Jung Mo Sung/Brazil, The Rev. Linda Thomas, PhD/USA, Prof. Dr. Detlov Tonsing/South Africa, Prof. Dr. Stylianos Tsompanidis/Greece, The Rev. Dr. Alicia Vargas/USA, Prof. Dr. Mammen Varkey/India, Prof. Dr. Petros Vassiliadis/Greece, Prof. Dr. Vuyani Vellem/South Africa, Prof. Anna Marie Vigen, Ph.D./USA, Dr. Klausdieter Wazlawik/Germany, Dr. Paul A. Wee/USA, The Rev. Dr. Paul Westermeyer/USA, The Rev. Josef Purnama Widyatmadja/Indonesia, The Rev. Prof. Philip L. Wickeri/USA/China, Dr. M. E. Greetje Witte-Rang/Netherlands, The Rev. Nancy Wright/USA.

Website: http://www.radicalizing-reformation.com/index.php/de

Introduction

The modern ecumenical movement has achieved tremendous rapprochement among Christian denominations, especially from the last third of the 20th century to the present. Bilateral and multilateral dialogues have attained unprecedented agreement about long disputed points of Christian teaching, resulting in many full communion agreements among Protestant denominations. A prominent instance is represented by the "Baptism, Eucharist, Ministry" statement and consensual process initiated by the World Council of Churches in 1982. The resulting ecumenical progress in the arena of Faith and Order is well known, documented, and celebrated.

Less well known or recognized are the signs of ecumenical convergence related to the most critical matters of Work and Life. The Radicalizing Reformation project, undertaken at the 500th anniversary of the Reformation in 2017, documents the consensus of an increasing number of progressive Christian scholars that the created world and humankind are facing crises of enormous and unprecedented proportions related to matters of global economic injustice, inherent equality among all people, the sustainability of the ecosystem, radical peacemaking in response to cultures and acts of violence, protecting the vulnerable (all persons and all creatures), and engaging in interreligious reconciliation. This volume, like the other four in this series, provides challenging and provocative evidence of this emerging consensus among Protestant scholars from around the globe about the most urgent ethical questions confronting humanity and the creation itself at this juncture in history.

This volume, *Liberation from Violence for Life in Peace*, provides particular historical analyses of the Reformation's failure to contribute to peaceful existence in the 16th century (especially with reference to the peasants, Anabaptists, Jews, and Muslims/Turks), draws appreciatively from the Mennonite tradition for constructive peacemaking, and explores the essential dimensions of *shalom* for our time. The authors of the chapters in this volume come from diverse Christian traditions – Lutheran, Reformed, Mennonite. While these traditions remained unreconciled with each other at the time of the Reformation – and in the case of the Mennonites, violated by the majority Protestant groups in the 16th century – here they join with one voice in an emerging ecumenical consensus regarding a response to the crises facing humanity at the present hour. This consensus comes to pointed expression in the "94 Theses – Provoked by the Bible and Today's Crises," the heart of the Radicalizing Reformation project. The chapters of this particular volume document research and articulate arguments undergirding claims made in the 94 Theses, particularly in six arenas that are indispensable to "the things that make for peace" (Luke 19:42): a summons to repentance, the imperative of global economic justice, heeding the cry of the earth, an appeal for radical peacemaking, the need for interreligious reconciliation, and the call for a New Reformation.

1. Summons to Repentance

Luther's first thesis from 1517 reads: "When our Lord and Master Jesus Christ said, 'Repent' (Mt 4:17), he willed the entire life of believers to be one of repentance." Luther added in his third thesis: "Yet it does not mean solely inner repentance; such inner repentance is worthless unless it produces various outward mortifications of the flesh." The signs of outward repentance in our time begin with confession and repentance in relation to all those who were victims of violence in the wake of the Reformation itself, in particular peasants, Anabaptists, and Jews. Not only are the acts of persecution and slaying of peasants during the peasant rebellion, the anathemas against and murdering of Anabaptists, and pogroms and killing of Jews reprehensible for the 16th century, but the historical trajectory of these acts of terror continued to run its course over the centuries, especially through the Holocaust of the 20th century and into our present context. Luther's own devolution to "religious identity politics" needs to be overcome through the exercise of a thoroughgoing "neighbor politics," if we are to begin to overcome the ethical deficits of Luther's legacy (Nessan). A parallel fusing of cross and crusade took particular shape during the time of colonialization (Chung), and in our time is most ominous in the Islamophobic rhetoric, threats of violence, and actual acts of violence against Muslim people. Could Charles Amjad-Ali be accurate in asking whether, without our historical or critical awareness, what Luther "wrote about the Jews could be quite easily applied to [Muslims]"?

Other aspects of the Reformation legacy also call out for repentance. An individualizing approach to Reformation theology, especially a focus on justification apart from attention to nature and community, necessitates ongoing reform (Butting). The Reformation teaching of justification needs to break through its encapsulation within Western possessive individualism and political quietism. Justification must be reclaimed as an expression of God's deep compassion for all in the death of Jesus Christ, promoting public responsibility for the political realm, economic justice, and recognition of the 'Other' (Chung).

2. Imperative of Global Economic Justice

Consistent with the other volumes in this series, the contributors to this book view transformation of the global economic (dis)order as the *sine qua non* of the Reformation needed in our time. The Christian who has been justified by God in Christ values all human life – with particular attention to the needs of the poor, disenfranchised, and marginalized – and is set free by the Gospel to work for the welfare of others. When the secular order becomes indifferent to the concerns of the poor, the Christian must not only disobey but resist such authorities (Sahayadoss). Such commitment requires a reappraisal of the protest character of the Gospel, especially in relation to the contributions of the Radical Reformers in their attempt to carry forward the implications of the Reformation, not only for religious justice but socio-economic justice for all. The Mennonite voices in this volume (González, Koop, Prieto) witness to the emerging consensus among progressive Protestant traditions today that the imperative of economic justice must be a consequence for every stream within Reformation theology. The inseparableness of orthopraxis from orthodoxy comes to pointed expression in Bonhoeffer's proposal of a worldly engaged Christianity, in which the Gospel must be translated as "prayer and righteous action" among humanity (Wind).

3. Heeding the Cry of the Earth

While many gains were achieved in the 16th century when the Reformers criticized the worship of material reality, some went too far in rejecting all notion of the sacramental by stripping away at material culture in a surge of iconoclasm. These Reformers failed to recognize that all of life is divinely infused and that finally the whole world is sacramental reality. While the Christian Gospel is certainly about reconciliation between God and humanity, as well as reconciliation among humans, if the Gospel does not succeed in reconciling the whole of creation, it is not the whole Gospel. God's communion with the world in Jesus Christ means that the followers of Jesus Christ are inextricably called into communion with the world – a this-worldly faith that is made real when we join in God's mission for the renewal of all creation (Koop).

Mother Earth is being crucified and all the creation – human beings, animals, plants, earth, air, water, and all elements – awaits a resurrection (Rom 8:18-22). The center of creation is not humanity but the Sabbath day (Gen 2:2). *Buen vivir* ("good life") does not aim at "having more," accumulation, and economic growth, but at social equilibrium as the foundation for "good life." All that we receive from the earth is pure gift from God, for which we are summoned to lives of gratitude and care for creation (Beise Ulrich). "The Gospel to all creatures" (Mark 16:15), the good news to the entire creation, is interrupted, if human beings, made in God's image, destroy God's created order through injustice. The Gospel to all creatures challenges us to preserve the creation as God's garden both through a righteous personal stance and through new economic, social, and ecological politics for the welfare of the entire creation and all people of the world (Prieto).

4. Appeal for Radical Peacemaking

The 94 Theses set forth in this Radicalizing Reformation project make a radical claim about the need for engaging in nonviolent methods of social change: "It is not possible to justify or legitimize violence; it is always illegitimate. There is no 'measured' violence, no 'just war', no 'justifiable' war. Luther, Zwingli, and Calvin only tolerated limited violence for minimizing greater violence. However, even this logic is anachronistic in face of modern weapons of mass destruction. Violence can never serve as a means for attaining any goal, for God has reconciled all things to Godself (Col 1:19-20)" (Thesis 52). This claim has direct consequences for how we conduct our lives: "Practicing peace means being dedicated to the common life of all in a political community that is uniquely characterized by peaceful practices. Practicing peace means following the consequences of this conviction, being realistic with regard to one's own responsibility, because only by doing so will peace prevail in the world (Mt 5:43-48)" (Thesis 57).

While an "ethics of responsibility" has been conventionally privileged on the basis of both theoretical and practical reasoning, thereby providing grounds for engaging in "just war," a close analysis of such arguments demonstrates their fallibility. An "ethics of conviction," by contrast, consistent with the practice of nonviolence, expresses universal responsibility in ways that are masked by appeals to "responsibility." The pacifism of Jesus, especially as it comes to expression in the Sermon on the Mount, demonstrates that the consistent practice of nonviolence is not only philosophically but also practically more compelling than the default to violence authorized by an ethics of responsibility (González).

5. Need for Interreligious Reconciliation

Interreligious reconciliation begins for Christians with repentance – as the point of departure for a truth and reconciliation process – in relation to the Jewish people. This entails for Christians a return to the unity of Scripture, which instructs us concerning the unity of God and summons us to participation in God's work of liberation. This means that the Reformation's turn to the Bible today must be undertaken as a turn to the Old Testament. The Psalms, in particular, provide ways of exercising the uniting of God's people – Jews and Christians – together with all creatures. We yearn for the day when the people of God are no longer divided by categories such as class, race, gender, sexual orientation, or even religion, but when God will be all in all (Butting). Of urgent concern at the 500th anniversary of the Reformation is the volatile relationship between the West and its perception of Islam. It is not only essential to deconstruct and reinterpret the writings of Luther and the Reformers in relation to the Jews, but especially their portrayal of Muslims and Islam. The Christian response to the "Other" finds its greatest ethical challenge today in how it negotiates neighbor love toward Muslims in the charged and historically unexamined contemporary context (Amjad-Ali).

The disciples of Jesus Christ announce the hope of understanding God in community with the sacred texts of divine revelation in other religious traditions and seek to construct a reconciled world together with Jews, Muslims, Hindus, Buddhists, and people of all religious faiths from every culture in every place: Africa, the Near East, Asia, Pacifica, Latin America, the Caribbean, North America, and Europe. The Gospel contradicts every form of cultural, religious, or military invasion (Prieto). A post-colonial reading of Reformation theology advances a project of enculturation, in order to underpin interreligious dialogue as prophetic dialogue, adopting a new departure in the critique of colonialism by Reformation theology and avoiding misuse of its scholarship in the service of the powerful (Chung).

6. Call for a New Reformation

We are in need of a "New Reformation" because the evangelical impulse is no longer recognizable in the churches of the Reformation. So announced Dorothee Sölle already in 1968. While people can undertake pious practices, the churches face increasing alienation from the realities of the actual world in which people live. As with Martin Luther, we need a renewal of language and a return to the liberating message of the Gospel in the proclamation of the church for the life of the world (Wind). This means the refurbishing of the theology of the cross as a theology of life (resurrection!) aligned with God's solidarity with the *minjung*, economic justice for all, and the integrity of the ecological web of life (Chung). The attainment of *buen vivir* ("good life") is predicated on love for nature and all forms of life, matters fundamental to the ethical life. All human beings and the whole of creation have need for and a right to "bread and roses." The emergence of a New Reformation involves struggle for and proclamation of the right to *buen vivir* for the whole creation (Beise Ulrich).

Collectively, the chapters of this book summon the church to a critical appropriation of Reformation history and theology for addressing the acute global crises facing humanity and the creation itself on the occasion of the 500th anniversary of Luther's publication of the 95 theses, which signaled the beginning of Protestant Reformation. The authors in this volume contribute to and demonstrate the emerging ecumenical consensus on the part of progressive Christian scholars about the way forward for engaging these crises in the spirit of an *ecclesia semper reformanda.*

Many thanks to Hans G. Ulrich for putting the book manuscript into print version.

Craig L. Nessan, Wartburg Theological Seminary, Dubuque, Iowa, U.S.A.

Good Friday/Easter 2015

BEYOND LUTHER TO ETHICAL REFORMATION: PEASANTS, ANABAPTISTS, JEWS

Craig L. Nessan

In the last decades attention has been given to the emergence of what political analysts have characterized as "identity politics." Although the critical discussion of this phenomenon, pro and con, may be recent – especially in an increasingly polarized political climate – the reality of identity politics is ancient.

At the 500th anniversary of the Reformation we must reckon with three tragic cases from the theological ethics of Martin Luther, repenting of how Luther's devolution into "religious identity politics" misled him to horrific conclusions, whose consequences continue to plague the world centuries later. These three cases involve Luther's stances against the Peasants, the Anabaptists, and the Jews. Rather than standing for their protection under the laws of society according to "neighbor politics," Luther resorted to religious rhetoric and appeals to violence that reverberate until today.

The logic of Luther's two strategies paradigm should have led him to different conclusions.[1] Luther articulated the centrality of neighbor love for ethics according to his concept of the two strategies, especially in his treatise, *The Freedom of a Christian*. However, in his polemic against the peasants, Anabaptists, and Jews, Luther operated according to a religious identity politics that negated the Greatest Commandment: to love God and one's neighbor as oneself (Mt 22:34-40). Instead of defending these oppressed groups according to the imperative of neighbor politics, they were targeted as ene-

---

[1] Luther's two kingdoms paradigm is here reconstructed as God's "two strategies." Cf. Craig L. Nessan, "Christian Political Responsibility: Reappropriating Luther's Two Kingdoms," in Paul S. Chung, Ulrich Duchrow, and Craig L. Nessan, *Liberating Lutheran Theology: Freedom for Justice and Solidarity in Global Context* (Minneapolis: Fortress, 2011), 46-52.

mies through the hermeneutic of a vicious religious identity politics. Luther's ethical conclusions require critique, deconstruction, and repudiation toward the reconstruction of theological ethics as neighbor politics.

1. Religious Identity Politics Today: Abortion, Homosexuality, and the State of Israel

In the United States the religious identity politics of the Christian religious right provides background for analyzing Luther's own religious identity politics against the peasants, Anabaptists, and the Jews. Three primary examples of religious identity politics by the Christian religious right involve stances on abortion, homosexuality, and the State of Israel. In religious identity politics the warrants for arguments come primarily, if not entirely, from sources of religious authority. Religion serves as a particularly powerful source for identity politics, insofar as those motivated by religious belief claim divine authorization for their cause.[2]

For the Christian religious right, warrants come primarily, if not entirely, from the Bible. Based on absolute claims about the plenary inspiration of the Bible and appeals to biblical literalism, the Christian religious right positions itself as an interest group with divine endorsement for its political agenda. There is a virtual one-to-one correspondence between the Biblicist arguments of the Christian religious right and its political agenda regarding abortion, homosexuality, and the State of Israel. This is a characteristic of all religious identity politics. Religious identity politics is motivated to maintain purity regarding its interpretation of God's will based on appeals to divine revelation in Holy Scripture. Due to veritable certainty about the truth of their conclusions, there is little or no room for compromise in relation to the possible needs of those neighbors, who might be negatively affected by their religious agenda. This also means there is virtually no ideological space for "neighbor politics."

Religious identity politics is central to the political agenda of the Christian religious right in relationship to abortion, homosexuality, and the State of

---

[2] Cf. Cressida Heyes, "Identity Politics," *Stanford Encyclopedia of Philosophy*, <http://plato.stanford.edu/entries/identity-politics/>, August 1, 2013.

Israel. In religious identity politics there is a direct linkage between a particular interpretation of the Bible and the warrants that are drawn for pursuing a particular political agenda. The ostensible one-to-one correspondence between biblical interpretation and a clearly defined political program lends passion to religious identity politics. Because God has purportedly authorized this agenda through divine revelation, the consequences for those negatively affected by such an agenda are discounted, sometimes even dealt with through sarcasm or ridicule.

Contrast religious identity politics with "neighbor politics." Neighbor politics is also grounded in religious or ideological motivations. However, neighbor politics resists the reduction of ethical deliberation to a one-to-one correspondence between divine authorization and political agenda. Neighbor politics introduces complexity into ethical deliberation and the emerging political agenda. The needs of all neighbors, especially those most negatively affected by a given political stance, are taken seriously in ethical deliberation.

The reductionist approach of the Christian religious right is overcome by including a range of other neighbors: not only the rights of an unborn child but the situation of the mother, father, extended family, and a host of other social, economic, and contextual factors; not only the norm of marriage between a man and a woman but the rights of gay and lesbian persons, the situation of their families and friends, and a host of other practical matters, civil rights, and legal issues; not only the sovereignty of the State of Israel but the legitimacy of its laws and policies, especially as these oppress the Palestinian people and negatively interact with other Mid-Eastern countries. Neighbor politics entails a differentiated method of ethical deliberation, weighing many competing factors that affect a range of other persons – including also the needs of creation and its creatures! – in arriving at a course of action.

Employing the distinction between religious identity politics and neighbor politics, we will examine how Luther himself, in controversy with particular religious opponents, departed from his otherwise clearly articulated neighbor politics to assume the posture of religious identity politics, in order to oppose and defeat particular religious foes. Notwithstanding that the religious opponents themselves – peasants, Anabaptists, and Jews – may have employed their own versions of religious identity politics, Luther's reversion to religious identity politics in his rhetoric, controversies, and writings against these groups not only had disastrous ethical consequences in his own time but his positions continue to undermine the integrity of Lutheran theological and ethical heritage 500 years later.

2. Religious Identity Politics in Luther: Peasants, Anabaptists, and Jews

Three particular instances of religious identity politics call into radical question the legitimacy not only of Luther's ethics but his entire theology: his writings against the peasants, the Anabaptists, and the Jews. The ethical integrity of the Lutheran Reformation is severely questionable, if the conclusions drawn by Luther in these three cases in the sixteenth century are not repudiated. Where did Luther go wrong? Is it possible to draw upon Luther's own theological arguments to arrive at other conclusions? One key for interpreting, criticizing, and deconstructing Luther's thought involves unmasking how religious identity politics undermined the foundations of neighbor politics as grounded by his concept of the two strategies. Only by confronting Luther's reasoning against the peasants, Anabaptists, and Jews is it possible to turn his thought toward a consistent neighbor politics.

2.1 Luther against the Peasants

Luther's writings against the peasants need to be understood within the historical context and currents of the early 16th century. The Reformation was a nascent movement, dependent upon favorable protection by the German princes who sheltered Luther and fostered the reforms undertaken through his theological program. Peasant uprisings had occurred in Europe already in the 14th century.[3] The German Peasants War began in 1524 and climaxed in March-May 1525. The poverty, economic suffering, and consequent social problems facing the German underclass were extreme. Theological and practical reforms introduced by Luther raised legitimate expectations that the living conditions of the peasantry would also be remediated.

---

[3] For this and the following, see Martin Brecht, *Martin Luther: Shaping and Defining the Reformation 1521-1532*, trans. James L. Schaaf (Minneapolis: Fortress, 1990), 172-173.

Luther took a prophetic stance against the practice of usury.[4] Initially Luther exercised measured support for the peasants' cause. Because Luther saw that the grievances of the peasants belonged to the responsibility of the civil authorities, he rejected their attempts to appeal to spiritual and biblical arguments as rationale for rebellion.[5] To a certain degree Luther may have operated according to a neighbor politics, holding that the peasants' call to arms would lead to their destruction. Once the crisis began to deteriorate into violence, however, Luther lacked imagination for a solution other than a return to the status quo. He defended the prevailing political order against the demands of peasants, arguing vehemently for the obligation of civil rulers to crush their efforts to reform society through violent revolutionary change. "Luther only partially grasped the complexity of the situation, and this must have had an influence on his judgment and reaction."[6] Revolt appeared to Luther as a sign of the arrival of the apocalypse.

Brecht comments on The Fundamental and Proper Chief Articles of All the Peasantry and Those Who Are Oppressed by Spiritual and Temporal Authority, otherwise known as the Twelve Articles, published in March 1525:

The common accusation that the gospel causes revolution was rejected. In desiring the gospel, the peasants were not revolutionaries. However – and this was a veiled threat – one could expect God to support his oppressed people. All of the articles were supported by Bible references in the margin.[7]

Although many peasant leaders, including the authors of The Twelve Articles desired peaceful change, violence broke out against rulers and monasteries at the end of March, culminating in April. Upon receiving this document in April, Luther prepared a response, *Admonition to Peace: A Reply to the Twelve Articles of the Peasants in Swabia*, which was published in early May. Luther was not persuaded of the Christian character of the peasant

---

[4] Ulrich Duchrow, "Property, Money Economies, and Empires: Contexts of Biblical, Reformation, and Contemporary Ecumenical Theology," in Chung, Duchrow, and Nessan, *Liberating Lutheran Theology*, 173-181.

[5] Johannes Heckel, *Lex Charitatis: A Juristic Disquisition on Law in the Theology of Martin Luther*, trans. ed. Gottfried G. Krodel (Grand Rapids: Erdmans, 2010), 78-80.

[6] Brecht, 173.

[7] Brecht, 174.

movement and was convinced that if the temporal order was threatened that the conditions would no longer allow the continuation of the Reformation.

Luther linked inseparably the maintenance of the existing civil order with freedom to proclaim the Gospel. While acknowledging the legitimacy of some peasant demands, Luther believed that God would be the judge of unjust rulers and argued against the use of violence by the peasants, particularly mindful of the precedents by Müntzer and Karlstadt.[8]

> "Now you can see how far these false prophets have led you astray. They still call you Christians, although they have made you worse than heathen. On the basis of these passages even a child can understand that the Christian law tells us not to strive against injustice, not to grasp the sword, not to protect ourselves, not to avenge ourselves, but to give up life and property, and let whoever takes it have it. We have all we need in our Lord, who will not leave us, as he has promised [Heb 13:5]. Suffering! Suffering! Cross! Cross!"[9]

Luther advised the peasants not to seek economic justice through force but to appeal to God for aid. He referred to his own example of protest in relation to pope and emperor and how he never fomented rebellion or took up the sword.[10]

The failure of Luther to advocate more strongly against the economic conditions suffered by the peasants, and instead his admonishing them to suffer and bear the cross, reveals something about his own self-interest in this conflict. The temporal order that protected his own reformation agenda would not tolerate, Luther reasoned, the kinds of material reforms demanded by the peasants. The turn to violence would jeopardize the temporal status quo and give occasion to suppression of everything thus far accomplished. Luther had scarce imagination for a reformation that moved beyond the feudal political order toward participatory social and economic justice, even though his theology formally acknowledged the requisites of the left hand kingdom. Luther writes against the third article:

> "This article would make all men equal, and turn the spiritual kingdom of

---

[8] *LW* 46:24-28.
[9] *LW* 46:29.
[10] *LW* 46:31.

Christ into a worldly, external kingdom; and that is impossible. A worldly kingdom cannot exist without an inequality of persons, some being free, some imprisoned some lords, some subjects, etc...."[11]

Moreover, Luther rejected the appeals to Scripture by the peasants as a kind of religious identity politics, countering with his own form of religious identity politics, to oppose their demands. Especially galling to Luther were the appeals to Scripture by the peasants to justify rebellion.[12] Luther feared that chaos would engulf Germany should the peasants persist on their violent course and recommended arbitration as the necessary alternative.[13]

Events overtook the publication of Luther's *Admonition to Peace* as he received reports of an escalation of violence on the part of the peasants in early May. Therefore Luther amended his earlier treatise, adding a devastating new section, *Against the Robbing and Murdering Hordes of Peasants*. Luther charged the peasants with violating their obligation of obedience to the rulers. Because they had turned to violence, Luther implored the authorities to crush the peasant rebellion:

> "For rebellion is not just simple murder; it is like a great fire, which attacks and devastates the whole land. Thus rebellion brings with it a land filled with murder and bloodshed; it makes widows and orphans, and turns everything upside down, like the worst disaster. Therefore let everyone who can, smite, slay, and stab, secretly or openly, remembering that nothing can be more poisonous, hurtful, or devilish than a rebel. It is just as when one must kill a mad dog; if you do not strike him, he will strike you, and a whole land with you."[14]

While Luther appealed to the rulers to negotiate where possible, the thrust of his argument was aimed at freeing their consciences to respond to the revolt with all necessary force to maintain good order. Even against those who against their own will had been compelled to join the rebellion, the rulers should "stab, smite, slay. If you die doing it, good for you! A more blessed death can never be yours, for you die obeying the divine word and com-

---

[11] *LW* 46:39.
[12] *LW* 46:34-36.
[13] *LW* 46:42-43.
[14] *LW* 46:50.

mandment in Romans 13 [1, 2], and in loving service to your neighbor, whom you are rescuing from the bonds of hell and the devil."[15]

Luther's defense of the established political and economic order was consistent with his concept of good government. As also in his writings against the Anabaptists and the Jews, Luther's imagination was bound by the constraints of his time regarding the requisites of political and economic justice. Caught in the rush of unfolding events, Luther's writings against the "robbing and murdering hordes" appear even more vicious to later generations, who know how these words also have contributed to the suppression of other movements for social change, such as advocated by liberation theologies.[16]

Even in the face of excesses by the rulers and the abiding resentment by the peasants, Luther remained adamant in righteousness about his stance. For example, Luther published four letters of Müntzer under the title, *A Dreadful Story and a Judgment of God against Thomas Müntzer*, to defend his views about how God judges rebels.[17] Luther made frequent reference to Müntzer in many of his later writings to justify his position in the peasants uprising: "I killed Müntzer; his death is on my shoulders. But I did it because he wanted to kill my Christ." Luther remained convinced that his role in the peasants' war, advising the authorities to negotiate with their subjects and calling them to arms in the event of rebellion, was justified.

Already in 1525, Luther was prepared to defend his position, composing *An Open Letter on the Harsh Book against the Peasants*. God so ordered the world that subjects owed obedience to their lords and those in authority owed wrath to disobedient subjects: "The peasants would not listen; they would not let anyone tell them anything, so their ears must now be unbuttoned with musket balls till their heads jump off their shoulders. Such pupils need the rod."[18] While Luther counseled mercy for those who surrendered, he defended his stance according to the two kingdoms:

---

[15] *LW* 46:54-55.

[16] Craig L. Nessan, *The Vitality of Liberation Theology* (Eugene: Wipf & Stock, 2012), 149-150.

[17] Brecht, 184-185, who also includes the following quote.

[18] *LW* 46:65.

"There are two kingdoms, one the kingdom of God, the other the kingdom of the world. I have written this so often that I am surprised there is anyone who does not know it or remember it. Anyone who knows how to distinguish rightly between these two kingdoms will certainly not be offended by my little book, and he will also properly understand the passages about mercy. God's kingdom is a kingdom of grace and mercy, not of wrath and punishment. In it there is only forgiveness, consideration for one another, love, service, the doing of good, peace, joy, etc. But the kingdom of the world is a kingdom of wrath and severity. In it there is only punishment, repression, judgment, and condemnation to restrain the wicked and protect the good. For this reason it has the sword and Scripture calls a prince or lord 'God's wrath,' or 'God's rod' (Is 14)."[19]

Luther in this case tragically failed to grasp the rudimentary obligation of the left hand kingdom to provide sufficient livelihood for the underclass. God had to teach the peasants the value of maintaining law and order, and instruct the lords "to rule justly and to keep order in their territories and highways."[20] While the peasants were interpreted according to the categories of rebels, thieves, murderers, and evildoers, Luther seemed oblivious that those in authority could be accused of the same through their establishment of structural injustice.[21] It is at this juncture that Luther's teaching about the two kingdoms requires severe criticism and revision, if it is salvageable at all. "What we miss completely is any sign of understanding for the oppressed and their problems."[22]

2.2 Luther against the Anabaptists

Luther's stance against the Anabaptists was based on his opinion that they were engaged in monastic withdrawal from the world. He criticized the Anabaptists, as he did monks, for attempting to "climb into heaven" to escape civil society and thereby failing to fulfill the basic obligations of neighbor love. Luther's views were, moreover, negatively affected by his inability to differentiate the views expressed by revolutionary leaders like Müntzer in the

---

[19] *LW* 46:69-70.
[20] *LW* 46:75.
[21] *LW* 46:80-81.
[22] Brecht, 188.

peasants' revolt from other Anabaptists.[23] The lack of first hand knowledge about the Anabaptists, due in part to lack of contact with actual representatives of the movement, led Luther to make generalizations that failed to take seriously many key features of Anabaptist thought and practice.[24]

Luther's stance against the peasants was driven both by his antipathy against their biblical appeals for their revolutionary cause and his fear of the loss of political support for his own reformation, should the rulers see a connection between Luther's program of reform and the peasants' demands for economic justice through revolt. In response to the religious identity politics of the peasants, Luther's retreated from neighbor politics to his own version of religious identity politics in order to oppose them. Luther's primary argument against the Anabaptists was that they, as Enthusiasts (*Schwärmer*), fomented the same seditious agenda as Müntzer. Luther was troubled by the apparent success of the Anabaptist movement, especially among the lower classes. He feared civil unrest would jeopardize the protection by the princes of his theological and practical reforms.

Although Luther's most extensive discussion of the Anabaptist movement was *Von Der Widdertauffe an zween Pfarherrn, ein Brief* (1528), his writings are filled with critical and disparaging comments against them.[25] The conservative character of Luther's reformation is demonstrated by his defense of Roman Catholic theology against the Anabaptists regarding the Lord's Supper, forgiveness of sins, the pastoral office, the Creed, and especially baptism.[26] Luther rejected Anabaptist views of baptism on several counts.

First, he criticized their reliance on the faith of the believer as the prerequisite for baptism.

"They cannot get out of the predicament but must reduce to mere human

---

[23] For this and the following references to Luther's 1528 treatise see, John S. Oyer, *Lutheran Reformers against Anabaptists: Luther, Melancthon, and Menius and the Anabaptists of Central Germany* (The Hague: Martinus Nijhoff, 1964), 249-252.

[24] Luther was, furthermore, overly beholden to the harsh rhetoric of Melancthon, against perceived Anabaptist errors.

[25] *WA* 26: 139-?

[26] Oyer, 117-121.

works even Baptism and the Sacraments, which are God's Word and institution. Thus the Anabaptists claim that Baptism is nothing if one is not previously sanctified. They do not want to acquire holiness through and from Baptism, but by their piety they want to make Baptism holy and wholesome."[27]

Thereby Luther distanced himself from the proposal of rebaptism by Balthasar Hubmaier.

Second, he rejected the Anabaptist claim that infant baptism made the believer uncertain about the validity of his/her own baptism.

"This is the true remembrance, to hear the Word of Christ. Thus all Sacramentarians and Anabaptists are Pelagians."[28]

To allow free choice in matters of the Gospel made salvation conditional on human will.

Third, Luther criticized the motives of the Anabaptists as a stance taken merely for the sake of opposing the pope.

Fourth, Luther criticized the Anabaptist reliance on Mark 16:16 ("The one who believes and is baptized will be saved") for making baptism too subjective.

"One must be on one's guard against the Anabaptists and the schismatic spirits, who speak sneeringly of Baptism and aver that it is mere water and of benefit to no one. They gaze at this sacred act as a cow stares at a new door. For they behold a poor preacher standing there, or, in an emergency, a woman who baptizes. They take offense at this and say: 'Well, what can Baptism accomplish.'"[29]

By contrast, Luther defended infant baptism as historic church practice, quoting other Scripture texts for his position (for example, Mt 19:14).[30] Because baptism is done at God's command, not according to human faith, infant baptism is efficacious and valid as a sacrament of the church.

---

[27] *LW* 14:39.
[28] *LW* 17:256.
[29] *LW* 22:173.
[30] Cf. *LW* 3:103.

Fifth, Luther charged the Anabaptists with works righteousness in their approach to baptism.[31] The act of performing baptism itself became among the Anabaptists a kind of monastic demonstration of good works.

> "These are the ravenous wolves in sheep's clothing, who have corrupted Christianity in every age. Until recently they were called monks; now they are the Anabaptists, the new monks."[32]

The Anabaptists' subjective approach to baptism, together with their biblical literalism, led Luther to identify the Anabaptists as Enthusiasts (*Schwärmer*).[33]

Luther's writings took an ominous turn when he identified the Anabaptists as blasphemers, a punishable crime. For example, in his *Commentary on Psalm 82* from 1530 Luther wrote:

> "If some were to teach doctrines contradicting an article of faith clearly grounded in Scripture and believed throughout the world by all Christendom, such as the articles we teach children in the Creed – for example, if anyone were to teach that Christ is not God, but a mere man and like other prophets, as the Turks and the Anabaptists hold – such teachers should not be tolerated, but punished as blasphemers. For they are not mere heretics but open blasphemers; and rulers are in duty bound to punish blasphemers as they punish those who curse, swear, revile, abuse, defame, and slander."[34]

Roland Bainton comments: "In 1530 Luther advanced the view that two offenses should be penalized even with death, namely sedition and blasphemy."[35]

Bainton describes Luther's endorsement of Melancthon's stance against the Anabaptists in two *Gutachten* from 1531 and 1536:

> "In a memorandum of 1531, composed by Melancthon and signed by Luther, a rejection of the ministerial office was described as insufferable blasphemy, and the disintegration of the Church as sedition against the ecclesial order. In a memorandum of 1536, again composed by Melanchthon and signed by Luther,

---

[31] Cf. *LW* 21:254.
[32] *LW* 21:258-259.
[33] Oyer, 124.
[34] *LW* 13:61.
[35] Roland Bainton, *Here I Stand: A Life of Martin Luther* (New York: Mentor, 1950), 295.

the distinction between the peaceful and the revolutionary Anabaptists was obliterated....Luther may not have been too happy about signing these memoranda. At any rate he appended postscripts to each. To the first he said, 'I assent. Although it seems cruel to punish them with the sword, it is crueler that they condemn the ministry of the Word and have no well-grounded doctrine and suppress the true and in this way seek to subvert the civil order.' Luther's addition to the second document was a plea that severity be tempered with mercy."[36]

"In 1540 he is reported in his *Table Talk* to have returned to the position of Philip of Hesse that only seditious Anabaptists should be executed; the others should be merely banished. But Luther passed by many an opportunity to speak a word for those who with joy gave themselves as sheep for the slaughter."[37]

Luther's invective against the Anabaptists contributed to defamation of character and charges of sedition and blasphemy.

"That seditious articles of doctrine should be punished by the sword needed no further proof. For the rest, the Anabaptists hold tenets relating to infant baptism, original sin, and inspiration which have no connection to the Word of God, and are indeed opposed to it....From all this it becomes clear that the secular authorities are bound...to inflict corporal punishment on the offenders...we conclude that the stubborn sectarians must be put to death."[38]

Such conclusions were justified by a harsh religious identity politics that claimed the executions of the Anabaptists were warranted because they were of Satan:

"Such is the religion of the Anabaptists today, although day by day they are betraying that they are possessed by the devil and are seditious and bloodthirsty men."[39]

"The Anabaptists were Satan's minions in a vast cosmic struggle. The Lutherans could detect the demonic character of their opponents by their doctrine and also by their secrecy in spreading their ideas. They preferred

---

[36] Bainton, 295.
[37] Bainton, 295.
[38] Martin Luther as quoted by Johannes Janssen, *History of the German People from the Close of the Middle Ages*, trans. A.M. Christie (St. Louis: Herder, 1910), 222-223.
[39] *LW* 27:88.

darkness to light."[40]

Such opinions became embedded in the authoritative writings of the Lutheran Church in the *Book of Concord*. They were only finally repudiated by the Lutheran World Federation in 2010 with the confession:

"So Lutherans, following the example of the returning exiles in Nehemiah 9, dare to ask for forgiveness for the harm that their forebears in the sixteenth century committed against Anabaptists, for forgetting and ignoring this persecution in the intervening centuries, and for all inappropriate, misleading and hurtful portraits of Anabaptists and Mennonites made by Lutherans authors, in both popular and academic publications, to the present day."[41]

2.3 Luther against the Jews

The conventional view – that Luther began his career with certain openness and generosity to the Jews in anticipation of their conversion to the Gospel, who only later in life turned toward animosity and hatred against them – is demonstrably false.[42] From his early writings onward, Luther demonstrated contempt for the Jewish people, not only on biblical grounds but especially due to their rejection of Jesus as the Christ both in the New Testament and especially in rabbinic Judaism.[43] Although one could not have predicted that his utterances against the Jews would lead finally to Auschwitz, the legacy of anti-Semitism ignited by his pen and perpetrated by his followers is the most disastrous of all Luther's ethical missteps.

Luther knew precious little about living Judaism: "He had neither Jewish conversation partners nor Jewish friends. His knowledge of Judaism was primarily dependent on what he read, and those readings were dominated by overtly anti-Jewish treatises, some of which were written by Christians and

---

[40] Oyer, 250.

[41] Healing Memories: Reconciling in Christ. Report of the Lutheran-Mennonite International Study Commission (Geneva: Lutheran World Federation, 2010), 102.

[42] Brooks Schramm and Kirsi I. Stjerna, eds., *Martin Luther, the Bible, and the Jewish People: A Reader* (Minneapolis: Fortress, 2012), 5-10.

[43] Eric W. Gritsch, Martin Luther's Anti-Semitism: Against His Better Judgment (Grand Rapids: Eerdmans, 2012), 35-36.

some by Jewish converts."⁴⁴ Luther consistently maintained the view that the Jews were an apostate people, based on their failure to receive Jesus as their Messiah, and therefore blameworthy for their own subsequent mistreatment in Christian history. He employed the argument that for 1500 years the Jews had been living in defiance of the Gospel of Jesus Christ. The only reasonable explanation was "that they had been handed over by God to the Devil. Thus their resistance to the gospel – and their resistance to admitting *the* reason for their exile – was willful and unforgiveable."⁴⁵

The Jewish people had abandoned their status as the "chosen people" due to their rejection of Jesus as Christ.

> "For Luther, the promise to Abraham's seed was in reality the promise of the Seed, that is the Messiah/Christ (Gen 3:15). The physical seed of Abraham, the Jews, were God's chosen instrument in Old Testament times to bear that promise. But Abraham's true descendents/seed, even in the Old Testament times, were always those who believed in the promise of the Messiah and not those who relied on the physical descent. This is the fundamental error, and sin, of the Jews, who trust as it were that they have been born into grace, that they are bound to God by birth, and thus that God owes them God's benevolence. For Luther, this constitutes a theological obscenity, because the grace and benevolence of God can *only* be accessed by faith, and it has never been otherwise."⁴⁶

Luther rejected Jewish "choseness" according to the terms of the old covenant, which led him to view the Jews as the apostate people. The Jews are fully culpable for their sins. The curse uttered by the Jewish crowds at the crucifixion of Jesus rightly falls upon the apostate Jews for all time: "His blood be on us and on our children! (Mt 27:25)."

Already in Luther's early Psalm lectures (1513-1515), there is evidence of this fundamental posture against the Jews.⁴⁷ Commenting on Psalm 1, Luther wrote: "For to deny that it is a sin to have crucified the Lord is worse than to

---

⁴⁴ Schramm and Stjerna, 5.
⁴⁵ Schramm and Stjerna, 6.
⁴⁶ Schramm and Stjerna, 7.
⁴⁷ The following citations follow the material documented in Schramm and Stjerna.

have perpetrated the sin itself, that is, to do the crucifying. Therefore the last error and the last sin are unforgiveable."[48]

> "To this very day they crucify him within themselves, as the apostle accuses them (Heb 6:6), because they keep the truth pierced through and continue to stab it with their extremely hard iron lies (which are their goads). Thus to this day they do not know what they are doing, just as they did not know then. They scourge, stone, and kill the prophets and scribes in the same way as did their fathers."[49]

The "1500 years of Jewish apostasy and exile" myth was embedded already in Luther's thought at this early stage. Regarding Psalm 78 Luther commented: "[God] made this a firm policy, and He punishes them permanently without ceasing, not in passing, like the godly, but over and over again. As a road is usually not made by one passing but by incessant footsteps, so by incessant tracks and signs of God's wrath, which we see in them, He has now, as it were, made a road, a road worn and indeed made firm."[50]

Luther held out hope that some Jews would be converted through the preaching of the Gospel as it was newly proclaimed through the reformation. In his Commentary on the Magnificat (1521), Luther wrote:

> "When Mary says, 'His seed forever,' we are to understand 'forever' to mean that such grace is to continue to Abraham's seed (that is, the Jews) from that time forth, throughout all time, down to the Last Day. Although the vast majority of them are hardened, yet there are always some, however few, that are converted to Christ and believe in Him...We ought, therefore, not to treat the Jews in so unkindly a spirit, for there are future Christians among them, and they are turning every day."[51]

Luther did not hold that all Jews would remain reprobate until the eschaton. However, conversion was the condition placed upon their being accepted. This view was elaborated in *That Jesus Christ Was Born a Jew* (1523): "If we really want to help them, we must be guided in our dealings with them not by papal law but by the law of Christian love. We must receive them cor-

---

[48] *LW* 10:13.
[49] *LW* 10:19.
[50] *LW* 11:80.
[51] *LW* 21:354-355.

dially, and permit them to trade and work with us, that they may have occasion and opportunity to associate with us, hear our Christian teaching, and witness our Christian life. If some of them prove stiff-necked, what of it? After all, we ourselves are not all good Christians either."[52]

One fascinating treatise for understanding Luther's Old Testament hermeneutics and thereby his concept of Judaism is *How Christians Should Regard Moses* (1525). Here Luther addressed the question: what from the Law of Moses, that is, the Old Testament still applies to Christians? He offers a threefold answer, each point related to his theological concept of law and Gospel. First, the Mosaic laws that conform to the natural law remain binding for Christians. All other laws, ceremonial or ritual specific only to Israel, are no longer binding.[53] Second, the Law of Moses is binding wherever it conveys Christ and the promise of the Gospel (for example, Gen 3:15 or Deut 18:15). Third, the Law of Moses is useful for instructing Christians through examples of righteous living, for instance, Abraham. While retaining key aspects of the Old Testament for Christian faith and life, Luther's hermeneutical method accords with his judgment of rabbinic Judaism as being apostate in the period following the New Testament.

In his correspondence, sermons, treatises, and biblical commentaries, Luther perpetrated to the end of this life a basic posture against the Jews. Commenting in 1538 on Genesis 17, Luther argued: "God does not lie. His promises are true and firm. They do not promise that some dregs of a people will come from Abraham; they promise kings and peoples. Where, then, has the kingdom remained during these 1500 years? Where have their laws remained, the institutions of the fathers, and their worship? What else are the Jews today than a body miserably torn to pieces and scattered throughout the world?"[54]

Luther's body of work against the Jews culminated in the treatise, *On the Jews and Their Lies* (1543). Contrary to conventional interpretations, his shocking recommendations to both civil authorities and clergy about how to

---

[52] *LW* 45:229.
[53] Cf. *LW* 35:165.
[54] *LW* 3:150.

deal with the Jews cohere with Luther's stance throughout his career.[55] The occasion for this writing was a rabbinic rebuttal of his own arguments against the Jews, which Luther earlier had published as *Against the Sabbatarians* (1538). At the same time, Luther was offended by slanderous claims against Jesus and his mother which were transmitted in a certain medieval Jewish text and by the information conveyed to him by a Jewish convert.[56]

Luther asserted his views regarding the Jewish problem of this own time, whether Jews should be tolerated or expelled. While he would prefer for Jews to take up residence in lands not occupied by Christians, Luther argues that the Jewish blasphemies can no longer be tolerated.

What shall we Christians do with this rejected and condemned people, the Jews? Since they live among us, we dare not tolerate their conduct, now that we are aware of their lying and reviling and blaspheming. If we do, we become sharers in their lies, cursing, and blaspheming. Thus we cannot extinguish the unquenchable fire of divine wrath, of which the prophets speak, nor can we convert the Jews. With prayer and the fear of God we must practice sharp mercy to see whether we might save at least a few from the glowing flames. We dare not avenge ourselves. Vengeance thousand times worse than we could wish them already has them by the throat. I shall give you my sincere advice...[57]

In *On the Jews and Their Lies* Luther makes his infamous proposals regarding policy against the Jews by both civil authorities and the clergy.[58] To the civil authorities Luther recommends the following measures: burn down synagogues, destroy Jewish homes, confiscate prayer books and Talmudic writings, forbid rabbis to teach, abolish safe conduct for Jews, prohibit usury by Jews, and enforce the Jews in manual labor. To the pastors and preachers he commends: burn down synagogues; confiscate prayer books, Talmudic writings, and the Bible; prohibit Jewish prayer and teaching; and forbid Jews

---

[55] Cf. Schramm and Stjerna, 99-163.

[56] For this and the following, see Schramm and Stjerna, 164-165.

[57] *LW* 47:268.

[58] *LW* 47:268-272, 285-287. Cf. the chart outlining the following measures in Schramm and Stjerna, 165.

to utter the name of God publicly. To the end of his life and even in his final public utterance, Luther advocated harsh treatment of the Jews.[59]

The force of Luther's public testimony against the Jews took on a life of its own over the centuries.[60] The path leading from Luther to *Kristallnacht* and Auschwitz is long and twisted. But one can arrive there from here.

In our post-Holocaust context, and knowing more than Luther did about just how far human beings – including Christians – can go down the road of Jew-hatred, we are following the tracks that are shameful and that require honest remembering. Because of the atrocities of the Nazi era, and because of ongoing expressions of anti-Semitism in our time as well, it is only proper to bring to continued inspection and prayerful reflection words such as Luther's, so that we better continue to tell the truth, repent, and strive for justice and protection of the dignity of life, in accordance with the worthy principles of our respective religions.[61]

Only in 1994 did the Evangelical Lutheran Church in America adopt a statement repudiating Luther's anti-Jewish writings and their legacy.[62]

3. Fallacy in Luther's Ethical Theology

Luther's ethical theology is embedded in the late medieval apocalyptic worldview that pitches God in a life versus death, cosmic battle against Satan.[63] Because the end of the world was drawing near, the Devil had intensified efforts to gain control of the world through those who sought to deceive and delude many from believing the Gospel of Jesus Christ. The peasants, Anabaptists, and Jews were among those (though not the only ones!) through

---

[59] See Admonition against the Jews (1546) in LW 58:458-459.
[60] Gritsch, 97-137.
[61] Schramm and Stjerna, 204.
[62] "Declaration of ELCA to Jewish Community," <http://www.elca.org/Who-We-Are/Our-Three-Expressions/Churchwide-Organization/Office-of-the-Presiding-Bishop/Ecumenical-and-Inter-Religious-Relations/Inter-Religious-Relations/Christian-Jewish-Relations/Declaration-of-ELCA-to-Jewish-Community.aspx>, August 14, 2013.
[63] Heiko Obermann, *Luther: Man between God and the Devil* (New York: Doubleday, 1992).

whom Satan was raging on the eve of the Apocalypse. Luther saw himself justified in waging war against these enemies of God.

Luther's writings against the peasants, Anabaptists, and Jews expose a tragic fallacy in Luther's ethical theology and pose penetrating and incisive questions that must be answered. Is there anything worth salvaging from the wreckage of Luther's intemperate and vilifying utterances, which not only have led to the suffering and death of many in the 1500s but also have contributed to the hatred, persecution, and even murder of countless vulnerable people in subsequent centuries? How might Luther's legacy of contempt and destruction as executed in the name of Jesus Christ finally be brought to an end? Is there any alternative to the outright rejection of Luther's theology, when the ethical consequences have been so lethal? Four correctives are imperative.

First, it is necessary to deconstruct Luther's binary thinking against enemies. While the apocalyptic battle between God and Satan was the framework for Luther's theology, wherever opponents become identified as Satan's minions, all things become possible as means to their destruction. Luther experienced spiritual attack (*Anfechtung*) with vivid reality. The devil and demons raged as agents, threatening his cause on every side. The danger, to which Luther succumbed, like the danger befalling contemporary expressions of religious identity politics, involved demonizing opponents. Once others are objectified through dehumanizing categories, every form of eliminationism is legitimated.[64] Luther's rhetoric against the peasants, Anabaptists, and Jews deprived them of their status as neighbors worthy of protection under the aegis of the law. It is imperative to guard theology against constructing binary opposites that authorize evil against those deemed less than human.[65]

Second, it is necessary to apply suspicion, based on the universality of human sinfulness, to one's own arguments. Luther constructed a thoroughgoing

---

[64] Daniel Jonah Goldhagen, Worse than War: Genocide, Eliminationism, and the Ongoing Assault on Humanity (New York: Public Affairs, 2009), 14-21.
[65] David Livingstone Smith, *Less than Human: Why We Demean, Enslave, and Exterminate Others* (New York: St. Martin's Press, 2011), 250-262.

doctrine of the universality of sin. Even those justified by grace through faith in Jesus Christ continue to labor under the reality of sin. Resisting Christian perfectionism, Luther insisted that Christian existence in this world always remains *simul justus et peccator* (simultaneously saint and sinner). However, in times of intense conflict Luther exempted himself from this cautionary proviso. Rather than acknowledging the limits of his own perspective and the possibility of this own fallibility, Luther assumed ethical absolutism against his enemies. It is imperative to guard theology against the demonization of others through genuine humility about the limitations of one's own ethical perspective due to the universality of sin, also among Christians.

Third, it is necessary without exception to safeguard by rule of law the status of neighbors, including those neighbors with whom we are in conflict for religious or ideological reasons. Luther advocated that by defending neighbors from harm, civil government contributes to preserving the common good. The primus usus legis belongs inherently to God's left hand kingdom/strategy. However, in his own brand of "enthusiasm" (Schwärmerei), Luther advocated harm against those neighbors – peasants, Anabaptists, and Jews – whom he opposed for religious reasons. Thereby Luther suspended his own theological logic about the proper function of government and succumbed to religious identity politics, summoning civil authorities to engage in violent action against certain neighbors, not only because he opposed their politics but especially due to their religious convictions. Although it is anachronistic to expect Luther to adhere to any modern doctrine of separation of church and state, the nascent foundation for such a doctrine is implicit in his own teaching about the two kingdoms/strategies. By failing to uphold the responsibility of the civil authorities for protecting neighbors according to the first use of the law, including those he opposed for religious reasons, Luther neglected the primary function for which God instituted government. It is imperative to restrain religious institutions from doing harm to religious enemies by upholding a universal rule of law that provides physical protection of all neighbors and safeguards their rights.[66]

---

[66] *Universal Declaration of Human Rights*, Article 18, December 26, 2013. <http://www.un.org/en/documents/udhr/>.

Fourth, it is necessary to repent of past failures not only by the confession of sins but through the restoration of right relationships with those who have been harmed. The 500th anniversary of the Reformation affords the occasion for the dominant Protestant churches to confess the sins of their forbearers against peasant, Anabaptist, and Jewish peoples at the time of the Reformation and to repent of the legacy of persecution in the subsequent centuries. Although there have been declarations of guilt[67] and processes of reconciliation[68] in recent ecumenical relations, the Reformation anniversary provides a kairos not only for solemn acts of contrition but the possibility for truth and reconciliation processes throughout the Lutheran communion, whose goal is the restoration of right remembering[69] and restoration of right relationships with the living generation of Anabaptist and Jewish people. While such truth and reconciliation processes needs to begin with formal actions by denominations and global church organizations, they also need to extend to local communities and congregations. From the side of Lutherans, this process needs to begin by remembering the history documented in this chapter and acknowledging the harm caused to millions of human beings as Luther's writings have contributed to an historical trajectory of defamation, persecution, and acts of physical harm, even murder. How can truth telling about the Lutheran heritage in relation to the peasants, Anabaptists, and Jews lead toward reconciliation with neighbors from these traditions in our times?[70]

---

[67] "Declaration of ELCA to the Jewish Community," adopted April 18, 1994, http://download.elca.org/ELCA%20Resource%20Repository/Declaration_Of_The_ELCA_To_The_Jewish_Community.pdf, December 26, 2013.

[68] "Action on the Legacy of Lutheran Persecution of "Anabaptists," adopted by LWF in July 2010, http://www.lwf-assembly.org/uploads/media/Mennonite_Statement-EN.pdf, December 26, 2013.

[69] "Right Remembering in Anabaptist-Lutheran Relations," Report of the Evangelical Lutheran Church in America-Mennonite Church USA Liaison Committee (Chicago: Department of Ecumenical Affairs, 2004), http://download.elca.org/ELCA%20Resource%20Repository/Right_Remembering_In_Anabaptist_Lutheran_Relations.pdf, December 26, 2013.

[70] Cf. *From Conflict to Communion: Lutheran-Catholic Common Commemoration of the Reformation in 2017* (Leipzig: Evangelische Verlagsanstalt/Bonifatius, 2013), #236-237, which includes a call for "Lutheran confession of sins against unity" in relation to both Roman Catholics and Anabaptists/Mennonites.

4. Reconstructing Luther's Two Strategies as Neighbor Politics, Beginning with the Least

The Gospel of Jesus Christ, proclaimed as Word and administered as sacraments, sets Christians free *from* the power of sin, death, and the devil and free *for* service of the neighbor. According to an ethics of the cross, Christian neighbor love pays particular attention to those neighbors who are the most vulnerable and in need of protection. The right hand (spiritual) strategy involves the work of God to accomplish salvation by grace through faith in Jesus Christ alone. This grace is not "cheap."[71] The death and resurrection of Jesus Christ takes place in the life of every Christian person as death to sin and resurrection to new life in discipleship. The Christian life entails participation both in God's right hand strategy of sharing the good news with others through evangelical listening and speaking the faith[72] and through engagement in God's left hand strategy of service to neighbors. The neighbors God gives us to serve as Christians include 1) members of our families, 2) those we encounter through our daily work, 3) those served through the efforts of religious institutions, and 4) those that we serve through collective political action.[73] It is this fourth group to whom we devote special attention in relation to the failures of Luther's social-political ethic.

One acute danger facing Christian social ethics is religious identity politics. This is patently manifest in the contemporary agenda of the Christian religious right with reference to abortion, homosexuality, or the State of Israel. Drawing a one-to-one correspondence between claims to biblical authority and an absolutist ethical stance, religious identity politics brackets out the complexity of the issues and narrows the range of neighbors needing to be served. Although his time and context were clearly different, Luther's social ethics succumbed to the logic of religious identity politics in his absolutist positions against the peasants, Anabaptists, and Jews. While there are re-

---

[71] Cf. Dietrich Bonhoeffer, *Discipleship*, ed. Geffrey B. Kelly and John D. Godsey, trans. Barbara Green and Reinhard Krausss (Minneapolis: Fortress, 2001), 53-56.

[72] Richard H. Bliese and Craig Van Gelder, ed., *The Evangelizing Church: A Lutheran Contribution* (Minneapolis: Fortress, 2005), 133-137.

[73] Craig L. Nessan, Shalom Church: The Body of Christ as Ministering Community (Minneapolis: Fortress, 2010), 22-25.

sources in Luther's thought that could have reframed his arguments into a consistent neighbor politics, in the end his appeals to Scripture led him to harsh condemnation of his religious enemies with grave consequences for their protection by the civil authorities.

Given Luther's failure to defend the peasants, Anabaptists, and Jews as neighbors who deserved the protection of civil law, we must, as an act of repentance, reconstruct his thought with more thoroughgoing consistency regarding the two distinct, yet dialectically related kingdoms, which describe God's ways of working in the world. It is crucial, first, to understand that these kingdoms are not to be interpreted spatially. One fundamental error, leading to a range of misunderstandings about the two kingdoms, imagines them according to a spatial metaphor, which inevitably leads to understanding them as separated and disconnected.[74] Therefore it is constructive to speak not of two "kingdoms" (*Reiche*) but of two "strategies" (*Regimente*). God has two distinct but indispensable strategies for ruling the world. Both are necessary to serve God's purposes of guarding against evil and bringing forth the kingdom of *shalom*.[75] These two strategies must be viewed in dialectical, not contradictory, relationship to one another. God is ambidextrous in ruling the world with two hands: through the spiritual strategy of the Gospel on the right and the civil strategy, entailing the first use of the law, on the left.[76]

Second, in the left hand strategy the civil law encompasses all people, not only Christians. All people "dance in God's masquerade," fulfilling their obligations to neighbors in the four stations belonging to the left hand strategy – through family, daily work, religious institutions, and political responsibility – whether they explicitly acknowledge God as the One whom they serve or not. God employs secular rulers as agents in this left hand strategy, whether these are the princes and lords of Luther's late medieval world or the elected officials in modern democracy. The scope of the enacted civil law, if

---

[74] Walter Altmann, Luther and Liberation:

[75] Cf. Paul Althaus, *The Ethics of Martin Luther*, trans. Robert C. Schultz (Philadelphia: Fortress, 1972), 52-53.

[76] Althaus, 54-56.

the law is to be equitable and just, must protect and safeguard all people, without exceptions based on race, class, gender, sexual orientation, or any other marker, including religion. It is the fallacy of religious identity politics, whether by Luther at his time or by contemporary representatives of the religious right, to exempt certain neighbors from equal protection under law on the basis of their appeals to religious (biblical!) authority.

Third – and in contradiction to the special pleading of religious identity politics – if there is bias exercised by Christians in the left hand strategy, it is not against those who fail to share a "Christian" religious worldview, but rather on behalf of those whom Jesus named "the least" – the hungry, thirsty, homeless, sick, or imprisoned ones – the most vulnerable, those at the margins of society in need of particular political advocacy (cf. Matt 25:31-46). What legitimates political engagement on behalf of the oppressed (including increasingly the oppression of the natural world) are not appeals to religious (biblical) authority. Rather, when Christians are involved in political advocacy, they are compelled to employ public arguments that aim to persuade all reasonable people about the legitimacy of a particular course of action apart from special pleading based on religious (Biblicist!) authority. The work of politics entails constructing coalitions to influence the balance of power in league with all those who share concern for the neighbor, beginning with the least. Religious identity politics must yield to a consistent neighbor politics, with *the welfare of the neighbor as the sole concern of Lutheran social ethics*, not religious self-righteousness.

Fourth, when civil authorities violate their God-given responsibility to protect and safeguard the rights of the people (especially minorities), Christians are called to engage in direct political action to make the government accountable for the proper exercise of its civil responsibility. According to Bonhoeffer:

> "There are thus three possibilities for action that the church can take vis-à-vis the state: *first* (as we have said), questioning the state as to the legitimate character of its actions, that is, making the state responsible for what it does. *Second* it is service to the victims of the state actions. The church has an unconditional obligation toward the victims of any societal order, even if they do not belong to the Christian community. 'Let us work for the good of all.' These are both ways in which the church, in its freedom, conducts itself in the interest of a free state. In times when the laws are changing, the church may under no circumstances neglect either of these duties. The *third* possibility is

not just to bind up the wounds of the victim beneath the wheel but to seize the wheel itself. Such an action would be direct political action on the part of the church. This is only possible and called for if the church sees the state to be failing in its function of creating law and order, that is, if the church perceives that the state, without any scruples, has created either too much or too little law and order. It must see in either eventuality a threat to the existence of the state and thus to its own existence as well."[77]

With this third possibility Bonhoeffer offers the needed correction to Luther's religious identity politics: the church must call for the state to fulfill "its function of creating law and order," not to impose its peculiar religious agenda on the state. Bonhoeffer (alongside the other conspirators) exercised this form of political responsibility by following the *ultima ratio* of planning *cout d'etat* against the dictatorship, a measure Luther never imagined within the legitimate scope of Christian political responsibility.

The limits of Luther's social ethics are profound. Luther's political reasoning and advocacy against the peasants, Anabaptists, and Jews must be rejected and repudiated. His counsel and conclusions reverberate across subsequent history in the arguments and actions of those who have appealed to his precedent, both by their rhetoric and through acts of persecution and violence. Only by deconstructing the logic of religious identity politics, both then and now, can Luther's ethical framework be reconstructed in service of a neighbor politics that has its sole purpose in defending the weak from harm and safeguarding the welfare of the most vulnerable in society, regardless of their religious convictions.

Abstract

Dieses Kapitel analysiert Luthers theologische Schriften gegen die Bauern, Täufer und Juden als eine Form „religiöser Identitätspolitik". Dieser Begriff wird auch in Beziehung auf heutige Formen theologischer Argumentationen angewendet, die bestimmte Fragen als „christlich" apostrophieren (wie z. B. Abtreibung, Homosexualität und den Staat Israel) und dabei besondere biblische Rechtfertigungen für die von ihnen gewünschten (politischen) Ergebnisse beanspruchen. Auf der Grundlage von Luthers eigenem Verständnis christlicher Ethik –

---

[77] Dietrich Bonhoeffer, "The Church and the Jewish Question," in Dietrich Bonhoeffer, *Berlin 1932-1933*, ed. Larry L. Rasmussen, trans. Isabel Best and David Higgins (Minneapolis: Fortress, 2009), 12:365-366.

wie in der Schrift „Von der Freiheit eines Christenmenschen" entwickelt und weitergeführt durch eine tiefer gehende und konsistente Darstellung von „Gottes Reich zur Linken", nach dem alle Menschen durch die Herrschaft des Rechts geschützt werden müssen –, hätte Luthers ethische Position eigentlich die Gestalt einer „Politik für die Nächsten" annehmen müssen, die die Rechte der Bauern, Täufer und Juden als schutzbedürftiger Nächster sichergestellt hätte.

Dieses Kapitel untersucht drei Fälle – nämlich seine Schriften gegen Bauern, Täufer und Juden – in ihrem historischen Kontext und analysiert sie mit Bezug auf jüngste Forschungen, besonders auf neuere Interpretationen der antijüdischen Schriften Luthers. Diese drei Fälle werfen radikale Fragen auf – nicht nur im Blick auf Luthers Ethik, sondern seine gesamte Theologie. Die ethische Integrität der lutherischen Reformation selbst steht ernsthaft in Frage, wenn die Schlussfolgerungen, die Luther in diesen drei Fällen zieht, nicht zurückgewiesen, korrigiert und überwunden werden.

Auf der Basis der Erkenntnis, dass Luthers ethische und theologische Argumente hier auf einem Irrtum beruhen, werden vier Schlussfolgerungen gezogen: 1. es ist notwendig, Luthers binäres Denken gegen Feinde zu dekonstruieren; 2. es ist notwendig, die Hermeneutik des Verdachts auf die eigenen Argumente anzuwenden, weil die menschliche Sündhaftigkeit universal ist; 3. es ist ohne Ausnahme notwendig, durch rechtliche Regeln den Status von Nächsten sicherzustellen – einschließlich solcher, mit denen wir aus religiösen oder ideologischen Gründen einen Konflikt haben; und 4. ist es notwendig, von vergangenem Versagen umzukehren – nicht nur durch ein Schuldbekenntnis, sondern auch durch die Wiederaufnahme gerechter Beziehungen mit denen, die wir geschädigt haben. Nur durch die Dekonstruktion der Logik „religiöser Identitätspolitik" kann Luthers ethischer Rahmen wieder rekonstruiert werden für eine „Nächstenpolitik", deren einziger Zweck darin besteht, die Wohlfahrt der Verwundbarsten in der Gesellschaft sicherzustellen, ohne Rücksicht auf religiöse Überzeugungen.

Im Gegensatz zu den besonderen Forderungen „religiöser Identitätspolitik" – wenn ChristInnen denn in der Strategie von „Gottes Reich zur Linken" einseitig Stellung nehmen sollen – sollten sie dies nicht gegen die tun, denen eine „christliche" Weltanschauung fehlt, sondern gerade für die, Jesus die „Geringsten" nennt, die Verwundbarsten am Rande der Gesellschaft. Wenn ChristInnen politisch für Menschen eintreten, müssen sie öffentliche Argumente vortragen, die alle vernunftbegabten Menschen von der Berechtigung einer bestimmten Handlungsweise ohne Rückgriff auf exklusive religiöse Argumente überzeugen – insbesondere nicht auf solche Argumente, die sich auf enge (biblizistische) Schrift-zitate berufen. Politische Arbeit schließt die Bündnisbildung mit anderen ein, die die Anliegen der betroffenen Nächsten, besonders der geringsten, teilen und sich deshalb gemeinsam für diese einsetzen. „Religiöse Identitätspolitik" muss deshalb durch echte „Nächstenpolitik" ersetzt werden – mit der Wohlfahrt der Nächsten und nicht religiöser Selbstgerechtigkeit als einzigem Anliegen lutherischer Sozialethik.

Prejudice and its Historical Application
A Radical Hermeneutic of Luther's Treatment of the Turks (Muslims) and the Jews

Charles Amjad-Ali

1. Introduction: Re-examining Fundamental "Truths" of Europe

Philosophically and theologically we live in a world in which dialogue (and its various synonyms), as well as an emphasis on multi-religious context, are not only ubiquitous but are regarded as historically unique and epistemologically central. Dialogue is therefore seen as providing novel potential for dealing with the perceived "new phenomenon" of religious and cultural pluralism. This, however, not only ignores the longstanding vibrant and robust experience of such dwelling in Asia and Africa, but also overlooks earlier similar experiences in Europe itself. Underlying this approach is a false and arrogant assumption that this context is incomparable and that the previous centuries had neither such contexts nor experiences and certainly did not have the wherewithal to deal with other religions. Thus Europe is assumed to have been exclusively Christian, in spite of the fact that the Iberian Peninsula (or Roman/Latin *Hispania*), the most western part of mainland Europe, had been ruled by Muslims for almost 800 years, and also had a huge and highly influential Jewish presence. Added to this was the Turkish imperial expansion starting in the 14th century which resulted in the Islamic control of most of central and eastern Europe. This was the immediate context in which Martin Luther was operating and writing from in the 16th century.

When dealing with Luther's understanding of Islam, it is therefore imperative to take these historical situations and traumas as part of his context. As Bernhard Lohse correctly points out "the history of Luther and the Reformation must always be seen in this larger context."¹ This perhaps provides some justification for the character of his writings about the Turks, even if not always for the content of his sophistry against Muslims, and even worse against the Jews. It must be noted here that while Luther's writings vis-à-vis the Turks and Islam can be somewhat justified, his extreme vitriol against the Jews has no such justification at all. Given this threat there had been many responses: "Catholic writers called for a united crusade to reclaim Constantinople and, occasionally, the Holy Land. Humanists and early Protestants, in addition to approving and urging defensive war strategies, began to study the Ottomans and their religion; some even optimistically hoped to instigate a missionary enterprise among them. And the radical authors of the Reformation urged a pacifist response to Ottoman imperialism with a few expressing hope in a Turkish conquest of Europe."² Luther had elements of all these responses but he also has criticisms, some theological, of all of them simultaneously. In this context, Adam Francisco provides a critical clue, stating that "when Luther began his inquiry into the religion of the Turks he would use... [the various earlier writings about Islam] in order to develop his own approach. They provided him information to which he would never be privy, for *he never once dialogued with a Muslim or came into contact with Islamic culture*. But once he decided that Islam needed to be responded to theologically he had to use what he could obtain in order to begin his own polemical and apologetical writing against the Turks and their religion."³

So we must look at Martin Luther as a theologian in this larger context. That he was dealing with other religions like Judaism (Jews) and Islam

---

[1] Bernhard Lohse, *Martin Luther: An Introduction to His Life and Work*, trans., Robert Schultz (Edinburgh: T & T Clark, 1987), 4.

[2] Adam S. Francisco, *Martin Luther and Islam: A Study in Sixteenth-Century Polemics and Apologetics* (Leiden: Brill, 2007), 31. This paper is deeply indebted for the comprehensive information this groundbreaking work provides. Although I do not always agree with his conclusions, there are few other sources that cover the topic of Luther and the Turks in such comprehensive breadth. For a comprehensive German approach to this issue, see also Johannes Ehmann, *Luther, Türken und Islam: eine Untersuchung zum Türken- und Islambild Martin Luthers (1515 – 1546)* (Gütersloh: Gütersloher Verlagshaus, 2008), which surveys the German scholarship on this subject.

[3] Francisco, 29-30, emphasis added.

(Turks) shows that, though he often wrote as if he was in a mono-religious Christian and mono-cultural milieu (with the heterodoxy of the Roman Catholics and the Anabaptists), he actually did his theology with these other monotheistic faiths in mind. And I would argue that Calvin, as on many other issues, followed him in this tradition also. Both encountered, did polemics, and apologetics vis-à-vis Islam and the Turks and the Jews, though not always in the most irenic, or even Christian way. This assumed mono-religious and, more critically, mono-cultural context is maintained by most Lutheran and Calvinist theologians, even today. Some work has been done on Luther's writings about the Jews, because of the use of those execrable texts by Hitler, and the Lutheran guilt vis-à-vis the holocaust, but his writings on the Turks have been largely ignored, including by most Lutheran theologians. However, I may quickly add that in many respects Luther's encounter and rhetoric vis-à-vis Islam is essentially not so different from some of our contemporary expressions of it, especially since September 11, 2001. Given the fact that what Luther said and wrote about Judaism was used some 400 years later in Germany, this makes me quite apprehensive about how some of Luther's writings vis-à-vis Islam could be utilized for our contemporary anti-Islamic prejudices, biases and victimization, in sum *Islamophobia*.

2. The Multi-Cultural and Multi-Religious Context of Europe

Europe at the time of Luther and his new theological concerns, was neither mono-religious, nor mono-cultural. It had had a series of historical developments over the last few centuries prior to the Reformation which reflected its highly multi-religious and culturally pluralistic context. These developments were still part of the collective memory, and in fact were the theological and epistemic foundations for the Reformation. Spain was under Muslim rule from 711[4] until the completion of the Reconquista of 1492 (i.e., the fall of Granada, which was the last Islamic state on the Iberian Peninsula). 1492 is now better recognized and famous for Christopher Columbus and the "discovery" (i.e., colonization) of the Americas under the patronage of the most Catholic Monarchs, Isabella and Ferdinand. After 1492 these monarchs

---

[4] When the Muslim General Tariq ibn Ziyad defeated King Roderic, the last of the Visigoth rulers of Hispania.

forcefully converted the Muslims and Jews of Spain to Christianity. The Muslim converts were referred to as Moriscos, i.e., Moorish.[5] The Jewish converts were known as Marranos – meaning pigs or swine, i.e., "filthy-dirty" and "unscrupulous."[6] The expulsion of the Moriscos from Spain began in 1609 and was finally completed in 1614.[7] The Jewish expulsion started earlier, after the genocide of 1391,[8] and is seen as the turning point for the Spanish (Sephardic) Jewish existence in Europe. It was the precursor to the Inquisition some 90 years later and to the expulsion of even the converted Jews which followed. The numbers of those expelled from Spain vary: Juan de Mariana estimates this number to be as high as 800,000;[9] while Rabbi Isidore Loeb estimates it to be as low as 165,000.[10] Loeb also shows that some 90,000 of these refugees migrated to Turkey as they were welcomed by the Sultan.

Besides this long term presence and influence of Muslims and Jews in western Europe, large portions of central and eastern Europe also lived under similar long term Muslim control, in this case of the Ottoman Turks. This

---

[5] The term Moriscos was largely applied to the indigenous Spanish Muslim converts and not so much to those of Arab descent.

[6] For Jews to be referred to as pigs or swine, especially in the context of 800 years of Islamic rule (which had similar religious purity laws), was highly derogatory, offensive, and obscene; their descendents, therefore naturally preferred the term *Anusim* – Hebrew for forced.

[7] In 1609 King Philip III issued an Act of Expulsion of the Muslims (*Expulsión de los moriscos*) who were left behind after 1492, because he saw them as having loyalty to the Ottoman Turks and therefore as a subversive fifth column in the Iberian Peninsula. This expulsion was finally completed in 1614. See, esp., Mary E. Perry. *The Handless Maiden: Moriscos and the Politics of Religion in Early Modern Spain* (Princeton: Princeton University Press, 2005).

[8] This genocide took place in different locations all across Spain: Seville, Cordoba, Toledo, Aragon, Catalonia, Majorica, Valencia, Palma, Barcelona, *et al.*

[9] de Mariana was a Spanish Jesuit, regarded highly for his sagacious research and accuracy. See his famous *Historiae de rebus Hispaniae,* a 20 volume work published first in Toledo in 1592 (trans. from Latin into Spanish and even into English by J. Stevens, as *The General History of Spain* in 1699).

[10] Loeb inaugurated and was the first editor of the Jewish journal *Revue des Études Juives*, in Paris, in which he proposes this figure in his article, "Le nombre des juifs de Castille et d'Espagne," in vol. xiv. 1887, 162–183.

started at least as early as the 1389 battle of Kosovo. With some permutations, this status remained largely unchanged until as late as the First World War, i.e., a period of over 500 years.[11] With the control of Constantinople in 1453, and all of Greece in 1460 (the cradle of the "western civilization"),[12] the Turkish Muslims had a comprehensive and long term presence in this part of Europe as well.

These two long-term multi-religious contexts in the western, central, and eastern parts of Europe, and the presence of the other two monotheistic faiths in "Christian" Europe, belies its mono-religious claim, on the one hand, and forces us to look at the epistemic significance of its multi-religious experiences and dialogical practices on the other. It also demands from us a more critical re-examination of this history and a demythologizing of it for a more honest theological and philosophical task.

Islam has had its own veracity amnesia: it uncritically accepts the "western" claim to the Mediterranean and its contributions. In this way Muslims can maintain the complete purity of their absolute Arabian causation and revelation. This is to preserve the myth that the Islamic resources are purely Arab and are neither influenced nor contaminated by the Mediterranean Greco-Roman world, nor by the Indian, Chinese/Mongol, or Zoroastrian worlds,

---

[11] This Turkish presence in Europe can be dated to as far back as the Battle of Maritsa in 1371 which the Ottoman Turks won, or to as late as the Turkish victory in the Battle of Kosovo in 1389. The latter has acquired a central role in Serbian folklore and is seen as the epic battle which heralded the beginning of bad luck for Serbia. This folklore played quite a significant role in the Yugoslav and Bosnian wars of the 1990s and the genocide of the Muslims there after some 600 years. It must also be remembered that the Ottoman Empire had taken over the Greek areas of Thrace and much of Macedonia after the Battle of Maritsa in 1371. Sofia fell in 1382, followed by Tarnovgrad in 1393, the state of Romania/Hungary after the Battle of Nicopolis in 1396. The Turkish victory over Hungarian forces in the Battle of Varna, in 1444, expanded their control over the Balkans and was of special concern to Calvin. See my article, "Debilitating Past and Future Hope: Calvin, Calvinism and Islam" in *Reformed World,* Vol. 61, No. 2 (2011), 120-133.

[12] What is now modern Greece was also part of the Ottoman Empire from the mid-15th century until its declaration of independence in 1821, a historical period also known as *Tourkokratia* in Greek (Τουρκοκρατία) or "Turkish rule."

etc. On the other side, when showing a more open approach, these Mediterranean and other sources are not only acknowledged, but the Muslim contribution to them is hyperbolized and exaggerated beyond any factuality and location in truth. The latter position is more for polemical and apologetic sophistry and ends up challenging the veracity of the deep interaction between the Mediterranean and the Muslim world. Some of the recent internal clashes between the different Islamic groups are based on the levels of purity from these Mediterranean and post-Mediterranean sources they wish to maintain and articulate.

3. Christianity as a Western Religion, Luther's Vitriol against Jews and Muslims

Both the amnesia of the West and that of the Muslim world, under even a minimum scrutiny, show that the foundations that each is claiming are not sustainable, even when the necessity of epistemic prejudice is accepted, a la Gadamer.[13] Yet huge epistemological edifices have been erected which take for granted that the West is Christian and the (middle) East is Muslim; this is the fundamental difference between occident *(abendland)* and orient.[14] This

---

[13] Hans-Georg Gadamer retrieves the epistemic location of *prejudicum* and sees the Enlightenment itself as having a prejudice against prejudice itself, and thus claiming a transcendent dislocated veracity which is not historically sustainable. See his, *Truth and Method* (New York: Seabury Press, 1975).

[14] See Edward Said, *Orientalism* (New York, Pantheon Books, 1978) and much of the subsequent literature on this theme and the de-privilegization of the taken-for-granted normatives. For a critical early read of this, see Henri Pirenne, *Mohammed and Charlemagne* (London: George Allen & Unwin Ltd., 1954) trans. of *Mohomet et Charlemagne* which was influential on Marc Bloch, among others, in the formation of the critical Annales School of History, from which emerged one of the most significant works on Mediterranean society by Fernand Braudel, *The Mediterranean and the Mediterranean World in the Age of Philip II,* trans. by Siân Reynolds (Berkeley, CA: University of California Press, 1996). For larger implications, see also the controversial work by Oswald Spengler, *The Decline of the West (Der Untergang des Abendlandes,* 1918-1922) which deals with the "oriental mind" and the morphology of cultures, two vols. (New York: Alfred A. Knopf, 1932). In Marxist circles, the concept of Oriental Despotism took on a special significance, see especially Karl A. Wittfogel, *Oriental Despotism: A Comparative Study of Total Power* (New Haven: Yale University Press, 1957).

This sophistry has continued and is now rearticulated in recent years as the clash of civilizations, and "the west versus the rest" (i.e. consumerist capitalism of the west ver-

edifice assumes first that Christianity is an exclusively Western religion, thus its non-acknowledgment of the churches in the East. On the other side, Islam makes itself an exclusively Arab religion, even though the majority of Muslims live in the non-Arab world. We have to undo these mythical stereotypifications if we are to live in a just and peaceful world and achieve truth for a righteous society based on common weal and social virtue.

Out of these series of prejudices, untruths, and distortions comes a now almost permanent misunderstanding on both sides. Since we are dealing largely with Luther, the Reformation and Islam in this paper, we must therefore seriously address the issues of centuries-old misunderstandings, and indeed the contrived vilification of the Muslims, their Prophet, their Scriptures, their religion, and their culture, and overcome the ignorance vis-à-vis Islam as a whole. What is even more distressing than this sheer ignorance is the conscious malice, vilification, and calculated distortions of Islam and its contributions, which has been part of the grammar in the west for well over six hundred years. When we give credit to the West and to Christianity for democracy, participatory rights, social justice, equality of genders, and freedom of sexual choice, etc., we conveniently forget that we are borrowing straight from secular sources of the Enlightenment, which actually attacked Christianity and vice versa, it being the only religion that was part of that discourse. This vilification was also the case with the Jews, at least until 1945, and from this period on there have emerged new and quite anachronistic readings of Jewish-Christian relations, thus for example the ubiquitousness of the term "Judeo-Christian" for ethics, morality, values, etc., as a retroactive historical-

---

sus the religious and tribal fundamentalism of Islam; and the advanced brilliant technology in the making of Lexus versus the oldest working technology of the Olive grove); in Samuel Huntington, *The Clash of Civilizations and the Remaking of World Order* (New York: Simon and Schuster, 1996); Benjamin Barber, *Jihad vs. McWorld: How Globalism and Tribalism are Reshaping the World* (New York: Random House, 1996); and Thomas Friedman, *Lexus and the Olive Tree: Understanding Globalization* (New York: Picador, 1999), among others.

ly permanent fixture,[15] and thus any critique of the state of Israel is perceived as a threat to this newly perpetuated mythology. So when we give credit to the West we locate and give undue credit to Christianity for the achievement of human values without actually paying attention to the religious distortions, challenges, and critiques of these Enlightenment ideologies.

Another social hermeneutical issue we face today is the difficulty of the widely present juxtaposition of incompatible and largely hostile systems of thought, morals, and beliefs. These are embodied in political and economic power(s) of impressive, if not awe-inspiring, presence. We sometimes talk as if this was a new problem – and certainly it is new to the modern world. The Western sense of superiority in every sphere of endeavor has scarcely been challenged for over three hundred years both in its colonial and post-colonial expressions. It has become part of our overall heritage, most painful to abandon as well as to morally adjust to. What is overlooked is the fact that Europe itself went through this painful experience well over a thousand years ago, through the hegemony of the Roman Empire and partly through the hegemonic Muslim expansion after the 7th century. Further, Europe lived with the Muslim challenge more or less permanently, starting at least with the conquest of Spain in 711, through the Crusades starting in 1095, and right up to the 17th century. There was rarely a period of complacency from this challenge throughout the Middle Ages and even well after the Reformation, our mono-religious hermeneutic of this history notwithstanding. The existence of Islam was one of the most far-reaching problems in medieval Christendom. It posed a problem at every level of experience. As a practical problem it called for action and discernment between the competing possibilities of crusade, conversion, coexistence and commercial interchange. As a theological problem it called persistently for some answer to the mystery of its existence. What was its providential role in history? Was it a symptom of the world's last days or a stage in Christian development; a heresy, a schism, or a new religion; a work of man or devil; an obscene parody of Christianity, or a sys-

---

[15] From the previously ubiquitous "Christ-killers" (till around 1939), to the current ubiquitous "Judeo-Christian" label, is a major epistemological shift and is not always a product of high ethical commitment.

tem of thought that deserved to be treated with respect? In different places, Luther argued each of these positions, however epistemologically discrete each argument may be in itself. So one finds elements of all these evaluations in various texts of Luther.

4. From Rome to Constantinople (the New Rum) and the Founding of Christendom

There are some typical, and clearly incorrect, assertions about the West that need to be examined as part of the larger context of Luther's approach on the issue of the Turks and the Jews. Briefly, the West views itself as being in direct continuity with the Mediterranean culture and civilization and as the successor of the Roman Empire (not simply of the "Western Roman Empire," whatever that term means),[16] without any mediation, much less a primary contribution, from Africa and Asia towards these developments. This historiographical sleight of hand is undertaken in order to emphasize the enduring continuity between "European" history and its "mother" Greco-Roman civilizations of the Mediterranean. Thus at least conceptually locating the Mediterranean[17] exclusively in Europe, even though geographically it is located between Africa, Asia and Europe.

What is critical to understand is the fact that the perception of unbridged Mediterranean continuity and Europe's mono-religious status evolved largely out of a Constantinian Christendom model. What is equally critical to remember, however, is that the location of the capital of this Constantinian

---

[16] This phrase seems to have been coined in modern historiography to define the Western provinces and courts of the Roman Empire and to give them equal footing with the "Eastern Roman Empire," because of Constantinople. Ostensibly this happened when the capital was shifted from Rome to Byzantium by Constantine in 330, and after his death the former was renamed Constantinople and remained the capital of the Roman Empire till 1204; whatever the status of Charlemagne's Carolingian rule (800-814) with a blessing of the Bishop of Rome (Pope Leo III). For this historiography, see esp. Edward Gibbon, *The History of the Decline and Fall of the Roman Empire* 6 vols. (London: Straham & Cadell, 1776-1789).

[17] The term itself derives from the Latin word *mediterraneus* (*medi-*: "middle" or "between"; + *terra*, "land, earth"): i.e., "in the middle of earth" or "between lands," it being the sea between the then three known continents of Africa, Asia and Europe. The German word for Mediterranean, correctly calls it *Mittelmeer*, i.e., the middle sea.

Christendom and Empire bordered Asia, if it was not directly in Asia itself, i.e., on the Bosphorus. It had no real contribution from, nor was it ever a direct product as such of, the so-called European "barbarian" tribes: Goths, Visigoths, Huns, Vandals, Franks, Angles, Saxons etc.,[18] who had threatened the Roman Empire. Their aggression and threats led to the move from Rome (Italy) to Byzantium/Constantinople (the New Rome on the Bosphorous) as the new capital of the Empire in the fourth century. It is critical to note that it is here that Christianity becomes the religion of imperial Rome. Constantinople, therefore, is the original location of what came to be called "Christendom," rather than what is now classified as Europe.[19]

Further, it should be remembered that at the beginning of this period there is only one Roman Empire (no such aberrations as the Western and Eastern Roman Empire) which moved its capital from Rome, south into or towards Asia, to a new capital, Constantinople. To the Muslims, this was the *Rum*, the only Rome they knew, having come into being after this shift. The Muslims became the inheritors of this Roman Empire and of most of the Mediterranean, beginning with the initial period of Islamic expansion and conquest, crescendoing finally with the capture of Constantinople in 1453 – the task was complete with *Rum* under the Muslims. With this they inherited the intellectual tradition of the Greco-Roman world, which was then transmitted to the West through Muslim scholars even for as central and pivotal a Christian theologian/philosopher as St. Thomas Aquinas. Sidney Griffiths therefore rightly points out that, "Al-Farabi (870-950), Ibn Sina/Avicenna (980-1037), and Ibn Rushd/Averroes (1126-1198), are the Muslim philosophers with the most immediate name recognition ... but they are far from being the only ones making major contributions. And, of course, their accomplishments

---

[18] These tribes were variously located in, or were part of, eastern Germany, Pomerania to the Black Sea, Scandinavia, Caucuses to Central Asia, Norman Germanic tribes controlling Portugal and Spain (*Hispania*), Southern Poland, Spain to some parts of North Africa and France, and Britain especially after the Romans left the area in 410 A.D.

[19] The first real state to adopt Christianity as its state religion was the Kingdom of Armenia in 301 AD, followed shortly thereafter by the Caucasus Albania (modern-day Azerbaijan), somewhere between 301 and 314. The Armenian and Azerbaijani Orthodox Churches proudly let you know that they were the first Christian kingdoms prior to the establishment of the Christian Imperial power in Constantinople.

sparked yet another translation movement in the eleventh and twelfth centuries, this time in the Islamo-Christian west, in places like Bologna, Toledo, and Barcelona, where eager minds translated philosophical texts from Arabic into Latin, and provided the impetus for the flowering of scholastic philosophy and theology in the works of Thomas Aquinas, Bonaventure, and Duns Scotus, through the earlier achievements of scholars such as Abelard and Albert the Great."[20] So it was not by sword that Albert the Great and St. Thomas Aquinas (1224-1274) accepted the Muslim masters for their philosophy (Avicenna and and Averroes), and dare I say also for their theology. It was in the light of these masters that Thomas reexamined Christianity and insisted on the perspicuity of the sacred text, as in Islam. This then influenced Luther's *sola scriptura*, with had little space for the mediation of *traditio*. On the other hand, it was Thomas' judgment and critique of these, his masters and teachers, and their Aristotelian philosophies, in *summa de veritate catholique fidei contra gentiles* (Treatise on the Truth of the Catholic Faith against Unbelievers),[21] which has determined our position on Islam and Muslims in the West, as well as on Aristotle in the Protestant circles. These were the predecessors and guides to Luther leading up to the Reformation.

The three monotheistic religious traditions certainly borrowed from one another in Muslim-ruled Spain, benefiting especially from the blooming of philosophy and the medieval sciences in the Muslim Middle East. There was

---

[20] Sidney H. Griffith, *The Church in the Shadows of the Mosque: Christians and Muslims in the World of Islam* (Princeton: Princeton University Press, 2008), 18. See also Majid Fakhry, *A History of Islamic Philosophy*, 3rd. edition (New York: Columbia University Press, 2004); Fernand van Steenberghen, *Aristotle and the West: The Origins of Latin Aristotelianism*, trans. by Leonard Johnston (New York: Humanities Press, 1970); Charles Burnett, "The Translating Activity in Medieval Spain" in *The Legacy of Muslim Spain* 2 vols., ed. Salma Khadra Jayyusi, vol. 2: 1036-58 (Leiden: E.J. Brill, 1994); Burnett, "Arabic into Latin: The Reception of Arabic Philosophy into Western Europe," in *The Cambridge Companion to Arabic Philosophy*, ed. Peter Adamson and Richard C. Taylor, 370-404 (Cambridge: Cambridge University Press, 2005); John E. Wansborough, *The Sectarian Milieu: Content and Composition of Islamic Salvation History* (Oxford: OUP, 1978). See also, the present author's *Islamophobia: Tearing the Veils of Ignorance* (Johannesburg: Ditshwanelo Car²as, 2005), specifically the first chapter.

[21] It has traditionally been dated to 1264, though some recent scholarship places it towards the end of Thomas' life, somewhere between 1270 to 1273.

more "tolerance" and coexistence than has been imagined or acknowledged. In spite of some recent scholars questioning this notion of peaceful coexistence of Muslims, Jews, and Christians – known as the *convivencia* – and wondering if it could be defined as "pluralistic,"[22] there was clearly much more interaction, conviviality, acceptance and tolerance for each other in Muslim Spain than in "Christian" Spain after 1492.

5. The Pervasive Fear of Islam and the Crusades

The fear of Islam is not new in Christendom and Christian history. It started with the Islamic conquests as early as the late 7th century, its rapid expansion, and its annexation of almost all the Biblical lands. This early expansion extended to the occupation of three of the five cities of the founding patriarchates (the Pentarchy) of Christianity, viz., Jerusalem, Antioch, and Alexandria; later even Constantinople. Rome was the exception in both cases, though it too came very close to being captured.[23] This was further exacerbated by the fear and awe generated by Muslims during the three centuries of the Crusades. The Christian inability to maintain the euphoric success at the capture of the holy land from the Muslims in the First Crusade, and its subsequent failure to sustain this occupation, shook Christianity hard. It generated serious difficulty for Christians, given the ubiquitous religious notion that success and victory shows that God is on our side because of our faith and piety; conversely the same idea provided succor to the Muslims precisely because of their high level of success in these centuries.

The Crusades became a self-justifying *cause célèbre* for Christianity and played a very significant role in most aspects of European medieval life, be it ecclesial, economic, political, cultural, or social. Having been put on a religious and spiritual footing by the popes starting with Urban II in 1095 at the Council of Clermont, who linked the call for crusade to the wars of independence by Christians taking place on the Iberian peninsula, they were cen-

---

[22] See for example Stephen O'Shea, *Sea of Faith: Islam and Christianity in the Medieval Mediterranean World* (New York: Walker & Company, 2006).

[23] Sultan Mehmet II of the Ottoman Empire clearly had his eyes set on Rome, having already captured Otranto in 1480, when he suddenly died and that expansion stopped because of internal Ottoman strife over the question of succession.

tral to the theological development of the Reformation, as I shall show. The Crusades were a series of Christian "holy wars" carried out from 1096 till 1270 against the Muslims in larger Syria and Palestine and subsequently elsewhere in the area. Steven Runciman, one of the major historians of the Crusades, correctly describes them as "a long act of intolerance in the name of God, which is a sin against the Holy Ghost."[24] Others have argued that, "[i]n a broad sense the Crusades were an expression of militant Christianity and European expansion."[25] There were of course the narrower market, economic, and capitalist interests such as those of Venice, and its trade interests with India and China. While Venice did not have a direct role during the crusades themselves, nonetheless it played a significant role in them, restricting this to trade and the political power needed to protect this trade. As the crusades began Venice dominated the Adriatic and eastern Mediterranean trade, especially within the Byzantium empire. With the victory of the first crusade, its merchants quickly established major trading relations with the new Crusader kingdom. Because it was one of the major naval powers of the Mediterranean it became one of the convenient points of departure for many a crusade.

There were at least 8 Crusades, of which the first four are the most relevant. The battle cry of the First Crusade that "God wills it" and "To free the Holy Land of the Infidels" became established as the overt *raison d'etre* for the subsequent crusades. The first crusade was successful and Jerusalem was taken over in 1099, establishing the crusader Kingdom of Jerusalem, which lasted until 1187. The second was a disaster. The third led to the Treaty of Ramla in 1192 between Saladin and Richard the Lionheart. It was highly favorable for Christians, as it allowed Christians pilgrimage to Jerusalem, despite Muslim control of the city. In the fourth, in 1204, the Crusaders sacked Constantinople (some 250 years prior to its subjugation by the Ottoman Muslims in 1453) desecrating many Orthodox churches including Hagia Sophia (built in 537), one of the most holy ecclesial sites in all of Christianity. As a

---

[24] Steven Runciman, *A History of the Crusades* (New York: Harper and Row, 3 volumes, 1967), 480.

[25] See, http://history-world.org/crusades.htm, as accessed on February 9, 2015.

result a new Latin Kingdom of Byzantium was established there which lasted for 60 years.

What is often forgotten, or not mentioned with any import, is the fact that besides killing an enormous number of non-combatant innocent Muslims, the crusades also killed a massive number of Jews both in Europe as well as in the near east.[26] These genocidal massacres were justified on the grounds that such killings were not sinful because the ones killed were not Christians but infidels (not of the faith). Gustavo Perednik, a scholar of Judeophobia, states "...the first half of this millennium witnessed genocides of Jews as the norm. And this is precisely when the Church reached the zenith of its power... the main genocides were the first three crusades and the four Jew-murdering campaigns that followed them."[27] And we can add here that the millennium also ended with a genocide of the Jews in the Holocaust.

---

[26] This generated a whole series of writings which rework the *Akedah* material (i.e., Abraham's sacrifice of Isaac) in Jewish Rabbinic theological and religious discourses and various art forms including folk songs and folk lore. For a very special treatment of this material during the crusade-based Jewish holocaust, see Shalom Spiegel, *The Last Trial: On the Legends and Lore of the Command to Abraham to Offer Isaac As a Sacrifice: The Akedah,* translated by Judah Goldin (Woodstock, VT: Jewish Lights Publishing, 1993, 3rd edition). For a critical read of the Akedah material for New Testament studies, see, Nils Alstrup Dahl, *Crucified Messiah, and Other Essays* (Minneapolis, MN: Augsburg Press, 1974). For more popular writing see among others Amos Oz's brilliant work, *Unto Death: Crusades and Late Love (Two Novellas)* (New York: Mariner's Books, 1978).

[27] Perednik also rightly points out that: "Pope Urban II called for a campaign 'to free the Holy Land from the Muslim infidel.'... The crusaders decided to start their cleansing on the 'infidels at home,' and pounced upon the Jews all over Lorraine, massacring those who refused baptism. Soon it was rumored that their leader Godfrey had vowed not to set out for the crusade until he had avenged the crucifixion by spilling the blood of the Jews, and that he could not tolerate the continued existence of any man calling himself a Jew. Indeed, one common denominator of the genocides... was the attempt to wipe out the entire Jewish population, children included." So that, "By the end of the 13th century Jews had been expelled from England, France and Germany." See, his "Judeophobia - Anti-Semitism, Jew-Hate and anti-"Zionism"" a series of lectures based on his book *La Judeofobia: Como y Cuando Nace, Donde y Por Que Pervive* (Mexico: Tusquets, 2001), made available online at http://www.zionism-israel.com/his/ judeophobia.htm.

6. The Turkish Threat and the Apocalyptic Visions

For Medieval Europe, Islam, now in the guise of the Turk, posed a threat of apocalyptic proportions. Starting with the fourteenth century this threat had become enough of a concern that it was part of various Medieval writings. By the sixteenth century a Turkish victory over Europe seemed palpably immanent: the fall of Constantinople in 1453 (just thirty years before Martin Luther's birth in 1483) was a devastating blow, but the north western expansion of the Ottomans, culminating in the attack on Vienna in 1529, was more existentially debilitating. Though this attack was repulsed by the Habsburgs, at the heavy cost of some 30,000 lives – dead or enslaved, it had not minimized the sense of this imminent threat of the Turks.[28]

The Crusades' anti-Jewish and anti-Islamic sentiments continued into the Reformation period, as is evident in Luther's writings and later even in Calvin. Both seriously polemicized against Islam; however, at the same time what is more significant, is the fact that they both saw Islam as a judgment of God upon a highly corrupt and venal Christianity, especially Roman Catholicism. Therefore, Luther could call Islam "the rod of God." Writing as early as 1518 Luther says that "To fight against the Turk is the same as resisting God, who visits our sin upon us with this rod."[29] So Luther sees the Turks as God's instrument of punishment against a sinful Christendom, and in response to Pope Leo X's call for a new crusade against the Ottoman Turks, Luther argues, in *Resolutiones disputationum de indulgentiarum virtute* (1518, a copy of which he sent to the Pope), that: "Many, however, even the 'big wheels' in the church, now dream of nothing else than war against the Turk. They want to fight, not against iniquities, but against the lash of iniquity and thus they would oppose God who says that through that lash he himself punishes us for our iniquities because we do not punish ourselves for

---

[28] Gregory Miller, "Holy War and Holy Terror: View of Islam in German Pamphlet Literature 1520-1545" (Ph.D.: Boston University, 1994), 67-68.

[29] See, Sarah Henrich and James L. Boyce, "Martin Luther—Translations of Two Prefaces on Islam: Preface to the Libellus de ritu et moribus Turcorum (1530), and Preface to Bibliander's Edition of the Qur'ān (1543)," in *Word & World,* Vol. XVI, No. 2, Spring 1996, 250-266, esp. 252, see their footnote 3 quoting from the *Explanations of the Ninety-Five Theses* in *Luther's Works,* vol. 31:91-92.

them."[30] Similarly, as late as 1529, he continues to describe the Turks as the "rod of God's wrath" by which "God is punishing the world."[31]

But these Reformers also saw Islam, along with Catholicism, as "the second horn on the head of the devil." Both these seemingly paradoxical positions vis-à-vis Islam were maintained by Luther and followed by Calvin.[32] For Luther, the Turks were both the rod of God's wrath, and also of Satan. As George Forell argues: "For Luther the devil was always God's devil, i.e., in attempting to counteract God the devil ultimately serves God."[33] So Satan (and thereby the Turks) was being used by God for God's purposes. This was further confirmed by an unjust war carried out exclusively for aggressive purposes rather than defensively which is the devil's *modus operandi*. The Turks were, according to Luther, thus the instrument "with which God is punishing the world as he often does through wicked scoundrels, and sometimes through godly people."[34]

Francisco points out that Luther rarely talks about the Turks without also mentioning the papacy:

> "His colleagues recorded him as suggesting that both were the Antichrist. 'The Pope is the spirit of the Antichrist, and the Turk is the flesh of the Antichrist. They both help each other to choke [us], the latter with body and soul, the former with doctrine and spirit.'[35] In his own writings ... he viewed the Pope as the Antichrist whereas the Turks were another sort of demonic aberration. Along with the rest of the Muslim world, they were followers of the

---

[30] See, *Explanations of the Disputation Concerning the Value of Indulgences,* popularly known as the *Explanations of the Ninety-Five Theses* in *Luther's Works,* trans. Harold J. Grimm and Helmut T. Lehmann, vol. 31. (Philadelphia: Muhlenberg Press and Fortress Press, 1957), 79-252, esp. 92.

[31] Henrich and Boyce, 252.

[32] See Amjad-Ali, "Debilitating Past," 120-133.

[33] George Forell, "Luther and the War Against the Turks," in William Russell (ed.), *Martin Luther, Theologian of the Church: Collected Essays* (St. Paul: Luther Seminary, 1994), 127.

[34] *On War Against the Turks,* LW 46:170. See Francisco, 80.

[35] *D. Martin Luthers Werke: Tischreden,* 6 vols. (Weimar: Bohlau, 1912–1921).1:135.15–17: 'Papa est spiritus Antichristi, et Turca est caro Antichristi. Sie helffen beyde einander wurgen, hic corpore et gladio, ille doctrina et spiritu'; cf. also 3:158.31–35.

beast of Apocalypse 20:10, which was Muhammad. The situation, according to Luther's exegesis of the passage was thus: Muhammad's kingdom (the beast) reigned in the East and the papacy (the false prophet of Antichrist) reigned in the West. Both were poised under the command of Satan waiting for orders to commence the final assault upon the church. 'Because the end of the world is at hand,' he wrote 'the Devil must attack Christendom with both of his forces.' Yet, interestingly, and probably due to proximity, Luther almost always viewed the papacy as the bigger threat than Muhammad and the Turks. He often remarked that compared to the Pope, 'Muhammad appears before the world as a pure saint.' Nevertheless, both played an integral role in his eschatological view of history and his assessment of the nature of the Turkish threat."[36]

7. Medieval Christendom's Approach to Islam and the Jews

Norman Daniel, a philosopher, political theorist, and ethicist at Harvard University, writing about the western 'scientific' approach towards Islam, rightly advises us that, "… even when we read the more detached scholars, we need to keep in mind how medieval Christendom argued, because it has always been and still is part of the make-up of every western mind brought to bear on the subject."[37] From a very different perspective, Colin Chapman, an evangelical missionary who had spent time in the Near East School of Theology, London Bible College and at various academic institutions in the UK, writes that, "At the time of the Reformation, Protestants saw Islam alongside Roman Catholicism as embodiments of the Antichrist, while Catholics saw in Islam many of the features they hated most in the Protestants. Then, with the coming of the Enlightenment, the rationalists took their turn to denigrate Islam and pour scorn on the Prophet."[38] What is consistent in these two critical quotes from highly divergent sources is the ubiquitous anti-Islamic attitude and judgment in Western history which has been the epistemic normative over quite a few centuries, even when the discourse involves interlocutors of very different, antagonistic, and hostile ideological starting points. The modern-day expressions of Islamophobia have roots in Christian faith history and

---

[36] Francisco, 83-4.

[37] Norman Daniel, *Islam and the West: The Making of an Image* (Edinburgh: Edinburgh University Press, 1960; revised edition 1993), 326.

[38] Colin Chapman, *Islam and the West: Conflict, Coexistence or Conversion?* (London: Paternoster Press, 1998), 11.

they have long term consistency even when the various social, ideological and structural permutations have changed, and even when our vocabulary of prejudice has undergone quite a few euphemistic alterations.

There are a significant number of publications covering the history of Christian-Muslim encounters (which have proliferated especially since 9/11). The quality varies widely, though some (mostly dating back a few decades prior to 9/11) are of a high quality. Most of the Christian theologians referenced in these texts, who had significant interactions with Islam prior to, and even during, the crusades, lived under Islamic rule. These theologians were religious minorities dwelling under Islamic control and the overall Islamic cultural milieu, and were therefore defined by it, their polemics against Islam notwithstanding. Albert Hourani rightly points out that "by the tenth century ... men and women in the Near East and the Maghreb lived in a universe which was defined in terms of Islam. ... Time was marked by the five daily prayers, the weekly sermon in the Mosque, the annual fast in the month of Ramadan and the pilgrimage to Mecca, and the Muslim calendar."[39] That they were for the most part able to carry out their apologetic and polemical work (especially against the Prophet Muhammad) whilst under exacting Muslim rule (in the larger Syria, Maghreb, Spain, and Turkey), shows the level of intellectual space that these societies must have had, despite the propaganda to the contrary.[40]

---

[39] See his, *A History of Arab Peoples* (New York: Warner Books, 1992), 54-57. This, by the way, is the experience of all Christians living in Islamic contexts even today, though the level of tolerance has decreased significantly in the recent years. Unfortunately these Christians are not fully a part of the contemporary ecumenical discussion vis-à-vis Christian-Muslim relations which is supervised by "Christian concern" in the Western context and by their "objective" approach.

[40] The most significant names are: John Sedra, a Monophysitic Jacobite patriarch of Antioch from 631-48; John of Damascus, a Malkite (d.749/764), arguably the author of the very first *Summa Theologica*; Theodore bar Koni, a Syriac Christian, (d. 792), author of *Scholian,* a commentary on the Old and New Testament; Patriarch Timothy I, of the Church of the East, (727/8-823); Theodore Abu Kurrah, a Malachite from Edessa who was the Bishop of Harran also in Syria (c. 755-830), who actually did his Christian theology in Arabic and wrote in both Syriac and Arabic; Hunayn ibn Ishaq (808-873) Nestorian physician, philosopher and translator, known for his translation into Arabic of Greek philosophical and scientific texts; Elyas of Nisibis, a Nestorian (975-1046); and

Though the Jews were theologically the closest and oldest neighbor to Christianity (the concepts of *praeparatio evangelica*, Messiah, etc.), they were a vulnerable victim to an aggressive Christianity immediately following Constantine's "conversion" in the early 4th century. Islam, on the other hand, being a major post-Christian religion, posed a serious challenge to the sufficiency and efficaciousness of Christianity. Just as Christianity saw Judaism as *praeparatio evangelica*, Islam saw both Judaism and Christianity (its monotheistic predecessors) as *praeparatio Islamica,* to coin a phrase. Its rapid phenomenal growth and conquests immediately following its founding were perceived by Islam as clear indications of the validity and efficaciousness of its cause. Therefore Islam was a challenge for Christians theologically, geographically, numerically, politically and economically. Located so close, it posed a threatening and confrontational challenge, a neighbor to be vilified and where possible rooted out. Philip Hitti, the great Lebanese Christian Arab historian, formerly at Princeton University, speaks of this relationship as: "The two communities have been yoked together through cooperation and conflict, tolerance and hatred, dialogue and diatribe, personal friendship and communal strife."[41] Hourani, formerly of Oxford University, also a great historian with a Christian Lebanese background, describes it as a "long and intimate, an ambiguous and usually painful relationship."[42] So in spite of the high theological claim and the great divine imperative of "loving our neighbors as ourselves," we Christians have hated to love and have loved to hate our closest neighbor, the Muslims.

Both Hitti and Hourani are correct in giving their respective evaluations of the paradoxical history of the Christian-Muslim relationship, especially vis-à-vis Western Christianity and Islam. Luther represents this ambiguity, and the seeming contradiction, in his attitude towards the Muslims. Over time he shows the same contradictory attitude towards the Jews, but there his negativity is much more vitriolic. This is clear in his total *volte-face* vis-à-vis the Jews. In his earlier writings, he has a relatively positive evaluation, especial-

---

Paul of Antioch (ca. 1180) Malachite bishop. Cf. Griffith, *op. cit.*; and Wansborough, *op. cit.*

[41] Philip Hitti, *Islam and the West* (Princeton, NJ.: Van Nostrand, 1962), 6.
[42] Albert Hourani, *Europe and the Middle East* (London: Macmillan Press, 1980), 71-2.

ly given the overall negative attitude towards Jews prevalent at the time. His first statement about the Jews comes from his letter of 1514, addressed to Pastor Georg Spalatin, the secretary/advisor to imperial Elector Frederick the Wise: "Conversion of the Jews will be the work of God alone operating from within, and not of man working — or rather playing — from without. If these offences be taken away, worse will follow. For they are thus given over by the wrath of God to reprobation, that they may become incorrigible, as Ecclesiastes says, for every one who is incorrigible is rendered worse rather than better by correction."[43]

Then in 1519 Luther challenges the doctrine of *Servitus Judaeorum* (Servitude of the Jews) established by Justinian I in *Corpus Juris Civilis* (Body of Civil Law) between 529-34 and the theologians defending it: "Absurd theologians defend hatred for the Jews... What Jew would consent to enter our ranks when he sees the cruelty and enmity we wreak on them – that in our behavior towards them we less resemble Christians than beasts?"[44] Luther makes the most comprehensive statement for the Jews in *That Jesus Christ was Born a Jew* written in 1523, again with a very heavy critique of those theologians who support an anti-Jewish position:

"If I had been a Jew and had seen such dolts and blockheads govern and teach the Christian faith, I would sooner have become a hog than a Christian. They have dealt with the Jews as if they were dogs rather than human beings; they have done little else than deride them and seize their property. When they baptize them they show them nothing of Christian doctrine or life, but only subject them to popishness and mockery... If the apostles, who also were Jews, had dealt with us Gentiles as we Gentiles deal with the Jews, there would never have been a Christian among the Gentiles... When we are inclined to boast of our position [as Christians] we should remember that we are but Gentiles, while the Jews are of the lineage of Christ. We are aliens and in-laws; they are blood relatives, cousins, and brothers of our Lord. Therefore, if one is to boast of flesh and blood the *Jews are actually nearer to Christ than we are...*

---

[43] Martin Luther, "Luther to George Spalatin," in *Luther's Correspondence and Other Contemporaneous Letters*, trans. Henry Preserved Smith (Philadelphia: Lutheran Publication Society, 1913), 1:29.

[44] Luther quoted in Elliott Rosenberg, *But Were They Good for the Jews?* (New York: Birch Lane Press, 1997), 65.

If we really want to help them, we must be guided in our dealings with them not by papal law but by the law of Christian love. We must receive them cordially, and permit them to trade and work with us, that they may have occasion and opportunity to associate with us, hear our Christian teaching, and witness our Christian life. If some of them should prove stiff-necked, what of it? After all, we ourselves are not all good Christians either."[45]

By 1543, however, with the publication of *On the Jews and their Lies,* Luther himself has become one of those "absurd" "dolts" and "blockhead" theologians, making highly immoral if not totally sinful, and scurrilous claims about the Jews. He says that they are a "*base, whoring people, that is, no people of God, and their boast of lineage, circumcision, and law must be accounted as filth,*"[46] in direct contradiction of what he said earlier.

"What shall we Christians do with this rejected and condemned people, the Jews?... we dare not tolerate their conduct, now that we are aware of their lying and reviling and blaspheming... I shall give you my sincere advice: First, to set fire to their synagogues or schools and to bury and cover with dirt whatever will not burn, so that no man will ever again see a stone or cinder of them... Second,... that their houses also be razed and destroyed... Instead they might be lodged under a roof or in a barn, like the gypsies... Third,... that all their prayer books and Talmudic writings, in which such idolatry, lies, cursing, and blasphemy are taught, be taken from them. Fourth,... that their rabbis be forbidden to teach henceforth on pain of loss of life and limb... Fifth,... that safe-conduct on the highways be abolished completely for the Jews... Sixth,... that usury be prohibited to them, and that all cash and treasure of silver and gold be taken from them and put aside for safekeeping... by it [usury] they have stolen and robbed from us all they possess. Seventh, I recommend putting a flail, an ax, a hoe, a spade, a distaff, or a spindle into the hands of young, strong Jews and Jewesses and letting them earn their bread in the sweat of their brow... we suffer as much as we do from *these base children of the devil, this brood of vipers... these venomous serpents and devil's children.*"[47]

---

[45] Martin Luther, "That Jesus Christ was Born a Jew," Trans. Walter I. Brandt, in *Luther's Works* (Philadelphia: Fortress Press, 1962), 200–201, 229, emphasis added.

[46] Martin Luther, "On the Jews and Their Lies," in *Luther's Works,* vol. 47: *The Christian in Society IV*, trans. by Martin H. Bertram (Philadelphia: Fortress Press: 1971), 268-293, emphasis added; see also Robert Michael, *Holy Hatred: Christianity, Antisemitism, and the Holocaust* (New York: Palgrave Macmillan, 2006), 111.

[47] Ibid., section 11, emphasis added.

Several months later still in 1543, Luther wrote Vom Schem Hamphoras und vom Geschlecht Christi (Of the Unknowable Name and the Generations of Christ):

> "Here in Wittenburg, in our parish church, there is a sow carved into the stone under which lie young pigs and Jews who are sucking; behind the sow stands a rabbi who is lifting up the right leg of the sow, raises behind the sow, bows down and looks with great effort into the Talmud under the sow, as if he wanted to read and see something most difficult and exceptional; no doubt they gained their Shem Hamphoras from that place."[48]

So Luther goes from giving the Jews a special significance, associating them with Christ, to a complete vilification, bile and calling them the Devil's progeny within a twenty year period. The reasons for this change of attitude are nowhere articulated in Luther and the suggested reasons by some scholars make little or no sense. He advised an almost bodily, material, and spiritual eradication of the Jews, in a litany eerily reminiscent of Hitler's Nazi regime – as they put into practice what Luther proscribed.

8. Luther's Seeming Contradictory Views of Islam and the Turks

So it is clear that Luther sits well within the tradition of negatively evaluating both Judaism and Islam. Nonetheless, he is one of the earliest of the major Western theologians to acknowledge the critical role of Islam, in spite of facing its threat and imminent conquest of Europe. This is present in many of his writings and not, as is so often portrayed, exclusively in his *On the War Against the Turks*. Luther advised that "in whatever way possible the religion and customs of 'Muhammadanism' be published and spread abroad."[49] It is particularly fascinating to recall that Luther towards the end of his life in 1543 was critically instrumental in the publication of a new translation of the

---

[48] *Schem Hamphoras* is the Hebrew rabbinic name for the ineffable name of God, the *tetragrammaton*. Luther's use of the term was in itself a taunt and insult to Jewish sensitivities. See Gerhard Falk, *The Jew in Christian Theology: Martin Luther's Anti-jewish Vom Schem Hamphoras, Previously Unpublished in English, and Other Milestones in Church Doctrine Concerning Judaism* (Jefferson, NC: McFarland & Company, Inc., 2013).

[49] op. cit. Henrich & Boyce, 255.

Qur'an into Latin by Theodore Bibliander.⁵⁰ This, for whatever reason is not given much publicity, perhaps because of the much more infamous publication of "On the Jews and their Lies," in the same year.

Bibliander had studied Arabic, and upon Luther's request he published a reworked version of the Latin Qur'an based on Robert Ketton's seminal, though not always accurate, translation (*Lex Mahumet pseudoprophete*, "The Law of Muhammad, the False Prophet") of 1143.⁵¹ In 1542, Luther used his influence on the Council of Basel which had banned and confiscated Bibliander's Qur'an. Persuaded by Luther's letter, the Council lifted the ban and released the text on the condition that both Luther and Melanchthon wrote prefaces to it. The Qur'an was finally published in 1543 along with these prefaces. Henrich and Boyce summarize that, "The main burden of Luther's preface ...was to argue once again for the clear presentation of the teachings of Muhammad so that by contrast they might be more readily refuted by the clear teachings of the church about Christ, the incarnation, his death for our sins, and the resurrection, and so that Christians might thereby be armed in conflict with the enemy by a sure and certain knowledge of the central tenets of their own faith."⁵²

Besides these warnings and critiques, Luther at the very end of his preface writes,

> "In this age of ours how many varied enemies have we already seen? Papist defenders of idolatry, the Jews, the multifarious monstrosities of the Anabaptists, Servetus, and others. Let us now prepare ourselves against Muhammad. But what can we say about matters that are still outside our knowledge? Therefore, it is of value for the learned to read the writings of the enemy in order to refute them more keenly, to cut them to pieces and to overturn them, in order that they might be able to bring some to safety, or

---

[50] Born in Bischofszell, Switzerland, *Theodor Buchmann* is known by his Greek name of *Theodore Bibliander*, a common practice (along with Latin) to raise the status of the person in middle Europe.

[51] It is worth mentioning, to quote Francisco, that, "There is certainly no reason to deny that Robert's translation is best described as a paraphrase and, likewise, that it served to fuel the majority of medieval anti-Muslim polemics," Francisco, 12.

[52] Henrich & Boyce, 256.

certainly to fortify our people with more sturdy arguments."[53]

So Luther's approach was to attempt to overcome the existing lacuna of knowledge vis-à-vis the religion of the Turks. According to Southern, this was because "he looked forward to the probability that Christendom would be engulfed in Islam."[54]

It is important to remember here that one of the most significant contributions of the Reformation was the de-priviligization of the *lingua sacra* or *religiosis* of Latin, and making the vernacular *lingua popularis* German operational both for the reading and hermeneutics of the sacred texts and religious rituals. This made religion more egalitarian, less sacerdotal, and more cognitive rather than superstitious and mysterious. Reformation Christianity, including the Anabaptists, at that juncture was the originary expression of this change, while other Christian expression continued in this distinction even in the West.[55] While epistemologically one may put down those religions (including many Christian communities) which maintain the distinction between the sacred value of the *lingua sacra/religiosis* and the comprehensive value of a vernacular language, many scholars continue to give Arabic Muslims a privileged position when dealing with Islam because of the sacred value of Arabic. Their numbers do not demand this privilege as at least 80% of Muslims are non-Arabic speaking.[56]

Luther did not have either of these problems and therefore when he looked at Islam he recognized the Arabic language as a *lingua sacra* and gave it a central place. He insisted on a new translation of the Qur'an into Latin and not German (still holding to the distinction between *lingua sacra* and *lingua popularis* in spite of his own theological emphasis on the latter as being valuable for both tasks – perhaps this was his way of maintaining the distinction

---

[53] Ibid., 266.

[54] R.W. Southern, *Western Views of Islam in the Middle Ages* (Cambridge, MA: Harvard University Press, 1962, 3rd printing 1982), 105-106.

[55] It took the Roman Catholics some 450 years to reach this position at the end of Vatican II (1963-65).

[56] One wonders whether this emphasis on Arabs and Arabic is not based on some self-interested understanding of the Islamic world and its geo-political and economic value – both for oil and for the state of Israel.

between the *lingua intelligentia/academia* and the *lingua popularis*). But it is important to remember that he was not looking at Arabic Islam; rather his understanding of Islam was based on equating it with the Turks, the contemporary imperial enemy. So he uses "Mohammedans" and "Turks" interchangeably when discussing Islam and Muslims.

Assessing the nature of the Muslim faith and culture and the threat that it posed to Christians, Luther argued, in his preface to *Libellus de ritu et moribus Turcorum* (1530), that it was critical for Christians to know the Islamic scripture and Muslim culture and to study it:

> "Since we now have the Turk and his religion at our very doorstep our people must be warned lest, either moved by the splendor of the Turkish religion and the external appearances of their customs or displeased by the meager display of our own faith or the deformity of our customs, they deny their Christ and follow Muhammad."[57]

Earlier in the text he argued,

> "... we see that the religion of the Turks or Muhammad is far more splendid in ceremonies – and, I might almost say, in customs – than ours, even including that of the religious or all the clerics. The modesty and simplicity of their food, clothing, dwellings, and everything else, as well as the fasts, prayers, and common gatherings of the people that this book reveals are nowhere seen among us ... which of our monks, be it a Carthusian (they who wish to appear the best) or a Benedictine, is not put to shame by the miraculous and wondrous abstinence and discipline among their religious? Our religious are mere shadows when compared to them, and our people clearly profane when compared to theirs. *Not even true Christians, not Christ himself, not the apostles or prophets ever exhibited so great a display.* This is the reason why many persons so easily depart from faith in Christ for Muhammadanism and adhere to it so tenaciously. I sincerely believe that no papist, monk, cleric, or their equal in faith would be able to remain in their faith if they should spend three days among the Turks. ... *Indeed, in all these things the Turks are by far superior.*"[58]

Very high praise indeed! Though clearly for a negative *telos*.

---

[57] op. cit. Henrich & Boyce, 260.
[58] op. cit. Henrich & Boyce, 259, emphasis added.

9. Contra-Catholic Crusade and Anabaptist Pacifism, Luther on Christian Vocation and the Two Kingdom Theory

In his earlier writings Luther did not explicitly endorse or condemn the various military measures taken against the Turks, but he did completely reject the idea of a new crusade. In 1518 when his opinion was solicited by George Spalatin vis-à-vis the papal plans for another crusade against the Turks, he responded

> "If I rightly understand you, you ask whether an expedition against the Turks can be defended by me on biblical grounds. Even supposing the war should be undertaken for pious reasons rather than for gain, I confess that I cannot promise what you ask, but rather the opposite... It seems to me if we must have any Turkish war, we ought to begin with ourselves. In vain we wage carnal wars without, while at home we are conquered by spiritual battles... Now that the Roman Curia is more tyrannical than any Turk, fighting with such portentous deeds against Christ and against his Church, and now that the clergy is sunk in the depth of avarice, ambition and luxury, and now that the face of the Church is everywhere most wretched, there is no hope of a successful war or of victory. As far as I can see, God fights against us; first, we must conquer him with tears, pure prayers, holy life and pure faith."[59]

Thus for Luther the real threat to Christianity was not so much from the Turks but rather from the "papacy's subjugation of the church to false doctrine."[60] We have already mentioned above Luther's response to Pope Leo X's call for a new crusade against the Ottoman Turks. And again, in *Von den guten Werken*, "Christendom is being destroyed not by the Turks, but by those who are supposed to defend it."[61] Luther's overall denouncement of the papacy, and particularly against the demand for a quite popular crusade/holy war in the face of an imminent Turkish invasion, had already angered the Roman Church. Luther's apparent lack of direct attack on the Turks further exacerbated the matter, so now with popular support the Roman Church sought his excommunication with a little more gusto. Luther in his personal

---

[59] *Luther's Correspondence*, 1:140-141, as quoted in Francisco, 68.
[60] Francisco, 68.
[61] *Von den guten Werken, Luther's Works*, Vol. 44:72, as quoted in Francisco, 69.

correspondence had been very negative vis-à-vis the Pope since as early as 1518, arguing that Rome was more tyrannical than the Turk.[62] Luther went further in 1518 and "publicly declared that the Pope was not only a 'tyrant' of Christianity but also the 'Antichrist'."[63] He made matters worse when, in 1520, he hyperbolized that the true "Turks" were the Pope's servants, his "lackeys and whores."[64] The Pope's response to this sustained attack was to threaten to excommunicate Luther in 1520. Among Luther's many alleged heretical and scandalous teachings denounced by the papacy in the bull, *Exsurge Domine* (1520), was a summary of an early statement he had made with regards to the Turks: "to fight against the Turks is to fight against God's visitation upon our iniquities."[65]

Luther's response to the Papal bull of excommunication was to maintain:

"This article does not mean that we are not to fight against the Turk, as that holy manufacturer of heresies, the pope charges. It means, rather, that we should mend our ways and cause God to be gracious to us. We should not plunge into war, relying on the pope's indulgence with which he has deceived Christians in the past and is deceiving them still... All the pope accomplishes with his crusading indulgences and his promises of heaven is to lead Christians with their lives into death and with their souls into hell. This is, of course, the proper work of the Antichrist. God does not demand crusades, indulgences, and wars. He wants us to live good lives. But the pope and his followers run from goodness faster than from anything else, yet he wants to devour the Turks... This is the reason why our war against the Turks is so successful – so that where he formerly held one mile of land he now holds a hundred. But we

---

[62] Cf. his letter to George Spalatin cited above, also see his letter to Wenzel Link (1483-1547), Johann Staupitz's successor as vicar general of the Augustinian order, in *D. Martin Luthers Werke: Briefwechsel*, 18 vols. (Weimar: Böhlau, 1930–1985) 1:270.13-14, as cited in Francisco, 69.

[63] Francisco, 69, quoting *Eyn Sermon von den newen Testament,* in *Luther's Works*, Vol. 35:107.

[64] *Luther's Works*, Vol. 35:90.

[65] 'Exsurge Domine', in Carl Mirbt (ed.), *Quellen zur Geschichte des Papsttums und das römische Katholizismus*, 2nd. edn. (Tübingen: J.C.B. Mohr, 1901), 184. Pope Leo X also sent a letter to Elector Frederick accompanying the bull, claiming that Luther 'favors Turks'. See Francisco, 70, footnote 11.

still do not see it so completely have we been taken by this Roman leader of the blind."[66]

This does not mean that Luther was a pacifist, something for which he strongly condemned the Anabaptists. Rather, he endorsed a military response against the Turks. See for example, the *Türkenbüchlein* – the so called Turkish writings, the most well known of which is *Vom Kriege wider die Türken (On War Against the Turks)* (1529). He writes the latter in order to counter those "stupid preachers amongst us Germans ... who are making us believe that we ought not and must not fight. Some are even so foolish to say that it is not proper for Christians to bear the temporal sword or to be rulers... some actually want the Turk to come and rule because they think our *German people are wild and uncivilized.*"[67] With the Ottoman Turks beginning to seriously encroach on Europe with Suleyman I's conquest of Belgrade in 1521, the Kingdom of Hungary in 1526, and the (repelled) Ottoman attack on Vienna in 1529, the threat of Ottoman occupation of Europe began to seem very realistic indeed. It was not so much a question of a crusade against the Turks (i.e., an offensive attack on Turkish territory outside of Europe), but rather now a very real possibility of having to defend western European territory against Ottoman occupation.

In *On War Against the Turks*, Luther argues that although in his earlier writings he had argued that Christians must fight their wars by spiritual means, i.e., through repentance and reform, and indeed this was still valid, he had maintained a non-fighting position vis-à-vis the Turks because the Pope had been pushing for this war as a Holy War to be undertaken in the name of Christ, something which Luther found extremely offensive. But he wanted to maintain that they must fight the Turks as part of their secular vocation. This was not to be a crusade, a holy war against the Turkish religion, but rather a secular war, led by secular not religious leaders, against an invader. If one were going to go to war against heresy, one would have to start with Roman Catholicism. "Let the Turk believe and live as he will, just as one lets the

---

[66] Luther's Works, vol. 32:89-91, as quoted in Francisco, 70. The Pope officially excommunicated Luther in 1521 via the bull *Decet Romanum Pontificem.*

[67] *Luther's Works*, 46:161–162, emphasis added.

papacy and other false Christians live."[68] Now, he urged everyone to take up arms against the Turks, not as a religious issue but yet as an issue of vocation, theologically expanding that concept beyond the exclusivity of the priestly calling. In *Eine Heerpredigt wider den Türken* (1530), he encourages Christians to embrace the vocation of soldiery, because "Such a person should know that they were merely defending themselves 'against the Turks in a war started by them,' which they were entitled and even obliged to do so... for in battling the Turks one was 'fighting against an enemy of God and a blasphemer of Christ, indeed, the Devil himself.'"[69]

Two of the central tenets of Luther's theology – the Two Kingdoms, and the concept of *vocatio dei* – were, I believe, deeply influenced by the context of the Turkish presence and the responses it generated from the Roman Catholic Church, invoking the crusade or, conversely, the pacifism of the Anabaptists. The latter, while agreeing with Luther that Islam was the Rod of God to purge Christianity from its sin and calumny, saw his resistance against the Turks as un-Christian, and against God's ordination and design. Unlike the pacifism of the Anabaptists, who were not worried about how they were perceived in society, Luther still needed the support of the people, especially his princely friends, and thus his correspondence with the Reverend Spalatin mentioned above. Therefore he develops a very novel and creative idea of seeing a broader notion of *vocatio dei,* rather than the already existing narrow understanding of restricting it exclusively to the sacramental and priestly duties. It is through this notion of soldiery as a vocation, and the vocation of a soldier, that he can counter both the crusading holy war Roman Catholic mindset, on the one hand, and the pacifist Anabaptist mindset, on the other. In this way Luther reconfigures the notion of a just war theory away from the Catholic notion of a religious war, and refutes the Anabaptist position of total pacifism with no place for warring of any kind. For Luther, therefore, at issue is not so much a definition of warring itself, but of two sets of governance – civil and religious –, as well as the notion of the Christian vocation being larger than residing exclusively in the priesthood. Warring is

---

[68] *Luther's Works*, 46:185–186.
[69] Francisco, 77, quoting *Eine Heerpredigt wider den Türken* in *Luther's Werken* 30/2:173.4–5, 9.

thus in the domain of the civil governance and to be initiated and conducted by this side of the two kingdoms and not to be undertaken as a holy war or crusade initiated by the Church where it had no place to be undertaking this vocation.

10. The Anachronism of Cuius Regio Eius Religio and the de facto Exclusion of the Other

It must be remembered that Luther's approach towards the Muslims, especially the Turks, was based on fear, dread and vulnerability and therefore had a profound apocalyptic dimension. His position vis-à-vis the Jews, on the other hand, is towards a highly vulnerable, weak, and constantly threatened minority. The Jews had lived with the Sword of Damocles hanging over their head throughout Europe, escalating especially after the Spanish massacre of 1391 and the beginning of the Jewish genocide and final expulsion from Spain a century later. The question in the western European context, which by the mid-nineteenth century was framed as the Jewish Question or *Judenfrage*, was whether Jews could be citizens: first, of the Holy Roman Empire, and then, post-Reformation, this was further expanded vis-à-vis the recently emerging independent autonomous princely states/fiefdoms, which Luther, for good or bad, had supported and been affiliated with. This was especially critical after the Peace of Augsburg between the Holy Roman Emperor, Charles V, and the forces of the Schmalkaldic League, the alliance of Lutheran princes, in September 1555. The agreement acknowledged the status of Lutheran Princes and the Augsburg Confession of 1530 and ratified a critical clause: "*cuius regio, eius religio*" (whose realm, his religion). This among other issues becomes one of the central clauses codified in the much more secular Treaty of Westphalia of 1648, which is seen as the founding of the modern nation state system.[70] The centrality of this concept even in the secular Treaty of Westphalia by default excluded the Jews and those Christians who had no such prince with a controlling realm, such as the Anabaptists. The Jews and the Anabaptists had to either convert or adopt the religion of

---

[70] Some form of "*cuius regio, eius religio,*" is *de jure* still present and applicable in many of the European nation-states which were not occupied by the Communists, even though *de facto* they may not see themselves as Christian states.

their local princes, giving up their respective faith positions or face persecution even unto death. A fate which both groups had to face on a number of occasions.[71]

11. The Essentialization of Islam, from Judenfrage to Muslimfrage and the Turkish Minorities in Germany

To search for the contemporaneous application and relevancy of Luther's discussions of the Turks and the Jews, especially in light of the horrific appropriation of Luther's anti-Jewish sentiments in Nazi Germany, a critical but brief examination of the situation of the Turks in contemporary Germany is vital. Much of what we see in Germany is equally applicable to the rest of Europe. With the overcoming of old nationalist identities generated after Westphalia in 1648 in mainland Europe, and the consolidation of a "united European identity," with similar transcendent nationalism as in the USA, the question of "the Other" acquires a critical importance. This applies especially to non-European immigrants (nationalised or otherwise), especially the Muslims, and in Germany, specifically the Turks. This has become even more crucial since September 11 and the growth of Islamophobic rhetoric. The contemporary presence of Islam, and its growing radicalization, has posed a whole series of questions, and challenges some of the fundamental assumptions behind liberal democracy and the rights regimes that have been in place in Europe. Issues such as freedom of speech versus hate speech; the character of religious freedom in a post-Christian secular context; the derogatory images of the Prophet Muhammad and the associated terroristic essentialization of Islam; the scare-mongering rhetoric of the imposition of Shariah law by Islam in secular Europe; the freedom of religion and expression embodied in the right to wear the veil versus the state imposition of a dress-code; the issue of Charlie Hebdo's freedom of press and speech, and the parameters of hate speech against foreigners; the rise of (neo-Nazi) organizations like

---

[71] A critical and highly scandalous example of this intolerance is the German Peasants' War of 1524-25 where a third of the peasants, approximately 100,000, were killed by the armies of the feudal princes, supported by Luther. The worst example of this is that just in the one-day battle of Frankenhausen, approximately 6,000 peasants were massacred. So in 1525 Luther pens, "*Wider die räuberischen und mörderischen Rotten der Bauern*" (*Against the Murderous, Thieving Hordes of Peasants*).

PEGIDA[72] and its xenophobic politics; nationalist political parties and their extreme xenophobia like Geert Wilders' *Partij voor de Vrijheid*, and Marine Le Pen's *Front National*; etc., all demand a serious reevaluation of democracy, the accepted human rights regimes, and the recognition of the reconstructive role of immigrants in European history after the second World War, and the role of compensatory justice.

Given the horrific history of the Holocaust, with some level of cooperation by most of Europe, or at least acquiescence through silence, (though there were clearly exceptional cases), it is rightly no longer acceptable to make anti-Jewish and "anti-Semitic" statements or to deny the Holocaust;[73] these are justly perceived as hate crimes. The same status however is not given to the Muslim minorities which now actually reside in Europe. Thus the anti-semitic language, imagery, political and military rhetoric once applied towards the Jews can now be used with impunity or little restriction against the Muslims and Islam, clearly with appropriate adjustments.

Our examination of the contemporary German context after the Second World War must begin with the critical reconstruction of a war-ravaged Germany destroyed by six years of devastation. The Germans at the time had no major colonies,[74] and a large number of their own young men had been killed

---

[72] *Patriotische Europäer gegen die Islamisierung des Abendlandes*, or Patriotic Europeans Against the Islamization of the West.

[73] Though when this valid restriction against the vilification of a people or individuals is expanded to cover the state, moral or otherwise, it entails taking away the right of ethical discourse itself, which is a *sine qua non* for modern democracy and transparent and accountable governance. So if any critique of the state, even for its most immoral acts, is seen as a pejorative judgment against a particular people, there is a serious confusion of categories. If this is not challenged then the issue of restorative justice which is supposed to be behind this position is itself seriously damaged, if not totally nullified, and the idea of critical virtuous thought and citizenship itself is put into serious question.The lack of these rights were central in generating the crimes against a people in the first place. So when a critique of this state is seen as anti-semitic and all critical conversation is shut down then we have a major confusion between the people (*demos*) and the state (*basileia*).This curtails the core value of the ability of moral discourse against the state and its coercive overreach.

[74] The division of Africa among the European states had taken place during the Berlin Conference of 1884-85, with representatives of: Austria-Hungary, Belgium, Denmark, France, Germany, Great Britain, Italy, the Netherlands, Portugal, Russia, Spain, Swe-

or seriously injured in the two World Wars (from 1914-1945). Germany therefore had to recruit foreign labor for their reconstruction and re-industrialization after the second world war.[75] The demands of the American Marshall Plan had already met some challenges with the loss of half of Germany to the Soviet Union (and later the building of the Berlin Wall in 1961), which seriously restricted the flow of labor for industrialization purposes and the ever expanding demands generated by the *Wirtschaftswunder* (economic miracle) of the 1950s. All this expanded the demand for labor with few indigenous resources to draw upon, so Germany entered into several bilateral labor agreements with different countries.[76] The largest portion of these laborers were from Muslim societies, most significantly from Turkey.[77] In 2009 it was estimated by Germany's Federal Office for Migration and Refugees that there were 4.3 million Muslims in Germany, i.e., 5.2% of the over-

---

den-Norway, *Turkey,* and *USA*, (emphasis added) and by 1914, Africa had been fully divided into fifty new states. After 1885 Germany was the third largest colonial presence in Africa, controlling Tanganyika (now part of Tanzania), Ruanda-Urundi (now Rwanda and Burundi), Wituland (part of Kenya) and Kionga Triangle (part of Mozambique) together they were called German East Africa; Namibia and part of present Botswana, were the German South-West Africa; and Togoland and Kamerun (which included besides Cameroon, the northern part of Gabon and Congo, western part of Central African Republic, southwestern Chad and the far eastern part of Nigeria). However, within thirty years, these colonies were occupied by its enemies during World War I and were completely confiscated in the Treaty of Versailles in 1919.

[75] Euphemistically referred to as *Gastarbeiter* (guest workers) as compared to the contextually more negative *Fremdarbeiter* (foreign or alien workers), which had referred to the forced labor conscripted from German-occupied Europe to work in agriculture and industry during the Second World War.

[76] The bilateral agreements which Germany entered for importing labor were with Italy (1955), Spain (1960), Greece (1960) (all three had been fascist societies; respectively under Mussolini, Franco, and Ioannis Metaxa), Turkey (1961), Morocco (1963), Portugal (1964), Tunisia (1965) and finally Yugoslavia (1968), while still under Tito's communist rule.

[77] See the highly critical study by Sonja Haug, Stephanie Müssig & Anja Stichs, *Muslimisches Leben in Deutschland im Auftrag der Deutschen Islam Konferenz*, (Berlin: Bundesamt für Migration und Flüchtlinger, 2009) [Muslim Life in Germany, published on behalf of the German Islam Conference by the Federal Office for Migration and Refugees], available at: http://www.bmi.bund.de/cae/servlet/contentblob/566008/publicationFile/31710/vollversion_studie_muslim_leben_deutschland_.pdf.

all population. Around 63% of these were of Turkish descent (i.e., 2.7 million, constituting 3.0% the total population). About 65% of these Muslims were fully German citizens. This gives some sense of the contemporary numerical context of religious minorities in Germany which becomes especially critical when compared to the Jewish population in the pre-WWII Germany: "In prewar central Europe, the largest Jewish community was in Germany, with about 500,000 members (0.75% of the total German population)."[78] If this small number of Jews was found unacceptable from 1933 onwards, and therefore there was widespread acceptance of the concentration camps and even genocide,[79] one wonders where the current much larger Turkish and Muslim presence could lead to if some trigger is set into motion. We have been facing the *Muslimfrage*, in various forms, now the worry is that it could be converted to a more violent structured removal of the contemporary Others like that exercised vis-à-vis the Jews during the Second World War.

In the contemporary context, the Turks in Germany are, on the one hand, a vulnerable, weak, and dependent ethnic and religious minority, like the Jews of Luther's time. They can be and are at times treated with capricious disregard and high moral and social coercion. Because of the causal link of being initially a "lower/laboring class" vulnerable ethnic minority, what Luther wrote about the *Ottoman* Turks does not apply directly to the contemporary *German* Turks. However, what he wrote about the Jews could be quite easily applied to them.

On the other hand, they are Muslims and thus are the new binary enemy after the Cold War and the collapse of the Soviet Union. They are therefore essentialized and stereotyped as part of the "War against Terror." The status of the Turks in Germany has undergone a major shift since September 11, 2001 (as was the case for all Muslim immigrants across Europe). From being a vulnerable blue-collar labor force, and therefore somewhat tolerated for

---

[78] See, "Jewish Population of Europe in 1933: Population Data by Country" in the United States Holocaust Memorial Museum's *Holocaust Encyclopedia*, at http://www.ushmm.org/wlc/en/article.php?ModuleId=10005161.

[79] For the comprehensive involvement of the German populace in this morally dark period in German history, see, Daniel J. Goldhagen, *Hitler's Willing Executioners: Ordinary Germans and the Holocaust* (New York: Alfred A. Knopf, 1996).

economic and social convenience, the Muslims have now come to represent the new *Inbegriff der Feindschaft* (enemy-ness) with almost apocalyptic implications for what Western social values stand for, and therefore are a threat and challenge to this "normative virtuous life." Here therefore, Luther's texts on the Ottoman Turks can be applied rather directly. This entailed a major shift, and with it new sets of prejudices: Islam and Muslims are no longer seen as a weak and vulnerable minority living in Europe in culturally and socially specific ghettos, but rather a highly hyperbolized threatening and very powerful enemy, both inside and outside, which could take over Europe at very short notice and impose its law (*Shariah*) on the local citizens and the European values and achievements. So vis-à-vis the current European Islamic presence, both of Luther's approaches towards the Jews and the Turks have application and possibilities.

12. The Use of Hermeneutical Subtilitas (Intelligendi, Explicandi, and Applicandi): Towards the Role of the Other in Human History

Hans-Georg Gadamer defines application as the integral part of the hermeneutical task, and he argues that this application entails the understanding of the text in the contemporary situation of the interpreter itself.[80] This is what completes the hermeneutical circle for him because it recognizes the location of the interpreter with all her/his existing pre-judgments (*prejudicium*, prejudices) as the *arche* and *telos* of the hermeneutical task. In this paper, I have tried to achieve such a hermeneutical task on Luther's texts vis-à-vis the Muslims (Turks) and the Jews, the historical events in which his writings emerged, and the overall the context of his work, in order to radicalize the Reformation in light of pre-judgments present against the "Other." Behind this hermeneutical task was a special concern for the development of Reformation theology with the focus on the religious Other(ness) of the Muslims (Turks) and the Jews during that period. It demanded a radical hermeneutic

---

[80] See his *Truth and Method* (New York: Seabury Press, 1975), 274, see also Haoming Liu, "Subtilitas Applicandi as Self-Knowledge: A Critique of the Concept of Application in Hans-Georg Gadamer's Truth and Method," in *The Journal of Speculative Philosophy, New Series*, Vol. 10, No. 2 (1996), 128-147.

of Luther's texts, both their larger and narrower contexts, and an assessment of the tradition of their interpretation within the European *prejudicium*.

If we take the triadic unity, or the three moments of the hermeneutical task (viz., *subtilitas intelligendi*, *subtilitas explicandi* and *subtilitas applicandi*), as being theologically and historically valid and essential, I hope I have achieved these three moments in this paper through a critical demythologizing of the taken-for-granted interpretation of certain ossified dogmas and positions. I have also tried to place different interpretations of the historical context in which Luther's texts emerged. *Subtilitas intelligendi* requires a sound understanding, a discernment whether we really understand a passage or the events surrounding it, and to pay attention to the difficulties that lie in the way of understanding it. The search for a proper approach and way of investigating the historical events or epochs lead to a radicalizing moment of understanding Luther's texts and biography. *Subtilitas explicandi* required a look at those historical events or epochs as having perspicuous argument and illustration, which I have tried to demonstrate and thus achieve some level of clarity. It also requires a demythologizing of the taken-for-granted fixed interpretation so that we may move beyond the ossified traditions and dogmas which have cast a veil on this self-explanatory perspicuity. At the same time I have placed the original events and texts themselves under the hermeneutical scrutiny of reason and struggle in order to overcome the obscureness which some of these events and epochs have generated. This then has its own radicalizing moment on the Reformation.

The *subtilitas intelligendi* and *subtilitas explicandi* though critical for the hermeneutical task are, however, incomplete without the *subtilitas applicandi*. The last not only demands the validity of the first two subtilitas in light of the ethical and moral application of ideas, but also as to what are the ethical and moral values of Luther's texts vis-à-vis the Other, and the surrounding events, for us today. In the context of this paper, it demanded an application of a critical hermeneutic to explain the spoken and unspoken contents and contours, so that we attempt and project their application vis-à-vis the contemporary "Other(s)." This was especially critical because of the horrendous effective history of the previous hermeneutic and (im)moral practice of the dominant "Christian" majority on a religious and cultural Jewish minority. The acknowledged, and even perhaps unconscious application of Luther's text, and moral standing and voice, to achieve these immoral acts left behind a history of their interpretation and debilitating "effective (or effectual) history" (*Wirkungsgeschichte*). This is to say that to understand the "effective/effectual history" of these texts, is also a study of their *subtilitas applicandi*. More than this it also defines the self-knowledge/prejudices which also lie behind this *subtilitas applicandi* and which makes it so poignant for the hermeneutical task and its radicalizing vocation.

The application of these texts, epochs, or events, have to be of value and must therefore be understood as being applicable to the present situation as well. For according to Gadamer "... if the heart of the hermeneutical problem is that the same tradition must always be understood in a different way, the problem, logically speaking, is that of the relationship between the universal and the particular."[81] This has a direct bearing on the task behind this project, namely, a way of radicalizing the Reformation. We must go beyond both the sanctification of the Reformation texts and events for generating doctrinal and dogmatic material and certitude, and also the self-justificational attitude we develop towards these Reformation texts. Rather the task should be to provide radical and critical clues for our own self-understanding in our situation and in our time for a more virtuous approach to the contemporary "Other;" so that justice and peace prevails and that with Aimè Cèsaire we can say:

> for it is not true that the work of man is done
>
> that we have no business being on earth
>
> that we parasite the world
>
> that it is enough for us to heel to the world whereas the work of man (sic) has only began
>
> and man (sic) still must overcome all the interdictions wedged in the recesses of his fervor
>
> and no race has a monopoly on beauty, on intelligence, on strength
>
> and there is room for everyone at the convocation of conquest.[82]

---

[81] *Truth and Method*, 278.

[82] Aimé Césaire, *Notebook of a Return to the Native Land*, trans. Clayton Eshleman and Annette Smith (Middletown, CT: Wesleyan University Press, 2001), 44. This long poem was originally published in Paris in 1939 and again in 1947 as *Cahier d'un retour au pays natal*.

Abstract

Zwar wurde angesichts des Holocaust in Luthers Schriften die „Judenfrage" gründlich untersucht, aber seine Haltung gegenüber Islam und Muslimen (im Allgemeinen verhandelt unter dem Stichwort „Türken") blieb fast völlig ignoriert. Das änderte sich nach dem 11. September 2001, der zu einem tiefen Antagonismus gegen die muslimischen Gemeinschaften führte, die jetzt bedeutende Minderheiten im europäischen Kontext darstellen. Einige Schriften Luthers wurden dazu benutzt, eine feindliche Rhetorik gegen den Islam und Muslime und gerade auch gegen die Türken hervorzurufen. Diese Rhetorik half auch, den Mythos der „Festung Europa" und die Betonung der Unvereinbarkeit zwischen „West und Ost" neu zu konfigurieren. So wurde die Religion eine wesentliche Trennlinie für die europäische Exklusivität (z. B. zwischen der EU und der Türkei) – und dies in einer in anderer Hinsicht stolz säkularen Kultur.

Diese europäische Exklusivität versäumte, verschiedene Tatsachen zur Kenntnis zu nehmen:

- der Islam war in Europa seit dem frühen 8. Jahrhundert in Spanien über fast 800 Jahre präsent

- die Kreuzzüge dominierten die allgemeine Politik vom Ende des 11. bis zum Ende des 13. Jahrhunderts, während der Reformationszeit selbst und in Osteuropa seit dem 15. Jahrhundert für ungefähr 600 Jahre.

Angesichts der gewollten Vernachlässigung oder bewussten Unkenntnis des Islams in der lutherischen akademischen Arbeit, ist es unbedingt nötig zur Kenntnis zu nehmen, dass Luther die Türken, ihre Religion und den Propheten Muhammad in vielen Bänden seiner gesammelten Werke erwähnt (oder mindestens Hinweise darauf). An manchen Stellen, selbst in seinen giftigsten, macht er dem Islam höchste Komplimente. Der Islam war für Luther keine kleine Frage. Wir haben hier also eine klare Lücke, derer sich lutherische Forschung ernsthaft annehmen muss. Angesichts des 500jährigen Reformationsjubiläums und in Verbindung mit der uns gestellten hermeneutischen Aufgabe ist das Studium des Islam und der Muslime, d.h. die Muslimfrage und Türkenfrage (in Bezug auf die „Judenfrage") von zentraler Bedeutung. Das gilt besonders im Blick darauf, dass diese Fragen große Teile des gegenwärtigen Diskurses bestimmen, und zwar nicht nur im Blick auf die Religion, sondern auf die Fragen des Friedens, der Theorien des gerechten Krieges, der Gerechtigkeit, der Menschenrechte und der politischen und ökonomischen Handlungsweisen.

DAS EVANGELIUM ALLER KREATUR.
THOMAS MÜNTZERS UND HANS HUTS BOTSCHAFT FÜR DIE HEUTIGE WELT
Jaime Adrián Prieto Valladares[1]

Einleitung

Im Jahr 2017 wird Europa das große Reformationsjubiläum feiern – 500 Jahre nachdem Martin Luther seine Thesen gegen den Ablass bekannt gegeben hatte.[2] Dieser Artikel zielt darauf ab, die Theologie und pastoralen Praktiken zweier großer deutscher Reformatoren, Thomas Müntzers und Hans Huts, bekannt zu machen. Müntzer und Hut hatten die reformatorische Botschaft von Andreas Rudolf Bodenstein (Carlstadt)[3] und Martin Luther gehört[4], die in Wittenberg entstanden war[5]. Von diesem Einfluss geprägt, ent-

---

[1] Ich danke Pfarrer Bernd Appel, Ev. Kirche in Hessen und Nassau, für die Korrekturen und Übersetzungen der deutschen Texte meines Beitrags.

[2] Evangelische Kirche in Deutschland: Perspektiven 2017. Schriften über die Reformation, Reformationsjubiläum 2017. Hannover, ohne Datum; Rat der Evangelischen Kirche in Deutschland: Rechtfertigung und Freiheit – 500 Jahre Reformation 2017. Gütersloher Verlagshaus, Gütersloh 2014.

[3] Andreas Rudolf Bodenstein, Theologe und Reformator (ca. 1480-1541) wurde in Karlstadt, Franken (Deutschland) geboren. Seit 1507 war er Professor der Theologie an der Universität Wittenberg. Während der Abwesenheit von Luther auf der Wartburg führte er in Wittenberg die Reform nicht nur auf biblischen Prinzipien, sondern durch eine starke spirituelle Führung weiter. Nach der Rückkehr von Luther und im Kontext des Bildersturms in dieser Stadt im Jahre 1522 wurde seine Predigt verboten und seine Bücher zensiert. Er fuhr 1523 fort, als Pfarrer der Reformation im sächsischen Orlamünde zu arbeiten. Aus Anlass seiner Annäherung an Ulrich Zwingli in dessen Auseinandersetzung mit Luther um das Abendmahl im Jahre 1524 und nach dem Bauernkrieg im Jahr 1525, musste er in die Schweiz fliehen, wo er als Professor und Pfarrer in Basel diente. Vgl. Calvin Augustine Pater: Karlstadt as the Father of the Baptist Movements. The Emergence of Lay Protestantism, Toronto-Buffalo-London: University of Toronto Press, 1984.

[4] Vgl. Roland H. Bainton: Luther, (Übersetzung von Raquel Ayala Lozada Torales), 2. Ausgabe, Buenos Aires. Editorial Sudamericana, 1978.

wickelten sie ihre eigene Theologie und pastorale wie liturgische Praxis zu Gunsten der am stärksten Benachteiligten, sie predigten das Evangelium und engagierten sich stark für soziale Veränderungen in Sachsen, Thüringen, Süd-Deutschland und dem Österreich des sechzehnten Jahrhunderts. In der Vergangenheit hatte die deutsche Geschichtsschreibung diese Reformer jahrelang vernachlässigt[6], aber heute erkennen wir, dass die Radikalität der Botschaft, das mystische Verständnis des Evangeliums und die Nachfolge Jesu uns bei den Herausforderungen unserer heutigen Gesellschaft behilflich sein können.

Zwar waren die historischen Quellen des sechzehnten Jahrhunderts von Christian Meyer[7], Karl Schornbaum[8], Grete Mecenseffy[9] und Lydia Müller[10] und der Zusammenhang zwischen der Botschaft und der sozio-kirchlichen Praxis von Müntzer und dem Täuferprediger Hut bereits bearbeitet worden;

---

[5] Zur Anwesenheit von Müntzer in Wittenberg von 1517 vgl. Günter Vogler: Thomas Müntzer. Berlin, Dietz Verlag, 1989, S. 43. Zur Anwesenheit von Hans Hut in Wittenberg in den frühen Jahren der Reformation und seine Teilnahme an theologischen Debatten und den Verkauf von Büchern vgl.: Hans Hut, Antwort auf die ihm vorgelegten Fragstücke 1527 (AR-A.38, 97, S. 104 Kopie. Auch im Mährischen Landesarchiv Brünn, Sammlung Beck Nr. 79, S. 4 ff.) in: (Hg.) Verein für Reformationsgeschichte: Quellen zur Geschichte der Wiedertäufer. II. Band, Markgraftum Brandenburg (Bayern I. Abteilung); Karl D. Schornbaum (Direktor des landeskirchlichen Archivs in Nürnberg), Leipzig: M. Heinsius Nachfolger, 1934, S. 41-44. Johan Loserth und Robert Friedmann: „Hut, Hans", in: D. Christian Hege und Christian Neff (Hg.) Mennonitisches Lexikon, Zweiter Band, Frankfurt am Main und Weierhof (Pfalz). Verlag der Herausgeber, 1937, S. 370-375.

[6] Der deutsche Philosoph Ernst Bloch macht ab 1921 Müntzer als „Theologe der Revolution" bekannt. Vgl. Ernst Bloch: Thomas Münzer als Theologe der Revolution. Frankfurt am Main, Suhrkamp Verlag, 1969.

[7] Christian Meyer: Zur Geschichte der Wiedertäufer in Oberschwaben 1: Die Anfänge des Widertäufertums in Augsburg, in: Zeitschrift des Historischen Vereins für Schwaben und Neuburg 1, 1874, S. 207-256.

[8] Dr. Karl Schornbaum, op. cit.

[9] Grete Mecenseffy: Die Herkunft des Oberösterreichischen Wiedertäufertums. Archiv für Reformationsgeschichte, XLVII, Heft 2, 1956, S. 252-258. Grete Mecenseffy: Quellen zur Geschichte der Täufer. Band XIII, Österreich, Teil II. Heidelberg. Verein für Reformationsgeschichte, Gütersloh, Gütersloher Verlagshaus, 1972.

[10] Lydia Müller (Hrsg.): Glaubenszeugnisse oberdeutscher Taufgesinnter. Quellen und Forschungen zur Reformationsgeschichte, Bd. XX, Leipzig 1938.

Das Evangelium aller Kreatur.

Historiker wie Gerhard Zschäbitz[11], Herbert Klassen[12], Gordon Rupp[13], George Huntston Williams[14], Rollin Stely Armour[15], Gottfried Seebass[16] und Hans Jürgen Goertz[17] vertieften jedoch die Einsichten über das Leben, die Schriften und Theologie der beiden Führer der Radikalen Reformation.

In der pastoralen und praktischen Theologie Huts und Müntzers ist der Missionsbefehl aus Markus 16,15 zentral. Dieser Vers wird das Zentrum des theologischen Denkens von beiden. Der Ausgangspunkt ist die Erkenntnis der Ordnung, die Gott in der Schöpfung festgelegt hatte, aus der die Ehrfurcht vor Gott folgt, also der Wunsch, seine Weisungen zu befolgen, wie es auch Elisabeth, Maria, Rahab, Ruth und Judith getan hatten. Der Missionsauftrag zeigt auf "gehet hin in die Welt", und bedeutet, das Evangelium aller Kreatur, allen Völkern, Kulturen und Religionen zu verkünden. Das Evangelium ist einfach und wird mit der Stimme verkündet, die aus dem täglichen Leben kommt – aus dem Bergbau, aus den ländlichen und bäuerlichen Bereichen, vom „gemeinen Mann" – und steht damit im Gegensatz zu dem Verständnis des Evangeliums, das vom katholischen Zentralismus Roms entwickelt wurde, aber auch in Spannung zu den Schriftgelehrten aus Wittenberg, die sich im Dienst der Fürsten von Sachsen befanden. Die Verkündigung des

---

[11] Gerhard Zschäbitz: Zur Mitteldeutschen Wiedertäuferbewegung nach dem großen Bauernkrieg. Berlin, Rütten & Loening, 1958.

[12] Herbert Klassen: Das Leben und die Lehre des Hans Hut, Teil II: Thomas Müntzer und Hans Hut, in: The Mennonite Quarterly Review, Volume XXXIII, Number Three. Goshen, Indiana, Juli 1959, S. 267-304.

[13] Gordon Rupp: Thomas Müntzer, Hans Hut und Das Evangelium aller Kreatur, in: Abraham Friesen und Hans-Jürgen Goertz: Thomas Müntzer. Darmstadt, Wissenschaftliche Buchgesellschaft, 1978, S. 178-210.

[14] George Huntston Williams: The Radical Reformation. Philadelphia, Westminster Press, MCMLXII.

[15] Rollin Stely Armour: Anabaptist Baptism. A representative study. Scottdale, Pennsylvania, Herald Press, 1966.

[16] Gottfried Seebass: Müntzers Erbe. Werk, Leben und Theologie des Hans Hut (1527), Habilitationsschrift an der Theologischen Fakultät der Friedrich Alexander Universität zu Erlangen – Nürnberg, 1972.

[17] Hans Jürgen Goertz: Innere und äußere Ordnung in der Theologie Thomas Müntzers. Leiden 1967. Hans Jürgen Goertz: Pfaffenhass und groß Geschrei. Die reformatorischen Bewegungen in Deutschland 1517-1529. München, Verlag CH Beck, 1987.

Evangeliums konkretisiert sich in der Erfahrung der Taufe mit Feuer, Wasser und Blut. Der Missionsbefehl in Markus 16,15 wird in der Nachfolge Jesu erfüllt, indem Christus in seinen Anhängern durch Leiden und Schmerzen Gestalt annimmt. Die Freundschaft Christi mit seinen Anhängern und Anhängerinnen äußert sich im Trost durch den Heiligen Geist, und sie zeigt sich unter den Anhängern Jesu durch die Verkündigung seines Evangeliums anhand konkreter Taten der Solidarität und Treue inmitten von Verfolgung und Tod.

1. "Geet hin in die Welt und predigent das Evangelion aller Creaturen" (Markus 16,15): Ordo Dei

Müntzer ist in der Radikalen Reformation eine wichtige Figur, die einen großen Einfluss auf seinen Schüler Hut ausübte, der wiederum als führender missionarischer Wiedertäufer und Evangelist Süddeutschlands und Österreichs betrachtet wird.[18] Die meisten Historiker vermuten, dass Müntzer zwischen 1488 und 1489 in der Stadt Stolberg (Sachsen) geboren wurde.[19] Auch im Fall Huts haben wir keinen genauen Zeitpunkt seiner Geburt. Man erwog die Aussage von Thomas Spiegels im Februar 1527, dass Hut "uber die dreissig biss in die vierzig Jare seins alters" sei[20], um zu bestätigen, dass Hut 1490 in der Grafschaft Heneberg an einem Ort, der bekannt ist als Haina im Grabfeldgau, geboren wurde. Müntzer studierte zwischen 1506 und 1512 Theologie an der Universität Leipzig und der Universität Frankfurt/Oder.[21] Hut widmete sich ländlicher Arbeit und Tischlerarbeiten, hatte jedoch eine große autodidaktische Begabung und brachte sich selbst bei, Latein zu lesen und zu

---

[18] Herbert Klassen: The life and teaching of Hans Hut, Part I: Hut's Life, in: The Mennonite Quarterly Review, Volume XXXIII, Number Three, Goshen, Ind., July 1959, S. 171-304

[19] Walter Elliger: Thomas Müntzer, Leben und Werk. Dritte Auflage, Göttingen, Vandenhoeck & Ruprecht, 1976, S. 17.

[20] Thomas Spiegels: Urgichten von Ostheim (19 Febr. bis 3. März 1527), in: Paul Wappler, Die Täuferbewegung in Thüringen von 1526-1584. Jena, Verlag von Gustav Fischer, 1913, S. 232, Nr. 1: 19, c. S. 232.

[21] Klaus Ebert: Thomas Müntzer. Von Eigensinn und Widerspruch. Frankfurt am Main, Athenäum, 1987, S. 68-72.

schreiben. Um circa 1515 heiratete er und hatte sechs Kinder mit seiner Frau, deren Name bis heute unbekannt ist.[22]

Am 31. Oktober 1517 beginnt die Protestantische Reformation, als Martin Luther seine 95 Thesen gegen den Ablass an Erzbischof Albrecht in Mainz schickt und sie an die Schlosskirche in Wittenberg hängt. Müntzer identifizierte sich von Anfang an mit der lutherischen Reformation. Ende 1518 begibt Müntzer sich nach Wittenberg, dem Zentrum der Protestantischen Reformation, wo er Martin Luther[23], Philipp Melanchthon, Konrad Glitzsch, Andreas Bodenstein (Karlstadt), Franz Günther, Nikolaus Hausmann und möglicherweise Johannes Agricola kennenlernte.[24] Eine sorgfältige Überprüfung seiner Vorgehensweise macht deutlich, dass er seit Beginn der Reformation der Theologie, Politik und Pastoral Karlstadts, dem Dekan der Universität Wittenberg, näherstand als dem Hauptreformator Luther.[25] Nach seiner Teilnahme am theologischen Disput Luthers und Karlstadts mit Johannes Eck über das Thema der Prädestination, der vom 27. Juni bis 16. Juli 1519 in Leipzig stattfand, sind sich verschiedene Historiker darüber einig, dass Müntzer sich möglicherweise in Orlamünde niederließ, wo Karstadt als Pfarrer diente.[26] Zentral in dieser Zeit ist sein Interesse an der mystischen Literatur, bekannt auch als „Theologia Deutsch", die sich in einen grundlegenden Anstoß verwandelte, welcher der Protestantischen Reformation vorausging; denn es war genau Luther, der im Jahre 1516, ein Jahr bevor er die Thesen

---

[22] Thomas Spiegels: Urgichten von Ostheim (19. Febr. bis 3. März 1527), in: Paul Wappler, op. cit.

[23] In seiner „Hochverursachte Schutzrede" von 1524 äußert Münzer, dass er seit sechs oder sieben Jahren Luther noch nicht wieder getroffen habe; was bedeutet, dass er im Jahre 1518 Martin Luther bereits kannte. Günther Franz (Hg.) unter Mitarbeit von Paul Kirn: Thomas Müntzer, Schriften und Briefe. Kritische Gesamtausgabe, Quellen und Forschungen zur Reformationsgeschichte XXXIII, Gütersloh, Gütersloher Verlagshaus, 1968, S. 341, 10 f. (Abkürzung: MSB).

[24] Günter Vogler: Thomas Müntzer, op. cit., S. 43.

[25] Von Leif Grane: Martin Luther und Thomas Müntzer, in: Abraham Friesen und Hans-Jürgen Goertz (Hg.): Thomas Müntzer. Darmstadt, Wissenschaftliche Buchgesellschaft, 1978, S. 54-73.

[26] Walter Elliger: Thomas Müntzer, op. cit., S. 66-73.

gegen den Ablass anschlug, die mystische Literatur veröffentlicht hatte.[27] Es war ein Thema, das Müntzer weiter vertiefte – mit den mystischen Schriften der Hildegard von Bingen, Elisabeth von Schönau, Mechthild von Hackeborn[28]; weiterhin den Schriften der Dominikaner Meister Eckhart, Johannes Tauler und Heinrich Seuse[29] – die er im Nonnenkloster Beuditz bei Weißenfels las, wo er von Herbst 1519 bis Anfang 1520 als Beichtvater arbeitete, was sich aus der entstandenen Korrespondenz mit einer als Ursula bekannten Nonne entnehmen lässt.[30]

Die "Theologia Naturalis" Müntzers stützte sich auf das Konzept des „ordo" (Ordnung), das seine Quellen in den Schöpfungserzählungen im Buch Genesis hat und sich durch die ganze Schrift zieht und damit bestätigt wird. Müntzer definierte Ordnung wie folgt: "Dye ordenunge zu betrachten un zcu machen, ist erstlich dye vier element unde der hymmel, dornach das gewechß, dornach das vihe, dornach der mensche, dornach Christus, dornach Got vater almechtigk, ungeschaffener, do vorstehet man alle ding yhnnen".[31] Luther hatte in seinem Kommentar zur Genesis geäußert, das erste Kapitel der Genesis sei „die Summe der ganzen Schrift" und Melanchthon betonte in seiner Lehre von der Naturfrömmigkeit eine Ordnung der Geschöpfe.[32] Für Müntzer wird das Konzept der „ordo" in den Erzählungen der Genesis, dem ersten Buch der Bibel, festgehalten. 1. Mose 1,1 erklärt: „Am Anfang schuf Gott Himmel und Erde" und erzählt dann, wie der Schöpfer weitermachte,

---

[27] Gerhard Wehr (Hg.): Theologia Deutsch. Eine Grundschrift deutscher Mystik. Diengfelder, Argo-Ausgabe Weisheit im Abendland, 1989, S. 20.

[28] Max Steinmetz: Thomas Müntzer. Weg nach Allstedt. Eine Studie zu seiner Frühentwicklung. Berlin, VEB Deutscher Verlag des Wissenschaften, 1988, S. 71.

[29] Über die gesammelt Aufnahme von Traditionen der Frauenmystik bei diesen Mystikern siehe: Herbert Grundmann: Die Frauen und die Literatur im Mittelalter. Ein Beitrag zur Frage nach der Entstehung des Schriftums in der Volkssprache, in: Herbert Grundman: Ausgewählte Aufsätze, Teil 3. Bildung und Sprache. Stuttgart, Anton Hiersemann, 1978, S. 67-95.

[30] Klaus Ebert: Thomas Müntzer. Von Eigensinn und Widerspruch, Frankfurt am Main, Athenäum, 1987, S. 72-81.

[31] Thomas Müntzer: Zwei Predigtentwürfe, in: Franz, MSB, a.a.O., S. 519, 17-20.

[32] Dieter Fauth: Thomas Müntzer in bildungsgeschichtlicher Sicht. Frankfurt am Main, Deutsches Institut für Internationale Pädagogische Forschung, Böhlau, 1993, S. 89-101.

Das Evangelium aller Kreatur.

alle Dinge und Wesen im Himmel und auf der Erde zu erschaffen. In den Schriften Müntzers erscheint das Konzept „ordo" als absolut oder auch in Beziehung mit einem untergeordneten genitivischen Attributivum ordo rerum, ordo creaturarum oder ordo dei.[33] Man spricht dann „von Gott und seyner Ordnung", also Gott, dem Schöpfer, der seine Herrschaft über die Menschen ausübt, und diese wiederum über die anderen Geschöpfe. Die Schrift Huts „Von dem Geheimnis der Taufe", die zwischen Juni 1525 und Mai 1526[34] verfasst wurde, entstand zwar später als die bereits zitierte Schrift Müntzers, aber auch hier finden wir das Prinzip der Ordnung Gottes. Dem Konzept der „göttlichen Ordnung" ging eine starke Kritik an den Wittenberger Theologen voran, die sie als die „wuchersüchtige, wollüstige, ehrgeizige und heuchlerische Schriftgelehrten" bezeichnete, die nur des Geldes wegen predigten. Hut kritisiert die Lehre jener, die sich auf den Imperativ "glaube" konzentrieren, aber nicht erklären, auf welche Art dieser Imperativ konkret werden kann. Für diesen Bauern ist die Antwort einfach: Zuerst müsse man die Ordnung Gottes in der ganzen Schöpfung erkennen, um danach das Urteil Gottes durch seine Gebote und sein Wort zu verstehen und zu erlernen.[35]

In Müntzers Konzept der ordo Dei, findet der „Anfang" statt, als Gott den Himmel und die vier Elemente unter diesem Himmel erschafft: Land, Wasser, Luft und Feuer. Diese vier Elemente sind in der Kosmologie des Mittelalters und in der theologischen Weltanschauung der Hildegard von Bingen vorhanden und werden den entsprechenden Temperamenten zugeordnet: melancholisch, ruhig, fröhlich und zornig; und ihren jeweiligen vier Eigenschaften: trocken, kalt, nass, und warm; und schließlich den entsprechenden vier Jahreszeiten: Frühling, Winter, Herbst und Sommer.[36] Es ist zu sehen, dass, nachdem der Anfang der Schöpfung des Himmels und der vier Elemente be-

---

[33] Ebd.
[34] Herbert Klassen: The life and teaching of Hans Hut, Part I: Hut's Life, Op. cit, S. 179.
[35] Hans Hut: Von dem Geheimnis der Taufe, in: Heinold Fast (Hg.): Der linke Flügel der Reformation. Glaubenszeugnisse der Täufer, Spiritualisten, Schwärmer und Antitrinitarier. Bremen, Carl Schünemann Verlag, 1962, S. 80-81.
[36] Hans Liebeschütz: Das allegorische Weltbild der Hildegard von Bingen. Berlin, Studien der Bibliothek Warburg XVI, 1930. Vgl. Fußnote zu dieser Monographie.

kannt gegeben wurde, die anderen Teile der Schöpfung in aufeinanderfolgender Weise beschrieben werden. Das Wort, das dafür verwendet wird, ist „dornach" und wird in der Beschreibung von Gottes Schöpfungsordnung stets wiederholt: dornach das gewechß, dornach das vihe, dornach der mensche, dornach Christus und schließt ab (Ende) mit „dornach Got vater almechtigk". Es besteht demnach ein ʿAnfangʾ in dem Creaturarum Ordo, der im Himmel und den vier Elementen besteht, gefolgt von der sukzessiven Erschaffung der anderen Lebewesen (Teile) und schließlich wird der Name des Schöpfers erwähnt (Ende).

In der Dynamik des ordo creurarum zeigt das „Ende", bevor sie als ein weiteres Stück der Schöpfung (Stückwerckischen) betrachtet wird, die Fülle dieses komplexen Ganzen. So könnte das „Ganze" zum Beispiel das Alte Testament oder die ganze Heilige Schrift sein, und die Menschen können darin diese „Teile" und das „Ganze" erkennen. Das „Ganze" könnte aber auch für den Geist Gottes stehen, der die volle Offenbarung Gottes aufzeigt, die in der Schöpfung und in der Heiligen Schrift zu finden ist. Diese Dynamik des ordo creurarem zwischen den „Teilen" und dem „Ganzen" finden wir im „Prager Manifest" wieder, wo Müntzer erklärt: „Ich habe gar von keynem gelerten dye ordnungk Gots in alle creaturn gsatzt vornommen ym allergrinsten wortlin, und das gantze eyn eynygher weck alle steyle czu erkennen, ist nye grochen von den, dye do woltn christen seyn, unde sunderlich von den vormaledeygthn pfaffen".[37]

Für Hut ist das Verständnis der Dynamik zwischen der Ordnung der Schöpfung und ihren Teilen stark in dem Wunsch verankert, Zeugnis zu geben mit einem Herzen, das nach Gerechtigkeit dürstet und hungert. Deutlich zu erkennen ist sein Interesse daran, dass das Evangelium aller Kreatur von den Armen her verstanden werden kann, wenn er sagt: „So ein hohes und unmögliches Ding ist es für einen fleischlichen Menschen, die Urteile Gottes wahrhaftig zu begreifen, wenn sie nicht mit allen Teilen in eine rechte Ordnung gestellt und verfasst werden. (...) Gott wolle sich erbarmen aller Menschen und vor allem der Armen!"[38]

---

[37] Thomas Müntzer: Das Prager Manifest, in: Franz, MSB, a.a.O., S. 491.
[38] Hans Hut: Von dem Geheimnis der Taufe, op. cit. S.83

Wer es schafft, die Ordnung Gottes zu verstehen, kann gleichzeitig das „Ganze" sehen und die „Teile" begreifen. Das ist die theologische Grundlage von Müntzer und Hut, durch die wir ihren Einfluss auf das Verständnis des großen Missionsbefehls in Markus 16,15 verstehen. Das Markusevangelium hat einen sehr wichtigen Platz in der Liturgie-Reform, die Müntzer im Jahr 1524 veranlasste. Er unterteilte den liturgischen Kalender in fünf verschiedene Zeiträume: Advent, Geburt, Passion, Ostern und Pfingsten. Der zu Ostern gelesene Haupttext ist Markus 16, 1-7, der davon spricht, wie Maria Magdalena, Maria Jacobi und Salome die Auferstehung Jesu erlebten. In den Liedern, die dieser Bibellese folgen, wird der „almechtige Got" gelobt, also Jesus Christus, der in Gottes Schöpfungsordnung zu finden ist, derselbe, der gekreuzigt und durch Gottes Kraft wieder auferweckt wurde.[39]

Der Hymnus „Conditor alme siderum", den Müntzer aus dem Lateinischen ins Deutsche übersetzte, drückt die Beziehung zwischen dieser Ordnung des Schöpfers, Christus und dem Evangelium aller Kreatur aus. Es ist eine kosmische Christologie, wie in Kolosser 1,16-23, wo Christus in die Schöpfungsordnung gestellt und der Wunsch ausgedrückt wird, sich seinen Urteilen zu unterstellen und seinen Willen zu tun.

„Alles, was durch yhn geschaffen ist,
dem gibt er krafft, wesen und frist
nach seynes willens ordnung zwar,
yhn zu erkennen offenbar.
Wir bitten dich, o heylger Christ,
wann du künfftiger richter bist,
lehr uns hyevor deynen willen thun
und im glauben nemen zu."[40]

In seinen theologischen Meinungsverschiedenheiten mit Johann Egranus Silvius kritisierte Müntzer dessen rationalistische Methoden, die keinen Raum dafür gaben, das Wirken des Heiligen Geistes in den Auserwählten zu verstehen. Und obwohl Müntzer der Behauptung Egranus', die den apokryphen Charakter der Passage in Markus 15, 9-19 hervorhob, nicht wider-

---

[39] Siehe die Hymne im Offertorium „Die Erde hat erbidmet und geruget, do Got wolt zcum Urteil aufferstehn", in: Franz, MSB, S. 197-199.
[40] Thomas Müntzer: Das ampt auff das advent, in: Franz, MSB, S. 48, 20-27.

sprach, relativierte und ironisierte er dessen Position, als er sagte, dass genau der zitierte Text die „coronis evangelica" sei.[41] Und dies war ohne Zweifel unter anderem seinem Verständnis zu verdanken, dass der große Missionsbefehl Jesu "geet hin in die Welt und predigent das Evangelion aller Creaturen" (Markus 16,15), ein Schlüsseltext war, um das Evangelium im Licht des Konzepts der ordo creaturarum zu verstehen.

Für Hut ist der Text aus Markus 16,15 auch zentral für sein Verständnis der Heiligen Schrift. Ab 1521 arbeitete Hut im Handwerk, kaufte Vordrucke, band sie in Bücher und verkaufte sie. Durch die enorme Verbreitung von Flugschriften und den Buchverkauf verbreitete er die Ideale der Protestantischen Reformation.[42] Er zog durch Würzburg, Bamberg, Nürnberg, Passau, bis Österreich und ließ sich dann in Wittenberg nieder. Hut war von der reformierenden Botschaft Luthers beeindruckt, nahm während seiner Aufenthalte in Wittenberg an den Gottesdiensten teil und hörte die Vorlesungen. Durch seine Reisen konnte er Schriften verbreiten und gleichzeitig auf dem neuesten Stand sein, wenn es um die Entwicklung der Reformationsbewegung ging.[43] Seebass bestätigte, es sei nicht unmöglich, dass Hut den Magister Thomas Müntzer auf einer seiner ersten Reisen nach Wittenberg kennengelernt und sich mit den hussitischen Schriften von Pastor Martin Reinhard in Jena vertraut gemacht hatte.[44] Als Autodidakt verfolgte Hut die Schriften der Reformation aus nächster Nähe und nahm seit 1521 die Spannungen zwischen Karlstadt und Müntzer gegenüber Luther wahr, da er als umherziehender Vertreiber von Büchern zwischen Wittenberg und Nürnberg herumreiste, was den Kontakt zu Karlstadt, der Pfarrer in Orlamünde und zu Müntzer, der Pfarrer in Allstedt war, erleichterte. Vor dem Hintergrund seiner ländlichen

---

[41] Der vollständige Satz lautet „Evangelium Marci in ultimo capite et apocriphum et coronis evangelica". Siehe: Thomas Müntzer: Angebliche Propositionen des Egranus. (Zwickau, vor April 1521, 16P), in: Franz, MSB, S. 514, 30-31.

[42] Herbert Klassen: The life and teaching of Hans Hut, Part II: Hans Hut and Thomas Müntzer, in: The Mennonite Quarterly Review, Volume XXXIII, Number Three, July 1959, S. 267-304, bes. 268.

[43] Wilhelm Neuser: Hans Hut. Leben und Wirken bis zum Nikolsburger Religionsgespräch. Berlin, Hermann Blanke's Buchdruckerei, 1913, S. 12; Herbert Klassen, The life and teaching of Hans Hut, Part I: Hut's Life", op. cit. S. 171-205.

[44] Gottfried Seebass: Müntzers Erbe, S. 169 (164-169).

Wurzeln stellt Hut den Text aus Markus 16,15 ins Zentrum seiner wichtigsten Schrift „Von dem Geheimnis der Taufe"[45], in der er die theologische und gesellschaftlich-kirchliche Bedeutung des Textes darlegt. Ich sage deshalb auch, dass Markus 16,15 im Mittelpunkt des Denkens von Hans Hut steht, weil er am 16. September 1527, im entscheidenden Moment seines Lebens, im Gefängnis und im Angesicht der Angst vor der Folter und dem Urteil, das sein Leben beenden würde, diesen Text verwendet, um von seinem Auftrag Zeugnis zu geben.[46]

2. „Geet hin in die Welt und predigent das Evangelion aller Creaturen" (Markus 16,15): Pflanzen und Tieren, allem Erschaffenem im Himmel und auf der Erde

Die Himmel und die Erde mit all ihren Geschöpfen verkünden das Werk von Gottes Händen und sind daher das Evangelium Gottes. Die Schöpfung ist das erste Evangelium Gottes. Dies ist eine Grundlage der mystischen Theologie Thomas Müntzers. Im Deutschen Kirchenamt, das von Müntzer in Allstedt eingeführt wurde, erscheint in der Liturgie der „Weihnacht" in der ersten „Antiphon" als Bibellese Psalm 19. Die ersten 7 Verse präsentieren die ganze Schöpfung als „die kunst Gottis", also „das Evangelion aller creaturen": „Der tag vorkleret das wort dem tage, und die nacht vorkündiget der nacht die kunst Gottis."[47] Die Offenbarung Gottes, das Evangelium, stellt sich hier nicht mit Worten, sondern als Schöpfung vor. Am Tag geht die Sonne zwischen den Bergen auf und beleuchtet alle Konturen der Erde, man kann bei Tagesanbruch ihre sanften Strahlen am blauen Himmelsgewölbe spüren und sehen, die Vögel flattern im Rhythmus des Windes. Am Tag erblickt man Wasserströme, die wie Schlangen durch die Wälder gleiten, und Fische, die zwischen ihren Wasserfällen umherspringen. Die Wälder offenbaren „die kunst Gottis", weil ihre Bäume von Zeit zu Zeit, je nach Jahreszeit, ihre Blätter wechseln, ohne dass sie dadurch aufhören, Früchte für die Ernäh-

---

[45] Hans Hut: Von dem Geheimnis der Taufe, in: Heinold Fast (Hg.): a.a.O., S. 79-99.
[46] Die Aussagen Hans Huts im Verhör am 16. September 1527. Augsburg StA, Wiedertäuferakten I, f. 4r-20v, ohne f. 10r-13v. Zitiert nach: Gottfried Seebass: Müntzers Erbe, S. 515ff. (Anhang, S. 31-42).
[47] Thomas Müntzer: Das ampt auff das fest der geburt Christi, in: Franz, MSB, S. 53, 4f.

rung der Tiere, Vögel und Menschen zu tragen. Der Psalmist stellt die Sonne als Bräutigam dar, der die Welt von Osten nach Westen bereist, um in die nächtliche Behausung seiner Geliebten, dem Mond, einzudringen. Auf seiner Tour hat er die Wärme des Lebens hinter sich gelassen, und am Ende der Reise sind die Berge, Wiesen und Himmel in Rot, Orange und zartes Gelb gemalt. Wenn es dunkel wird, dann erscheint der Mond, begleitet von Lichtern, blauen, grünen und scharlachroten Sternen, die vor Melancholie und Schönheit zittern. Keine Worte ... aber die Stimme Gottes leuchtet in der Symphonie des Universums. Keine Worte ... aber seine Stimme wird „in den grentzen des umbkreyß der erden" gehört. Dies ist das Evangelium aller Kreatur: keine Worte sind nötig, um das Evangelium bekannt zu machen, weil die Schöpfung in ihrer ganzen Größe und Schönheit „die kunst Gottis" offenbart.[48]

Wenn Müntzer von der Genesis und dem Buch der Psalmen ausgeht, um sich auf das „Evangelium aller Creaturen" zu beziehen, dann beginnt Hut direkt beim Mandat Jesu Christi in Markus 16,15 und beim Text aus dem Brief an die Kolosser 1,23, wo der Apostel Paulus sagt: „...das Evangelium, das Euch gepredigt wird, ist in allen Kreaturen". Und um die Bedeutung dessen zu erklären, sagte Hut: „Hier ist nicht gemeint, dass das Evangelium den Kreaturen gepredigt werden soll, wie Hunden und Katzen, Kühen und Kälbern, Laub und Gras, sondern, wie Paulus sagt, das Evangelium, das euch gepredigt wird, ist in allen Kreaturen."[49] Wie Müntzer hielt auch Hut die ganze Schöpfung für das erste Buch, das das Evangelium Gottes zum Ausdruck bringt.

Der erste Teil von Psalm 19 stellt „das Evangelion aller creaturen" in Bezug auf „die kunst Gottis" vor (V. 1-7), aber der zweite Teil des Psalms setzt es in Beziehung zum „gesetz Gottis" (V. 8 -15). Gott hat seinen Geschöpfen seinen Geist eingehaucht, und die Kreaturen, die in seinem Ebenbild geschaffen und ihm ähnlich sind, als sie diesen Geist des Lebens empfingen, können

---

[48] Über die Sprache Müntzers, um Himmel, Atmosphäre, Erde, Pflanzen, Tiere und Mensch zu beschreiben, vgl. Hans Otto Spilmann: Untersuchungen zum deutschen Wortschatz in Thomas Müntzers Schriften. Berlin-New York, Walter de Gruyter 1971, S. 14-35.

[49] Hans Hut: Von dem Geheimnis der Taufe. in: Heinold Fast (Hg.), a.a.O., S 85.

seinen Garten mit Rechtschaffenheit und Weisheit bebauen und verwalten. In der Übersetzung des biblischen Textes wird das Wort „Außerwelten" verwendet, um die von Gott geschaffenen Menschen zu bezeichnen, die bereit sind, sich der Ehrfurcht und den Geboten Gottes, der Himmel und Erde gemacht hat, zu unterstellen. So stellt der Psalmist „das gesetz Gottis" in der folgenden Übersetzung vor, die im Deutschen Kirchenamt verwendet wird:

„*Das gesetz Gottis ist reyn, zu bekeren die hertzen der außerwelten.*
Das gezeugknis Gottis est warhafftig, die weyßheit die kleynen zu leren.
Die war gerechtigkeit Gottes erfrawet die hertzen der außerwelten.
Das gebot Gotes erleuchtet scheynparlich ire augen.
Die forcht Gottis ist reyn un weret ewiglich.
Die waren urteyl Gottes seint rechtschaffen an yhn selbest."[50]

„Das Evangelion aller Creaturen" wird durch die „kunst Gottis" und das „gesetz Gottis" ausgedrückt. Letzteres lässt den Menschen die Ordnung alles Erschaffenen verstehen und bewirkt so Bewunderung für und Ehrfurcht vor Gott und Weisheit und Gerechtigkeit im Herzen der „Außerwelten". Sowohl in Müntzers Schriften als auch bei Hut kann die intrinsische Beziehung wahrgenommen werden zwischen dem Schöpfungsakt Gottes, der allen Geschöpfen das Leben gibt, und dem Geist Gottes, der auf das Herz seiner Geschöpfe schreibt, noch bevor die Gebote niedergeschrieben wurden. In seiner Schrift „Von dem Geheimnis der Taufe" drückte Hut es so aus: „Denn die ganze Welt mit allen Kreaturen ist ein Buch, in dem man alles im Werk sieht, was im geschriebenen Buch gelesen wird. Denn alle auserwählten Menschen von Anfang der Welt bis zu Mose haben in dem Buch aller Kreaturen studiert und dabei das erkannt, was ihnen von Natur durch den Geist Gottes in das Herz geschrieben ist (Röm. 2,14 f.), weil das ganze Gesetz mit kreaturischen Werken beschrieben ist."[51]

Wenn wir Müntzers Exegese dieses Textes mit der seines theologischen Gegners Egranus vergleichen, sehen wir, dass es in der Interpretation einen großen Unterschied gibt. In der Interpretation Egranus' werden die „kunst Gottis" und „das gesetz Gottis" im Psalm 19 von Christus überschattet. „Al-

---

[50] Thomas Müntzer: Das ampt auff das advent. in: Franz, MSB, S. 53.
[51] Heinold Fast (Hg.): Der linke Flügel der Reformation. op. cit., S. 90.

so ist Christus \ eyn frolicher freudereicher breutgam \ der freude austeylet und gibt \ lest sich darumb sehen \ und tuht sich herfur \ das er yderman mit freude und friede uberschutte. Das seyn di hymelischen benedeyung \ damit uns Gott gebenedeyet hat."[52] Was das „gesetz Gottis" und die Auslegung des 10. Verses in Psalm 19 betrifft, so sagt Egranos: „Wer Gottes werck ym Evangelio durch Christus freundtlikeyt erkennet\ dem ist das gesetz\ zeugniss\ rechte und sitten Gottes lieber denn silber und goldt das ist\ er acht alle dinge \ die gros \ hoch \ suss \ und lieplich seyn vor der welt fur nichts \ gegen dissem schatze.\"[53]

Nach dem Verständnis Müntzers ist eine solche Exegese nicht möglich, denn Egranus kehrt die Reihenfolge der Schöpfung um. Es sind die Schöpfungsordnung und die Gebote, die durch Mose gegeben wurden, anhand derer die Menschen sowohl die „kunst Gottis" als auch das „gesetz Gottis" verstehen. Egranos interpretiert, dass das Evangelium nur im Licht Christi interpretiert werden kann. Müntzer glaubt, dass die gesamte, im Alten Testament beschriebene Schöpfung des Universums und die Gebote Gottes sich in der Ordnung Gottes wiederfinden, und dass das Neue Testament dem nicht widerspricht, sondern dass die Inkarnation und das Wirken Jesu diese Ordnung ergänzen. Egranos interpetiert, dass das Evangelium nur im Licht Christi interpretiert werden kann, während Müntzer bei der Schöpfung des Universums und den Rechtsvorschriften des Gottes des Universums beginnt, um die Menschwerdung und Auftrag Jesu zu verstehen: „geet hin in die welt und predigent das evangelion aller creaturen" (Markus 16,15).

Wenn Müntzer sich hinsetzt, um die Natur (kunst Gottis) zu betrachten und zu bewundern, denkt er gleichzeitig über die Weisungen Gottes (gesetz Gottis) nach. Ein Beispiel dafür finden wir im Manifest von Prag, wo er mit reformerischem Eifer gegen jene religiösen Führer predigt, die die Menschen nicht mit dem lebendigen Wort Gottes ernährt hatten: „Sye sint nicht wie Christus, unser lieber Herre, der sich vorgleicht einer hennen, dye do warm macht yhre kynder. Sie geben auch keine milch den trostlossen vorlassenen

---

[52] Ludwig Fischer (Hg.), Die lutherischen Pamphlete gegen Thomas Müntzer, München: Deutscher Taschenbuch-Verlag, Tübingen: Niemeyer, 1976, S. 70.
[53] Ebd., S. 74

menschen vom brun der unausscheplichen vormanunge Gots. Den sie haben den glauben nicht vorsucht. Sie sein wie der storch, der do in den wisen und sumpem die frossche auffleseth, dornach speiget er sie alzo rohe yns nescht zu seinen jungen."[54]

„Das Evangelion aller Creaturen", das heißt, die gute Nachricht Gottes, die durch die gesamte Schöpfung und sein Gesetz sichtbar wird, wird unterbrochen, wenn der Mensch, der nach dem Bild Gottes geschaffen ist, aus dieser Ordnung ausbricht, um Ungerechtigkeit zu üben (Römer 1,18-20). Gottes Reaktion auf die menschliche Ungerechtigkeit gegenüber dem „Evangelion aller Creaturen", verstanden Müntzer und Hut[55] im Lichte dessen, was der Apostel Paulus sagte: „Denn Gottes Zorn offenbart sich vom Himmel her über alle Gottlosigkeit und Ungerechtigkeit der Menschen, die die Wahrheit durch Ungerechtigkeit niederhalten. Denn was man von Gott erkennen kann, ist unter ihnen offenbar; Gott hat es ihnen offenbart. Denn Gottes unsichtbares Wesen, nämlich seine ewige Kraft und Gottheit, wird seit der Schöpfung der Welt an seinen Werken mit der Vernunft wahrgenommen, so dass sie keine Entschuldigung haben" (Römer 1,18-20).

Müntzer nahm eine prophetische Haltung ein, um die Bedeutung des „Evangelion aller Creaturen" anzukündigen, als sich die Herren und Fürsten alle Geschöpfe für ihr Wohlergehen aneigneten und als diese und die Schriftgelehrten – er führt Luther mit auf – die Ehrfurcht vor Gott verloren hatten, indem sie die „kunst Gottis" zerstörten und „das Gesetz Gottis" zu ihrem Vorteil und gegen die Armen verdrehten. „Sich zu, die grundtsuppe des wuchers, der dieberey und rauberey sein unser herrn und fürsten, nemen alle creaturen zum aygenthumb. Die visch im wasser, die vögel im lufft, das gewechß auff erden muß alles ir sein, Esaie. 5. Darüber lassen sy dann Gottes gepot außgeen unter die armen und sprechen: Got hat gepoten, du solt nit stelen; es dienet aber in nit. So sye nun alle menschen verursachen, den armen ackerman, handtwerckman und alles, das da lebet, schinden und schaben, Michee. 3. capitel, so er sich dann vergreifft am allergeringesten, so

---

[54] Das Prager Manifest. 1. und 25. November 1521. Erweiterte deutsche Fassung, in: Franz, MSB, S. 500, 24-29 und 501,1.
[55] Hans Hut: Von dem Geheimnis der Taufe, op. cit., S. 90-91.

muss er hencken: Do saget denn der doctor lugner: Amen. Die herren machen das selber, dass in der arme man feyndt wirdt. Dye ursach des auffrurß wollen sye nit wegthun, wie kann es die lenge gut werden? So ich das sage, muß ich auffrürisch sein, wol hyn."[56]

Obwohl die Texte Müntzers[57] seit seiner Fürstenpredigt (1523)[58] einen schärferen und sarkastischeren Ton gegen die Fürsten und Luther haben als die Hans Huts[59], kann man bei beiden Pastoren eine konstante Bezugnahme auf die paulinischen Texte aus dem Brief an die Römer erkennen. Sie taten das, um gemeinsam mit dem Apostel Paulus zu untermauern, dass Geschöpfe nicht den Geist der Knechtschaft, sondern von Gott den Geist der Kindschaft erhalten haben (Röm. 8,14-17).[60] Denn beide waren der Ansicht, dass die Zeit gekommen war, dass das Wasser, die in der Luft fliegenden Vögel, Tiere, Pflanzen, die Bäuerinnen und der „arme Mann" sich danach sehnten, aus der Knechtschaft heraus in die Freiheit der Söhne und Töchter Gottes zu kommen. „Denn wir wissen, dass die ganze Schöpfung bis zu diesem Augenblick gemeinsam seufzt und in Wehen liegt. Aber nicht nur sie, sondern auch wir selbst, die wir den Geist als Erstlingsgabe haben, seufzen in uns selbst und warten auf die Kindschaft, die Erlösung unseres Leibes." (Römer 8,22-23).

3. "Geet hin in die Welt und predigent das Evangelion aller Creaturen" (Markus 16,15): in der Ehrfurcht Elisabeths, Marias, Rahabs, Ruths und Judiths

Einer der schwierigsten Aspekte im „Evangelium aller Geschöpfe" von Müntzer und Hut ist die Berücksichtigung der biblischen Texte, deren Para-

---

[56] Thomas Müntzer: Hochverursachte Schutzrede, in: Franz, MSB, S. 329, 18-29.
[57] Einige der von Müntzer geschrieben Texte, die sich auf das 8. Kap. des Briefes von Paulus an die Römer beziehen, sind: Das Prager Manifest, 1. und 25. November 1521. in: Franz, MSB, S. 492, 5 bis 17; Auslegung des unterschieds Danielis (1524) in: MSB, 251 S. 14-19; Von dem gedichteten Glauben (1524) in: MSB, S. 224, 4-8.
[58] Die Predigt wurde am 12.02.1523 geschrieben, aber im folgenden Jahr veröffentlicht.
[59] In seiner Schrift „Von dem Geheimnis Taufe" zitiert Hut Kap. 10 des Briefes des Paulus an die Römer. in: Heinold Fast, a.a.O., S.79-99
[60] Thomas Müntzer: Deutsches Kircheamt (1523). in: Franz, MSB, S. 145,1-6.

digma der Glauben und das Handeln von Frauen ist. Müntzer nutzt die Reflexionen der Elisabeth und Maria im Lukasevangelium, wohingegen Hut Judith erwähnt. Aber beiden Autoren ist gemeinsam, dass sie Texte von Frauen reflektieren, die sich in Situationen der Unterdrückung befinden, die angesichts der Gegenwart Gottes in Staunen versetzt werden, die durch Schwangerschaft das Wunder des Lebens empfangen und die an den Kämpfen des Volkes Gottes teilhaben.

Es ist sehr gut möglich, dass die gleichen Umstände, in denen Müntzer gelebt hatte, ihn dazu führten, die entscheidende Rolle von Frauen in der Geschichte der Kirche, der Reformation und der Bauernaufstände zu erkennen. Ihre Überzeugung, dass Gott in der Bibel, durch die Geschichte und in der Gegenwart durch Träume sprach, hat ihren Anhaltspunkt in den Erfahrungen und Schriften dreier wichtiger Mystikerinnen des Mittelalters.[61] Im Werk der Hildegard von Bingen (1098-1179), das als „Scivias Domini" („Wisse die Wege des Herrn") bekannt ist, wird die Sicht auf die Heilsgeschichte seit dem Fall Adams bis zum Gericht und dem ewigen Leben betont. Charakteristisch für ihre Anschauung und Gemälde ist die natürliche und spirituelle Perspektive auf das Gleichgewicht und die Harmonie des Kosmos, der von Gott geschaffen wurde. Im Werk der Elisabeth von Schönau (1129-1164), das als „Liber viarum Dei" (Buch der Wege Gottes) bekannt ist, ist die Sicht auf die Auferstehung der Jungfrau Maria vorrangig. Und schließlich, im Werk Mechthilds von Hackeborn (1241-1299) „Liber speciales gratiae" (Buch der besonderen Gnade), wird auf die Mystik des Herzens Jesu hingewiesen, in der Jesus mehr als der erhabene Christus dargestellt wird als der im Fleisch Gedemütigte.[62]

---

[61] Die Arbeit, die Müntzer in seiner Bibliothek hatte, und die er verwendete, um die genannten Autoren zu lesen, war: Jacobus Faber Stapulensis (Hg.) TRIUM virorum ET LIBER TRIUM SPIRITUALIUM Virginum, Paris, 1513. Zitiert von Reinhard Schwarz: Thomas Müntzer und die Mystik, in: Helmar Junghans und Siegfried Bräuer (Hg.): Der Theologe Thomas Müntzer. Göttingen, Vandenhoeck & Ruprecht, 1989, S. 283-301, bes. 297.

[62] Dieter Fauth, op. cit., S. 158-166.

Was wir über seine Frau, die Nonne Ottilie von Gersen[63], wissen, ist, dass sie mit einer Gruppe von 15 Nonnen das Kloster Wiederstedt verließ, und sie zusammen mit 10 dieser Nonnen Zuflucht in Schlössern in Allstedt suchte.[64] Diese Umstände deuten darauf hin, dass die Heirat von Müntzer und Ottilie von Gersen eine Liebe zur Grundlage hat, die wegen ihrer theologischen und ideologischen Entscheidungen in einem großen Spannungsfeld entstand und wuchs, und sie beide vergleichbare Vorstellungen über die politischen, sozialen und religiösen Veränderungen hatten, die in der Nähe Mansfelds vor sich gingen. Seine Gedanken über die Schwangerschaft von Elisabeth und Maria im Lukasevangelium zeigen sich ein Jahr nach seiner Heirat mit Ottilie von Gersen und dreieinhalb Monate nach der Geburt ihres Sohnes.[65]

Die Frau ist Teil der Schöpfung Gottes und hat eine wichtige Rolle in der Heilsgeschichte, wenn sie ihren Platz in der Ehrfurcht Gottes gefunden hat. In seinem berühmten Text „Ausgedrückte Entblößung" sind Elisabeth und Maria zusammen mit Zacharias die zentralen biblischen Figuren in den Überlegungen Müntzers über das erste Kapitel des Lukas-Evangeliums. Die zentrale Frage, mit er der die Zuhörer und Leser durch seine Predigt herausfordert, ist die gleiche wie in Jesaja 53,1 und Römer 10,14-21: „Meynstu wenn des menschen sun kummem wirt, das er werd glauben finden auff erden?"[66] Und er selbst beantwortet diese Frage der genannten Texte, indem er betont, dass diejenigen, die offenbar geglaubt hatten – es sei das Christentum – , ihren Glauben an Gott aufgegeben hatten. Und dann führt er den Glauben der Elisabeth und Maria als Vorbild an.

Zacharias zweifelt angesichts der Botschaft des Engels, dass seine Frau Elisabeth, die bereits in die Jahre gekommen war, einen Sohn gebären würde. Aber Elisabeth, die Ehrfurcht vor Gott hat und die Hoffnung nicht aufgegeben hat, ein Kind zu bekommen, glaubt und nimmt das Wunder Gottes in ihrem Körper an. Maria ihrerseits freut sich über die Botschaft, dass obwohl

---

[63] Gerhard Brendler: Thomas Müntzer, Geist und Faust. Berlin, VEB Deutscher Verlag der Wissenschaften, 1989, S. 84.
[64] Walter Elliger, op. cit., S. 375.
[65] Nach den Äußerungen Agricolas wurde Müntzers Sohn am Ostertag 1523 geboren. Walter Elliger, op. cit., S. 375-376.
[66] Thomas Müntzer: Ausgedrückte Entblössung (1523), in: Franz, MSB, S. 265-319.

Das Evangelium aller Kreatur.

sie noch mit keinem Mann geschlafen hatte, aus ihrem Schoß Jesus geboren werden würde und singt ein Lied großer Freude. Aus diesem von Maria gesungenen Magnificat betont Müntzer den folgenden Satz: „Sein Name ist heilig und seine Gnade währt von Geschlecht zu Geschlecht, für die, die ihn fürchten" (Lk. 1,49b-50). Dies bedeutet, dass sowohl Elisabeth als auch Maria innerhalb der Schöpfungskette, die Gott durch Adam begann, über Abraham bis hin zu ihrer Zeit, das Evangelium Gottes verkündigen. Sie sind Kreaturen aus Ton aus der Hand des schöpferischen Töpfers, der ihren Mutterleibern jetzt seinen Geist einhaucht, um Leben und Hoffnung zu erzeugen (Jesaja 64,7). Und während sie mit Ehrfurcht vor dem Schöpfer bleiben, können sie auch mit ihrem Lied die verwandelnde Kraft des Evangeliums Gottes zum Ausdruck bringen. Und es ist gerade wegen der Ehrfurcht vor Gott, in der Maria und Elisabeth lebten, dass Gott Israel Rettung durch ihre Kinder (den Propheten Johannes der Täufer und Jesus von Nazareth) bringen würde.

Die Erwähnung Johannes des Täufers sieht Müntzer im Zusammenhang mit der Herrschaft des Herodes. In diesem Kontext kann man Veränderungen in seiner Schrift „Die Fürstenpredigt" feststellen, weil seine Beschwerde sich hier nicht nur gegen die Schriftgelehrten richtet, die die Bedeutung des Evangeliums stehlen, sondern auch gegen die Herrscher („Menschen-Regiment") seiner Zeit, die die Armen unterdrücken. Müntzer fragt sich, ist es möglich, dass Marias Lied, das Gott preist, weil er die Armen erhöht und den Gewaltigen vom Thron stößt, seinen Platz im Leben des Volks nicht finden kann, da eben dieser Täufer seinen Kopf ja angesichts der Macht des Herodes verlor? Wenn die Situation, in der sich „gemeine Mann" vor den Fürsten in den deutschen Gebieten befand, ähnlich war wie die Unterdrückung, die die Juden in Rom erlitten, und durch die der Täufer starb, wie könnte es dann möglich sein, auf dieser Erde Glauben zu finden?

Und wieder antwortet er auf diese nagende Frage mit dem Argument, dass die Ehrfurcht vor Gott, die im Herzen von Maria ist, das ist, was sie ausrufen lässt: „Der Allmächtige tut große Dinge zu meinen Gunsten." Was dem Menschen unmöglich erscheint, wird dann möglich. „Denn nichts ist unmöglich bei Gott" (Lukas 1,37), denn er setzte Johannes den Täufer und Jesus durch seinen Heiligen Geist in den Schoß der Elisabeth und der Maria. Es ist das Ausharren in der Ehrfurcht vor Gott, dem Schöpfer, das Maria, eine arme Frau aus dem Volk, ein Instrument des Segens für alle Generationen sein lässt. Bezogen auf die synoptischen Evangelien fordert Müntzer seine Leser auf, zu berücksichtigen, dass jede Kreatur, die den Willen Gottes tun möchte, das Evangelium verkündigen kann: „Seht, das sind meine Mutter und meine Brüder! Denn wer Gottes Willen tut, der ist mein Bruder und meine Schwester und meine Mutter" (Markus 3,35.)

In dieser Predigt greift Müntzer auch auf den Evangelisten Matthäus zurück, um „das Evangelion aller Creaturen" anhand der Erfahrung Ruths und Rahabs zu verkünden. Er erwähnt nicht nur Elisabeth und Maria als direkte Nachkommen von Abraham, dem Freund Gottes. Er beachtet nicht nur Maria als arme Frau des jüdischen Volkes, sondern erwähnt Rahab, die Hure, und Ruth in der Genealogie Jesu, um aufzuzeigen, dass alle Frauen, ob Kanaaniterinnen, Moabiterinnen, Jüdinnen, Türkinnen oder Heidinnen, als Schöpfung Gottes sein Evangelium verkünden; und dass diese, seien sie aus der einen oder anderen Nation, in der Ehrfurcht vor Gott, vom Geist erfüllt, das Evangelium der Gnade Gottes von Generation zu Generation[67] predigen können.

Vor allem nach der Niederlage der Bauernaufstände in Deutschland im Jahr 1525 veränderte sich Huts Familienleben sehr. Er musste aus Bibra fliehen und sich ständig von einem Ort zum anderen bewegen, erstens wegen des Rufs Gottes, das Evangelium aller Kreatur zu predigen, und zweitens, um vor den Behörden zu fliehen. Aus diesem Grund wurden seine Frau, seine Kinder, die dem Täuferglauben treu waren, Teil der frühen Täufer-Gemeinden und erlitten als solche die Ablehnung der Gesellschaft und der etablierten Kirchen. Durch diese Doppeldynamik des Umherziehens im südlichen Deutschland und den österreichischen Territorien war er in der Lage, sein Zeugnis mit vielen Frauen und Männern zu teilen. Die Liste der Männer und Frauen, die sein Wort hörten und von ihm getauft wurden, ist sehr groß und ist nur teilweise dokumentiert. Durch die Eigenschaften dieser frühen Täufer-Gemeinden kann bestätigt werden, dass die Unterstützung für den Dienst Hans Huts, während er von einer Stadt zur anderen zog, dank der Solidarität vieler Bäuerinnen möglich war.

---

[67] Ebd., S. 311-312.

Das Evangelium aller Kreatur.

Die mystische Theologie der Hildegard von Bingen, Elisabeth von Schönau, Mechthild von Hackeborn, Meister Eckhart, Tauler und Seuse beeinflusste die Theologie und die deutsche idealistische Philosophie der Zukunft.[68] Bei Hut wie bei Müntzer kann man dieses Erbe wahrnehmen, das durch den revolutionären Anstoß der Taboriten und der biblisch-apokalyptischen Literatur geschürt wurde. Für Müntzer gewinnt das Buch Daniel besonders an Interesse, weil er in dessen Traum die Offenbarung von Gott erkennt, wie die mittelalterlichen Strukturen entlarvt werden, die den „gemeine Mann" unterdrückten.[69] Bei Hut bekommt das Lesen des deuterokanonischen Buchs Judith große Relevanz, um seinen Glauben in konkreten Situationen der Trübsal und Verfolgung zu stärken, daher erwähnt er Judith auch in seinen Reflexionen über die Taufe im Blut.[70] Sowohl das Buch des Propheten Daniel als auch das Buch Judith beziehen sich auf den historischen Moment, in dem sich das Volk Israel im Exil unter der Macht Nebukadnezars befindet. Judith ist die jüdische Frau, die Holofernes, dem Kapitän der Armeen Nebukadnezars, König von Babylon, die Stirn bietet. Judith ist die Geschichte einer klugen, mutigen und schönen Frau, die als Witwe der jüdischen Frömmigkeit treu bleibt und sich so der Mutlosigkeit ihres unterdrückten Volks entgegenstellt. Mit ihrer List verführt Judith den Soldaten Holofernes und enthauptet ihn, sobald dieser betrunken ist; die Feinde fallen in Verzweiflung und das jüdische Volk wird freigelassen. Judith repräsentiert die Treue Gottes zu einer Nation, die kurz vor der Ausrottung steht, und hat didaktisch gesehen einen Aspekt der universellen Erlösung.

In den kurzen Schriften von Hans Hut, zu denen wir Zugang haben, gibt es keine so explizite biblische Exegese über Frauen wie jene, die bei Müntzer vorliegt, aber dennoch ein Gedankenkontinuum, das sich bei der Gestaltung der frühen Täufer-Gemeinden festigt. In seiner Schrift „Vom Geheimnis der Taufe" beginnt er genau damit, die Mitglieder der Gemeinde, Männer und

---

[68] Herbert Grundmann: Die geschichtlichen Grundlagen der Deutschen Mystik. In: Herbert Grundmann: Ausgewählte Aufsätze, Teil 1, Religiöse Bewegungen, Stuttgart: Anton Hiersemann, 1976, S. 243-268.

[69] Thomas Müntzer: Auslegung des anderen Unterschieds Danielis, in: Franz, MSB, S.241-263.

[70] Hans Hut: Von dem Geheimnis der Taufe, in: Heinold Fast, a.a.O., S.91-92...

Frauen, herauszufordern, sich, bewegt durch den Heiligen Geist, der Ehrfurcht vor Gott zu unterstellen: „Die reine Furcht Gottes wünsche ich zum Anfang göttlicher Weisheit allen Brüdern und Schwestern im Herrn, der reinen und rechtgeschaffenen Christenheit, der Gemeinde Gottes, der einzigen Ehefrau und Braut Christi, die aus Bewegung des Heiligen Geistes durch das Band der Liebe vereinigt, und allen, die mit betrübtem Herzen und zermahlenem Geist Verlangen haben nach der ernsten Gerechtigkeit des gekreuzigten Sohnes Gottes, und allen denen, die begehren, gespeist zu werden: denen wünsche ich Gnade und Friede im Heiligen Geist."[71]

Bei den Beispielen Huts, die zeigen, wie das Evangelium in der ganzen Schöpfung zum Ausdruck gebracht wird, finden wir auch jene expliziten über die Rolle der Frauen. Er bezieht sich nicht auf Maria und Elisabeth, wie wir in den Überlegungen Müntzers sehen, erwähnt dafür aber den Fall anderer schwangerer Frauen. Das erste Beispiel zitiert der Prophet Jesaja in Kapitel 26,17-19 und deutet den Schmerz des Volkes als Schmerzen der Frauen bei der Geburt. Hier gibt es die Hoffnung, dass die neugeborenen Töchter und Söhne das Erbe und das Heil der Menschen gewährleisten können. Das zweite Beispiel wird von Jesus gegeben, als er das Evangelium als eine Frau darstellt, die bei der Geburt viel leidet (Johannes 16,21), die aber, sobald sie ihr Kind geboren hat, ihre Leiden vergisst wegen der Freude, ihre neugeborene Tochter oder Sohn zu sehen. Das dritte Beispiel findet sich in Kapitel 12 der Offenbarung, in dem es um die Vision von der Frau geht, die gebären soll, und um einen Drachen mit sieben Köpfen, der auf die Geburt des Kindes wartet, um es zu verschlingen.[72] Alle diese biblischen Beispiele spiegeln die Verfolgungsangst der frühen Täufer-Gemeinden wider: zwischen 1527 und 1581 wurden in Bayern insgesamt 223 (Wieder)Täufer hingerichtet; im Tal von Tirol wurde zwischen 1527 und 1530 der Tod von etwa 1.000 Täufern gezählt, und in Linz wurden seit 1529 etwa 70 Brüder und Schwestern hingerichtet.[73]

---

[71] Ebd., S.79-80.
[72] Hans Hut: Von dem Geheimnis der Taufe, in: Heinold Fast, a.a.O., S. 87.
[73] John Jorsch: Persecution of the Evangelical Anabaptists, in: The Mennonite Quarterly Review, Volume XXII, Goshen, Indiana, 1938, S. 3-26.

Im persönlichen Zeugnis der Familie Hut nimmt man auch diese Ehrfurcht vor Gott wahr, die in seiner Frau, Töchtern und Söhnen gewachsen war; auch sie litten aufgrund der Nachfolge Jesu. Eine der Töchter Hut, deren Name nicht aufgezeichnet ist, wurde festgenommen und wegen ihrer anabaptistischen Überzeugungen am 25. Januar 1527 in Bamberg ertränkt.[74] Sie führte den Weg des Martyriums an, den Monate später auch ihr Vater Hans Hut begehen würde. Wie auch Huts Tochter wurden unzählige Täufer-Frauen aus Frankreich, Deutschland, der Schweiz und Holland ins Gefängnis gebracht, dem folgte ein Gerichtsprozess und danach wurden sie durch öffentliche Verbrennung zu Tode gemartert, wieder andere wurden an Händen und Füßen gefesselt und in die Flüsse geworfen, um ihre Strafe als „Ketzer" mit dem Tod durch Ertrinken zu verbüßen.[75] Die Lieder der Täufer-Gemeinden, die aufgrund der Predigten Huts entstanden waren, bezeugen dies:

„Man hat sie an die Bäum gehenkt,
erwürget und zerhauen,
heimlich und öffentlich ertränkt
viel Weiber und Jungfrauen.
Die haben frei
ohn alle Scheu
der Wahrheit Zeugnis geben,
dass Jesus Christ
die Wahrheit ist,
der Weg und auch das Leben".[76]

---

[74] Wilhelm Neuser: Hans Hut. Leben und Wirken bis zum Nikolsburger Religionsgespräch, op. cit., S. 9-10. Johann Loserth: Hut, Hans, in: Christian Hege und Christian Neff (Hg.) Mennonitischee Lexikon, Zweiter Band, Frankfurt am Main und Weierhof, 1937, S. 370-375, bzw. S. 373.

[75] C. Arnold Snyder and Linda A. Huebert Hecht (Ed.): Profiles of Anabaptist Women. Sixteenth-Century Reforming Pioneers. Studies in Women and Religion, Volume 3, Waterloo: Wilfrid Laurier University Press, 1996.

[76] Lienhart Schiemer: Wie köstlich ist der Heilgen Tod, in: Heinold Fast (Hg.): Der linke Flügel der Reformation. Bremen, Carl Schünemann Verlag, 1962, S. 100-103 bzw. S. 102.

4. „Geet hin in die Welt und predigent das Evangelion aller Creaturen" (Markus 16,15): Nationen, Kulturen und Religionen

Das Mandat des auferstandenen Jesus „geet hin in die Welt und predigent das Evangelion aller Creaturen" erwarb im Denken Müntzers und Huts im 16. Jahrhundert große Bedeutung, wenn wir es in Bezug setzen zu der Ausbreitung des türkischen Reiches, dem Antisemitismus in Europa und dem Vorhandensein von heidnischen Sklaven, die aus Afrika[77] und der Neuen Welt ankamen[78]. Nach dem Fall Konstantinopels 1453 setzte das Osmanische Reich der Türken im 16. Jahrhundert seine Expansion in den Osten fort, bei dem die Gebiete Armenien, Mesopotamien, Syrien und Ägypten unter die Hand Süleymans II. (1520-1566) inkorporiert wurden. Es war der Sultan Süleyman II., der große Befürchtungen in Europa verbreitete, indem er Richtung Mitteleuropa vordrang, im Jahre 1521 Belgrad, 1525 Mohács (Mohatsch) und große Teile des ungarischen Gebiets eroberte, bis er im Jahre 1529 die Tore Wiens erreichte.[79]

Nach Ebermann[80] geht die protestantische Reformation hervor aus einer Bevölkerung, die der, von Rom angetriebenen, heiligen Kriege gegen die muslimische Welt überdrüssig waren. Die Idee eines neuen, von der römischen Herrschaft unabhängigen Nationalstaats verbindet sich mit den reformatorischen Gedanken und auch mit einer gewissen Sympathie für die Politik der Osmanen wegen der religiösen Toleranz, die sie während ihrer Ausbreitung nach Mitteleuropa anwendeten. Man konnte sie auch für ein Mittel der Strafe Gottes wegen der Korruption des Christentums halten, wie wir es

---

[77] Zur Expansion der Portugiesen in Afrika und den Sklavenhandel siehe: José Gebühr Rodriguez: Brasilien und Afrika: Outro Horizont, Rio de Janeiro: Editora Brasileira SA Civilização 1961, S. 2-34.

[78] Zu der deutschen Beteiligung an der Eroberung von Amerika vgl. Georg Friederici: El carácter del descubrimiento y de la conquista de América, Tomo II, México: Fondo de Cultura Económica, 1987, S. 204-248.

[79] Johannes Irmscher: Das Türkenbild Thomas Müntzers, in: Max Steinmetz (Hg.): Der deutsche Bauernkrieg und Thomas Müntzer. Karl-Marx-Universität Leipzig, 1976, S. 137.

[80] R. Ebermann: Die Türkenfurcht. Ein Beitrag zur Geschichte der öffentlichen Meinung in Deutschland während der Reformationszeit. Dissertation, Halle, 1904. Zitiert nach Johannes Irmscher, a.a.O., S. 137-138.

bei Müntzer und Luther[81] sehen. In der deutschen Literatur präsentiert das Gedicht „Des Türken Fastnachtsspiel", das im Jahre 1456 von dem Nürnberger Kupferschmied Hans Rosenplüt geschrieben wurde, den Sultan (der aus dem Fernen Osten kommt, wo Frieden herrscht und wo die Menschen steuerfrei leben) in der (vorgestellten) Situation, als er die christlichen Länder von Nürnberg erreicht und die Klagen der Verkäufer und Bauern über ihren Adel und das Raubrittertum hört.[82]

Die Öffnung Müntzers gegenüber Türken, Juden und Heiden ist seit den Anfängen seines Dienstes als Pfarrer in Zwickau in seiner Anschauung „Das Evangelium für/von alle/aller Kreatur" zu finden. Müntzer hatte seine Arbeit in der Marienkirche aufgrund der Empfehlung Luthers am 17. Mai 1520 begonnen. Nach der Rückkehr des Pastors Johann Silvius Egranus in die Marienkirche, setzte Müntzer seine pastoralen Aufgaben in der Kirche St. Katharinen (Zwickau) fort. Im April 1521 begann Müntzer theologische Diskussionen mit Egranus. Letzterer hielt dafür, dass die Gnade Christi als Befreiung von Sünden zu verstehen ist, die nur durch das Leiden und den Tod des Sohnes Gottes möglich ist. Egranus sah das Kreuz Christi als das Zentrum des Heils für die gesamte sündige Menschheit an; und dass es vor Christus nicht möglich gewesen war, weder volle Seligkeit noch die Fülle der Sündenvergebung zu erlangen. In Bezug auf Juden und Heiden erklärte Egranus: „Im Paradeiß hatt ehr (Christus) sich beweißtt den Juden und heiden, den heiden, die nach der vernunfft gelebt haben, die ein erbarlich, from leben gefuhrett haben etc. Den Juden, die das gesetz gehalden haben."[83]

---

[81] Sermón de campaña contra los turcos (1529), in: Martin Lutero, Obras de Martin Lutero, Volumen 2, Buenos Aires: Paidós-Aurora, S. 205-233. Luther, infolge seiner Angst vor einer Invasion der Osmanen 1529 bei Wien und seiner Sicht von den zwei Reichen, glaubt, dass die Christen sich im Kampf gegen die Türken im Namen der weltlichen Behörden (Fürsten) verteidigen müssen. Vgl. Walter: Lutero e Libertação. Releitura de Lutero em perspectiva latino-americana, São Paulo: Sinodal-Editora Ática, 1994, S. 229-240.

[82] H. Pfeiler: Das Türkenbild in den deutschen Chroniken des 15. Jahrhunderts. Dissertation, Frankfurt, 1956, S. 9 ff. Zitiert nach Johannes Irmscher, op. cit. p. 138.

[83] Johannes Sylvius Egranus: Ungedruckte Predigten des Johann Egranus Sylvius. Hg. v. Georg Buchwald, in: Quellen und Darstellungen aus der Geschichte des Reformations-

Müntzer widersprach der Theologie Egranus' anhand von drei Feststellungen.[84] In der ersten und dritten argumentiert er, dass für Juden und Heiden die Möglichkeit der Erlösung außerhalb von Christus und außerhalb des Gesetzes bestand, nicht nur, weil Christus und das Gesetz zeitlich nach der Schöpfung kamen, sondern auch weil er meinte, dass Gott seinen Geschöpfen, von dem Moment der Schöpfung an, den göttlichen Atem und die nötige Kraft gegeben hatte, um richtig zu handeln. Mit der zweiten Feststellung kritisierte Müntzer die Position Egranus', weil er meinte, dass diese den Glauben auf eine historische und intellektuelle Interpretation reduzierte, auf eine billige Gnade, bei der die Frucht des Kreuzes Christi letztendlich nur die war, gute Werke zu tun. Die Einschätzung Müntzers ist radikaler; seine Leidenstheologie fordert den Christen heraus, den Fußstapfen seines Lehrers zu folgen, an Christi Leiden und Schmerzen teilzuhaben.

Zu Beginn seines Dienstes in der Kirche St. Katharinen schloss Müntzer sich den ärmsten Zweigen der Tuchmacher an, vor allem den Zwickauer Propheten und Nikolaus Storch, der ihn mit der apokalyptischen Theologie der Taboriten beeinflusste und mit dem ihn eine innige Freundschaft verband.[85] Anschließend änderte sich die Zusammensetzung des Zwickauer Rats und Müntzer war nicht mehr so begünstigt wie zuvor. Des Aufruhrs beschuldigt, flieht Müntzer aus der Stadt und geht nach Prag, der Stadt, wo die Vor-Reform-Bewegung von Hans Hus geboren wurde. Wir wissen nicht, ob Müntzer jüdische und türkische Freunde hatte, aber sicher ist, dass die Reise nach Prag es ihm erlaubte, Menschen aus anderen Sprachen, Kulturen und Religionen kennenzulernen. Im Prager Manifest kann man bereits diese Sympathie für andere Völker und Nationen erkennen und seinen innigen Wunsch, dass die Christen den Türken und Juden ein wahrhaftiges Zeugnis

---

jahrhunderts. Bd. 18, Leipzig, 1911, S. 116. Zitiert nach Walter Elliger: Thomas Müntzer, S. 134-135.

[84] Thomas Müntzer: Angebliche Propositionen des Egranus (Zwickau?, 1521, vor April 16?), in Franz, MSB, S. 513, 1-2.

[85] Annemarie Lohmann: Zur geistigen Entwicklung Thomas Müntzers. Beiträge zur Kulturgeschichte des Mittelalters und der Renaissance. (Walter Goetz, Hg.), Band 47, Hildesheim, Verlag Dr. H.A. Gertenberg, 1972, S. 3-18.

ihres Glaubens bieten könnten.[86] Nachdem er Herzog Johann und Kurprinz Johann Friedrich von Sachsen am 13. Juli 1523 seine Botschaft aus dem Buch Daniel vorgestellt hatte, begriff Müntzer, dass man seitens der Fürsten der deutschen Gebiete und auch von den Wittenberger Reformatoren keine großen Veränderungen in Bezug auf die Erneuerung des Christentums und die Anforderungen des „gemeinen Mannes" erwarten konnte, die nach seiner Interpretation der Heiligen Schrift nötig gewesen wären. Zur gleichen Zeit war er auch Zeuge der schweren Krise Mitteleuropas im ersten Quartal des 16. Jahrhunderts: der Anwesenheit heidnischer Völker auf der anderen Seite des Meeres; den türkischen Invasionen in den christlichen Ländern, des Kampfes der deutschen Fürsten, die sich von der römischen Herrschaft trennen wollten; der Korruption des mittelalterlichen Christentums und der Aufstände der Bergleute, der Bauern und des Handwerks aufgrund ihrer unglücklichen wirtschaftlichen Lage.

Es war der Einbruch einer neuen Zeit, und er sah sich als von Gott gesandt, um die Ausgießung des Geistes Gottes unter den Völkern und Nationen, Türken und Heiden zu predigen. In seiner Schrift „Ausgedrückte Entblößung"[87], einer Interpretation des Glaubens Marias und Elisabeths im ersten Kapitel des Lukasevangeliums, kann man jene Aspekte bemerken, die der Grundlage seiner Theologie des ordo creaturarum Kontinuität geben, indem die weitreichende Bedeutung einer universellen Erlösung sichtbar wird. In dem vorherigen Schreiben, also in der „Fürstenpredigt" schien er die Hoffnung gehabt zu haben, die Fürsten würden seiner Offenbarung als neuem Propheten „Daniel" Beachtung schenken, und bereit sein, sich nicht nur von der Zentralmacht Roms zu distanzieren, sondern auch ihr Schwert in den Dienst der Bauern zu stellen. Als er sich der vollen Ablehnung seiner Botschaft seitens der Gelehrten und der Fürsten von Sachsen bewusst wird, fühlt sich Müntzer wie der Apostel Paulus von seinen eigenen Landsleuten abgelehnt und dazu berufen, das Evangelium den Türken und Heiden zu predigen. Das Prinzip

---

[86] In der Ausgabe von Franz Günther finden sich drei Fassungen des Prager Manifests: a) Kürzere deutsche Fassung b) Erweiterte deutsche Fassung und c) Lateinische Fassung. Vgl. Thomas Müntzer: Das Prager Manifest. 1. und 25. November 1521, in: Franz, MSB, S. 491-512.

[87] Thomas Müntzer: Ausgedrückte Entblösung, in: Franz, MSB, S. 265-319.

„ordo creaturarum" öffnet ihm die Tür dieser Bibelauslegung, denn wenn Gott der Schöpfer aller Lebewesen ist, dann auch der Heiden, Juden und Türken.

In einem Kontext, in dem das Christentum durch die Invasion der Türken, bedroht wird, die sich bereits den Toren Wiens näherten, erreicht Müntzers Predigt eine umstürzlerische Radikalität. In seiner offenen Auseinandersetzung mit den reformatorischen Führern Wittenbergs wirft Müntzer die folgende brennende Frage auf: „Was wissen dy torhafftigen menschen, was sie doch beweget, christen und nicht heiden zu sein, ader warumb das der alchoran nicht also warhafftig sey wie das evangelium?"[88] Und dies entwickelt sich nicht nur zu einer rhetorischen Frage, sondern entspricht seinem Verständnis von Gottes Wort. Er erachtet, dass die Überlegenheit des Evangeliums gegenüber dem Koran, dem heiligen Buch der Muslime, in der Schöpfungsordnung und der Ehrfurcht vor Gott erkannt werden sollte. Was die Herzen der Menschen berühren soll, ist nicht, die heiligen Schriften der Muslime zu disqualifizieren, wenn man denkt, dass nur die Offenbarung der Bibel die Wahrheit enthält, sondern zu verstehen, dass Gott mit dem Finger auf die Herzen seiner Geschöpfe schreibt, und das steht vor dem toten Wort. Sich an die Worte Jesu in Joh 6,45 anlehnend, erklärt Müntzer, im Geist des Propheten Jesaja (Jes. 54,13), dass Gott selbst unser Lehrer sein wollte. Dabei knüpft Müntzer an 1 Kor 1,18-31 an, wo Paulus die Weisheit Gottes, die Machtlosen und Verachteten zu erwählen, als Verrücktheit vor der Welt bezeichnet, und gleichzeitig die umgekehrte Weisheit der Welt als Verrücktheit vor Gott.[89] So bezeichnet er die Theologen, Schriftgelehrten, die keine Bereitschaft zur Busse, Schmerz zeigen, als die "Hochvertockten des Unglaubens" und schreit ihnen zu, dass die Türken, Juden und Heiden, die Menschen aus anderen Kulturen, auch Geschöpfe Gottes sind, die als solche direkt von Gott gelehrt werden können.

---

[88] Thomas Müntzer: Sendbrief an die Brüder zu Stolberg vom 18 Juli 1523, in: Franz, MSB, S. 23,19-21.

[89] Vgl. Franz J. Hinkelammert: Der Fluch, der auf dem Gesetz lastet. Paulus von Tarsus und das kritische Denken. Luzern: Exodus, 2011, 19ff.

Das Evangelium aller Kreatur 171

Müntzer behauptete, dass sich sein Wissen über die türkische Perspektive im Licht des Koran gebildet hatte[90], und trotz späterer Diskussionen über diese Behauptungen[91] basiert seine Schrift „Ausgedrückte Entblößung", in der wir das Thema des Evangeliums an Türken, Juden und Nichtjuden finden, auf den Texten des ersten Kapitels des Lukasevangeliums. Wenn wir diese Texte mit dem Koran[92] (a) Sure Nr. 3-Ãl-'Imrãm, ayat (Vers) Nr. 32-45 und b) Sure Nr. 19-Maryam, ayat (Vers) Nr. 1-41) vergleichen, werden wir die große Ähnlichkeit ihres Inhalts bemerken. Von den vier Evangelien enthält nur das Lukasevangelium diese beiden Erzählungen: a) die des Zacharias b) die Erscheinung des Engels bei Maria, der die Geburt Jesu ankündigt. Auf der anderen Seite sind die erwähnten Texte von Lukas die Erzählungen des Neuen Testaments, die im Koran am meisten widergespiegelt werden. Die Personen, deren Namen in beiden heiligen Büchern genannt werden, sind Zacharias und sein Sohn, der Prophet Johannes der Täufer (Yahya im Koran), Maria und ihr Sohn, Jesus von Nazareth. Dass der Schlüsseltext in „Ausgedrükte Entblößung" darin besteht, das Evangelium den Juden, Türken und Heiden zu predigen, führt uns zu der Annahme, dass Müntzer ausreichende Korankenntnisse hatte, die es ihm erlaubten, das erste Kapitel des Lukas als Anknüpfungspunkt und für das Verständnis der heiligen Bücher der erwähnten Völker zu wählen. Sowohl Zacharias wie Maria, Charaktere in beiden heiligen Texten, werden als Beispiele für einen Glauben gegeben, der wie ein Senfkorn wächst.

---

[90] Thomas Müntzer: Protestation oder Erbietung, in: Franz, MSB, S. 232,20-23.

[91] Arnulf Zitelmann bestätigt, dass Müntzer den Koran las. Siehe Arnulf Zitelmann: „Ich will donnern über sie!! Die Lebensgeschichte des Thomas Müntzer. Weinheim, Basel, 1989, S. 18. Dieter Fauth behauptet, dass Müntzer den Koran nicht gelesen haben konnte, weil die erste lateinische Ausgabe des Koran nicht vor dem Jahr 1543 erschien und die Toletaner Handschrift in Basel von ihm nicht herangezogen werden konnte, als Müntzer „Ausgedrückte Entblößung" schrieb, da sein erster Aufenthalt in Basel nicht vor dem Ende des Jahres 1524 war. Dieter Fauth, op. cit., S. 113.

[92] O sagrado Al-Corão. Texto arabe e tradução portuguêsa, Publicado sob os asuspicios de Hazrat Mirza Tahir Ahmad Quarto Sucessor do Missias Prometido Chefe do Movimento Ahmadiyya do Islá, Islam International Publications Ltda., Printed in Breat Britain at the Alden Press, Oxford, 1988, S. 51-54 und 289-292.

Müntzer sah eine große Einmischung der Juden, Türken und anderer heidnischer Nationen (Heiden) in Europa voraus, als er sagte: „Ist aller geprechen im selbigen, das keiner der türcken, heiden, juden und aller unglawbigen will in der ankunfft seines glawbens gleich sein, sundern ein ieder nutzet und putzet sich mit seinem glauben und wercken, welcher beyder er widder grund nach podem weys."[93] Vor und nach dieser Aussage steht eine harte Kritik an der mittelalterlichen Christenheit, um den Bereich des Evangeliums für die Türken, Juden und Nichtjuden zu öffnen. Müntzer stützt seine Position auf das Evangelium des Matthäus 9,10-13, wo Jesus und seine Jünger dafür kritisiert werden, im Gespräch mit den Zöllnern und Sündern zu sein. Der andere Text, den er angibt, ist 1. Petrus 3,18-21, in dem es heißt: „Denn auch Christus hat `einmal` für die Sünden gelitten, der Gerechte für die Ungerechten, damit er euch zu Gott führte, und ist getötet nach dem Fleisch, aber lebendig gemacht nach dem Geist. In ihm ist er auch hingegangen und hat gepredigt den Geistern im Gefängnis, die einst ungehorsam waren, als Gott harrte und Geduld hatte zur Zeit Noahs, als man die Arche baute, in der wenige, nämlich acht Seelen, gerettet wurden durchs Wasser hindurch. Das ist ein Vorbild der Taufe, die jetzt auch euch rettet. Denn in ihr wird nicht der Schmutz vom Leib abgewaschen, sondern wir bitten Gott um ein gutes Gewissen, durch die Auferstehung Jesu Christi." Er meinte, dass, wenn Jesus in seiner Zeit auf der Erde die Zöllner und Sünder wichtig waren, und er sogar bis in den Tod ging, um denen aus der Zeit Noahs zu predigen, es mit viel mehr Grund notwendig wäre, auch im hier und jetzt das wahre Evangelium Christi zu hinterlassen, in den Herzen der Menschen, die nicht Teil dieses korrupten Christentums waren.

Wenn es darum ginge, die Schöpfungsordnung durch die Erfüllung der Gebote Gottes aufrechtzuhalten, so wie es das korrupte Christentum tat, wäre das laut Müntzer für Türken, Juden und Heiden keine schwierige Aufgabe gewesen. Und er verspottet die Unbeständigkeit der Christenheit in ihrem eigenen Glauben und sagte: „Das kanstu woll abnemen, wenn ein Jud oder Türk unter uns solte seyn und solte durch disen glauben, den wir noch zur

---

[93] Thomas Müntzer: Von dem gedichteten Glauben, in: Franz, MSB, S. 221,13-16.

zeyt haben, gebessert werden, da solt er wol vil gewinß treyben, als vil ein muck auf irem schwantz möcht wegfüren, ya noch vil weniger."[94]

In den Schriften von Hans Hut, die nach den Veröffentlichungen Müntzers erschienen, finden wir Anklänge an seinen Lehrer. In seiner Schrift „Von dem Geheimnis der Taufe" bezieht er sich zwar nicht so deutlich wie Müntzer auf die Türken, aber wir finden klare Hinweise auf Heiden und Juden. Der Ausgangspunkt des „Evangeliums aller Creatur" ist immer vorhanden, die Tiere haben den göttlichen Atem erhalten, und bevor es das geschriebene Gesetz gab und Jesus von Nazareth geboren wurde, ist in der ganzen Schöpfung der Wille ihres Schöpfers niedergeschrieben. So erklärte Hut es in seiner Schrift: „Und alle Menschen gehen auch so mit den Kreaturen um (wie das Gesetz es darstellt), auch die Heiden, die das schriftliche Gesetz nicht haben und doch das Gleiche tun, was die tun, welche das schriftliche Gesetz haben. Das schriftliche Gesetz zeigt, wie man die Tierlein schlachten muss, ehe man sie Gott opfert. Danach wurden sie erst gegessen. So tun es auch die Heiden, die das Gesetz der Natur haben. Sie essen kein Tier lebendig. So müssen wir zuvor der Welt absterben und in Gott leben. Im Gesetz hat man bei den Ampeln eine kleine Lichtschere. So haben es auch die Heiden für ihre Leuchter und so fast in allen Zeremonien und Geboten. Darum beschreibt Moses sein Buch mit solchen Zeremonien der Kreaturen, auf dass er die Menschen erinnert und ermahnt, dass sie Gottes Willen darin erforschen und erlernen. Wie deshalb das Gesetz in allen Kreaturen beschrieben und dargestellt ist, so lesen wir es täglich in unsern Wirken. In diesem Buch gehen wir täglich um, und die ganze Welt ist voll und voll des Willens Gottes geschrieben."[95]

Müntzer verstand die gefährliche Zeit, in der er lebte, in apokalyptischen Begriffen, sah die Christen zusammen mit allen Auserwählten, Nationen und Konfessionen vor dem Angesicht des Boten (Offenbarung Kap. 10), wo sie vor dem Thron des Gerichts Rechenschaft geben mussten, dazu auch die, die sich wirklich unter der Furcht Gottes befanden. Der Glaube der Türken, Juden und Nichtjuden würde wachsen müssen wie Zacharias' und Marias Senf-

---

[94] Thomas Müntzer: Ausgedrückte Entblößung, in: Franz, MSB, S. 312, 22-30.
[95] Hans Hut: Von dem Geheimnis der Taufe, op. cit., p. 90.

korn-Glaube, der in der Furcht Gottes zu finden war, sie würden ihren Unglauben und ihre Ängste überwinden müssen. Und er, Müntzer, fühlt sich dazu ausgesendet, die Ausgießung des Geistes Gottes unter den Türken und Heiden Gott zu predigen, weil Gott, wie auch Jesus mit dem römischen Hauptmann (Matthäus 8,11), alle Konfessionen und Nationen zu Tisch geladen hatte. Während die natürlichen Erben (Juden) ausgeschlossen wurden, gingen die Nationen an seinem Tisch essen. Für diesen in Stolberg geborenen Prediger ist es die gleiche Fülle des Geistes in den Körpern von Elisabeth und Maria (wie im Lukas-Evangelium beschrieben), die in der Apostelgeschichte Kapitel 10 am Werk ist, als Gott die gottgläubigen Gebete und die Ehrfurcht des römischen Hauptmanns Cornelius hört; Gott spricht im Traum dann zu Petrus, um die natürlichen Erben zu beschämen und zu zeigen, dass die Verheißung des Evangeliums allen Geschöpfen gilt.

Der Prophet mit dem felsenfesten Glauben bezieht die Worte des Apostels Paulus in Antiochia in Pisidien (Apostelgeschichte 13,47 und 49) auf sich selbst, die wiederum aus Jesaja 49,6 stammen: „...ich habe dich auch zum Licht der Heiden gemacht, dass du seist mein Heil bis an die Enden der Erde." Und über die „Besitzung" Gottes in jedem Geschöpf verkündet er: „Ich sag es euch, allerliebsten brüder, es ist mir nicht zu verschweygen, ich wolt ehe heyden, Türcken und Juden unterrichten mit dem allergeringsten wort, von Gott und seyner ordnung zu reden, von der besitzung nach uns und zu Got zu rechen..."[96]

Die Predigt Müntzers macht den Widerspruch von Johannes dem Täufer und Jesus gegen Herodes und Schriftgelehrten deutlich. Danach identifiziert er seine prophetische Stimme mit dem Wirken Johannes' des Täufers. Drittens bezichtigt er die Schriftgelehrten seiner Zeit, sie verdeckten mit dem Evangelium die Realität der Unterdrückung von Bauern, Bergleuten und Handwerkern. Für eine Christenheit, die seit mehreren Jahrhunderten „heilige Kriege" mit dem Islam führte, wurde der vierte Aspekt unerträglich, da Gott angekündigt hatte, er wolle ein neues Reich bauen, das „niemals zerstört werden würde" (Daniel 2,44), in dem alle Auserwählten der Welt seien, d.h.

---

[96] Thomas Müntzer: Ausgedrückte Entblößung, in: Franz, MSB, p. 314,3-10.

solche, die aus Ehrfurcht vor Gott seine Gebote halten und diese könnten Christen, Juden, Türken und Heiden sein.

Die Vision von einer gerechteren Welt, an der Menschen unterschiedlicher Sprachen, Christen, Juden, Türken und Heiden gemeinsam teilhaben können, hat für Müntzer und Hut drei Ausgangspunkte: a) Alle Völker der Erde, unabhängig von Kultur und Religion,[97] haben den göttlichen Atem des Lebens, sind Gottes Geschöpfe. b) Alle Völker der Erde, unabhängig von Kultur und Religion, können, wenn sie Gott fürchten und seine Gebote halten, in der gleichen einzigartigen, von Gott geschaffenen, Welt zusammen leben. c) Die Türken werden im Endgericht Instrumente Gottes gegen die Korruption des Christentums sein. Andere Denker jener Zeit wie Johannes Cochläus, ein erklärter Feind der protestantischen Reformation, verfälschten diese universelle Botschaft und den Aufstand der Bauern so: a) Rechtfertigung der Gewalt der Fürsten gegen die Bauern, die ihr Recht einforderten; b) Ausnutzung der mittelalterlichen Menschenfeindlichkeit gegen Juden, Türken, Heiden, um die Tötung von Bauern zu rechtfertigen; c) Indem dem Evangelium die Grundlage entzogen wurde, die der „gemeine Mann" im Aufstand für seine Rechte einsetzte; d) Verurteilung der Aufständischen zur ewigen Verdammnis.[98]

---

[97] Hans Jürgen Goertz (Hg.): Radikale Reformatoren. 21 biographische Skizzen von Paracelsus bis Thomas Müntzer, München 1978.

[98] Johannes Cochläus' (1479-1552) Antwort auf Luthers Schrift, in: Klaus Ebert (Hg.), Thomas Müntzer im Urteil der Geschichte. Von Martin Luther bis Ernst Bloch, Wuppertal, Hammer, 1990, S. 61. Cochläus, erklärter Feind der Reformation, traf Luther beim Reichstag in Worms (1521). Cochläus glaubte, Luther sei für den Aufstand der Bauern verantwortlich. Diese hätten Thüringen und auch noch nicht ganz Deutschland erreicht, seien (aber) angeregt durch die Predigten und die Schriften von Martin Luther.

5. "Geet hin in die Welt und predigent das Evangelion aller Creaturen" (Markus 16,15): der „gemeine Mann"

Max Steinmetz[99] sowie Günter Vogler[100] betrachten die Jahre zwischen 1517 und 1525/1526 als Schlüssel für die Entstehung der protestantischen Reformation und den Höhepunkt der Bauernkämpfe. Dieser Zeitraum, interpretiert anhand der historischen Prämissen Lenins und Marx', wird als "reifere Stufe" der frühbürgerlichen Revolution in Deutschland bezeichnet. Und sie wird gekennzeichnet durch eine erhöhte Produktion seitens der Arbeiter (Bergarbeiter) dank einer Reihe technischer Entdeckungen, das Wachstum der Textilindustrie, die Entstehung eines nationalen Bewusstseins nicht nur bei Adel und Bürgertum, sondern auch bei den einfachen Leuten, die Krise des mittelalterlichen Feudalismus und die Entstehung der ausbeuterischen Beziehungen im aufkeimenden Kapitalismus. In diesem Zusammenhang entstehen der Protestantismus, die antiklerikalen Kämpfe gegen die katholische Kirche, der Kampf des Fürstentums gegen die Zentralgewalt (Adel), die Kämpfe der Stände gegen die Kirche, sowie die Bauernkriege gegen die Fürsten und die großen mittelalterlichen Lehen. Eine andere Perspektive der Interpretation dieses historischen Moments geht von den Prämissen Max Webers aus[101], bei dem der Impuls für die strukturellen Veränderungen herrührt aus der Reformbewegung, die durch den Zusammenschluss der protestantischen Ethik mit dem Geist des Kapitalismus entstand. Eine weitere Sichtweise ist die Peter Blickles, der die Aspekte des gesellschaftlichen sowie theologischen Wandels berücksichtigt, um zu bestätigen, dass strukturelle Veränderungen das Ergebnis der „Auseinandersetzung zwischen Feudalismus und Kommunalismus" sind.[102] Jedoch ist sowohl für die Theoretiker

---

[99] Max Steinmetz: Die frühbürgerliche Revolution in Deutschland 1476-1535, in: Max Steinmetz (Hg.): Die frühbürgerliche Revolution in Deutschland. DDR, Akademie-Verlag Berlin, 1985, S. 38-48.

[100] Günter Vogler: Revolutionäre Bewegung und frühbürgerliche Revolution, in: Max Steinmetz (Hg.): Die frühbürgerliche Revolution in Deutschland. a.a.O., S. 202-223

[101] Max Weber: Die protestantische Ethik und der Geist des Kapitalismus. in: ders., Gesammelte Aufsätze zur Religionssoziologie I, Tübingen 1972 S. 17-206.

[102] Peter Blickle: Die Reformation im Reich. Stuttgart, Verlag Eugen Ulmer, 1982, S. 159.

der „frühbürgerlichen Revolution" wie für Peter Blickle die Rolle des „gemeinen Mannes" (Handwerker, Bergknappen, Bauern) in der protestantischen Reformation und der Bauernrevolution von grundlegender Bedeutung. Thomas Müntzer und Hans Hut waren von 1517 bis 1527 die Protagonisten der Reformation und der Bauernaufstände mit einer theologischen, politischen und pastoralen Vision, die vom „gemeinen Mann" ausging und aus der sich ihr Verständnis des Missionsbefehls „geet hin in die Welt und predigent das Evangelion aller Creaturen" (Markus 16,15) entwickelte.

Müntzers Sympathie für die Reformationsbewegung, die Luther im Jahre 1517 in Wittenberg initiiert hatte, verfestigte sich, als er wiederholt die theologischen Diskussionen in Wittenberg besuchte. Bereits 1520 beginnt Müntzer auf Empfehlung Luthers, seine Arbeit als Pfarrer in der Marienkirche in Zwickau und später in der Katharinenkirche. Letztere war eine aus Handwerkern und Bergknappen bestehende Gemeinschaft, reichlich beeinflusst von den Zwickauer Propheten, deren Leiter Nikolaus Storch war.[103] Die Linie der theologischen Überlegungen und des pastoralen Engagements für den „gemeinen Mann" kann von seinen frühen Schriften im Jahre 1521 bis zu Müntzers Tod 1525 während des Bauernkriegs gesehen werden. Der Bauer und Handwerker Hut wurde seinerseits im gleichen Zeitraum einer von Müntzers Jüngern und treuen Anhängern bis zu Huts Tod im Gefängnis im Jahr 1527.

Vom theologischen Standpunkt aus verstand Müntzer die Schöpfung als das erste Buch, in dem Gott sich offenbarte. Und heraus aus seiner detaillierten Beobachtung des Lebens des „gemeinen Mannes" inmitten der Schöpfung, setzte er diesen in Beziehung mit dem Evangelium. Seine erste Schrift „Das Prager Manifest"[104] von 1521 ist, im Einklang mit der antiklerikalen Predigt Luthers, eine Beschwerde gegen die Gelehrten und Pfaffen, die den Sinn des Wortes verdrehen, so dass es gegen die Interessen des Volkes steht. In seiner Predigt vor den Fürsten im Schloss Allstedt am 13. Juli 1524 kann man wahrnehmen, dass er das Evangelium jeder Kreatur aus der Perspektive

---

[103] Paul Wappler: Thomas Müntzer in Zwickau und die Zwickauer Propheten (1908). Gütersloh, Gütersloher Verlagshaus, 1966.
[104] Thomas Müntzer: Das Prager Manifest. Erweiterte deutsche Fassung. In: Franz, MSB, S. 495-505.

des „gemeinen Mannes" beurteilt. Das Christentum wird angesehen wie die Menschen in Israel, d. h. wie ein Weinberg, der von Gott gepflanzt, gepflegt, gedüngt und umzäunt wurde, der aber zur Zeit der Ernte nur saure Trauben produzierte. Der Schöpfer hatte Früchte der Gerechtigkeit erwartet, hörte aber nur Schreie der Ungerechtigkeit (Jesaja 5,1-7, Psalm 80,9-14). Die neutestamentlichen Texte, die diese Schilderung begleiten, sind Markus 4,26-29 und Lukas 8,5-15, um zu zeigen, dass Christus, die Apostel und Propheten ein rechtschaffenes und reines Christentum begonnen hatten. Das Herz der Lebewesen ist zu sehen wie der Garten, den Gott bebaut, um die Samen des Evangeliums hinein zu säen. Aber die Realität war, dass die Christenheit korrupt geworden war und aus ihrem Schoß der Drachen, das Tier und die unreinen Geister der falschen Propheten gekomen waren, die sich mit den Königen der Erde verbündeten, um gegen Gott zu kämpfen (Offenbarung 16,13).[105]

Hut, der Bauer, der die letzten Jahre seines Lebens damit verbrachte, die Ideale der Radikalen Reformation durch Flugblätter und die Bücher der Reformer, die er einband, zu verbreiten, berichtet auch von der Bedeutung des Evangeliums ausgehend vom „gemeinen Mann", wenn er sagt: „Weil man aber Gottes Kraft und Gottheit oder sein unsichtbares Wesen wahrnehmen und erkennen kann an den Werken oder Kreaturen aller Geschöpfe von der Welt an, so muss man aufmerken und betrachten, wie Christus dem gemeinen Mann das Himmelreich und die Kraft des Vaters stets darstellt in einer Kreatur durch ein Gleichnis, durch Handwerk in allen Werken, mit denen die Menschen umgeben. Den armen Mann hat er nicht auf die Bücher verwiesen, wie jetzt unsere Schriftgelehrten ohne Verstand tun, sondern hat das Evangelium bei ihrer Arbeit gelehrt und bezeugt, den Bauern bei Acker, Samen, Disteln, Dornen und Fels (Matth. 13,3 ff.; Markus 4,3ff.; Luk. 8,4ff.; Joh. 12,24)."[106] Und dann fügt er hinzu: "Den Gärtner lehrt er das Evangeliums durch das Beispiel der Bäume, den Fischer durch das des Fischfangs, den Zimmermann durch das Beispiel des Hauses, den Goldschmied durch das der Läuterung des Goldes, die Weiber durch das Beispiel des Teigs (Matth.

---

[105] Thomas Müntzer: Auslegung des anderen Unterschieds Daniels. In: Franz, MSB, S. 243

[106] Hans Hut: Von dem Geheimnis der Taufe. op. cit., S. 86.

Das Evangelium aller Kreatur.

13,33; Luk. 13,20 f.; I Kor. 5,6; Gal. 5,9), die Weingärtner am Beispiel von Weingarten, Weinstock und Reben (Jes. 5,1 ff.; Jer. 2,21; Matth. 20, 1 ff.; Luk. 20,9 ff.; Joh. 15,1 ff.), die Schneider durch den Flecken auf einem alten Kleid (Matth. 9,16)."[107]

Wenn der Kontext der Reformation für alle Reformer derselbe war, wie ist es dann möglich, dass Müntzer und Hut mit Luther eine direkte Konfrontation über den „gemeinen Mann" begannen? Historisch kann man sagen, dass Luther von den Fürsten von Sachsen darin unterstützt wurde, die Erneuerungsbewegung der Reformation möglich zu machen. Müntzer radikalisiert Luthers Vorschläge, indem er nicht nur an die nationalistischen und antiklerikalen Kämpfe gegen Rom dachte, sondern auch das Stöhnen des „gemeinen Mannes" angesichts der Unterdrückung durch die Fürsten hörte. Müntzers theologische Sicht des „gemeinen Mannes" war immer der Horizont, der ihn dazu führte, der Theologie, die von Wittenberg ausging, zu misstrauen; und als die Fürsten im Jahr 1524 ablehnten, seine apokalyptische Botschaft des Buches Daniel zu berücksichtigen, war dies der Höhepunkt, der seine Hoffnung zerschlug, dass die Fürsten den Prozess der sozialen Transformation unterstützen würden, welche die armen Leute erstrebten. In der „Fürstenpredigt" wird deutlich, dass er die Bilder aus der Zerstörung der irdischen Reiche im Traum von König Nebukadnezar auf das „Evangelium allen Geschöpfen" aus der Perspektive des „gemeinen Mannes" überträgt. Bei der Kritik an den beliebten Götzenbildern von Jesus, der in einer Krippe geboren wurde, glaubte Müntzer, dass es nicht möglich sei, dass Jesus Christus als „menlín" gemalt würde. Vergleicht man die Gesellschaft seiner Zeit mit den Weinberg-Gleichnissen, störte Müntzer sich an den Mächtigen, die Jesus Christus als „Vogelscheuche" aus Stroh betrachteten, die inmitten der Aussaat stand, leblos war und vom Wind hin- und her bewegt wurde. Müntzer interpretierte Jesus Christus als „Eckstein", der, wie zur Zeit des Römischen Reiches, die alten Strukturen des mittelalterlichen Christentums zerspalten würde.

Als die Reformation und die Kämpfe des „gemeinen Mannes" voranschritten, war der einzige gemeinsame Punkt zwischen Luther und Müntzer die antiklerikale Bewegung und der Kampf gegen Rom. Die harten Bezeichnun-

---

[107] Ebd., S. 87.

gen, die Müntzer und Hans Hut später für Luther verwendeten, sind identisch: „Bruder Mastschwein", „Bruder Sanftleben", und sie beschreiben die Rolle des Schriftgelehrten als jemand, der ein komfortables Leben in den Schlössern der Fürsten führte und das Evangelium nach deren Interesse auslegte. Der Brennpunkt der Uneinigkeit zwischen Müntzer und Hut auf der einen und Luther auf der anderen Seite hat mit den theologischen und pastoralen Entscheidungen über den „gemeinen Mann" zu tun. In den Erklärungen Müntzers, nachdem er ins Gefängnis gebracht und bevor er im Mai 1525 öffentlich hingerichtet wurde, erfahren wir von seiner Beteiligung an der Entwicklung von 12 Artikeln, die zum fordernden Programm des „gemeinen Mannes" wurden.[108]

Die Lehre von den zwei Regimentern, die die Trennung der feudalen Königreiche der Fürsten von der geistigen und wirtschaftlichen Zentralmacht der Kirche in Rom erlaubte, war die gleiche, die für Luther die Grundlage bildete, um die Niederschlagung der Bauern, Bergleute und Textilarbeiter durch die Armeen der Fürsten zu unterstützen. Beide Prediger gehen in ihren Überlegungen von Römer 13,1-7 aus. Luther betont die Verse 1 und 2, um die revoltierenden Bauern dazu aufzurufen, sich der von Gott eingesetzten Autorität unterzuordnen. Dahingegen geht Müntzer von den Versen 3 und 4 aus, um zu unterstreichen, dass das Schwert von den Behörden verwendet muss, Gutes zu tun, für Gerechtigkeit zu sorgen, und nicht als Mittel der Repression dem gegenüber, der Gutes tut. Nach Müntzer ist der Fürst nicht der über dem Gesetz stehende absolute Herrscher, sondern ihm ist das Schwert gegeben, um Gottes Willen auszuführen. Wenn der Fürst das Schwert dazu missbraucht, das Volk zu unterdrücken, dann ist es dessen Recht, ihm das Schwert zu entreißen.[109]

Die zwölf Artikel der Bauern sind eine Beschwerdeschrift, denn sie erheben Einspruch gegen die Wirtschaftsbedingungen, den begrenzten Zugang zu Jagd und Fischerei, die beschränkte Verwendung von Brennholz aus dem

---

[108] Bekenntnis Thomas Müntzers vom 16 Mai 1525. in: Franz, MSB, S. 544, 11-15.
[109] Eike Wolgast: Die Obrigkeits- und Widerstandslehre Thomas Müntzer. in: Siegfried und Helmar Junghans (Hg.): Der Theologe Thomas Müntzer. Untersuchungen zu einer Entwicklung und Lehre. Göttingen, Vandenhoeck & Ruprecht, 1989, S. 62-83, bzw. S. 195-220.

Wald, den Verlust der gemeinsamen Produktionsgrundstücke und die unbegrenzten Dienstforderungen, durch die sie seitens Fürsten unterjocht waren. Die zwölf Artikel wurden zur Reformagenda des „gemeinen Mannes", weil sie eine Befreiung von den alten feudalen Verpflichtungen verlangten, die sie von den Feudalherren abhängig machten. Während sie sich wünschten, von den Strafen befreit zu werden, denen sie nach dem römischen Recht unterworfen waren, sollten die Feudalherren auf den Tribut verzichten, den Witwen zahlen, wenn ihre Ehemänner starben, weswegen diese und die Waisen arm wurden; der Zehnte für die Unterstützung des Klerus sollte auf den „großen Zehnten" (Weizen und andere Agrarprodukte) beschränkt werden, während der kleine Zehnte (Anteile des Viehs und Milchprodukte) auslaufen sollte; sie forderten das Recht der Gemeinde, ihre eigenen Pfarrer zu wählen. Alle Artikel werden von biblischen Texten einschließlich Galater 3,28 unterstützt „Hier ist kein Jude noch Grieche, hier ist kein Knecht noch Freier, Hier ist kein Mann noch Weib; denn ihr seid allzumal einer in Christo Jesu." Der letzte Artikel besagt, dass, wenn einer der Artikel der Heiligen Schrift widerspreche, die Bauern zustimmen würden, diesen zurückzuziehen, vorausgesetzt, es wird festgestellt, dass dieser nicht im Einklang mit Gottes Wort ist. Die zwölf Artikel sind ein revolutionäres Manifest, da sie der bestehenden wirtschaftlichen und sozialen Ordnung trotzen und verlangen, dass diese Ordnung gemäß dem von Gott gegebenen Recht, das heißt im Einklang mit dem Evangelium, transformiert wird.[110]

Luther reagierte mit seiner Schrift "Ermahnung zum Frieden auf die zwölf Artikel der Bauerschaft in Schwaben" zunächst mit der Anerkennung vieler Beschwerden der Bauern und war auf Ausgleich bedacht, verbot aber dem „gemeinen Mann", das göttliche Recht und das Evangelium als Grundlage für ihre Forderungen in den 12 Artikeln zu nutzen: „Lieben brueder, yhr fueret den namen Gottes, und nennet euch eyne Christliche rotte odder vereynigung vnd gebt fur, yhr woellet nach dem goettlichen recht faren vnd handeln,

---

[110] Günther Franz: Die Entstehung der „Zwölf Artikel" der deutschen Bauernschaft. Archiv für Reformationsgeschichte, Nr. 36, 1939, S. 193-213. Peter Blickle, op. cit., S. 104-105.

Wolan, so wisset yhr ia auch, das Gottes name, wort vnd titel, soll nicht vergeblich noch unnuetze anzogen werden..."[111]

Müntzer im Gegenzug hört im schmerzvollen Aufschrei der Bauern und Bäuerinnen, der Witwen, der Waisen, der Armen – d. h. des „gemeinen Mannes", die Stimme der Propheten des Evangeliums. Der „gemeine Mann" ist Teil des Evangeliums aller Kreatur, nicht nur in dem Maße, dass er als Kreatur das Bild Gottes widerspiegelt, oder weil er das Evangelium in der hinreichenden Evidenz der Schöpfung und durch die große Schaffenskraft ihrer Hände erkennt, sondern auch, weil er aufgrund der erlebten Ungerechtigkeiten und Schmerzen zu Gott schreit. Er wendet sich an die Gebote des Evangeliums, die in der Thora, den Propheten, durch Jesus und die Apostel ausgedrückt werden, um seine Rechte als ein Geschöpf Gottes einzufordern.

Das Ergebnis der Aufstände des „gemeinen Mannes" durch sein Manifest der 12 Artikel hatte im Jahr 1525 eine große Wirkung in Deutschland. Die Fürsten und Herren der großen feudalen Gebiete, die noch immer getrennt waren durch die Uneinigkeiten, die die protestantische Reformation hervorgebracht hatte, schlossen ihre Armeen gegen die Aufständischen zusammen. Am 12. Mai wurden die Aufständischen von Württemberg in Böblingen, am 15. Mai die Thüringer Aufständischen auf den Feldern von Frankenhausen geschlagen, am 16. Mai wurden die Elsässer Aufständischen in Zabern und am 2. Juni die Aufständischen aus Franken in Königshofen besiegt. Nach den Berechnungen jener Zeit starben etwa 100.000 Bauern, Bergleute und Textilarbeiter auf dem Schlachtfeld oder durch den Galgen und Hunderte von Dörfern wurden verbrannt, zerstört und in Staub und Asche gelegt.[112] Die von Luther ausgerufene Lehre von der Rechtfertigung durch den Glauben, vermischt mit der Lehre von der Unterwerfung unter die Autoritäten, verlor im Rahmen der revolutionären Forderungen des „gemeinen Mannes" ihre anfängliche prophetische Pracht, die sie als antiklerikaler Aufruf und als antirömische Nationalbewegung gehabt hatte. Unterdessen nahm Müntzer in dieser schwierigen Zeit sein pastorales Engagement für den „gemeinen Mann" auf sich und nahm dessen Forderungen im Einklang mit der Ankün-

---

[111] Martin Luther, Werke. Weimarer Ausgabe 18, 1908, S. 305 bzw. 301 f.
[112] Peter Blickle. op. cit., S. 109.

Das Evangelium aller Kreatur.

digung der Propheten und des Evangeliums wahr: „Ir werdt sehen, Got wyrt euch beystehen. Forcht, dicht nicht, du kleyns heufleyn, dan es gefelt dem starken Got von Sabaoth, seynen namen eyn mall lassen vor der prechtygen welt sehen. (...) Ir musth das ampt teglich treyben myt dem geleß des gesetz der propheten und evangelisten, auff das die text dem gemeynen manne gleych so leuftig seynt wie dem prediger (...)."[113]

Hut wurde in Frankenhausen Zeuge der Verkündigung Müntzers, der die Bauern in ihrem Kampf gegen die Armeen der Fürsten ermutigte, und behauptete, den Regenbogen gesehen zu haben, von dem Müntzer angekündigt hatte, er würde dem Bund Gottes mit seinem auserwählten Volk Glaubwürdigkeit verleihen. Danach, erschreckt durch die Tausenden von enthaupteten Bauern auf den Feldern von Frankenhausen, flüchtete Hut. Müntzer und der Pfarrer von Mühlhausen, Pfeiffer wurden lebendig gefangen und ins Gefängnis gebracht, wo sie gefoltert und dann öffentlich hingerichtet wurden. Müntzer war konsequent in der Ausübung seiner pastoralen Entscheidungen und in seinem Verständnis der Verkündigung des Evangeliums aller Geschöpfe ausgehend vom „gemeinen Mann". In seinem letzten Brief an die Bürger von Mühlhausen[114] und seinem Widerruf[115] aus dem Gefängnis, in dem er um Schutz für seine Frau und seinen Sohn bittet, offenbart er seinen Zustand, der dem der Bauern und dem „gemeinen Mann" gleicht, er ist bekümmert von der vollständigen Schutzlosigkeit seiner Familie nach der Niederlage gegen die Armeen der Fürsten. Hut seinerseits, der lebend aus dem Krieg fliehen konnte, hatte sich in sein Dorf in Bibra begeben, und hatte noch die frischen Erinnerungen an den ungleichen Kampf zwischen den Bauern und den schwer bewaffneten, an die Kreuzzugskriege gewöhnten Soldaten, das schaurige Geräusch galoppierender Pferdehufe und die erschreckenden Schreie derer, die gerade durch das Schwert gestorben waren, vor Augen, und konnte nicht aufhören über sein Verständnis der Bedeutung der Taufe, über die Kommunion und den Götzendienst zu predigen. In seiner Botschaft hallten die Worte Müntzers wider: gegen die Geistlichen, die von den erzwungenen

---

[113] Thomas Müntzer: Brief Müntzers an seinen Freund Jeori, undatiert, in: Franz, MSB, S. 426.
[114] Müntzer an die Mühlhäuser. Heldrungen, 17. Mai 1525. in: Franz, MSB, S. 473, 15-18.
[115] Thomas Müntzers Widerruf. Heldrungen, 17. Mai 1525, in: Franz, MSB, S. 550, 28-30.

Zehnten profitierten und die angeblich das Evangelium predigten; gegen die Ungerechtigkeit der Fürsten, indem er (Hut) das Evangelium ausgehend vom „gemeinen Mann" prophezeite.[116] Wegen seiner radikalen Predigt zwangen ihn die örtlichen Behörden im Juni 1525, Bibra zu verlassen, weshalb er seine Frau und Kinder zurücklassen musste. Durch sein Umherziehen durch viele Orte belebte Hut sein Verständnis des Auftrags „gehet in die Welt und predigt das Evangelium aller Kreatur", und entwickelte sich dadurch zu dem eifrigsten anabaptistischen Missionar im südlichen Deutschland und Österreich.

6. „Geet hin in die Welt und predigent das Evangelion aller Creaturen" (Markus 15,16): Taufe in Feuer, Wasser und Blut

In den Schriften von Müntzer und Hut wird der Missionsauftrag in Markus 16,15 mit unterschiedlichen Interpretationen der Taufe in Verbindung gebracht. Obwohl es Unterschiede in der Wahrnehmung der Taufe gibt, kann man bei beiden Theologen sehen, wie sich die Bedeutung der Taufe mit den Dimensionen Feuer, Wasser und Blut durchzieht. Bei Müntzer finden wir eine sehr starke Beschwerde gegen die Mönche, die das Volk und die Nicht-Gläubigen täuschten, weil sie predigten, dass das Ritual der Wassertaufe für die Erlösung ausreichend sei. Bei den Kreuzzügen der Christen gegen Mauren und Türken, und später bei der Eroberung der Neuen Welt, wurde die Taufe als Zeichen der Errettung dargestellt, und verwandelte sich gleichzeitig auch in ein Symbol der Eroberung, denn es war das Ritual, das bei den Menschen angewandt wurde, damit diese ihre bisherigen Gottesüberzeugungen verließen und Teil des Christentums würden.[117] Im Prager Manifest bezeichnet Müntzer jene (Christen) als „teuffels Pfaffen", weil „Sie sprechen mit bloßen worthen: 'Wer do gleubet und ist getaufft, der wirdt selig'."[118] D.h. sie

---

[116] Wilhelm Neuser: Hans Hut, op. cit., S. 22-23.

[117] Bei der Eroberung der Neuen Welt unterschieden sich die Aktionen der Deutschen nicht von den spanischen und portugiesischen, wie Bartolomé de las Casas mit Bezug auf das von den Welsern erworbene Venezuela berichtet. Vgl. Georg Friederici, op. cit. S. 227-248.

[118] Thomas Müntzer: Das Prager Manifest, in: Franz, MSB, S. 503, 15-16.

verfälschten die tiefere Bedeutung von Markus 16,15 in dem Ausmaß, dass weder Türken noch Juden die „unüberwindliche Begründung" des Glaubens der Auserwählten hören könnten.

Während seiner Amtszeit als Pfarrer in verschiedenen Gemeinden und Kirchen führte Müntzer die Praxis der Kindertaufe fort, ohne ihr aber die Bedeutung zuzuschreiben, die die Kirche ihr traditionell gegeben hatte; denn er sah die Wassertaufe als symbolische Praxis an, und er hatte im Neuen Testament keine Grundlage dafür gefunden, dass Christus, Maria oder die Apostel die Kindertaufe durchgeführt hätten. Das heißt, das Heil eines Menschen war nicht davon abhängig, ob dieser getauft war oder nicht.[119]

Müntzer unterschied zwischen externer Taufe und interner Taufe. Seine Tauftheologie gründete sich auf die Worte Jesu: „niemand kann in das Reich Gottes kommen, wenn er nicht aus Wasser und Geist geboren ist" (Joh. 3,5). Die interne Taufe war demnach die Erfüllung der Tiefe der Seele durch den Geist Gottes und stimmte mit der Einladung Jesu überein: „Wen da dürstet, der komme zu mir und trinke! Wer an mich glaubt, wie die Schrift sagt, von dessen Leib werden Ströme lebendigen Wassers fließen" (Joh. 7,37-38).[120] Hut erhielt dieses Erbe der inneren Taufe durch das prüfende Feuer und Wasser sowohl von Karlstadt als auch von Müntzer. In seiner „Predigt vom Stand der christgläubigen Seelen, von Abrahams Schoss und Fegfeuer"[121] verstand Karlstadt das Fegefeuer als die totale Vernichtung aller menschlichen Werke und Wünsche sowie dies, dass alle kreatürlichen Lüste durch die Sehnsucht verzehrt wurden, von Gott abhängig zu sein, welche wiederum aus dem Glauben und der Liebe geboren wurde. Hans Hut drückte sich über die Taufe in Feuer und Wasser, die der Verkündigung des „Evangeliums Aller Kreatur" folgte, folgendermaßen aus: „Feuer und wasser rainigen alle ding, es ist aller ding rainigung in der zeit es sei durch wasser oder feuer. Was waich ist und feuer nit leiden kan, wirt duchs wasser gfegt von unrainen, was aber hert ist als kupfer, gold, silber, eisen, zinn wirt durchs feuer geschmelzt und von

---

[119] Thomas Müntzer: Protestation oder Erbietung, in: Franz, MSB, S. 228, 3-11.

[120] Thomas Müntzer: Protestation oder Erbietung Protestation, in: Franz, MSB, 228, 13-29. Vgl. Rollin Stely Armour, op. cit. S. 60-62.

[121] C.F. Jäger: Andreas Bodenstein von Carlstadt. Ein Beitrag zur Geschichte der Reformationszeit aus Originalquellen gegeben. Stuttgart, Rudolf Besser, 1856, S. 302-311.

zuesatz gfegt. Daher bildet uns der geist Gottes für wasser und feuer als ein gegensatz, darunter die vernunft in creaturischen werken beschlossen wirt undern gehorsam Christi."[122] Die Taufe mit Feuer und Wasser standen für das Werk Gottes, der den Menschen durch Leiden reinigte und rechtfertigte.

Bereits der Reformator Heinrich Bullinger[123] hatte versucht zu erklären, dass die Täuferbewegung ihre Wurzeln in der Tauftheologie Müntzers hat, aber historisch können wir sagen, dass Hans Hut als Schüler Müntzers der Kindertaufe keine Bedeutung zumaß, und als 1524 sein Sohn geboren wurde, ließ er nicht zu, dass dieser getauft würde. Hans Hut stimmte mit der inneren Bedeutung der Taufe, die Müntzer gepredigt hatte, überein, formulierte aber die Rolle und die Bedeutung der Wassertaufe neu. Es gibt immer noch Fragen zu den Personen, zur Zeit und den Orten, die der äußeren Wassertaufe neue Bedeutung gaben. Ein Beispiel ist Katharina Kreutter, die im Juni 1526 im Alter von sechzehn Jahren ins Gefängnis gebracht und dort gefoltert wurde wegen ihrer antiklerikalen Überzeugungen und ihres Kampfes gegen die kirchliche und säkulare Macht. Sie hatte sich im Krieg gegen die Bauern in Mühlhausen erhoben. Durch das „Kreutter Bekenntnis" wurde registriert, das ihr vorgeworfen worden war, sie habe sich in einem Kübel taufen lassen. Diesen Vorwurf leugnete sie nicht, sondern bekräftigte: „Sie seis also gelernt vom Pfeiffer und seiner geselschaft."[124]

Im Fall Huts können wir mit Bestimmtheit sagen, dass sein Wiedersehen mit dem anabaptistischen Apostel Hans Denck, von dem er im Mai 1526 mit

---

[122] Müller, Glaubenszeugnisse, op. cit., S. 27.

[123] Ernst Koch: Bullinger und die Thüringer. in: Ulrich Gläber und Erland Herkenrath (Hg.): Heinrich Bullinger 1504-1575. Gesammelte Aufsätze zum 400. Todestag, Bd. 2, Zürich, 1975, S. 315-318.

[124] Walther Peter Fuchs (Hg.): Geschichte des Bauernkriegs in Mitteldeutschland, Bd. II, Aalen (Neudruck) 1964, S. 754, Anm. In ihrer Interpretation dieses Ereignisses meint die Historikerin Marion Kobelt-Groch, Katharinas Aktion könnte eine antiklerikale Verspottung des Taufsakraments gewesen sein; sie könnte aber auch so interpretiert werden, dass die von Müntzer und Pfeiffer in Mühlhausen angestoßenen kirchlichen Reformen nicht nur zur Einführung der „Evangelischen Deutschen Messe" führten, sondern auch ein neues Verständnis der Erwachsenentaufe förderten. Vgl. Marion Kobelt-Groch: Aufsässige Töchter Gottes. Frauen im Bauernkrieg und in den Täuferbewegungen. Frankfurt / New York, Campus Verlag, 1993, S. 147-154.

Das Evangelium aller Kreatur.

Wasser getauft wurde, maßgeblich war für die Neuformulierung der Bedeutung der Wassertaufe.[125] In seinem „Geheimnis der Taufe" ist Hut klar in der Angabe der Schritte, die im Missionsbefehl in Markus 16,15 vorgegeben sind: 1) Geht und predigt das Evangelium aller Kreatur, 2) der, der glaubt und 3) getauft wird, wird errettet werden. Die neue Bedeutung, dies die Wassertaufe erlangt, ist mit anderen Worten die eines neuen externen Bundes, der dem internen Bund mit Gott entspricht. Die Erwachsenentaufe, und nicht die eines Säuglings, führt die Täuflinge öffentlich in die Gemeinschaft der Gläubigen ein. Diese externe Wassertaufe verkündet öffentlich einen Bruch mit der Einheit Kirche-Staat dadurch, dass sie die Kindertaufe ablehnt und so den Weg öffnet für die Entstehung einer freiwilligen Gemeinschaft von Anhängern und Anhängerinnen Jesu.

Eine weitere Dimension, die der Märtyrer-Theologie einen Raum öffnet, ist das Verständnis der Taufe im Blut, das wir sowohl bei Müntzer als auch bei Hut finden. In den liturgischen Reformen, die Müntzer in Allstedt eingeführt hatte, ist die Bemühung zu finden, sich nicht nur von den mittelalterlichen Taufzeremonien, die die sozialen Hierarchisierungen seiner Zeit widerspiegeln, zu distanzieren, um damit auf das Seufzen des „gemeinen Mannes" einzugehen, sondern auch zu versuchen, der Taufe ihre wahre Bedeutung in der Nachfolge Jesu zu geben. So finden wir zu Beginn der liturgischen Reformen, die Müntzer für die Taufe einführt, die Lesung von Psalm 69 in Deutsch, dessen erste Verse ausrufen: „Gott, hilf mir! Denn das Wasser geht mir bis an die Kehle. Ich versinke in tiefem Schlamm, wo kein Grund ist; ich bin in tiefe Wasser geraten, und die Flut will mich ersäufen. Ich habe mich müde geschrien, mein Hals ist heiser. Meine Augen sind trübe geworden, weil ich so lange harren muss auf meinen Gott" (V. 2-4). Und dann folgt die Lesung des Evangeliums nach Matthäus 3,13ff. – der Text der Taufe Jesu im Jordan.[126] Der Schrei des Schmerzes des Psalmisten kündigt bereits den

---

[125] Günter Goldbach: Hans Denck und Thomas Müntzer – ein Vergleich ihrer wesentlichen theologischen Auffassungen. Eine Untersuchung zur Morphologie der Randströmungen der Reformation. Dissertation zur Erlangung der Doktorwürde der Evang.-Theologischen Fakultät der Universität Hamburg, Hamburg, 1969.

[126] Thomas Müntzer: Ordnung und Berechnung, in: Franz, MSB, S. 214,12-36 und S. 215, 1-6.

Beginn des Auftrags Christi an, der mit seiner Taufe eröffnet wird, und der sein Dienst und sein Tod am Kreuz folgt. Das Ausmaß der Taufe im Blut drückte Müntzer auch in seinem Brief an Christoph Meinhard am 30. Mai 1524 aus, in dem er sich mit der Taufe des Johannes des Täufers und den Worten Jesu in Lukas 7,49-50 identifiziert: „Ich muss mit einer anderen Taufe übergossen werden, als mit der Taufe des Johannes und ich werde sehr gepeinigt, weil ich solches vollführe."[127]

Diese Dimension der Taufe im Blut drückte auch Hut mit den folgenden Worten aus: „Deshalb ist das Wasser aller Trübsal das rechte Wesen und die Kraft der Taufe, in dem der Mensch in den Tod Christi versinkt."[128] Leonhard Schiemer, ein österreichischer Franziskaner, der während einer Predigt Hans Huts zum Täufertum übergetreten war und im November 1527 festgenommen und im Januar 1528 wegen seines Glaubens enthauptet wurde, bezog sich in einem Vers eines Liedes, das er komponiert hatte, auf folgende Weise auf die Taufe im Blut:

„Wie köstlich ist der Heilgen Tod,
vor deinem Angesichte!
Drum haben wir in aller Not
ein tröstlich Zuversichte
zu dir allein;
sonst nirgend kein
Trost, Fried noch Ruh auf Erden.
Wer hofft auf dich,
wird ewiglich
Nimmer zu Schanden werden."[129]

---

[127] Brief von Thomas Müntzer an Christoph Meinhard in Ersleben zur Auslegung des Psalms 19. Allstedt, 30. Mai 1524. in: Thomas Müntzer, Schriften und Briefe (Hg. von Gerhard Wehr), Gütersloh, Gütersloher Verlagshaus, 1978 S. 135.

[128] Hans Hut: Von dem Geheimnis der Taufe, a.a.O. S. 93.

[129] Lienhart Schiemer: Wie köstlich ist der Heilgen Tod. in: Heinold Fast (Hg.): Der linke Flügel der Reformation, a.a.O., S. 100-103, hier S. 102.

7. "Geet hin in die Welt und predigent das Evangelion aller Creaturen" (Markus 16,15): „Christusförmig" werden und der wahre Freund Christus (verus Amicus Cristus)

Müntzer und Hans Hut hörten die Schmerzensschreie der Geschöpfe, und ihre eigenen Schmerzenserfahrungen öffneten ihnen den Weg zur „Theologia Deutsch"[130], durch die sie eine universelle Sicht erwarben, um das Geheimnis Gottes zu verstehen. Alle Geschöpfe, d.h. Pflanzen, Fische, Vögel, Flüsse, Wälder; Kinder, Frauen, Männer, Greise; verschiedene Nationen unabhängig von ihrer Kultur, Religion oder Nationalität, wurden in diesem historischen Moment durch die universelle Erfahrung von Schmerz verbunden. Die „Theologie des Kreuzes" umfasst als mystische Erfahrung die drei Sphären des Weges hin zu Gott: spirituelle Reinigung, Erleuchtung und die schlussendliche Vereinigung mit Gott (Unio mystica). Von dieser Spiritualität her erklang der Missionsauftrag Christi: „Gehet hin in alle Welt und predigt das Evangelium aller Kreatur"" (Markus 16,15) als eine Herausforderung, Christus zu gleichen und seine Freunde und Freundinnen zu sein.

Müntzer geht vom Fundament der „Ordnung Gottes in allen Kreaturen" aus, um auf Christus zu verweisen. Das Deutsche Kirchenamt übersetzt die erste Strophe des Liedes „Veni redemptor gentium" wie folgt:

„O Herr, erlöser alles volcks,
kum zeych uns die geburt deyns sons,
es wundern sich all creaturen,
dass Christ also ist mensch worden."[131]

Die Christologie Müntzers mit ihrem mystischen Erbe gründet sich in der von Gott geschaffenen Heilsordnung. In diesem Lied bringen alle Geschöpfe das Evangelium und Wunder der Menschwerdung Christi zum Ausdruck. Durch die Menschwerdung Jesu als dem zweiten Adam wird die Wiederherstellung der Schöpfung, die durch die Sünde des ersten Adams beschädigt worden war, möglich. Der zweite Adam stellt in vielerlei Hinsicht den ersten Adam dar, denn er ist ein fleischgewordener Mensch. Müntzer nimmt die

---

[130] Gerhard Wehr (Hg.): Theologia Deutsch. Eine Grundschrift deutscher Mystik. Nürnberg 1989.

[131] Thomas Müntzer: Deutsches Kirchenamt, in: Franz, MSB, S. und S. 45,24 46,1-4.

Menschwerdung ernst, und das bedeutet auch, dass er die Tatsache, dass der Mensch Fleisch ist, positiv bewertet. Hier beginnt sich das große Geheimnis Gottes zu offenbaren, das die mystische Theologie Müntzers[132] und Huts[133] durch 1. Kor 1,27 unterstützte: „Das Törichte hat Gott erwählt, dass er die Weisen zuschanden mache." Es handelt sich hierbei um das Geheimnis der Offenbarung Gottes, die sich im gekreuzigten Jesus zeigt.

Sowohl bei Müntzer und Hans Hut auf der einen Seite als auch bei Luther[134] auf der anderen Seite finden wir eine Theologie des Kreuzes, aber in der hermeneutischen Perspektive und der praktischen Anwendung auf den Status des „gemeinen Mannes" schlugen sie unterschiedliche Wege ein. Müntzer und Hut und distanzierten sich von Martin Luthers Rechtfertigungslehre, als sie merkten, dass diese Theologie die Schreie der leidenden Geschöpfe und den „gemeinen Mann", der unter der Unterdrückung der Fürsten stöhnte, nicht mehr berücksichtigte. Für Müntzer und Hut findet sich das große Geheimnis der Menschwerdung Gottes im Kreuz Christi, aber der Schwerpunkt fällt nicht auf den forensischen Aspekt, sondern sie betrachten ihr Leben im Einklang mit dem des Gekreuzigten. „Christus ist einmal für uns gestorben, damit er in uns nicht sterbe, und sein Sakrament ist nicht für uns zum Trost und sein Beispiel ist nicht zur Nachahmung zu verwenden. Im Amt der Messe erlangen wir, dass wir in dieser Welt nicht leiden mögen."[135] Der Gekreuzigte kann nur dann gepredigt werden, wenn der Jünger sich nicht über seinen Lehrer erhebt. Deshalb verstand Müntzer, dass die Verfolgung,

---

[132] Corpus Scriptorum Latinorum ecclesiasticorum, Wien 1866, 70, 196, 3-8; 198, 40 f; Top. 16. Zitiert in Martin Brecht: Thomas Müntzers Christologie, in: Siegfried Bräuer und Helmer Junghans (Hg.): Der Theologe Thomas Müntzer. op. cit., S. 62-83, bes. S. 81.

[133] Hans Hut: Von dem Geheimnis der Taufe, op.cit. S. 84.

[134] Martin Luther: Heidelberger Disputation und Beweise der Thesen (1518), in: Martin Hoffmann: Martin-Luther-Studienbuch. Grundtexte und Deutungen, Leipzig, Evangelische Verlagsanstalt, 2014, S. 32-35.

[135] Müntzer an Luther. Zwickau, 13. Juli 1520, in: Franz, S. 359, 8-11. "Cristus semel mortuus est, ne in nobis moriatur neque suum sacramentum nobis in consolationem sit nec suum exemplum in imitationem transformetur. In missarum offitio consequimur, ne paciamur in hoc *mundo*." Dies hört Müntzer Luther sagen.

die er erlitt, Teil seines Schicksals als Prediger des Evangeliums war, wie er es in seinem Brief an Hausmann im Jahre 1521 zum Ausdruck brachte.[136]

In dem Lied „Des königs panier gehn hervor", das aus dem Lateinischen „Vexila regis prodeunt" übersetzt wurde, kann man erkennen, wie der Tod des Dieners paradoxerweise einen rettenden Effekt hat. Das Geheimnis des Kreuzes ist, dass Christus durch seine Menschwerdung am menschlichen Leiden teilhat. Und die Reinigung des Menschen auf seinem Weg zu Gott bedeutet, auf die Sünde zu verzichten, indem man das Kreuz Christi auf sich nimmt, das heißt, an den Leiden Christi in der Welt teilhat. In der Menschwerdung, durch die schmerzhafte Erfahrung des Kreuzes, stellt Jesus Gottes Schöpfung wieder her. Sein Tod am Kreuz lädt uns auch dazu ein, ihm zu folgen und an seinem Schmerz teilzuhaben, die Welt neu zu erschaffen. Der Schwerpunkt liegt nicht auf der Rechtfertigung durch den Glauben, sondern in der Nachfolge des gekreuzigten, des bitteren Christus.

Das Abendmahlslied „Wir danksagen dir, Herr Gott der eeren" ist das einzige, das Müntzer ohne Vorlage erstellte. Die dritte Strophe heißt:

„Aller meniglich mitzuteylen,
so under des kreuz tund eylen,
nach seinem willen hie auf erden,
ihm gleychförmig möchten werden,
mit unserm leyden
in dem Herren
des vatters reych tun erwerben."[137]

Der Tod Christi ermöglicht die Befreiung aller Kreaturen. Christus ist das Weizenkorn, das durch den Schmerz des Kreuzes gemahlen wurde, um alle Menschen wiederherzustellen. Er ist das Brot des Lebens, das in den Tod am Kreuz gegeben wird. Dieses Brot kann nur von denen empfangen werden, die ihm gleich werden wollen. Sein Wille ist, dass wir an seinem Leiden teilhaben, um die Schöpfung zu transformieren. Das Reich Gottes wird denen

---

[136] Brief von Thomas Müntzer an Christoph Meinhard in Ersleben zur Auslegung des Psalms 19. Allstedt, 30. Mai 1524. Dies hört Müntzer Luther sagen. In: Thomas Müntzer, Schriften und Briefe (Hg. von Gerhard Wehr), a.a.O., S. 135.

[137] Thomas Müntzer: Abendmahlslied, in: Franz, MSB, S. 529, 15-21.

vererbt, die völlig auf Sünde verzichten, die an den Schmerzen Christi teilhaben, um ihm ähnlich zu werden, denen, die am Kreuz Christi teilhaben.

Die Bedeutung „christusförmig" betont Hut in der kollektiven Dimension der Geschöpfe Gottes und derer, die Glieder seines Leibes sind: „Aus solchen Gleichnissen soll der Mensch mit Fleiß wahrnehmen, dass, wie alle Kreatur das Werk des Menschen Leiden muss und so durch Schmerzen zu ihrem Ende kommen, zu dem sie geschaffen sind, so auch kein Mensch zur Seligkeit kommen kann außer durch Leiden und Trübsal, die Gott an ihm wirkt; wie auch die ganzen Schrift und alle Kreatur nichts anderes darstellen als den leidenden Christus in allen seinen Gliedmaßen."[138]

Die Unio mystica zu erreichen, ist nur möglich, indem wir Christus erlauben, sich in uns durch die Erfahrung des Kreuzes zu bilden. Und in diesem Zusammenhang gedeiht das Konzept, ein Freund oder eine Freundin Gottes zu sein. Man folgt Jesus Christus nicht nur als Einzelperson, sondern auch als Gemeinschaft. Sowohl in den Kreisen, in denen die „Theologia Deutsch" geboren wurde, als auch in den Gemeinschaften, in denen Müntzer und Hut teilnahmen, wurde Freundschaft als jene überquellende Freude derer verstanden, die sich unter der Ehrfurcht vor Gott befanden, so wie es beim Treffen von Maria und Elisabeth geschehen war. So drückte Müntzer es aus: „Es findet der außerwelt freünd Gottes ein wunsamme, überschenckliche freüd, wenn seyn mitbrüder auch also durch solche gleychformige ankunfft zum glauben kumen ist wie er".[139] Hut seinerseits verstand auch die enge Beziehung zwischen unio mystica, Erfahrung des Kreuzes und Freundschaft, als er bezogen auf die Taufe im Blut sagte: „Diese Taufe ist nicht erst zur Zeit Christi eingesetzt, sondern ist von Anfang an gewesen. Mit ihr sind alle auserwählten Freunde Gottes von Adam bis heute getauft worden, wie Paulus zeigt (Joel 3,1, I Kor. 10,1 ff.; Judith 8,20 f.)."[140]

Inmitten seiner verwirrten Aussagen kommen die Worte „Omnia sunt communia" aus dem Mund Müntzers – nach seiner Folterung im Gefängnis

---

[138] Hans Hut: Von dem Geheimnis der Taufe, S. 87-88.
[139] Thomas Müntzer: Ausgedrückte Entblößung, in: Franz, MSB, S. 309, S. 39 und 310,1-7.
[140] Hans Hut: Von dem Geheimnis der Taufe, S. 93-94.

Das Evangelium aller Kreatur.

und kurz vor seinem Tod.[141] Aus seinem bestraften Körper sind dies die relevanten Wörter, die sich darauf beziehen, was es bedeutet, ein wahrer Freund, eine wahre Freundin in der kollektiven Dimension der Gemeinschaft zu sein. „Omnia sunt communia" erinnert Müntzer nicht nur an den solidarischen Lebensstil der ersten Gemeinden, die Jesus gefolgt waren[142], sondern auch an seine Erfahrungen von Freundschaft und Solidarität seiner Freunde und Freundinnen auf seiner historischen Reise durch die Gemeinden in Jüterbog, Zwickau, Böhmen, Allstedt und Mühlhausen. Für seinen Schüler Hut verwandelt „Omnia sunt communia" sich auch in das Siegel der Freundschaft, den Nexus dafür, die Mission weiterzuführen, den Wunsch, eine Gemeinschaft von Anhängern Jesu zu bilden, in der sich die freiwillige Bereitschaft zeigt, die eigene Habe mit den ärmsten und bedürftigsten Mitgliedern der Gemeinde zu teilen.[143] Hut hatte eine klare Vorstellung davon, dass die Nachfolger und Nachfolgerinnen Christi einen Leib bilden, die Gemeinde Christi, in der Liebe und Solidarität freiwillig praktiziert wird. Das Prinzip „Omnia sunt communia" ist bei Hut das Verständnis davon, dass alle Habe, Auszeichnungen und alles Lob dem Heiligen Geist hingelegt werden, dergestalt, dass im Reich Gottes alle Dinge der Gemeinschaft gehören und nicht privater Natur sind.[144] Diese Dimension, ein wahrer Freund, eine wahre Freundin Gottes zu sein, die alle Habe miteinander teilten, war das, was es den Gemeinden, die durch die Verkündigung Huts in Süddeutschland und Mähren entstanden waren, ermöglichte zu überleben, obwohl ihre Häuser verbrannt, ihre Gärten zerstört, und viele von ihnen als Märtyrer auf dem Scheiterhaufen starben oder in Flüssen ertränkt wurden.[145]

---

[141] Thomas Müntzer Bekenntnis, 16. Mai 1525. in: Franz, MSB, S. 548, 13.

[142] Dies bezieht sich auf die folgenden Texte: „Alle aber, die gläubig waren geworden, waren beinander und hielten alle Dinge gemein. Ihre Güter und Habe verkauften sie und teilten sie aus unter alle, nach dem jedermann not war" (Apg. 2:44). "Die Menge aber der Gläubigen war ein Herz und eine Seele; auch keiner sagte von seinen Gütern, dass sie sein wären, sondern es war ihnen alles gemein" (Apg. 4:23).

[143] Lydia Müller (Hg.): Glaubenszeugnisse oberdeutscher Taufgesinnter, op. cit., S. 22.

[144] Ebd., S. 36.

[145] Die Betonung der Unterordnung von Eigentum und Besitz unter die Kirche als Bruderschaft war eine der Grundlagen der Hutterer Gemeinden, wie der Brief von Wolfgang Brandhuber angibt, ein beliebtes Dokument unter der Hutterern in den ersten Jah-

Schließlich, das Pfingstlied „Kumm zu uns schoepffer, heylger geyst" (Veni creator spiritus) kommuniziert eine Theologie, die nicht von den Eigenschaften des Geistes ausgeht, sondern von seiner Rolle als Tröster:

„Der du ein warer tröster bist,
ler uns erkennen deynen Christ,
im rechten glauben sicherlich
seyner zu nyessen ewiglich."[146]

Dies bedeutet, dass Gottes Freundschaft mit den Auserwählten nicht nur in der Menschwerdung seines Sohnes Jesus Christus besteht, sondern auch in deren Ausstattung mit dem Heiligen Geist, um diejenigen zu trösten, die an der Erfahrung, „christusförmig" zu werden, teilhaben möchten. „Wenn der Mensch nach allem Leiden und Trübsal im Heiligen Geist wiederum getröstet wird, dann wird er dem Herrn bereit und zu allen guten Werken verfügbar. (...) Da kommt der Mensch wiederum aus der Tiefe der Hölle und gewinnt Freude und Mut im Heiligen Geist."[147] Die Pneumatologie hat nicht die Funktion, eine dogmatische Trinitätstheologie zu unterstützen, sondern steht in Bezug auf die Nachfolge Jesu. Wenn wir Jesus persönlich und als Gemeinschaft mitten im Leiden nachfolgen, werden wir ihm ähnlich. Und der Geist stärkt uns individuell und als Leib Christi inmitten der Trübsal, und lässt so die Liebe Gottes in uns als heiße Glut wachsen:

„Also ißt man den leib des Herren,
wenn wir von heylgen gayst tund lernen,
got warhaftiglich erkennen;
göttliche liebe soll in uns brennen,
die macht uns zu reben

---

ren nach ihrer Gründung. Lydia Müller (Hg.): Glaubenszeugnisse oberdeutscher Taufgesinnter, op. cit., S. 137-143. Vgl. Karl Kautsky: Vorläufer des neueren Sozialismus, Zweiter Band, Berlin-Bonn, Verlag JHW Dietz Nachf., 10. Auflage 1981, S. 125-228.

[146] Thomas Müntzer: Deutsches Kirchenamt, in: Franz, MSB, 153, 5-8. Hinweis: Dieses und die drei vorangegangenen Zitate stammen von Herbert Klassen: Community of Goods, in Herbert Klassen: The Life and Teaching of Hans Hut, Part I, op. cit., S. 191-192.

[147] Hans Hut: Von dem Geheimnis der Taufe, S. 93-94, 97-98.

der gayst gibts leben:
Also wirt uns der leyb Christi gegeben."[148]

Der Bauer Hut war in der Nähe Müntzers in den entscheidenden Momenten der sozialen Bauernumwälzungen, die sie im Jahr 1525 auf dramatische Weise miterlebten. Nach der Teilnahme an der Synode der Märtyrer von Augsburg, wurde er im September 1527 verhaftet und kam ins Gefängnis, wo er im Einklang mit der „Constitutio criminalis Bambergensis" schrecklichen Verhören unterzogen wurde.[149] Er wurde in der Zelle, in der er gefangen gehalten wurde, verbrannt und starb am 6. Dezember 1527[150]. So hatte er an den Grundlagen seines Glaubens und an den Worten und der Praxis seines Lehrers und Freundes Jesus festgehalten: „Niemand hat größere Liebe als die, dass er sein Leben lässt für seine Freunde. Ihr seid meine Freunde, wenn ihr tut, was ich euch gebiete." (Joh. 15,13-14)

8. Schlussfolgerungen für die Welt von heute: "Geet hin in die Welt und predigent das Evangelion aller Creaturen" (Markus 16,15)

Zur Feier des 500. Jahrestages der Reformation verweisen uns das Leben, Denken und Zeugnis Huts und Müntzers auf den Missionsauftrag Jesu Christi: „Gehet hin in alle Welt und predigt das Evangelium aller Kreatur" (Markus 16,15). Sie laden uns dazu ein, diese Botschaft in der gebrochenen Welt von heute zu verkünden. Das Evangelium aller Geschöpfe, vom Beginn des „Ordo Dei" (Genesis 1) aus gesehen, führt uns dazu, über das Geheimnis der Schöpfung zwischen den Teilen und dem Ganzen zu meditieren. Die Schöpfung wurde in einem nachhaltigen Gleichgewicht geschaffen, weshalb die gesamte Menschheit von der Welt als Ganzem abhängt. Einzelpersonen und Familien, Gemeinschaften und Völkern können nicht überleben, wenn die Ordnung der Natur und der Ökosphäre zerstört wird. Es ist notwendig, das Evangelium, das die Teile und die bestehende Wechselbeziehung zwischen diesen Teilen und dem Ganzen in Gottes Schöpfung anerkennt, öffentlich zu verkünden. Die große Familie der Menschheit muss erkennen, dass sie nur

---

[148] Thomas Müntzer: Abendmahlslied, in: Franz, MSB, S. 530, 13-19.

[149] Eberhart Schmidt: Einführung in die Geschichte der deutschen Strafrechtspflege. 3 Auflage, Göttingen, 1965, S. 122-130.

[150] George H. Williams, op. cit., S. 191-210.

ein Teil des großen Ganzen ist. Ihr ist, nach dem Bild Gottes geschaffen, die Verantwortung übergeben, nicht nur sich selbst zu organisieren, sondern die ganze Schöpfung zu pflegen, um die Balance aller Teile, die das Leben auf dem Planeten Erde möglich machen, zu gewährleisten.

Das theologische Verständnis, dass jedes Geschöpf das Evangelium Gottes bereits verkündet, lädt uns zu einer neuen Haltung ein, uns wieder von dem ersten Buch der Offenbarung verzaubern zu lassen, welches Gottes Schöpfung selbst darstellt. Im Denken und tagtäglichen Verhalten der Reformer Müntzer und Hans Hut kann man die Bewunderung und Dankbarkeit gegenüber dem Gott der Schöpfung fühlen. Alles Erschaffene, die Schönheit der Jahreszeiten, die bunten Blumen, die Vielfalt der Früchte, Bäume und Nahrungsmittel verkünden das Evangelium Gottes. Die Liebe Gottes für alle Geschöpfe wird empfunden wie die Wärme der Sonne, die ihren Weg läuft, um inmitten der Nacht voller Sterne, Funken und Lichter das Zelt ihrer Geliebten zu erreichen. Gleichzeitig gibt es die Gebote Gottes, die von dem Moment unserer Erschaffung an und durch das Erbe Moses, der Propheten und Evangelisten als ethische Forderung in unsere Herzen gesät wurden und die so die Offenbarung ergänzen, d. h. das Evangelium, das in der Schrift zum Ausdruck gebracht wird (Psalm 19). Von der Bewunderung des großen Buches Gottes, d. h. der Schöpfung und der Gebote der Schrift her müssen wir das Evangelium verkünden, indem wir auf das Seufzen der Abholzung, der Zerstörung von Flora und Fauna, der Luftverschmutzung, der Verschmutzung von Land, Süß- und Salzwasser achten. Das kann dadurch seinen Ausdruck finden, dass wir Gebete sprechen und konkrete Maßnahmen umsetzen, wie z.B. das Pflanzen von Bäumen, den Schutz von Flussbecken, den verantwortungsvollen Umgang mit Wasser und jede Initiative, welche die befreiende Offenbarung Gottes fordert (Römer 8,20-22), damit in seinem Garten wieder unbändige Ströme lebendigen Wassers fließen können (Jesaja 58,11). Der Keimgedanke der Harmonie und des kosmischen Gleichgewichts, der Beziehung zwischen den Teilen und dem Ganzen, des Verständnisses vom Menschen, der als Mikrokosmos von der Liebe Gottes durchdrungen ist, um die Schöpfung in einem Bund mit dem zweiten Adam (Christus, dem Sohn Gottes) zu schützen – er wird geboren aus den biblischen Schöpfungstexten, in den Visionen von Frauen wie Hildegard von Bingen erneuert und an Reformer wie Müntzer und Hans Hut weitergereicht. Mit mehreren Beispielen zeigt uns das Evangelium für/von alle/r Kreatur die wichtige Rolle der Frauen in der Heilsgeschichte. Es ist die Ehrfurcht vor Gott und die Fülle seines Geistes, dass Rahab, die kanaanitische Hure, Ruth, die Moabiterin, und Judith, die Jüdin, von Gott dazu erwählt sind, unterdrückende Strukturen zu konfrontieren und sich so maßgeblich an der Rettung des ausgewanderten, armen und gefangenen Volks Israel zu beteiligen. Aus Ehrfurcht vor Gott und in Erwartung seiner Versprechen in Zeiten der römischen Gefangenschaft, gebar Elisabeth den Propheten Johannes den Täufer, und Maria gebar Jesus, den Sohn Gottes, der das Evangelium des Reiches verkünden würde. Das ist die wunderbare Erfahrung kämpferischer Frauen, die der Welt mit ihren Söhnen und Töchtern wieder Freude bereiten, von denen sie nicht nur die Neuschöpfung der großen Familie der Menschheit erwarten, sondern eine neue Generation, die das Evangelium mit einem Lebensstil verkündet, das dem Bild Gottes entspricht. Es liegt an den alltäglichen Kämpfen, dem Engagement für Gerechtigkeit, dem Zeugnis und den Gedanken vieler Frauen, dass die heutige Kirche und Gesellschaft sich erneuert und voller Freude das "Evangelium für/von alle/r Kreatur" verkündet.

„Das Evangelium für/von alle/r Kreatur" verlangt von uns, wie von Müntzer und Hut, die Augen auf Gott zu richten durch das erste Buch der Offenbarung (d. h. durch die Schöpfung), um seine kreative Arbeit zu bestätigen, so dass in unserem Sein ein Versprechen geboren wird, das Universum neu zu erschaffen, indem wir unsere Herzen dafür öffnen, einen Dialog mit der lebendigen Spiritualität anderer Religionen, Völker, Kulturen und Geschöpfe Gottes zu halten. Das Evangelium im Gesicht, den Augen, der Stimme, im Körper und Geist der Schwestern und Brüder anderer Religionen, Völkern und Kulturen zu erkennen, erfordert, dass wir die wahren Beweggründe der Aggression, Dominanz und aller religiösen Vorurteile aufdecken, die seit der Zeit der Kreuzzüge im Mittelalter im Namen des „Evangeliums" Kriege und die Vernichtung unserer Nachbarn rechtfertigten. Am heutigen Tag erinnern wir speziell an alle Kinder, Jugendlichen und Waisen in Palästina, im Irak und Nahen Osten und fordern alle Kirchen in der ganzen Welt dazu auf, für den Frieden zu beten und die subtilen und anhaltenden Vorurteile, die kolonialen Bestrebungen Europas und der Vereinigten Staaten gegen diese islamischen Völker öffentlich zu verurteilen. Wir warnen vor jeder Theologie, die das biblische Zeugnis von der Erwählung des Alten Israel als Bundesvolk Gottes für Gerechtigkeit ideologisch umdeutet in ein ethnisches Privileg und Herrschaftsinstrument des heutigen Staates Israel – auf Kosten des Lebens der benachbarten Brüder und Schwestern, die doch den gleichen Vater, Abraham, und Gott, den Schöpfer aller Völker, haben. Wir fordern die Kirchen auf, finanziell und mit verschiedensten solidarischen und humanitären Maßnahmen zum Wiederaufbau dieser Völker beizutragen, und in ihren Kirchen und Gemeinden Programme zu entwickeln, die den Frieden zwischen den Kulturen, Völkern und Religionen fördern.

Der „gemeine Mann" ist, wie man aus den Schriften von Müntzer und Hut klar entnehmen kann, Teil des „Evangeliums für/von alle/r Kreatur"; nicht nur in dem Maße, dass er eine Kreatur ist, die im Bild Gottes geschaffen wurde oder weil er das Evangelium in der großen Manifestation der Schöpfung und durch die große Kreativität der Hände Gottes erkennt, sondern auch, weil er durch die erlebten Ungerechtigkeiten und Schmerzen zu Gott schreit. Er beruft sich auf die Gebote des Evangeliums, die in der Thora, den Propheten, durch Jesus und die Apostel ausgedrückt werden, um seine Rechte als Geschöpf Gottes einzufordern. Wir fordern eine Theologie, deren Evangelium sich in jedem und für jedes Geschöpf ausdrückt, und durch die in der Nachfolge Jesu das Herz Gottes in uns geboren wird, dem „gemeinen Mann" von heute zu dienen: Migranten und Migrantinnen, die vom Land in die großen Städte ziehen; solche, die aus Afrika, Asien und Lateinamerika in die Vereinigten Staaten und nach Europa kommen, weil sie ihre Familien unterstützen wollen; die Bauern, Ureinwohner und Lateinamerikaner afrikanischer Abstammung, deren Ländereien von Großgrundbesitzern und multinationalen Unternehmen enteignet wurden, und die in die Randgebiete der großen Städte zogen, wo sie unter miserablen Bedingungen leben. Es geht darum, zur Ankündigung des auferstandenen Jesus zurückzukehren, „zu gehen und zu predigen das Evangelium für/in jede/jeder Kreatur", indem man den „gemeinen Mann" beachtet, die ausgebeuteten Arbeiter und Maurer, die hungrigen und verlassenen Kinder, die Frauen, die unermüdlich für wenig Geld in den Häusern der Wohlhabendsten und in den modernen Textilfabriken der neo-kapitalistischen Industriegesellschaft arbeiten.

Bei der Auslegung des Missionsauftrags von Markus 16,15-16 sind sowohl bei Müntzer als auch bei Hut drei Formen der Taufe zu finden: Geistestaufe, Wassertaufe und die Taufe im Blut. In der postmodernen Welt von heute, die durch die Verehrung der Technologie und des Hedonismus und das totale Desinteresse an leidenden Kreaturen gekennzeichnet ist, brauchen wir die Taufe des Geistes Gottes. Dies bedeutet eine Abkehr von der Sünde des Konsumzwangs und das Zulassen, von Gottes Geist überflutet zu werden, damit in uns die Freude entfesselt wird, mit anderen zu teilen. Es bedeutet, uns selbst aufzugeben, und dem Geist Gottes zu erlauben, Raum in unserem Körper, Gedanken und Leben einzunehmen. Die Wassertaufe muss über das reine Ritual hinausgehen, um stattdessen ein bedeutendes Zeichen dafür zu sein, dass man Jesus folgt und freudig an der Gemeinschaft des Glaubens und dem Schicksal unserer Völker teilnimmt. In einem Haus, das von Gott bewohnt wird, sollte die Wassertaufe, die in vielen Religionen und Kulturen so präsent ist, uns wieder geistlich mit all den über die Jahrhunderte hinweg geschätzten Weisheiten verbinden und sie sollte uns auch wieder mit dem Süß- und dem Salzwasser auf diesem Planeten verbinden und sich dann in einen geistlichen Ausdruck verwandeln, der uns erlaubt, die von Gott geschaffenen Quellen, Flüsse, Seen und Meere zu genießen und zu schützen. Die Bluttaufe steht für die Entscheidung, sogar unser Leben zu opfern, um die Anforderungen des Evangeliums zu leben. Die Taufe durch Blut in der mystischen Theologie der Radikalen Reformation ist mit dem Konzept der Theologie des Kreuzes und der Nachfolge Jesu verbunden.

Wir werden gefragt, was die wahre Verpflichtung in der imitatio Christi und die Bedeutung des verus amicus Christus ist. Und wir entgegnen, dass der Auftrag von Jesus Christus „Geht und predigt das Evangelium in/für aller/alle Kreatur", den der auferstandene Jesus ausgesprochen hatte, die schwierige Anforderung mit sich bringt, an seinem Kreuzestod teilzuhaben. Der Tod Jesu am blutigen Baum ist das größte Zeichen seiner Liebe für die ganze Menschheit. Er, der sein Versprechen mit dem Reich Gottes einhielt, wurde ausgepeitscht und öffentlich am Kreuz vorgeführt, vor seinen Freunden, seinen Verwandten, dem jüdischen Volk, den römischen Soldaten, seinen Feinden und den erstaunten Zuschauern, die nicht anders konnten als ihr Gesicht vor so viel Schmerz zu verbergen. Müntzer und Hut waren treue Freunde Jesu und nahmen an seinen Schmerzen teil, indem sie im Gefängnis geschlagen, öffentlich gemartert und erhängt wurden – den Witwen und Waisen der Bauern, die auf dem Schlachtfeld gefallen waren, vor ihren Freunden, ihren Verwandten, vor den Soldaten der Fürsten von Sachsen und Augsburg, vor ihren Feinden und den staunenden Zuschauern, die nicht anders konnten als ihr Gesicht vor so viel Schmerz zu verbergen. Anhängerinnen und Freundinnen von Jesus, so wie Katharina Kreutter, wie Ottilie von Gersen und ihr Sohn, wie die Tochter Huts und viele andere Frauen und Männer der Radikalen Reformation, wurden aus der Geschichte gelöscht, indem sie wegen ihres Zeugnisses öffentlich gefoltert, verbrannt, gemartert oder ertränkt wurden. Die Worte Jesu, die sich in die Herzen der Radikalen Reformer einbrannten, tragen seinen Willen noch immer weiter: „Es gibt keine größere Liebe, als sein Leben für seine Freunde zu lassen. Ihr seid meine Freundinnen und meine Freunde, wenn ihr den Willen meines Vaters tut." Die Herausforderung des „Evangelium von/für aller/alle Kreatur", Christus ähnlich zu werden und in der heutigen Welt seine Freunde und Familie zu sein, beginnt mit unserer Sensibilität, den universellen Schmerzensschrei aller Geschöpfe zu hören: der Atmosphäre; der Mutter Erde; der Pflanzen, Vögel, Wälder, Flüsse und Meere; der älteren Menschen und Frauen, Mädchen und Kinder; der Gefangenen in den Gefängnissen, der Kulturen, Religionen und der leidenden Völker, die sich danach sehnen, befreit zu werden.

Abstract

"The Gospel to all creatures" (Markus 16:15), that is to say, the good news of God through all that is created and through God's commandments (Psalm 19), appears interrupted when the human being, made in the image of God, destroys this order by practicing injustice (Romans 1:18-20). The Gospel challenges us to preserve creation, the garden of God, with right personal attitudes, and with new economic, social, and ecological policies for the good of all creation and all the peoples of the earth.

Proclaim to Christians that "the Gospel to all creatures" means: 1) rejecting all cultural, religious, economic, and military invasion by the Western Christian World of the Islamic world and the countries of the "Third World," and 2) announcing with hope the yearning for understanding of the mystery of God in co-existence with other texts of divine revelation, the joy to strengthen dialogue, and to build a better world with Muslims, Jews, Hindus, and each of the religions, local cultures, and religions of Africa, North America, Latin America, the Caribbean, Asia, the Middle East, Oceania, and Europe (Isaiah 49:6).

Teach every Christian that the missionary sending, "Go into all the world and proclaim the Gospel to all creatures" (Mark 15:16) requires from each of us a posture of contemplation, spiritual cleanliness, illumination, and submission to the will of God. When we hear the voice of God in the fear of Rahab (Joshua 2), and of Mary and Elizabeth (Luke 1), and we allow the flood of the spirit of God into the abysses of our being (John 7:37-39), we begin the journey of the imitation of Christ. We acquire the form of Jesus, following his footsteps. Even beyond the pain that we experience when we are in solidarity with nature as it groans (Romans 8:18-21), with the child who cries, with the oppressed woman, with the poor who die for lack of bread, or the prisoners without freedom (Matthew 25:31-46), we encounter the sense of being true friends of Christ, true friends of God (John 15:12-17).

THE RESPONSIBILITY OF CONVICTION: CHRISTIAN PACIFISM[1]

Antonio González Fernández

In ethical and political debates, appeal is frequently made to "responsibility," in order to avoid onerous obligations imposed by ethics or to justify decisions (sometimes brutal ones) that seem to contravene certain moral values. Such appeals to responsibility are often made when there is a question of justifying the use of violence. From the point of view of "responsibility," for example, one might affirm the need to use violence to defend the democratic political system, to insure access to petroleum, or to bring about the triumph of a particular social revolution. Given such a perspective, pacifists are seen as irresponsible; they can afford to reject violence only because there are other, more "responsible" persons and institutions that *use* violence to defend political systems, which allow for conscientious objection and for criticism of military ventures.

This chapter will analyze the difference between the "ethics of conviction" and the "ethics of responsibility," paying special attention to the pacifist position as an instance of what we might call "responsible conviction." In this context we will offer some considerations about the traditional doctrine of the "just war," and articulate the pacifism that characterized early Christianity.

1. Responsibility and Conviction

The distinction between these two types of ethics comes from the philosophy of Max Scheler, who distinguished between an "ethics of success" (*Erfolgsethik*) and an "ethics of conviction" (*Gesinnungsethik*). For Scheler, this distinction served as a defense against the possible Kantian accusation that a material ethics is always an ethics of results whereas true ethics is always an ethics of intentions. By introducing the concept of "conviction" (*Gesinnung*), as opposed to mere intention (*Absicht*), Scheler intended to show that convic-

---

[1] This text first originated in a conference on "Philosophy and Theology of Peace," held at the Universidad Centroamericana of San Salvador in September 2012.

tions are oriented to values, that is, to concrete contents, and these concrete contents are precisely what characterize his project of a "material ethics" in the sense of an ethics with contents. These values, however, are not to be identified with results. For Scheler, as for Kant, it is absurd to make the moral character of practical conduct depend on a calculation of the conduct's probable results; rather, conviction has in itself a substantive value independent of the results of the actions.[2]

This distinction was taken up again by the sociologist Max Weber in a conference in 1919 called "Politics as Vocation,"[3] but with an intention radically opposed to that of the philosophers. For Weber, the social and political chaos in Germany during those years was directly related to the extreme positions of persons who had made radical decisions based on their convictions, yet without taking into account the results of their actions. That is why Weber speaks of an "ethics of responsibility" (*Verantwortungsethik*) and not an "ethics of results," as Scheler did. Weber held that the ethics of responsibility, in contrast to the ethics of conviction, should take into account the consequences of one's actions; it therefore privileges those actions which have real possibilities of success. For example, a politician would not be responsible if he wanted to spend the whole available budget on social measures which resolved immediate needs but failed to guarantee that in the long run those needs would disappear. If the budget were spent in that way, then even greater needs might appear in subsequent years. By the same logic, a "responsible" politician could never base his actions on pacifist convictions but would have to have recourse to violence to combat crime or defend the borders of his state.

Max Weber recognized that the ethics of conviction did not disavow responsibility, just as the ethics of responsibility did not disavow convictions.[4] Nevertheless, his negative conception of the ethics of conviction led him to define it mainly in terms of its option to justify moral actions by their intrin-

---

[2] Cf. M. Scheler, *Der Formalismus in der Ethik und die materiale Wertethik* (Halle: Niemeyer Verlag, 1916, 1st ed. 1913), 109-161.

[3] Cf. M. Weber, *Politik als Beruf*, in his *Gesammelte Politische Schriften* (Tübingen: J.C.B. Mohr, 1988, 5th ed.), 505-560.

[4] Cf. *ibid*, 551-552.

sic value rather than by their results.[5] He argued that those who act on the basis of the ethics of conviction are not concerned about results; they may leave the result in the hands of God, for example. On the other hand, Weber held that the ethics of responsibility has definite convictions, and that these convictions are precisely what allow it to prefer certain results rather than others. Thus, for example, when a politician orders a particular violent action, such as the repression of a demonstration or the start of a war, he does so responsibly if he understands that failure to order such action would produce greater harm from an ethical point of view, for example, a greater loss of human lives. This kind of responsibility clearly presupposes prior conviction about the value of human life, which is precisely what allows one to act in a "responsible" way.

2. The "Just War"

The doctrine of the "just war" may in principle be considered to exemplify the ethics of responsibility. The ethics of "just war" theory can be found in the Roman philosopher Cicero, but its main development took place in the context of medieval thought. For the pagan mentality, war was something almost natural. Christianity, however, had its origins in pacifist convictions, and so it had to find a way to resolve the contrast between those convictions and the emergent alliance of the church with the Roman empire, especially from the fourth century on. The first great Christian theoretician of the "just war" was Augustine of Hippo. He acknowledged the value of pacifist attitudes in both private and monastic life, but he also claimed that the Roman empire had a right to defend itself and that "lay" Christians were obliged to contribute to that defense. Augustine also argued that the imperial authorities were obliged to persecute schismatic or heterodox Christians.[6]

Medieval and modern theology continued to develop the doctrine of the "just war" in interesting ways. Thomas Aquinas distinguished a "double ef-

---

[5] Max Weber: Der Sinn der 'Wertfreiheit' der soziologischen und ökonomischen Wissenschaft, originally published in 1917, in: Gesammelte Aufsätze zur Wissenschaftslehre (Tübingen: J.C.B. Mohr, 1988), 467ff.

[6] This is the famous *cogite intrare* of his letter 93 to Vincentius, inspired by a peculiar interpretation of Luke 14:23. Cf. Migne, *PL* 33, cols 323-30.

fect" in his analysis of violent action. On the one hand, a person being attacked is "allowed" to act violently to defend his own life when he has a right to defend it. In fact, argued Thomas, one is more obliged to defend one's own life than the life of another. On the other hand, the defensive violent action causes as a secondary effect serious harm or even death to the aggressor. The person defending himself can desire only the first effect (defense of his own life); he accepts the second effect (the death of the aggressor) as an inevitable consequence which was not sought for its own sake.[7] Thomas insisted that in cases such as these, there has to be proportionality between the effects desired and those not desired. It would not be proportional, for example, to eliminate a whole family or a whole village in order to defend oneself against a single aggressor. This perspective helps us understand why Thomas defended the doctrine of the "just war." Not every war would be just, but a particular war may be just, if it fulfills certain conditions. For Thomas war can be just only when it is begun by a legitimate authority, when its cause is just, and when the intention of the belligerents is upright.[8]

In later centuries other thinkers added other motives that would justify war. Francisco de Vitoria, for example, considered the particular conditions of the conquest of the Americas. For Vitoria, the valid motives which would allow "legitimate authority" (the king of Spain) to initiate a "just war" included the right of persons to free movement (including the right to trade), the removal of impediments to preaching the Gospel, the forceful conversion of idolaters, the resolution of conflicts between the pope and Indian leaders converted to Christianity, the overcoming of tyrannical pagan governments, the subjection of Indians to governance by the Spanish, and the enforcement of obligations imposed by alliances established with friendly groups.[9] On the other hand, Vitoria denied legitimacy to other motives frequently used to justify the conquest of the America. These included the presumed universal dominion of the Spanish emperor, the universal authority of the pope, the right of discovery,

---

[7] Thomas Aquinas, *Summa theologiae* (London/New York: Blackfriars, 1964), II/II, q. 64., a. 7.
[8] *Ibid.*, II/II. q. 40.
[9] Cf. F. de Vitoria, *Relectio de Indis* (1539), (Madrid: CSIC Press, 1989), 99-112.

the rejection of the faith by a person, the sins of the Indians, the rejection of Spanish dominion, and the idea of a special donation of God.[10]

The new Protestant churches emerging from the Reformation maintained the territorial structure of Catholicism, and they received support from the respective governments of the emerging European nations. Despite some initial doubts, the Protestant theologians maintained the Roman Catholic "just war" doctrine but added some interesting commentary. Luther, for example, held that a person could "for evangelical reasons" renounce self-defense, but he could not renounce defense of his neighbor. Actually, Luther strongly supported the repression of the peasant rebellions by the German princes. For their part, the peasants justified their rebellions as the only way they could gain freedom to read and interpret the scriptures.[11] Other Protestant thinkers, working within the context of the religious wars of Europe, introduced some important reflections on the "just war" doctrine. Hugo Grotius taught, for example, that it is never legitimate to wage "preventive wars" in order to contain the growing power of an adversary.[12] Reflecting on the rights of the defeated, Grotius also taught that they should not be subjected to burdens greater than those caused by their original aggressions or greater than the damage suffered by the victors.[13]

With the exception of Christians like Erasmus of Rotterdam and the 16th-century Anabaptists, the "just war" doctrine dominated the thought of the "established" churches until very recent times. The Roman Catholic Church's official catechism still enunciates that doctrine; it explains several traditional criteria for discerning between just wars, which should always be of a defensive nature, and unjust wars. Some of the conditions mentioned are the following: the existence of serious, certain, and lasting damage inflicted by the

---

[10] Cf. *ibid.*, pp. 75-97.

[11] Cf. M. Luther, "Wider die räuberischen und mörderischen Rotten der Bauern", *WA* 18: 357-361.

[12] Cf. H. Grotius, *De iure belli ac pacis* (Amsterdam: The Hague, 1948), Book II, chap. 1, par. 17.

[13] Regarding the right of the defeated, Grotius taught, for example, that rape should be punished equally in war and in peace. Nevertheless, he still thought that it was legitimate to enslave the defeated.

aggressor; the exhaustion of all alternative measures; serious possibilities of success; and proportionality between the damage caused by the use of arms and the evils which the war seeks to avoid.[14]

The 20th century brought some important new developments with regard to this doctrine. First, Pope Paul VI in his encyclical *Populorum Progressio* effected what might be considered a "broadening" of the right to wage a "just war" by applying the traditional criteria to popular insurrections. A popular uprising could be considered legitimate in the face of evident and prolonged tyranny that violated the fundamental rights of persons and the common good of the citizens of a country.[15] The criterion of "legitimate authority" was thus applied to the concept of the ultimate sovereignty of the people. In any case, this doctrine has not appeared again in official documents of the Roman Catholic Church, perhaps because of its revolutionary implications and the use to which it was put in the sphere of liberation theology.

Second, Pope John Paul II moved in a somewhat opposite direction by opposing the second Gulf War. He sent a special envoy to President Bush to state his view that any military action without United Nations support would be unjust. This was a significant intervention, because, curiously, the "just war" doctrine had never been explicitly used in the course of the centuries to declare that a war was unjust, despite the many criteria that were available for making such a judgment. In fact, the authorities of the established churches of the different "Christian" countries always held that the military campaigns of their respective armies were "just," even when they were fighting against another "Christian" army.

Finally, another idea has been gaining strength within the sphere of official Roman Catholic doctrine and teaching, namely, that it would be very difficult for a modern war to be considered just because of its necessarily massive character and the devastating consequences it would inevitably have on the civilian population.[16]

---

[14] Cf. *Catechism of the Catholic Church* (Mahwah, NJ: Paulist Press, 1994), no. 2309.

[15] Pope Paul VI, *Populorum Progressio* (Mahwah, NJ: Paulist Press, 1967), no. 31.

[16] Some of these Catholic positions can be seen in the book edited by Joan Gomis, *La iglesia y la Guerra del Golfo (*Barcelona: Christianisme i Justicia, 1991).

However, it should be noted that even in such interpretation the "just war" doctrine is not fundamentally changed. In principle, it is still thought to be possible to wage just wars. What is changed is the application of the doctrine. Particular wars, or even all wars, begin to be classified more or less explicitly as unjust because they do not fulfill the proper conditions for a "just war." This judgment is made after applying the classical criteria, such as the existence of a legitimate authority (in this case, the United Nations) or the due proportionality between the good that war seeks to protect and the damage that it will necessarily cause.

It is important to consider to what extent the ecclesiastical version of the "just war" doctrine is fully compatible with the ethics of responsibility. Naturally, the traditional criteria presuppose the responsible use of violence. The idea that we are responsible for the results of our actions could lead us to think that in certain situations, at least theoretically, we would be irresponsible if we did not take violent action. If it was judged that a war was just, then not going to war would seem to be unjust. We could consequently ask whether, from the perspective of the "just war" doctrine, every pacifist position regarding a "just war" would be ethically untenable. It could at least be thought that part of the population would be acting immorally, if they did not go to war – for example, the soldiers or everyone who has sworn to defend the country. However, it is not clear that such an obligation extends to the whole population. In fact, those who defend "just war" theory agree that clergy should be exempt from military service.[17] This position is rather surprising, since it would seem that the clergy should be among the first people to act "justly." It seems to be the case, however, that a certain amount of bad conscience exists regarding the "just war" doctrine, perhaps as a remnant of the pacifist convictions of the earliest Christians.

Thus strict application of the ethics of responsibility could lead us to think that pacifism, even for the clergy or other sectors of the population, would be simply irresponsible. Is this the case? In order to probe deeper into the question, we need to examine the concept of responsibility more carefully.

---

[17] Thomas Aquinas, *Summa theologiae* II/II, q. 40, a. 2.

3. Analysis of Responsibility

First, the ethics of responsibility speaks of "giving an account" of one's own actions, as opposed to forgetting about the consequences of the actions or simply leaving them in God's hands. This brings out an important aspect of this ethics, namely, its assumption of power. The ethics of responsibility presupposes that the ethical subject is capable of controlling with some degree of certainty the foreseeable consequences of one's actions. That is why it is an ethics that Weber attributes specifically to politicians but that can naturally be extended to other persons as well, such as those who advise politicians or, more generally, to all those who have the ability to exercise some type of control over the consequences of their actions. In this sense, it is perfectly understandable that the abandonment of pacifism in the history of Christianity coincides, at least generally, with the church's gaining power in the fourth century through its alliance with the Roman Empire.

Second, responsibility obviously has something to do with "responding." In the case of political ethics, this "responding" or "giving an account" conveys the idea of some type of "democracy" in the broadest meaning of the expression. The responsible politician, for example, is the one who is ready to give the citizens an "account" of the consequences of his actions. When, for example, a politician refuses to assist people in their immediate needs, when he authorizes an industrial project that can cause environmental damage, or when he gets his country involved in a war, he does so with the belief that any other option would have even worse consequences than the foreseeable consequences of his actions, and that the citizens to whom he is responsible would find such consequences more difficult to accept.

Third, the "responsible" politician shares a whole series of convictions with the citizens to whom he is accountable. Decisions are therefore made in relation to those convictions with the result that those measures are preferred which will possibly produce the results most in accord with the convictions shared by the citizens to whom the politician must respond. Naturally, these convictions can be of different types, and they are sometimes far from altruistic. For example, the politician will always have to consider that the citizens will possibly value their own interests, including the preservation of their own lives, more than they value the interests of people in other societies, including the desire of those people to preserve *their* lives.

We see some of the difficulties arising from the ethics of responsibility:

1) First, a frequent criticism of the ethics of responsibility stresses the often unpredictable nature of the results of our actions. From the perspective of that ethics, however, there is an easy answer to that objection. One is responsible only for the foreseeable consequences of one's actions, not for the unforeseeable ones. In any case, what can certainly be affirmed from an ethical viewpoint is that responsibility includes an obligation to know as well as possible all the consequences that can derive from our actions.

2) A second difficulty in the ethics of responsibility has to do with its "democratic" dimension. In a democracy, a politician has a responsibility to all the citizens, but in fact his ethics of responsibility tends to be restricted to accountability to those persons or instances that are more capable of pointedly questioning the politician regarding the consequences of his actions. Thus, in calculating the consequences of his actions, the "responsible" politician also tends to calculate who the persons are who are going to demand that he account for his actions. It may be, for example, that a minority that is not going to fight in a war (because they are wealthy) are nevertheless those who will most insist that the politician foment war because of their particular economic interests.[18]

3) Third, this circumstance indicates that the ethics of responsibility seems to be characterized by a tendency to reduce moral criteria to mere pragmatism. Even if the politician has true moral convictions, what determines the course of "responsible" action are not his own convictions but the convictions of those to whom he must give an account. And even if these are not the most powerful figures but simply the general citizenry, still the politician in question would act according to true ethical criteria only if the majority of the citizens were guided by them as well. It is most certain, then, that the politician's personal convictions are beholden to criteria that go beyond morality. The ethics of responsibility would appear to have an almost inevitable tendency not only to make us accountable for the results of our actions but

---

[18] The same can happen with intellectuals, clergy, or similar ecclesiastical figures who, because they have in some cases great social influence, can promote a war (or revolution) even though they will not directly participate in it.

also to ensure that our actions are ultimately justified by the results they produce.

Of course, the politician can decide that he will be responsible not to the electorate or to the power groups that support him but "to his/her own conscience." When that happens, the differences between the ethics of conviction and the ethics of responsibility begin to fade, at least if it is granted that the ethics of conviction also has a place for responsibility. In any case, the usual criticisms of the ethics of responsibility target its principal difficulty but never formulate it completely, as we will demonstrate below. Before considering this difficulty, however, we need to ask whether the ethics of conviction is really devoid of a sense of responsibility.

4. Responsible Conviction

As we saw, the ethics of conviction is usually characterized as not take the consequences of one's actions into account. But what do we understand as the "consequence" or the "result" of an action? Every action produces something or attempts to do so, and that which is produced or attempted is precisely a result. If, for example, I want to avoid killing another human being and in fact avoid doing so, then that is a "result" of my action. Of course, another "result" of the same action could be that that same human being will kill me or other persons, if I have not killed him. As Thomas Aquinas stated well, an action can have multiple results, but those results must be willed when we act. We cannot claim that in firing a rifle what we want is peace, when the action of firing has the "double effect" of making the bullet enter the skull of the enemy. When we fire the rifle, we also want the bullet to enter the enemy's skull. Precisely for that reason, the ethics of conviction, far from ignoring the results of our actions, seeks to take *all* the results into account. In doing so, it understands that foreseeable future results cannot change the moral character of the immediately willed results, for the willing is a quality of the moral act that is inseparable from what is immediately willed.[19]

---

[19] That is why the actions themselves cannot be put on the same plane as their results, as if the actions could be justified by the results; cf. Antonio Gonzalez, *Teología de la praxis evangélica* (Santander: Editorial Sal Terrae, 1999).

This does not mean that the ethics of conviction prescinds from the ulterior results of one's actions, the results which one does not immediately will. Those results also belong to the action, but they are more intricate and complex than anything suspected by the ethics of responsibility.

1) We might say, for example, that the ethics of conviction has a "humanist" type of responsibility in the following sense: it holds that any sacrifice of human lives that is justified in function of the ulterior results of our actions *also* results in the general devaluation of human life. This conclusion clearly is true in all cases, where the human lives are sacrificed (by violence or omission) in function of any result other than the preservation of human life itself. But it can even be true in cases where there is a "calculation" of human lives and some lives are sacrificed in order to save others. Such a calculation, insofar as it trivializes homicide and makes it part of the culture or even a heroic value, can also result in the devaluation of human life in general. As the Talmud pointed out long ago, whoever kills an individual also kills in some way the whole of humankind.[20] But that is not all. When calculations are made regarding human lives, a difference is usually affirmed between "their" lives and "our" lives, so that a foreseeable result of such decision-making processes is the strengthening of nationalism, racism, or xenophobia. Moreover, the politicians charged with the task of making such calculations are placed in a position of deciding about human lives, with the foreseeable result that their tendencies toward authoritarianism, militarism, or dictatorship will be reinforced.

2) These considerations present us with a second type of responsibility that characterizes, or may characterize, the ethics of non-violence. It is what we might call "alternative" responsibility. As we saw, the doctrine of the "just war" sensibly recommends that we take into account the possibility of success when we use violence – for example, to overthrow a monstrous dictator-

---

[20] "God created Adam to teach us that the person who saves a single human being saves the entire world and that if a person kills a single human being, it is as if he were killing all humanity. The reason why God created a single man is to show us that all men are brothers, so that no one can say to another: 'My father is superior to yours.' God made just one man also so that the pagans could not claim that in heaven there are various divinities." Cf. *Sanhedrin*, 37a.

ship. Now it is important for us to be aware that when we confront violence with violence, an essential requirement for success is having a destructive capacity that is reasonably greater that the enemy's, and that means that the foreseeable result of such dynamics is what might be called "monster-making." In order to triumph over a violent aggressor, one would have to become in many ways similar to the aggressor. The foreseeable result is that one would assume the methods, values, and even the aims of the aggressor. This is an important consideration, even when the initial aggression takes the form of "institutionalized" or "structural" violence. A violent response to it is very likely to end up institutionalizing the very violence that made victory possible. On the other hand, the refusal to respond to the oppressor by using the same violent means has as a foreseeable result the development of alternative ways of acting that would avoid the need for the victims of aggression to become similar to the aggressors.

3) This brings us to a third type of responsibility, which can be present in the ethics of conviction. We can call it "anticipatory" responsibility. When the ethics of responsibility *justifies* its present actions in function of their foreseeable future results, in reality it is not opening up any new avenues to the future. What it calculates as a foreseeable result is simply a perpetuation of the modes of action that are normal present practice. In contrast, when a pacifist ethics renounces any pragmatic justification for its actions, it produces as a foreseeable result a demonstration that it is possible, now in the present, to live (and even to die) in another, different way. In this way individual and collective practice gives historical demonstration that another world *is* possible, and such a demonstration is particularly important in a global situation characterized by despair. In refusing to justify the future results of actions, pacifist ethics has the paradoxical result of anticipating a future that is different from the present, thus becoming the "first fruits" of a hope that can be understood even by those who do not share pacifist convictions. In some way, the ethics of conviction has the foreseeable result of precipitating a future that is different from and better than the present.

4) In the fourth place, we might say that that the responsibility of conviction is "polyarchic". The very fact that pacifist ethics does not expect to have its actions justified by results, for which it would have to give account before the general population, implies that moral pluralism already exists and should be allowed to exist. Certainly it is possible to be pacifist "and" anar-

chist, in the sense of rejecting the existence of an institution such as the state, which is essentially violent. As Weber put it, the state has a monopoly of legitimate violence in a given territory.[21] It therefore has an "avenging" nature, and that was how the first Christians saw it.[22] But anarchism, which seeks to do away with the state, is not the only possible alternative. It is also possible, for example, to allow for the existence of the state, in which not everyone necessarily has pacifist convictions. In that case, the foreseeable result of actions that are guided by pacifist convictions is the requirement of pluralism and the consequent differentiation of state and society. One cannot demand that the state be pacifist – that would go against its very essence as state – but one *can* demand the right not to be a state and not to behave like a state. Therefore, the foreseeable result of actions that are in accord with pacifist convictions is the growth of genuine ethical pluralism.

All the foregoing shows us that, paradoxically, the refusal to *justify* one's actions by their results is not an abandonment of responsibility but an eminent exercise of responsibility. Nevertheless, there is yet a fifth form of responsibility, which deserves to be analyzed more carefully.

5. Universal Responsibility

To illustrate the fifth type of responsibility proper to conviction, we begin with an anecdote that we understand to be a true story, though its usefulness does not depend on its authenticity. A young man, who was a member of the pacifist religious group called the Amish, was summoned to the recruitment office in his country. He was being drafted to take part in one of the wars waged by the United States during the 20th century. When the young man stated that his Christian convictions prevented him from killing another person, he was subjected to ridicule by the soldiers and the other young men being recruited. An angry officer told him: "If everyone were like you, then

---

[21] This is precisely the thesis that M. Weber defends in the 1919 work cited above, *Politik als Beruf*. From there it follows that the establishment of every state is usually linked to bloody battles aimed at consolidating a monopoly of violence in the hands of those who become the rulers of a determined territory. It also follows that there is no state without forces that specialize in the exercise of violence.

[22] Cf. Romans 13:4.

the communists would win the war and conquer the world." However, another officer felt moved to defend the youth and responded: "No, if everyone were like him, there would be no communists and no wars."

It is interesting to observe that both statements attempt to account in a "responsible" way for the youth's actions, and curiously, both statements are true, or at least they appear true. If everyone were like the Amish youth, there would be no possibility of resisting the enemy and the enemy would triumph. On the other hand, it is also true that if everyone were like the Amish youth, there would be no enemies to resist. When two apparently contradictory statements are true at the same time, we are confronted with what Kantian philosophers call a "paralogism,"[23] and in this case it is a paralogism of practical reason, not pure reason. The apparent contradiction of the paralogism is resolved by showing that one term has been used with two different meanings so that there is no real contradiction.

In these two statements the crucial word is "everyone." In the first statement ("if everyone were like you, the communists would win the war"), the word "everyone" refers to the citizens of the United States and perhaps to those of its allies. And it is true that, if everyone recruited from those nations refused to fight, their enemies would win the war. In the second statement ("if everyone were like you, there would be no wars"), the word "everyone" refers to all human beings in every part of the world. Clearly, if everyone in the world were like the young Amish man, there would be no wars. That is why both statements can be true at the same time without being contradictory: they are speaking of different groups of persons. It is important to observe that both statements are also conditional: they suppose that "everyone" would behave like the Amish youth, even though in reality not "everyone" behaves like him now. Both statements consider the possible consequences, were the Amish man's behavior to become widespread. Consequently, the two statements speak about responsibility but do so with regard to different sectors of humankind. In the first statement, the consideration of what is responsible makes a distinction between "them" and "us," while in the second statement responsibility includes everybody, all humanity.

---

[23] Cf. I. Kant, Kritik der reinen Vernunft, B 399ff.

A pacifist responsibility of conviction is truly universal, whereas the ethics of responsibility does not reach the level of universality that is demanded of all ethics, at least from a certain viewpoint.[24] From the perspective of the ethics of responsibility, for example, when aid is denied to regions suffering hunger, when aid is given to projects that are potentially harmful to the environment, or when war is being waged, what is happening normally in such cases is that the politician considers "responsibility" to be limited only to certain groups of people, such as to the inhabitants of certain countries as opposed to "enemy" countries, or to the present generation as opposed to future generations, who will suffer the ecological harm stemming from present actions.

The universal character of the responsibility inherent in the ethics of conviction obliges us to ask to what extent the so-called "ethics of responsibility" truly makes a claim to universality. We also can see that the perspective provided by the ethics of conviction is the only one that can do justice to the idea of the basic equality of all human beings. The ethics of conviction therefore corresponds closely with our aspirations toward something like "worldwide democracy," in which all the inhabitants of the planet will have an equal right to take part in collective decisions about matters that are of concern to everybody.

6. The Pacifism of Jesus

The foregoing considerations help us to understand Christian pacifism, although it would perhaps be better to speak about the "pacifism of Jesus" since Christians, as Gandhi said, seem to be the only people who have failed to grasp that Jesus was pacifist. In any case, the pacifism of the founder of Christianity is inscribed within the traditions of Israel. It has been shown that during the first century the Jewish people, independently of Christianity, on many occasions practiced pacifist resistance against the Roman authorities, and they did so with notable success. Consequently, in order to understand the position of Jesus, we need to insert it into its Jewish context.

---

[24] Cf. Xavier Zubiri, *Sobre el hombre* (Madrid: Allianza, 1986), 431.

1) The way "humanist" responsibility was understood in the religion of Israel should be seen against a very definite background. In the biblical traditions, the idea of creation implied a radical "de-divinization" of the universe. The idea of creation by God's word indicated a radical difference between Creator and creatures, so that creatures could in no way be considered as an emanation or part of the divinity. The realities that were considered divine in other Semitic religious contexts (sun, moon, stars) were seen by the Hebrews as mere creatures placed at the service of human beings ("lights" in the sky). Human beings were creatures, but unlike all other creatures, they were the "image and likeness" of God. This meant that just as the biblical God was radically distinct from his creation, human beings were not destined to be subject to any of the powers of this world. This is something that was affirmed of "Adam," that is, of every human being (*adam* in Hebrew). There was no created reality that could be considered superior to the human being; there was nothing to which humans could be sacrificed.[25]

2) Second, the appeal Jesus made to the Jewish tradition about "God's kingdom" captured the essence of how Israel understood itself in relation to the nations. In this self-understanding, Israel was called by God to be a *distinctive* people precisely in order to show the other nations what happens when God governs a people directly ("kingdom of God") and grants it proper "instruction" (*torah*) for living justly. The aim of the Torah was to prevent human beings from being subjected to the powers of this world, and so it included many measures designed to guarantee the fundamental equality of all Israelites. Thus according to Scripture, on a regular basis debts had to be canceled, slaves had to be liberated, and people had to be allowed to recover the ancestral lands they had lost through debt. In this way major differences between social groups were not allowed to form. When Jesus summoned people to the kingdom of God, he was assuming the validity of all these traditions, just as the early Christian church assumed their validity. This is what we mean by "anticipatory responsibility." The followers of Jesus had the task of showing their contemporaries that a different world *was* possible, and pre-

---

[25] Cf. Genesis 1-2.

cisely for that reason the kingdom of God is not to be experienced just as a utopia of the future but also as a present reality.[26]

3) Third, these traditions indicate a perspective that corresponds to what we have called "polyarchic" responsibility. The idea of the "reign of God," far from seeking to legitimize a monarchy in Israel, had rather the opposite purpose. From the Jewish viewpoint, if God is King, then it does not make consistent sense for a human being to be one. If God is Master, than slavery is called into question. If God is the "Lord of Hosts," then it doesn't make sense to build up a country's military power, etc.[27] Acknowledging God's sovereignty calls into question all the other powers that can never attain to reigning completely and totally over human beings. Human beings, living under God's reign, may sometimes accept other sovereignties, but only to a certain extent. Whenever there is conflict, they must obey God rather than human beings.[28]

The intention of Jesus was not that the people of God should be organized in the form of a state, as was the custom among the "nations."[29] Consequently, the early generations of Christians, remaining faithful to Jesus' intention, organized themselves into communities that resided in different states but nevertheless maintained a relative independence of the states, thus contributing to tolerance for pluralism. Clearly, Christianity could fulfill this role of promoting tolerance only insofar as it was a group to which people freely belonged. When Christianity became generally identified with society, that polyarchic responsibility could not be exercised fully, with the result that Christianity itself practiced various forms of intolerance. Needless to say, when this happened, Christian pacifism was necessarily replaced with formulas that were more pagan than evangelical, such as those used in "just war" theory.

---

[26] Cf. John Howard Yoder, *The Original Revolution* (Scottdale, PA: Herald Press, 2003); *The Politics of Jesus: Vicit Agnus Noster* (Grand Rapids: Eerdmans, 1994, 2nd edition).
[27] Cf. 1 Sam 8; 1 Sam 12; Judges 7-9; Deut 17; etc.
[28] Acts 5:29.
[29] Luke 22:24-27.

This "non-state" characteristic of Jesus' pacifism distinguishes itself decisively from the pacifism of Mahatma Gandhi. Gandhi's pacifism was practiced within the framework of a state, the country of India. States by their nature exercise a monopoly on legitimate violence within a determined territory. Consequently, Gandhi's pacifism had the paradoxical function of minimizing the use of violence during the period when the monopoly on violence was being transferred from the British Empire to the new national rulers. In contrast, Jesus' pacifism consisted in the explicit renunciation, by him and his followers, of Israel's configuration as a state. Consequently, Jesus could aspire to a type of radical universality that would be impossible in any purely nationalist project. This also explains Jesus' particular rejection of violence, which involves another paradox. Jesus was recognized by his followers as the Messiah, but the original significance of the term "messiah" was primarily political rather than mystical or spiritual. The Messiah was to be the anointed king of Israel. This king from Nazareth, however, "takes God's side" ("standing at his right hand") and calls into question the configuration of Israel as a state, just as the ancient prophets had done, and he does so in the name of the same God.

4) The pacifist proposal of Jesus is characterized also by what we have called "alternative responsibility," the nature of which can be easily surmised from all that has gone before. In the "Sermon on the Mount" Jesus uses two diverse approaches in bidding people to love their enemies: the first is a positive approach, telling them to imitate their heavenly Father who makes the sun rise on both the just and the unjust; the second is negative, chiding them for behaving like pagans when they should behave like God's people. The pagans also love those who love them and there is no "grace" in doing the same as they do.[30] In a world ruled by violence, the pacifist conviction has as its "responsible" aim the introduction into the world of new criteria of behavior, which can result in a renewed praxis.[31]

---

[30] In Luke 6:32-34 Jesus asks his disciples three times what "grace" (*charis*) they deserve for acting in the same *quid pro quo* fashion as the Gentiles. Curiously, that word is usually translated as "merit" or "credit," not as "grace."

[31] Cf. the "Sermon on the Mount" in Matthew 5-7.

Many of the examples Jesus gives are aimed precisely at introducing a different kind of praxis. A person who is struck on the right cheek is normally struck by the backside of the hand. That is a gesture of contempt such as a farm owner might show to his day laborers or a master to his slaves. When the person struck turns his left cheek to the oppressor, the latter experiences certain confusion and is forced to reflect. Likewise in the Hebrew culture, a person who is left naked in a courtroom causes considerable shame for all who are present. The saying about walking an extra mile is a clear reference to the Roman legions who measured distance in miles. In this case, a Jewish peasant who offered to carry the equipment of the Roman army an extra mile would be violating the regulations of the Romans themselves and would be getting the soldiers in trouble. In each of these cases, an attempt is made to introduce a different sort of behavior, one that helps to bring about something new by questioning of the logic of oppression and providing an opportunity to make the oppressors reflect on their own behavior.[32]

5) In all the foregoing we can also detect what we have called "universal responsibility." Such responsibility comes when there exist in the world a people who behaves distinctively but whose distinctive behavior is characterized precisely by universal openness. What characterizes other peoples is their insistence on the difference between "us" and "them." This difference can take on various forms, including racism, xenophobia, and nationalism. The very concept of citizenship implies a distinction between those who are citizens of a particular state and those who are not. Jesus took a different stance: while remaining within Jewish traditions, he stressed the idea that Israel was a universal person that was radically distinct from other peoples. But its distinctiveness consisted not in its cultural or ethnic differences but precisely in its universality. For Jesus, love of enemies meant being radically different from other people but the difference consisted precisely in *not making* distinctions. In this way Jesus assumed the universal mission of Israel and radicalized it.

---

[32] Cf. Matt 5:38-48. See also W. Wink, Engaging the Powers. Discernment and Resistance in a World of Domination (Minneapolis: Fortress, 1992).

Christian pacifism here takes on a very concrete aspect: the perspective of the oppressed. Those who were forced to carry the Roman army's equipment a mile, those who were ordered to hand over their tunics in a courtroom, or those who were struck by the back of the hand were not the priests who presided in Jerusalem, nor were they the Jewish nobles who administered a vassal state. They were the little people, the humiliated and the subjugated. The perspective of the ethics of responsibility is that of the politicians and those who hold power, but the perspective of Jesus is that of the least and the last. Those who promote war or revolution are not usually the ones who are killed on the fields of battle or the bombarded villages. The pacifism of Jesus does not adopt the viewpoint of the belligerent intellectuals or the combative clergy but rather that of the people who are forced to suffer the unrelenting institutionalized violence of social and political systems. With these people Jesus takes up once again Israel's ancient task of proposing to all humankind a universal alternative. That is the originality and the radicality of his "social theology."

7. Conclusion

Our review of some of the ethical difficulties presented by the contrast between the ethics of conviction and the ethics of responsibility has allowed us to reflect on some of the philosophical and theological problems presented by pacifism in general and by Jesus' pacifism in particular. There is no way that pacifism involves any sort of irresponsible conviction. Rather, it requires very serious forms of responsibility: humanist responsibility, alternative responsibility, anticipatory responsibility, polyarchic responsibility, and universal responsibility. Pacifism differs from other types of presumably responsible ethics by embracing a radical universality. Such universality in no way needs to be abstract. In the concrete case of Israel, as Jesus understood it, universality was to come about through the existence of a concrete people that was nevertheless also universal. Such people make their appeal not to the founders of new states (whether violent or peaceful) but to those who usually suffer violence. That is why pacifism in general, and Jesus' pacifism in particular, is especially relevant in an age characterized by individualism, oppression, and violence.

Max Weber held that the ethics of conviction ignores the consequences of one's actions, leaving them in the hands of God. We have seen that this is not the case. Pacifism involves, or can involve, responsible conviction. Moreover, Christian pacifism has an explicit dimension of faith. The idea of "God's kingdom" certainly implies confidence that God directs human history. More precisely, it implies confidence that God leads his people, even in the Old Testament, to a reduction of armed forces. This confidence does not refer to the foreseeable consequences of one's actions, for which pacifists *do* take responsibility. Rather, this confidence refers to the unforeseeable consequences of our actions. There is no need to appeal to scientific and philosophical theories of chaos to recognize that in human history the majority of the consequences of our actions are unforeseeable. For just that reason, faith is always in essence efficacious, for it is precisely faith that allows us to adopt modes of behavior which would never come about if we depended only on the foreseeable. In this sense also, faith moves mountains.

Abstract

Wir müssen Max Webers Gegenüberstellung von „Gesinnungsethik" und „Verantwortungsethik" überwinden. Einerseits gibt es verschiedene Verantwortungen, die die „Verantwortungsethik" nicht berücksichtigt. Andererseits enthalten verschiedene Arten der sog. „Gesinnungsethik" spezifische Verantwortungen, die eine wichtigere Bedeutung haben, als gewöhnlich angenommen. Die „Gesinnungsethik" enthält mindestens 1. eine humanistische Verantwortung, 2. eine Verantwortung für Alternativen, 3. eine Verantwortung der Antizipation, 4. eine Verantwortung für Pluralität und 5. eine sehr bedeutsame universale Verantwortung.

Migrations Of Enchantment In The Radical Reformation
The Undoing of a Material and Natural World

Karl Koop

The idea that the modern world has become disenchanted probably took its most enduring form in Max Weber's *The Protestant Ethic and the Spirit of Capitalism*, first published in 1904-05.[1] Weber believed that in the modern period the world had lost some of its allure and had become lifeless.[2] He saw this as a part of a great historic secularizing process tied to capitalism, the industrial revolution, the rise in science and technology, and the rationalistic world view of the Enlightenment.[3] He also linked the notion of disenchantment with the sixteenth-century Reformation, particularly the way in which Protestants rejected the sacramental world as a means of salvation and upheld a more intellectualized religion, in which mystical and spiritual forces were removed from common life.[4]

Weber was neither the first nor the last to draw connections between the Reformation and secularism. In the nineteenth century the Spanish philosopher, Jaime Balmes linked Protestant perspectives to the ascendant secularism of his day,[5] while Weber's contemporary, Ernest Troeltsch, viewed the

---

[1] Max Weber, *The Protestant Ethic and the Spirit of Capitalism*, trans. Talcott Parsons (London: Unwin Hyman, 1989).
[2] Patrick Sherry, "Disenchantment, Re-enchantment, and Enchantment," *Modern Theology* 25 (July 2009): 369. Sherry notes that the term had been used in various grammatical forms by writers before Weber, such as Wieland and Schiller, the latter using the verb *"entzaubern"* to mean something like "losing its magic."
[3] Sherry, "Disenchantment, Re-enchantment, and Enchantment," 370.
[4] Alexandra Walsham, "The Reformation and 'The Disenchantment of the World' Reassessed," *The Historical Journal* 51 (June 2008): 498.
[5] Ephraim Radner, "The Reformation Wrongly Blamed," *First Things* (June/July, 2012): 47-48.

Reformation as a catalyst of modernity, although in an indirect fashion. More recently these perspectives on the Reformation have proven to be remarkably resilient and have re-emerged in revised iterations in works such as Charles Taylor's *A Secular Age* and Brad Gregory's *The Unintended Reformation*.[6]

Nevertheless, Weber's views have also come under serious critique. In her review essay examining the relationship between the Reformation and the process of "disenchantment," Alexandra Walsheim attributes much of the recent criticism to the late Robert Scribner, who argued that the Reformation played a rather marginal role in the process of desacralization. Attending to the sensibilities of popular culture, Scribner found significant continuities between various medieval and Protestant mentalities, concluding that Protestantism "did not entirely dispense with holy persons, places, times, or objects; it engendered rituals and even a magic of its own."[7] Walsham's perspectives have been influenced by Scribner but also take into account the notion of a "Long Reformation," where religious reform and renewal extends over several centuries. Walsham sees dynamic processes evolving over a lengthy period of time whereby "the early Reformation (both Catholic and Protestant) grew out of and embodied a moment of scepticism and 'rationalism' that slowly faded, giving way in later generations to a fresh receptiveness to the supernatural and sacred."[8] She contends that theories of history that privilege linear and mono-directional historical trajectories need to be rejected in favour of reciprocal and dialectical patterns, which also may be found in other periods of history, not just the Reformation era.[9]

This chapter begins with the assumption that dialectical patterns of enchantment are observable throughout Christian history, with the late medieval and Reformation eras demonstrating an inward turn. I use the term "enchantment" to refer to the sacred and to the way in which the divine is pre-

---

[6] Charles Taylor, *A Secular Age* (Cambridge, MA: The Belknap Press, 2007); Brad S. Gregory, *The Unintended Reformation: How a Religious Revolution Secularized Society* (Cambridge, MA: The Belknap Press, 2012).
[7] Walsheim, "The Reformation and 'The Disenchantment of the World' Reassessed," 500.
[8] Walsheim, "The Reformation and 'The Disenchantment of the World' Reassessed," 527.
[9] Walsham, "The Reformation and 'The Disenchantment of the World' Reassessed," 527-28.

sent in the world. In focussing on Anabaptism in the Radical Reformation, I argue that the Anabaptists did not disregard the idea of the sacred but tended to shift its location away from the realm of nature and materiality to the realm of anthropology and ecclesiology. There were certain gains that were achieved in this shift. Nevertheless, I contend that there was a certain kind of undoing in that the Anabaptists, together with the other Reformers, lost the conceptual framework for thinking positively about the material and natural world. Modern day inheritors of the Reformation do well to retrieve theological frameworks that undergird the material and natural world, particularly in light of the challenges facing our modern civilization – the desecration of land, water, and air, and the over-consumption of resources. Such retrieval would be in keeping with certain theological traditions of the early Christian era and with the spirit of the Reformation, which initially called for faithfulness to the biblical witness and the importance of addressing the pressing issues of the times.

1. Dialectical Patterns of Enchantment

Already in the first centuries of Christian experience, the sacred was subjected to dialectical patterns of enchantment. Christianity was birthed in the context of the Greco-Roman world, influenced by Neo-Platonism, which tended to negate the natural and material world. In such an intellectual environment, influenced by their Jewish heritage, Christians advocated a distinctive world-affirming view that their neighbors found shocking and offensive. Christians believed that all temporal materiality, all nature, while not yet perfected, was the ground of God's self-revelation, worthy of reverence and redemption. "The world was not an evil imprisonment, not a dispensable illusion, but the bearer of God's glory."[10] The "Word made flesh" at Christ's incarnation was "an unparalleled development" in world history, representing "not nature's antithesis, but its fulfillment."[11] The Christian theme of resurrection held forth the promise that all of humankind, all materiality and all

---

[10] Richard Tarnas, The Passion of the Western Mind: Understanding the Ideas that have Shaped our World View (New York: Ballantine Books, 1991), 127.

[11] Tarnas, The Passion of the Western Mind, 139.

physical reality would be swept up in a final consummation. Nothing would be left out of God's perfecting salvation.

Yet this affirmation of the natural and material world was not embraced by all Christians. Under the influence of Neo-Platonism, many believers viewed the body as the residence of sin and evil, while the human soul was the exclusive recipient of divine redemption. The attention to trans-worldly reality reinforced a metaphysical dualism that in turn gave way to a moral asceticism, which augmented the mystical and the interior dimension of Christian experience.[12] The most radical expression of this metaphysical dualism was probably held by Gnostic thinkers who refused to embrace both the created order and its creator. So the followers of Marcion rejected the notion of the incarnation of the divine logos and posited a deep gulf between "between the beneficent Father of Jesus Christ and the malignant demiurge of creation."[13]

Gnostic tendencies were found especially among Christian communities of asceticism, but they were also met with strong opposition by Christian apologists such as Irenaeus (c. 130-202) who fiercely argued that the material world was a direct product of God's creation, and that the body was the essential link between the material and the immaterial world.[14] In the writings of Athanasius (c. 296-373) and Cyril of Alexandria (c. 376-444) the importance of the incarnation as the means of salvation was likewise upheld,[15]

---

[12] Tarnas, *The Passion of the Western Mind*, 140-148. Of course not all forms of asceticism accentuate this metaphysical dualism. For a discussion on this, see Philip LeMasters, "Incarnation, Sacrament, and the Environment in Orthodox Thought," *Worship* 81 (May 2007): 219-221.

[13] Jan Milic Lochman, *The Faith We Confess: An Ecumenical Dogmatics*, trans. David Lewis (Philadelphia: Fortress Press, 1984), 59.

[14] John D. Zizoulas, "The Early Christian Community," in Bernard McGinn, John Meyendorff, and Jean Leclercq, eds., *Christian Spirituality: Origins to the Twelfth Century* (New York: The Crossroad, 1997), 1:36. See, for example, selections of Irenaeus's work *Against Heresies* in Cyril C. Richardson, ed. and trans., *Early Christian Fathers*, The Library of Christian Classics (Philadelphia: The Westminster Press, 1953), 1: 358-397.

[15] Athanasius, "The Incarnation of the Word" in Philip Schaff and Henry Wallace eds, *Nicene and Post-Nicene Fathers of the Christian Church* (Grand Rapids, MI: Wm. B. Eerdmans, 1953), 4: 36-67. Alexander Schmemann refers to Cyril of Alexandria as a central teacher of the incarnation as well. See Alexander Schmemann, *Historical Road*

while early Rules of Faith and creedal expressions, along with the Christological formulas articulated at Nicaea, Constantinople, and Chalcedon, all affirmed the created order together with the human nature of Christ as the means of salvation.

Further, most of these confessional statements reflected an eschatological hope that rested upon the conviction that the body would experience resurrection.[16] In these various ways a major element within Christianity brought a "materialistic" world view to the Greco-Roman world through which the material acquired decisive significance while seeking to maintain a healthy distance from pantheism. In reaction to the rhetoric of the iconoclasts who sought to eradicate the visual dimension of liturgical experience, John of Damascus (c. 676-749) defended the use of icons and linked their presence with the incarnation: "I do not worship matter. I worship the Creator of matter who became matter for my sake, who willed to take his abode in matter, and who through matter wrought my salvation."[17]

This movement that valued the material and the natural world was not linear or mono-directional. Some very influential thinkers of the classical period tended to polarize spirit and matter, body and soul, and the propensity to view all of nature as corrupt, lived on.[18] Within the Alexandrian School, particularly in the thought of Origen, the distinction between spirit and matter persisted as it also did in the "uplifting" mystical spirituality of Pseudo-Dionysius.[19] Under the lingering influence of Neo-Platonism and Manichaean dualism, the distinction between spirit and matter continued with Augustine, who clearly exemplified an interior otherworldly religiosity, even while

---

to Orthodoxy, translated by Lydia W. Kesich (Crestwood, NY: St. Vladimir's Seminary Press, 1977), 124-136.

[16] Zizioulous, "The Early Christian Community," 36.

[17] John of Damascus, *On the Divine* Images 1.16, trans. by David Anderson (Crestwood, NY: St. Vladimir's Seminary Press, 1980), 23, quoted in Leonid Ouspensky, "Icon and Art," *Christian Spirituality*, 384.

[18] Tarnas, The Passion of the Western Mind, 139.

[19] See Paul Rorem, "The Uplifting Spirituality of Pseudo-Dionysius" in *Christian Spirituality*, 132-149

affirming God's gracious fecundity in bringing forth creation.[20] Augustine's more inward and otherworldly spirituality dominated much of the Middle Ages and would only be seriously challenged after the West came under Aristotelian influence. In the thirteenth century Thomas Aquinas asserted that nature itself could reflect divine wisdom and that it had "inherent religious value"; it was "not just as a dim reflection of the supernatural."[21] This "worldliness" came about through a deep reverence of the incarnate Word.[22] While not forsaking the transcendent in Augustine's theology, Thomas Aquinas reminded Christians of the intrinsic worth and dynamism of this world and that everything should be viewed as good in so far as it existed.[23]

Thomas' "worldly" influence continued beyond the high Middle Ages, but it was also met by counter forces that would come to dominate late medieval and Reformation thinking. One of those forces was a return of Platonism, ushered in by Petrarch's renaissance, and humanist desire to re-educate Europe.[24] Another force was a wave of mystical fervor that swept the Rhineland environs involving thousands of women and men, both lay persons and spiritual elites. The mystics were intensely devotional, Christ-centred, and ultimately concerned about achieving inner union with God.[25]

The fountainhead of German mysticism was Meister Eckhardt, whose metaphysical vision involved partaking of the divine nature, experiencing divinization, and leading a sanctified life involving love and service.[26] Werner Packull has observed that Eckhardt's mystical Christianity transcended ordinary sense perception, in which all externals, including the body, were to be subordinated to the soul. "For only in total detachment (*Gelassenheit*) from

---

[20] Tarnas, *The Passion of the Western Mind*, 148, 154. For a further discussion on Augustine's inward turn, see Jürgen Moltmann, *The Spirit of Life: a Universal Affirmation*, trans. by Margaret Kohl (Minneapolis: Fortress Press, 1992), 89-93.

[21] Tarnas, The Passion of the Western Mind, 180.

[22] Josef Pieper, "Of the Goodness of the World," *Orate Fratres* 25 (September 1951): 435.

[23] Pieper, "Of the Goodness of the World," 434.

[24] Tarnas, The Passion of the Western Mind, 209-219.

[25] Tarnas, The Passion of the Western Mind, 197.

[26] Tarnas, The Passion of the Western Mind, 197.

all creatureliness could the 'inner Word' be apprehended."[27] Eckhardt warned believers not to be dependent on the outer and the sensual. Those who displayed false confidence in the mediating power of the sacraments, for example, would never know Christ in truth. Salvation, according to Ekhardt's *theologia mystica*, involved a gradual disengagement from externals climaxing in union with the Divine.[28] Since mystical union included a unity of wills, following after Christ meant that the Christian life included strong ascetic and moralistic overtones.[29] Meister Eckhardt gave the mystical tradition distinct definition but later mystics, such as Johannes Tauler and the author of the *Theologia Germanica*, were clearly influenced by Eckhardt, establishing his mysticism as the devotional lingua franca in the late medieval period. Treading the same path was the *devotion moderna* of the Brethren of the Common Life, whose best known leader was Thomas a Kempis, the likely author of *The Imitation of Christ*. In this devotion, great emphasis was put on private prayer, introspection, the practice of journaling, and contempt for the world (*contemptus mundi*).[30]

In the sixteenth century Martin Luther's reforming interests in many ways countered the inward turn of the *via mystica*. Luther believed that Christians were called into worldly vocations and were meant to engage social, economic, and political realities. Nevertheless, Luther had a well-informed interest in German and Latin mysticism and even published versions of the *Theologia Germanica*.[31] The internalizing and individualizing emphasis in mysticism would find an echo in Luther's emphasis on personal faith and the

---

[27] Werner O. Packull, Mysticism and the Early South German-Austrian Anabaptist Movement 1525-1531 (Scottdale, PA: Herald Press, 1977), 22.

[28] Packull, *Mysticism*, 23. Martha Kirkpatrick takes a somewhat different view of Eckhart as well as the mystic, Hildegard of Bingen. See "'For God so loved the World'": An Incarnational Theology," *Anglican Theological Review* 91 (2009): 197 and 211.

[29] Packull, *Mysticism*, 24.

[30] Taylor, *A Secular Age*, 70.

[31] On Luther's relation to mysticism see Steven Ozment, *The Age of Reform 1250-1550: An Intellectual and Religious History of Late Medieval and Reformation Europe* (New Haven: Yale University Press, 1980), especially 239-244.

individual conscience.[32] Moreover, while Luther sought to retain the corporeal reality of the divine presence in the Eucharistic ritual, his confidence that material elements might themselves have saving power, by comparison with the established Roman Catholic doctrine, was diminished. This shifting away from viewing material reality as a means of grace was accentuated further by Ulrich Zwingli, who viewed the Eucharist as a memorial meal, and who understood spiritual baptism, not water baptism, as the primary "means by which individuals were drawn into the orbit of divine salvation."[33]

These desacralizing tendencies in Luther and Zwingli found wide-spread approval among sixteenth century reformers who not only questioned medieval understandings of baptism and Eucharist but also took critical aim of the entire sacramental world view that had assumed that the material world was holy and divinely infused. Material culture became suspect such that "altars, priestly vestments, church music, paintings, and sculptures were stripped down in a surge of iconoclasm that took these 'signs and wonders' of God for idols."[34] In this way, the Protestant Reformers chipped away at the sacred as it had been experienced for centuries, and moved in the direction of favoring a spirituality more subjective than what had been experienced in the Thomistic era that counted on the natural and material world to convey divine grace. With the Reformer's increased distinction between the Creator and creature, between divine transcendence and the world's contingency, the early moderns of the Reformation era increasingly viewed nature's character as mundane. In these developments, according to Richard Tarnas, there was also increasing emphasis given to humanity's dominion over creation contributing to humanity's sense of superiority over the natural and material world.[35]

---

[32] See Ulrich Duchrow, "Luther's Stellung zum Individualismus des modernen Geldsubjekst", in: Bd. 1 dieser Reihe, 142ff.

[33] Timothy George, *Theology of the Reformers* (Nashville: Broadman Press, 1988), 139.

[34] Regina Mara Schwartz, *Sacramental Poetics at the Dawn of Secularism: When God Left the World* (Stanford: Stanford University Press, 2008), 11.

[35] Tarnas, *The Passion of the Western Mind*, 241. Jan Milic Lochman suggests that in Luther's interpretation of the Creed in his Small Catechism of 1529, there was a noticeable shift in emphasis from affirming the Creator of heaven and earth to focussing attention on the confessing subject. He states that "by transferring the main weight of the confession from faith in the Creator to the vital interests of the confessing Christian, charac-

2. Anabaptists and the Sacred

The Anabaptists embraced the Protestant Reformation program with its message of salvation by grace through faith but were critical of the notion that grace could be received through the church's sacraments. Influenced by the late medieval mystical traditions, they also incorporated in their theology an inward and other-worldly orientation, which was accentuated in times of persecution. In their reforming efforts they did not desacralize the world, but re-imagined the sacred, for the most part shifting its location away from a natural and material jurisdiction to the realm of the anthropological and the ecclesiological. In some of their commentaries on the Creed, the Anabaptists interpreted the theology of the first article in personal and subjectivist terms.[36] Among others, a two-kingdom theology encouraged dualistic thinking leading some to associate natural creation with the fallen world.[37]

---

teristic tendencies in Protestantism were reinforced that led in the direction of a privatization of the faith in creation. It also lent credence to the assumption that the world had been created exclusively for humanity's sake, as our object, our domain" (Lochmann, *The Faith We Confess*, 67). Lochman's perspective needs further analysis in light of Luther's other writings, and perhaps does not sufficiently take into account the genre of catechetical writing that by nature will be more personal and individualistic in tone. I wish to thank Ulrich Duchrow for drawing my attention to this observation.

[36] See, for example, Anabaptist interpretations of the creed, such as Hubmaier's "Twelve Articles in Prayer Form," in H. Wayne Pipkin and John Howard Yoder, trans. and eds., *Balthasar Hubmaier: Theologian of Anabaptism* (Scottdale, PA: Herald Press, 1989), 235; Leonard Schiemer, "The Apostles Creed: An Interpretation," in Cornelius J. Dyck, ed., *Spiritual Life in Anabaptism* (Scottdale, PA: Herald Press, 1995), 31-32; "A Confession of Faith by Jörg Maler," in Karl Koop, ed., *Confessions of Faith in the Anabaptist Tradition 1527-1660* (Kitchener, ON: Pandora Press, 2006), 38-39.

[37] Thomas Finger, "An Anabaptist/Mennonite Theology of Creation," in *Creation and the Environment: An Anabaptist Perspective on a Sustainable World*, ed. Calvin Redekop (Baltimore: Johns Hopkins University Press, 2000), 154. For other perspectives on Anabaptism and creation, see other essays in the volume by Redekop as well as Calvin Redekop, "Mennonites, Creation and Work," *Christian Scholar's Review* 22 (June 1993): 348-66; Calvin Redekop, "Toward a Mennonite Theology and Ethic of Creation," *Mennonite Quarterly Review* 60 (July 1986): 387-403; Royden Loewen, "The Quiet on the Land: The Environment in Mennonite Historiography," *Journal of Mennonite Studies* 23 (2005), 151-64; Dan Epp-Tiessen, ed., *Vision: A Journal for Church and Theology,* vol. 9 (Spring 2008), entire issue. I wish to thank Kathy McCamis, a student at Canadian Mennonite University, for making me aware of this literature.

To be fair, there were Anabaptists from the South German environs who believed that the divine was at work through the natural order, particularly in their teaching on "The Gospel of All Creatures." The teaching "incorporated the medieval assumption of a hierarchical chain of being. God had structured creation so that the lower orders found their fulfillment in submission to the rule of the higher."[38] Thus animals were ordained to serve humanity, while humanity was created to serve God. Hans Hut, a key proponent of this "Gospel" likely drew his ideas from Thomas Müntzer, as well as conclusions drawn from Genesis 1:28, where humankind was instructed to subdue and have dominion over creation. Hut examined the world of nature, convinced that it was a source of revelation, and that "the principle of fulfillment through suffering [was] revealed in every creature."[39] As Werner Packull has noted, "it was Hut's achievement that he gave the external witness of the creatures a greater autonomous role."[40] The divine order that was infused in nature revealed "the principle of redemptive and restorative suffering" whereby creation "not only mirrored the omnipotence of the Creator, but revealed His redemptive activity."[41] For a time Hut even emphasized that the witness in nature was a reflection "of the crucified Son and of the cathartic quality of suffering."[42] Followers of Hut, such as Leonhard Schiemer and Hans Schlaffer, assimilated some of Hut's ideas, as did Pilgram Marpeck who linked "the suffering of the creatures to the suffering of Christ and the believer."[43]

---

[38] Packull, *Mysticism*, 69.

[39] Rollin Stely Armour, *Anabaptist Baptism: A Representative Study* (Scottdale, PA: Herald Press, 1966), 81. For an extended discussion on "The Gospel of All Creatures," see Armour, *Anabaptist Baptism*, 64-68, 71-74, 80-83. For a rendition of Hut's teaching see his "The Mystery of Baptism," in Walter Klaassen, ed., *Anabaptism in Outline: Selected Primary Sources* (Scottdale, PA: Herald Press, 1981), 48-53.

[40] Packull, *Mysticism*, 70.

[41] Packull, *Mysticism*, 70.

[42] Packull, *Mysticism*, 70.

[43] Neal Blough, *Christ in Our Midst: Incarnation, Church and Discipleship in the Theology of Pilgram Marpeck* (Kitchener, ON: Pandora Press, 2007), 32. The teaching on "The Gospel of All Creatures" probably extended to the Marpeck circle, although in a reduced form. For example, see in "A Confession of Faith by Jörg Maler (1554) accord-

For most Anabaptists, however, the divine was not to be found in nature, but in the realm of anthropology and ecclesiology. Hans Denck, for instance, maintained that the sacred was lodged within humanity that contained a divine spark, presupposing divine immanence, leading to cooperation between the human and divine in the process of salvation.[44] Denck could not accept the Lutheran teaching of salvation *via iustitia aliena* of Christ, nor the formula *simul iustus et peccator* which conflicted with his understanding of gradual deification or divinization. Denck's internalizing religion also challenged sacramentalism, which insisted on grace being transmitted to the believer by external means. Grace, according to Denck, "was the divine Word itself effecting a transformation in the sinner and enabling him to imitate Christ's holy example."[45] The divine Word, which Denck located within the believer, was the logical corollary leading to outward action. Not some outer reality, but the inner Word was the ontological basis for holiness and a life of discipleship, which mirrored *actual* righteousness, rather than *imputed* righteousness of a Lutheran kind. As the inner reality of the believer was being transformed in union with Christ, so the outward expression of the Christian life was placed in conformity with the life of Christ through the power of the Holy Spirit.[46]

A similar theological trajectory existed among first generation Anabaptists in the Low Countries. A starting presupposition among these radical reformers, however, was not the belief in the presence of a divine spark within every human being, but the conviction that earthly flesh was thoroughly corrupted due to the fall that took place in the Garden of Eden when Adam and Eve disobeyed God. With this belief and consequences of the fall, these Anabaptists questioned how a Savior with an earthly body could be an adequate sacrifice, strong enough to overcome the powers of evil that now dominated the

---

ing to the Treasures of the Holy Scriptures," in Koop, *Confessions of Faith in the Anabaptist Tradition*, 38-39. Cf. also J. Prieto, above 143ff.

[44] Discussion on the divine spark, for example, can be seen in Denck's essay, "Concerning True Love," in *The Spiritual Legacy of Hans Denck: Interpretation and Translation of Key Texts,* by Clarence Bauman (New York: E. J. Brill, 1991), 182-203.

[45] Packull, *Mysticism,* 52.

[46] For a summary of Denck's thought, see Packull, *Mysticism*, 35-61.

world and all flesh.[47] Melchior Hoffman, who brought Anabaptists ideas to the Low Countries in the first place, concluded that Jesus Christ had indeed become incarnate in bodily form but his flesh must have had heavenly origins. The Word had indeed become flesh but could not have received his flesh from Mary, since all human flesh must have been corrupted through the fall. Only heavenly flesh, Hoffman reasoned, was sufficiently strong enough to overcome the powers of evil.[48]

These ideas were picked up by second generation leaders in the north, Menno Simons and Dirk Philips, even as they attempted to maintain a Chalcedonian Christology, affirming both Christ's deity and humanity. Like Hoffman, Menno Simons and Dirk Philips asserted that the flesh of Jesus could not be associated with Mary's flesh in any way because of its earthly association. Jesus was conceived *in* Mary, not *of* Mary.[49] This had implications for believers and their transformed status. Through the experience of the new birth, believers became partakers of Christ's nature, experiencing a form of divinization and regeneration. The regenerated life of the Christian had its ontological basis in the heavenly flesh of Christ; for this flesh indeed had the power to be truly transformative. While human beings were born with a corruptible nature, the rebirth provided the basis for outward holiness and faith active in love. With God becoming human, through the power of the Holy Spirit, humanity could become divine, receive eternal life and become clothed with divine moral characteristics.[50] The corporate expression of this new humanity was the community of saints, the church, a regenerated

---

[47] Karl Koop, Anabaptist-Mennonite Confessions of Faith: The Development of a Tradition (Kitchener, ON: Pandora Press, 2004), 92.

[48] See Melchior Hoffman's "Truthful Witness," in Klaassen, *Anabaptism in Outline*, 27-28.

[49] See, for example, Menno Simons, "The Incarnation of our Lord," in *The Complete Writings of Menno Simons,* trans. Leonard Verduin, ed J. C. Wenger (Scottdale, PA: Herald Press, 1984), 785-834; Dirk Philips, "The Incarnation of our Lord," in *The Writings of Dirk Philips 1504-1568*, trans. Cornelius J. Dyck, William E. Keeney, and Alvin J. Beachy (Scottdale, PA: Herald Press, 1992), 134-151. Although this view deviated from classical formulations, it was consistent with the common wisdom of the day that assumed that women did not contribute anything biologically of themselves to their offspring.

[50] Koop, Anabaptist-Mennonite Confessions of Faith, 100.

body "without spot or wrinkle," maintaining Christ-like ethical standards guaranteed through the practice of church discipline. Salvation was experienced through participation in this community with its liturgy, ceremonies, and discipline. But here the sacramental dimension was not as much present in the specific elements of bread, wine, liturgy, and discipline. Far more, Menno Simons and Dirk Philips viewed the church itself as sacrament.

On the question of the individual sacraments, such as the Eucharistic meal, Anabaptists everywhere were in essential agreement with Zwingli in their denial that the elements mediated grace. Ostensibly, the meal was seen a memorial of Christ's death, and a sign of fellowship and Christian unity. Commonly citing the Creed, they noted that Christ had ascended into heaven and that he presently sits at the right hand of the Father. Thus, Christ's flesh and blood were not actually present in the elements themselves. Against the backdrop of the Roman Catholic Church espousing a doctrine of transubstantiation, the Anabaptists stated in countless court records that the bread was only bread, the wine only wine.[51] But in practice and beyond the reaches of courtroom rhetoric, most Anabaptists did not view the elements lightly. They wrote extensively about the profound meaning of the Supper and they participated in the meal with reverence and deep devotion.

Pilgram Marpeck stood out as an Anabaptist who actually came very close to Roman Catholic teaching, articulating a view that the sacraments themselves involved mediating grace. Marpeck believed that the elements of water, bread, and wine were physical windows and doors which participated in the divine and through which the divine could be known. They were "physical means of growth into divine love and the mature spiritual life.[52] Yet, among the Anabaptists, Marpeck's perspective was unique. Anabaptists were far more likely to view the elements as subordinate to the more important experience of the believer that takes place inwardly. Conrad Grebel, writing

---

[51] C. Arnold Snyder, "Was the Bread only Bread, and the Wine only Wine? Sacramental Theology in Five Anabaptist Hymns," *Conrad Grebel Review* 24 (Fall 2006): 26.

[52] C. Arnold Snyder, *Anabaptist History and Theology: An Introduction* (Kitchener, ON: Pandora Press, 1995), 362. See Pilgram Marpeck, "A Clear and Useful Instruction," in *The Writings of Pilgram Marpeck*, trans and ed. William Klassen and Walter Klaassen (Scotdale, PA: Herald Press, 1978), 69-106.

within a Swiss context, referred to outer baptism as that which signifies the Christian walk more deeply rooted in inner baptism.[53] Other Anabaptists inferred that the elements were sacred in a spiritual sense. Menno Simons, for instance, stated that the Supper was a "holy sacramental sign," "an emblem of Christian love," and "a communion of the flesh and blood of Christ," which brought about a spiritual communion with Christ.[54] Likewise, Dirk Philips referred to the eating in the communion meal as a spiritual activity, not of the body but of the "mouth of the soul."[55] What these Anabaptists had in common was not a belief that the body of Christ was physically present in water, bread, and wine, but that Christ was in fact truly present in the believer. This supposition became the basis of a further understanding of the corporate body of Christ, the church, as the primary locus of Christ's presence.

In the Roman Catholic Church, the sacraments were viewed in the elements of the Mass, in physical images, in the juridical structures of the church, in the priesthood, and in the magisterium. This, together with other Protestants, the Anabaptists repudiated. Nevertheless, they believed that the people of God, the visible community gathered locally, were members of Christ's body. Far from being a metaphor for the church, the language concerning the body of Christ was intended as a literal description.[56] Christ was indeed present through the church together with its words and good deeds with the relation to Christ being one of incorporation.[57]

This idea of incorporation and living as members of Christ's body was especially prominent in the theology of Pilgram Marpeck, who grounded his ecclesiology in the incarnation. Marpeck believed that "not only did a good God bring a good creation into being, the centrality of the physical side of creation in the saving process was revealed, confirmed, and cemented by the

---

[53] See Klaassen, *Anabaptism in Outline*, 164-65; 191-92.
[54] Klaassen, Anabaptism in Outline, 208-210.
[55] Klaassen, Anabaptism in Outline, 206.
[56] Snyder, Anabaptist History and Theology, 355.
[57] Brian Hamilton, "The Ground of Perfection: Michael Sattler on 'the Body of Christ,'" in Abe Dueck, Helmut Harder, and Karl Koop, *New Perspectives in Believers Church Ecclesiology* (Winnipeg, MB: CMU Press, 2010), 143.

incarnation."[58] Accordingly, salvation came through the humanity of Christ with the clearest expression of divine love taking place within the community of love, the church, which was understood as the "primary place of God's presence and action."[59] The church as the body of Christ was "a sacramental offer of God's grace, mercy, and salvation for all."[60] As in the incarnation, Marpeck believed that God's presence would continue to be offered "through the physical Body of Christ to individuals and to the world by means of external and visible testimonies, ceremonies, and acts of love."[61] Marpeck's logic was further drawn from the writings of the Gospel of John that included trinitarian dimensions. In the same way that the Word had become flesh, in Jesus the Word was "prolonged throughout history in the concrete life of the believing community through the power of the Holy Spirit."[62] As the Father had sent Jesus into the world, Marpeck reasoned, so also the church was now being sent into the world to be a witness to the world (John 20: 21-22) through worship, love, and service.[63]

This emphasis of the church as a sacramental body was also a part of the ecclesiology of Michael Sattler, a leader among the Swiss Anabaptists. Scholars in the past have tended to emphasize the voluntary aspect of willing disciples that constituted Swiss Anabaptism.[64] But as Brian Hamilton has noted, this definition of the Christian community fails to fully explain the essential necessity of the church for the Anabaptists. For Sattler, the church was essential because she was the body of Christ, "and because unity with Christ's body [was] itself the essence of salvation."[65] In this way reconciliation and the atoning work of Christ could not be separated from the life of

---

[58] Snyder, Anabaptist History and Theology, 361.
[59] Blough, Christ in our Midst, 246.
[60] Snyder, Anabaptist History and Theology, 362.
[61] Snyder, Anabaptist History and Theology, 362.
[62] Blough, Christ in our Midst, 246.
[63] Blough, Christ in our Midst, 245-46.
[64] Hamilton, "The Ground of Perfection," 143.
[65] Hamilton, "The Ground of Perfection," 143-144. For a compendium of Sattler's writings, see John Howard Yoder, ed. and trans., *The Legacy of Michael Sattler* (Scottdale, PA: Herald Press, 1973).

the church. Sattler insisted on the union between Christ and the Christian community, what Augustine had referred to as "the *totus Christus, caput et membra*, the whole Jesus Christ, head and members."[66] For this reason, ethical issues, such as taking up the sword, or swearing oaths, could also not be set aside merely on the grounds that they were contrary to the teachings of Christ. More fundamentally, disobedience to Christ's teachings and example was problematic because such action destroyed the ontological and sacramental unity that was presumed when the believer was incorporated into Christ's body.

These teachings on the church illustrate the extent to which Anabaptists were willing to maintain a belief in the divine presence existent in the church, and they are yet another illustration of how they found ways of envisioning the sacred outside of the natural and the material world. Whether Anabaptists emphasized the holy presence of the divine in the individual, in ethical action, or in corporate expression, they did not disenchant the world as Weber might have it, but facilitated migrations of enchantment so as to re-enchant their world in a new format. In Marpeck's theology and in some other South German expressions of "The Gospel of All Creatures," we see glimpses of a theology affirming the natural and material world. Far more conspicuous in Anabaptist thought, however, was a heightened awareness of the sacred located in the realm of anthropology and ecclesiology. The sacred was not denied but present within the divinized new humanity, within the believer who had experienced the new birth, and within the body of Christ, the community of saints. If we were to take the time to contemplate the longer view, the "Long Reformation" of Anabaptism, we would most certainly see a continuation of this tradition, less attentive to the natural and the material world, and more deeply invested in anthropological and ecclesiological concerns. If we were to examine two of the most significant movements in which Mennonites were engaged from the seventeenth to the nineteenth centuries – the Dutch Collegiant and Pietist movements – we would see this on-

---

[66] Hamilton, *The Ground of Perfection*, 149. Hamilton is drawing on Augustine's *In Johannis Evangelium Tractatus*, XXVIII.1, in Corpus Christianorum Series Latina 36, ed. R. Willems (New York: Brepols, 1954).

going attention to the anthropological and the ecclesiological; we would not see much emphasis on the natural and material world.[67]

The Protestant radicals brought a new sense of the divine presence in the realm of the individual and the communal. But their contributions raise questions as to what may have been lost in these migrations of the sacred. Could it be that the Anabaptists, along with other Protestants, lost the ability to speak constructively about the material and the natural world – a language that we desperately need in view of the environmental challenges facing us in our time (Thesis 35)?

3. Retrieving other Imaginaries

Our judgements of the Reformation era need to be measured with care. We must recall that the late middle ages and Reformation eras were periods in which Europeans were living with much anxiety. The anxiety was linked to a preoccupation with suffering and death that was brought on by the twin experiences of famine and plague. The agrarian crisis was so severe in the early fourteenth century that in some regions people resorted to cannibalism. The pandemics that swept Europe reached their climax with the bubonic plague of 1349 that brought death to about one third of Europe's population. Added to these calamities were economic and politic instabilities, and the savageries of warfare with the introduction of the gunpowder canon – all of which contributed to a morbid preoccupation with death.[68]

Because death brought every individual before the terrifying judgement seat of a holy and wrathful God, it was particularly moral anxiety that became the preoccupation of late medieval and early modern Christians. Luther's struggle to find a gracious God was thus clearly paradigmatic for his

---

[67] See Andrew Fix, Prophecy and Reason: The Dutch Collegiants in the Early Enlightenment (Princeton: Princeton University Press, 1991); Robert Friedmann, Mennonite Piety through the Centuries: Its Genius and its Literature (Goshen, IN: The Mennonite Historical Society, 1949). The question of the extent to which Mennonites of the early enlightenment would have been attuned to aesthetics, or the extent to which later Pietists were influenced by German Romanticism, where nature becomes divinely infused, requires further examination.

[68] See Karl Georg Zinn, Kanonen und Pest: Über die Ursprünge der Neuzeit im 14. und 15. Jahrhundert (Oplanden: Westdeutscher Verlag, 1989).

time. As Timothy George has put it, Luther was "just like everybody else, only more so."[69] His doctrine of justification by grace through faith was a direct response to the issues and concerns of his age. In addition to moral anxieties, Europe longed for alternative forms of community, the sharing of economic resources, and new social patterns of interaction as the emerging capitalist economy was calling into question older patterns of relationship. All of these concerns were at the forefront as both magisterial and radical reformers discussed the importance of personal justification by grace through faith, the divinization or rebirth of the individual, and the holy nature of the church.

But our age is a different one. To be sure we long for a gracious God, and the questions about what it means to be authentically human or what it means to be authentically in community persist. But these longings and questions have changed in complexity in light of the challenges of globalization, growing economic disparities, and technological advances which appear to be beyond our control. At present we are also facing human engineered environmental devastation of unprecedented proportions. From the loss of glacier fields and the visible contamination of air and water to waste dumps and species extinction, "the planet is facing assaults from human activity as never before."[70] As Martha Kirkpatrick has put it, "the decline in the natural systems that sustain life and the rising aggregated social demand due to population and consumption increases are on a collision course. This makes the environmental crisis one of the most pressing and immediate problems of our age."[71]

We have recognized this crisis of our planet for decades, but many Christians have resisted the seriousness of the situation, either questioning the science of global warming, or perhaps dismissing environmental concerns because they appear to be politicized. Yet the preoccupation with science or politics is wrongly placed. Christians should not, in the first instance, be

---

[69] George, The Theology of the Reformers, 23.

[70] Martha Kirkpatrick, "'For God so Loved the World': An Incarnational Ecology," *Anglican Theological Review* 91 (2009): 191.

[71] Kirkpatrick, "'For God so Loved the World,'" 192.

solely preoccupied in affirming or denying the science of global warming – as important as the science surely is. Nor should Christians, in the first instance, solely concern themselves with whether the environmental discussion is ideologically driven – as surely as it is driven from both the left and the right. It is far more important, in the first instance, that Christians begin to seriously ask what it means when the Bible tells them that "the earth is the Lord's and all that is in it" (Ps. 24:1). It is far more urgent for them to contemplate the importance of the stewardship of creation (Gen. 1: 26-28) and fully come to terms with the fundamental Christian conviction that God so loved the world that the "Word became flesh and lived among us" (Jn. 1:14). It is also imperative that they begin to ask what it means when Scripture reveals that all of creation longs for the redemption that is to come (Rom. 8; see Thesis 33 and 34).

Some pre-modern traditions seem to be in a better position than the Reformation traditions in addressing environmental concerns. In antiquity and in the middle ages we see a posture attentive to the natural and the material world that is less apparent in modern times. This is particularly the case when we consider the incarnational theology of Irenaeus, the embrace of the material and iconic in John of Damascus, or the appropriation of a natural theology in Thomas Aquinas, who sees all of reality as divinely infused. These ancient and medieval thinkers, along with their associates, had a profound sense of the divine in all of reality. It is therefore not surprising that contemporary theologians rooted in the pre-modern era continue to reflect positively on the material and natural world.

Philip LeMasters notes that "the incarnation of Jesus Christ is the lynchpin of Orthodoxy's view of the place of matter in our life before God."[72] Writing from the perspective of the Eastern Orthodox tradition, Alexander Schmemann has argued for the importance of seeing "the world as sacrament," and that now in modern times "the world must be recovered."[73] He maintains that everything that exists is a divine gift to humanity and everything that exists is

---

[72] LeMasters, "Incarnation, Sacrament, and the Environment in Orthodox Thought," 212.
[73] Alexander Schmemann, *The World as Sacrament* (London: Darton Longman & Todd, 1966), 12.

intended to make God known and to bring about communion with God: "God blesses everything he creates, and, in biblical language, this means that he makes all creation the sign and means of his presence and wisdom, love and revelation. 'O taste and see how gracious the Lord is.'"[74] After centuries of denominational absolutism, surely the Reformation traditions would be enriched if they would open themselves to learning from the Orthodox and Roman Catholic traditions, which have a better sense of God's presence in the natural and material world.

Yet perhaps there is also a constructive potential within the Reformation itself. In the sixteenth century, confidence in the Apostles' Creed as a foundation for Christian understanding was an almost universal conviction among the varying proponents of reform.[75] Especially a re-reading of this text in light of its polemic against Gnostic tendencies in early Christianity might shed new light on the inherent value of God's creation, the affirmation of the humanity of Christ, the presence of the Spirit in the world, and the resurrection of the body. A further resource from the Reformation is the emphasis on peace, which was an important theme of a number of Anabaptist Reformers. If peace and reconciliation is at the heart of the message of Jesus,[76] the church will not only need to consider how the neighbor and enemy are to be treated as a faithful response to the cross, but they will also need to consider what it means to be reconciled and at peace with the whole of God's creation.

---

[74] Schmemann, *The World as Sacrament*, 14. For another eastern perspective, especially in light of the views of Gregory of Nazianzus see Sigurd Bergmann, *Creation Set Free: The Spirit as Liberator of Nature* (Grand Rapids: Eerdmans, 2005).

[75] See Russel Snyder-Penner, "The Ten Commandments, the Lord's Prayer, and the Apostles' Creed as Early Anabaptist Texts," *Mennonite Quarterly Review* 68 (July 1994): 318. For Luther's view on the Creed, along with the Ten Commandments and the Lord's Prayer, see Martin Luther, "A Short Exposition on the Decalogue, the Apostles' Creed and the Lord's Prayer," in Bertram Lee Woolf, trans. and ed., *Reformation Writings of Martin Luther*, The Basis of the Protestant Reformation (New York: Philosophical Library Inc., 1953), 1:71.

[76] See, for instance, John Howard Yoder, *The Politics of Jesus: Vicit Agnus Noster*, 2nd edition (Grand Rapids: Eerdmans, 1994).

Finally, the theme of grace, which was a central motif for both magisterial and radical reformers, needs deeper consideration.[77] Norman Wirzba has observed that the language of grace is important because it points to our being called into intimacy with God, who is also intimately in communion with the world.[78] When we acknowledge this grace and live out our unique calling in God's image, "we learn to highlight, promote, and make concrete God's loving, life-giving intentions for the whole world."[79] Because "Christ is the one through whom all things are created (cf. John 1:3; Col 1:15-20), we should not be surprised to learn that in Christ 'all things' will also be redeemed."[80] If Wirzba is correct, then true faith is not about migrating into an otherworldly orientation. The language of grace is an invitation to draw nearer to the heart of the world "and there discover the life of God at work"[81] (Thesis 36). If the Reformers – both mainline and radical – were living in the present age, they would call for nothing less.

Abstract

Während die Täufer bedeutsame Beiträge zur Theologie der Reformationszeit entwickelten, waren sie nicht in der Lage, positiv über die materielle und natürliche Welt zu denken, wie dieses Kapitel argumentiert. Heutige Erben der Reformation tun gut daran, biblische und andere vormoderne Begriffskategorien wiederzuentdecken, um über die materielle und natürliche Welt nachzudenken – besonders angesichts der Herausforderungen, vor denen die moderne Zivilisation steht: der Schändung des Bodens, des Wassers und der Luft sowie Überkonsum der Ressourcen. Solche Wiederentdeckungen würden ganz im Geist der Reformation selbst sein. Denn sie rief zur Treue dem biblischen Zeugnis gegenüber auf und hielt es für wichtig, eine Antwort auf die brennenden Fragen der Zeit zu finden.

---

[77] For a study on grace in the radical reformation see Alvin J. Beachy, *The Concept of Grace in the Radical Reformation* (Nieuwkoop: B. De Graaf, 1977).

[78] Wirzba, "Agrarianism," 246.

[79] Wirzba, "Agrarianism," 247.

[80] Wirzba, "Agrarianism," 247-48. Jürgen Moltmann develops a cosmic Christology along these lines. See especially *The Way of Jesus Christ: Christology in Messianic Dimensions* (San Francisco: Harper SanFrancisco, 1990), 274-291.

[81] Wirzba, "Agrarianism," 250.

REFORMATION RADIKAL: „BUEN VIVIR" – EIN BEITRAG AUS LATEINAMERIKA

Claudete Beise Ulrich

Die Erde ist des HERRN und was darinnen ist, der Erdkreis und die darauf wohnen.
Denn er hat ihn über den Meeren gegründet und über den Wassern bereitet.
Wer darf auf des HERRN Berg gehen, und wer darf stehen an seiner heiligen Stätte?
Wer unschuldige Hände hat und reinen Herzens ist;
wer nicht bedacht ist auf Lug und Trug und nicht falsche Eide schwört:
der wird den Segen vom HERRN empfangen und Gerechtigkeit von dem Gott seines Heils.
(Ps 24,1-5)

Vom baum lernen

Vom baum lernen
Der jeden tag neu
Sommers und winters
Nichts erklärt
Niemand überzeugt
Nichts herstellt

Einmal werden die bäume lehrer sein
das wasser wird trinkbar
und das lob so leise
wie der wind an einem septembermorgen[1]

Einleitung

Eine der tiefsten Krisen, die die Menschheit und die ganze Welt erreicht hat, ist die globale ökologische Krise. Die globale ökologische Krise ist ein

---

[1] Dorothee SÖLLE. Vom baum lernen, aus: Fliegen lernen. Gedichte. Wolfgang Fietkau Verlag, Kleinmachnow, 1. Aufl. 2000, 40.

zentrales öffentliches Thema, das verschiedene Aspekte beinhaltet. Aus meiner Sicht ist die ökologische Krise das Ergebnis einer sozialen Krise mit einer planetarischen Dimension. Sie trifft vor allem arme soziale Menschen. Viele Arme leben in sensiblen Regionen, die von Dürre, Hochwasser, Überschwemmungen getroffen sind. Sie leiden auch unter Hunger und Not. Leonardo Boff hat in einem „Offenen Brief an Papst Franziskus: Einberufung einer Versammlung zum Schutz des Lebens" geschrieben:

> "Das Leben ist heute tödlich verletzt: durch Hunger (900 Millionen Menschen weltweit), durch Durst (1,2 Milliarden Menschen mangelt es an täglichem sauberen Trinkwasser, und 2,4 Milliarden Menschen haben keine elementare sanitäre Einrichtung), durch Krieg, durch Zerstörung der Umwelt (Boden, Wasser, Artenvielfalt, Luft), und vor allem sind die Menschheit und alle Lebensarten durch den unglaublichen Klimawandel bedroht."[2]

Allerdings, überall in der Welt, wachsen Bewegungen und Widerstand gegen das System der Herrschaft des globalisierten Kapitals von multilateralen Großunternehmen, Konzernen und Agrarunternehmen. Es entstehen immer mehr Bewegungen für Umwelt und soziale Gerechtigkeit in der Wahrnehmung der Zusammenhänge zwischen sozialer Ungleichheit und Umwelt-Ungerechtigkeit. Die Basis dieser sozialen Bewegungen sind immer die solidarische Ökonomie, in Bezug auf die Zyklen der Natur, Respekt vor Mutter Erde, natürlichen und nicht genveränderten Samen, eine Ökonomie im Dienst des Lebens und nicht des Kapitals. Ein wichtiges Ziel ist auch der Aufbau einer nachhaltigen Sozialpolitik, wobei die Hauptbasis Gastfreundschaft, Toleranz, Zusammenarbeit, Solidarität unter den verschiedenen Völkern und die Achtung der Mutter Erde sind. Die globale ökologische Krise ist ein Thema, das ein radikales neues Denken und Handeln erfordert.

In Lateinamerika gibt es verschiedene soziale Bewegungen und Projekte wie die solidarische Ökonomie, Biobauernfamilien, saubere Energiealternativen, Via Campesina, Landlosenbewegung (Movimento dos Trabalhadores Rurais Sem-Terra), Bewegung gegen den Bau von Staudämmen, Frauen-

---

[2] Leonardo BOFF. Offener Brief an Papst Franziskus: Einberufung einer Versammlung zum Schutz des Lebens. 08/10/2013 In: http://leonardoboff.wordpress.com/2013/10/08/offener-brief-an-papst-franziskus-einberufung-einer-versammlung-zum-schutz-des-lebens/.

bewegung gegen Gewalt in der Stadt und Land, etc. Sie kämpfen für eine bessere Welt und reflektieren über Wege zu Gerechtigkeit und Frieden. In diesem Text wollen wir über „Buen Vivir"/gutes Leben nachdenken. Dieses Konzept und diese Praxis entstammen der Bewegung der indigenen Völker aus Lateinamerika und haben meines Erachtens eine universelle Bedeutung.

Über „Buen Vivir/Bem Viver/Gutes Leben" zu reflektieren, hat sowohl mit unserem alltäglichen Leben als auch mit unserem christlichen Glauben zu tun. Bei „Buen Vivir" geht es um eine Ethik der Beziehung mit der Natur und allen Geschöpfen, um die Gemeinschaft, um Frau, Mann, Kinder, Alte etc..

1. „Buen Vivir", Bem viver", „Gutes Leben" – Begriff und Konzept

„Buen Vivir" – „"Recht auf gutes Leben", unter diesem Stichwort wird in den Andenländern Ecuador, Bolivien, Peru und auch in anderen Regionen Lateinamerikas das Konzept auf Spanisch „Buen Vivir" oder auf brasilianisch „Bem Viver"[3] diskutiert. Dieser Begriff, Konzept und Lebenserfahrungen, kommt von indigenen Völkern und hat mit Respekt vor der Natur, fremden Kulturen und auch mit dem Zusammenleben in der Gemeinschaft zu tun. Nach Graciela Chamorro:

> "Wenn wir uns mit den Konzepten und Praktiken von Indigenen in Bezug auf das ‚Gute Leben' auseinandersetzen, stoßen wir auf Metaphern, die das Ideal eines erfüllten Lebens beschreiben. Ein solches Ideal ist den Völkern, deren Religion im Einklang mit der Natur steht, nicht fremd, und es hängt zusammen mit einer Wiederverzauberung des Lebens und einer spirituellen Erfahrung, die verankert ist im Vertrauen auf eine göttliche Präsenz in Geschichte und physischer Welt."[4]

Chamorro macht deutlich, dass „Buen Vivir" mit dem ganzen Leben zu tun hat, vor allem mit dem Respekt gegenüber der Natur. Dieses Konzept ist nicht neu. Es war schon immer Teil der Geschichte und Kultur der indigenen

---

[3] Cledes MARKUS. Renate GIERUS (Hg). O Bem Viver na criação. São Leopoldo: Oikos, 2013, 168.

[4] Graciela CHAMORRO. Der Nationalplan für das Gute Leben. In: Sehnsucht nach dem Guten Leben. Die Theologie des Lebens als Thema in Mission und Ökumene. Jahresbericht 2012/2013 des Evangelischen Missionswerks in Deutschland, Hamburg, September 2013, 34.

Völker des amerikanischen Kontinents, genannt *Abya Yala* (traditioneller Ausdruck für den amerikanischen Kontinent). Heute neu ist, dass wir dieses Konzept in der Theologie, Philosophie und Sozialwissenschaften diskutieren. Die Professorin für indigene Geschichte an der Universidade Federal do Grande Dourados/Mato Grosso do Sul in Brasilien schreibt:

> "Anmerken müssen wir jedoch, dass die Art und Weise der Indigenen, vom ‚Guten Leben' zu sprechen oder es zu erfahren, vorher kaum Beachtung fand. Deutlicher gesagt, wurde in Theologie und Philosophie vorher nicht ernsthaft darüber diskutiert, auch nicht von solchen Richtungen, die sich für eine gerechtere, friedlichere, kreativere und nachhaltigere Gesellschaft eingesetzt haben, als sie das kapitalistische System vorschlägt."[5]

Auf der Suche nach Alternativen zu einem Wirtschaftssystem und Lebensstil, die allein auf Wachstum ausgerichtet sind und auf der Ausbeutung von Mensch und Natur basieren, nähern wir uns an das Konzept „Buen Vivir" der indigenen Völker an. Bei der Suche nach dem „Guten Leben" stehen also nicht das wirtschaftliche Wachstum und der materielle Wohlstand im Vordergrund, es geht nicht um „Mehr haben", sondern um einen Gleichgewichtszustand, um eine neue Beziehung des Menschen zur Natur und auch zu den Menschen. Alles ist gleich wichtig und alles miteinander verbunden. Soziale Ungleichheiten sollen verringert und die bisherige Wirtschaftsweise überprüft werden. Es geht um einen zivilisatorischen Wandel, um die materielle, soziale und spirituelle Zufriedenheit für *alle* Menschen der Gesellschaft, jedoch nicht auf Kosten anderer Menschen oder der Natur.

Buen Vivir ist die spanische Übersetzung für *sumak kawsay* (Quechua/ Ecuador), suma qamaña (Aymara/Bolivia), Qhapaq Ñan (Quechua/Peru), Ñande Reko (modo de ser/Seinsweise Guarani) Tekó Porã (Guarani/ Paraguay/Brasilien), Maloka (Amazonas). Auch die Mapuche (Chile) und Kolla (Argentinien) vertreten ähnliche Ansätze einer Kosmovision, die auf kommunitäre und nicht-kapitalistische Wurzeln zurückgreift und dem anthropozentrischen westlichen Weltbild eine integrierte Lebensweise zwischen Mensch und Natur entgegen hält.[6] Im Mittelpunkt für Indianervölker aus den

---

[5] Ebd.
[6] Definiciones: El Buen Vivir/Vivir Bien desde los pueblos indígenas y originarios. In: http://filosofiadelbuenvivir.com/buen-vivir/definiciones/ Zugang: 28.01.1014.

Andenländern steht *Pachamama* „Mutter Erde", die allen Kreaturen das Leben schenkt, sie erhält und nährt.[7] Sumak Kawsay kann somit als „Zusammenleben in Vielfalt und Harmonie mit der Natur" verstanden werden. Die Guaraní haben ein anderes Bild von der Erde. Für die Guaraní ist die Erde ein Körper mit Haut, Haar und mit Ornamenten bedeckt. Sie haben von der Erde einen visuellen, plastischen Eindruck, und sie können auch die Erde hören.[8]

Ohne den Anspruch, der Komplexität dieses Entwurfes gerecht zu werden, versuche ich, den Begriff *Sumak Kawsay* kurz zu erläutern[9], um ein besseres Verständnis der Tragweite dieses Konzepts im gesellschaftlichen Diskurs zu ermöglichen:

Sumak – Fülle, Größe.

Kawsay – Das Leben als dynamischer, sich ständig ändernder Prozess, Interaktion alles Existierenden, institutionelles Ordnungsprinzip.

Sumak Kawsay – bedeutet somit mehr „Gutes Leben" und kann eher als „Zusammenleben in Vielfalt und Harmonie mit der Natur" (als integrierte Lebensweise in Gemeinschaft und Harmonie der Natur) verstanden werden. Leben im Einklang mit der Natur, den Göttern, und den Schutzgeistern des bestehenden Lebens auf dem Lande, in Wäldern, Flüssen, Himmel, Seen, etc..

2. Buen Vivir – Prinzipien und Wissen

„Buen Vivir"/Gutes Leben bedeutet für die indigenen Völker eine Reihe von Prinzipien, Wissen, Ideen und Vorschläge, in denen der Respekt vor der

---

[7] Luis MACAS. El Sumak Kawsay. In. Gabriela WEBER: Debates sobre Cooperácion y Modelos de Desarrollo – Perspectivas desde la Sociedad Civil en Ecuador. Quido, Centro de Investigaciones CIUDAD – Observatorio de la Cooperación al Desarrollo en Ecuador, Quito, 47-60.

[8] Bartomeu MELIÁ. El Buen vivir guaraní: Teko Pora: Agenda Latinoamericana ano 2012. In: http://servicioskoinonia.org/agenda/archivo/obra.php?ncodigo=762, 3. Meine Übersetzung aus dem Spanischen: Esta imagen no es común ni típica de los guaraníes; la tierra es para ellos, más bien, un cuerpo cubierto de piel y pelos, revestido de adornos. El guaraní tiene de la tierra una percepción visual y plástica, y hasta auditiva.

[9] Luis MACAS, a.a.O, 51-52.

Natur und das Gemeinschaftsleben im Mittelpunkt stehen. Wichtige Grundlagen des „Buen Vivir"[10] sind:

- Das Leben muss an erster Stelle stehen. Alle Formen von Leben sind wichtig. Das Leben steht vor allem! Nicht nur der Mensch steht im Mittelpunkt (Antropozentrismus), sondern auch die anderen Lebensformen, also die Vielfalt des Lebens in ihrem Gleichgewicht.

- Die Suche nach dem allgemeinen Konsens. Dialog statt Misstrauen.

- Unterschiede zu respektieren; lernen, die Anderen zu respektieren; lernen zu hören; lernen zu tolerieren; Komplementarität als Ordnungsprinzip: Die Menschen ergänzen sich gegenseitig, und so stehen auch Mensch und Natur nicht im Widerspruch, sondern ergänzen sich gegenseitig. Ein neuer Umgang mit der Natur, der die Komplementarität betont und in dem der Mensch die Natur nicht mehr beherrscht und unterwirft. Leben in Harmonie mit der Natur. Gut leben ist ausgeglichenes Leben mit allen Lebewesen in der Gemeinschaft. Respekt vor Ähnlichkeiten und Unterschiedlichkeit. Gutes Leben ist, in Komplementarität mit seinen Mitmenschen und den Anderen zu leben. Wertschätzung der Identität verschiedener Völker. Die Anerkennung der Anderen in der Konzeption der plurinationalen Staaten bezieht explizit auch nicht-indigene Gruppen (Afrodeszendente, mestizische Bevölkerung) ein. Die Geschichte, Mythen, Feiern, geistiges Leben, Gemeinschaftswerte, Art des Seins und Lebensweise sind wichtig. Die Gedanken und Lebensweisen des kolonialen Modells müssen entkolonisiert werden.

- Reziprozität – Dieses Lebensprinzip erzeugt Harmonie und ein Leben in Gerechtigkeit in der Dorfgemeinschaft. Die einzelnen Mit-

---

[10] Siehe dazu: Resgatar e valorizar outros pilares éticos: o Bom Viver in: http://rio20.net/pt-br/documentos/resgatar-e-valorizar-outros-pilares-eticos-o-bom-viver/ Zugang: 31.03.2014. Siehe auch dazu: Luis MACAS. El Sumak Kawsay. In. Gabriela WEBER: Debates sobre Cooperácion y Modelos de Desarrollo – Perspectivas desde la Sociedad Civil en Ecuador. Quido, Centro de Investigaciones CIUDAD – Observatorio de la Cooperación al Desarrollo en Ecuador, Quito, 2011, 52-60.

glieder der Gemeinschaft können nur leben und überleben, wenn sie sich gegenseitig helfen. Nach Frank Tiss[11] bedeutet es für die Kulina (Amazonas) eine Schande, nicht mit Manako (Geben und Nehmen/Reziprozität) zu leben. Die ganze Gemeinde schämt sich, wenn das passiert.[12]

In diesem Sinn schlagen Vertreterinnen und Vertreter[13] des *Buen Vivir* drei wesentliche Gegenentwürfe zum bisherigen abendländischen Modell vor:

- Dem westlichen *Anthropozentrismus,* der die Menschen als Maßstab aller Dinge sieht, steht das Modell des *Biozentrismus* gegenüber, in dem alles Lebendige gleich wichtig ist.

- Dem *Androzentrismus,* der den Mann zum Maß aller Dinge erklärt, steht das Modell der *Komplementarität* gegenüber, in dem sich die Geschlechter gegenseitig ergänzen.[14]

- Dem Modell der kolonialen Denkweise und der Trennung von Rassen steht das Modell der Pluralität indigener Gemeinschaften gegen-

---

[11] Frank Tiss war als Missionspfarrer des „Ev.-lutherischen Missionswerks in Niedersachsen" seit 1994 für den Indianermissionsrat der „Ev. Kirche lutherischen Bekenntnisses in Brasilien" beim indigenen Volk der Kulina, in der Region des mittleren Juruá-Flusses im Südwesten des Bundesstaates Amazonas tätig und seit 2000 gemeinsam mit seiner Frau, der Ärztin Christiane Tiss.

[12] Frank TISS. Interreligiöser Dialog und ethnisches Selbstbewusstsein bei den Kulina, 12. Dieser Artikel ist nicht in Deutscher Sprache veröffentlicht. Der Autor hat mir den Artikel per E-mail zur Verfügung gestellt. Dieser Artikel ist in Brasilien veröffentlicht. Siehe dazu: Frank TISS. Diálogo inter-religioso e autoconsciência étnica entre os Kulina. In: Um só Deus Criador – Diálogo intercultural e inter-religioso com povos indígenas. Cadernos do COMIN, vol. 11. Est, Oikos, Comin, 2012, 9-33.

[13] Siehe dazu: Alberto ACOSTA. El Buen Vivir en el caminho del post-desarrollo. Alguns reflexiones al andar. In: Gabriela WEBER. Debates sobre Cooperácion y Modelos de Desarollo – Perspectivas desde la Sociedad Civil en Ecuador. Quido, Centro de Investigaciones CIUDAD – Observatorio de la Cooperación al Desarrollo en Ecuador, Quito, 2011, 61-82.

[14] Diálogos Complexos: Olhares de mulheres sobre o Buen Vivir. in: http://www.cotidianomujer.org.uy/sitio/pdf/relatoria_indigenas_br.pdf. Articulacion Feminista Marcosur. 44 s. Zugang: 28.03.2014.

über, in dem alle Gesellschaftsgruppen gleichberechtigt nebeneinander leben. Nach Thomas Fatheuer: "Für alle Vertreter des Buen Vivir ist es Teil eines Prozesses der De-Kolonisierung und der Schaffung einer neuen Hegemonie, die auf der Diversität der Kulturen aufbaut."[15]

Das Konzept des *Buen Vivir* stellt durch seine Berufung auf den traditionellen Wissens- und Erfahrungsschatz und die traditionellen indigenen Prinzipien des *Sumak Kawsay* in mehrfacher Hinsicht einen Bruch mit herkömmlichen Modellen dar. Dadurch, dass die Vertreterinnen und Vertreter des *Buen Vivir* auf ihre nicht-kapitalistischen Wurzeln zurückgreifen und dem westlichen Weltbild die Lebensweise eines gemeinschaftlichen Lebens im Einklang mit der Natur entgegengehalten, leiten sie einen geistigen „Entkolonialisierungsprozess" ein.

Zum anderen brechen sie mit traditionellen Entwicklungsmodellen und mit der linearen Vorstellung von Entwicklung, indem sie die Beziehung zur Natur und die menschliche Gemeinschaft in den Mittelpunkt stellen und sie zum Fundament der Ethik machen. Leonardo Boff drückt es so aus: „Das *bien vivir* („gut leben") zielt auf eine Ethik des Genug für die gesamte Gemeinschaft und nicht nur für den Einzelnen."[16] In der Mitte steht nicht das Individuum, sondern die Gemeinschaft. Die Menschen sind Teil der ganzen Schöpfung. Zusammenfassend formuliert Leonardo Boff:

"Das *bien vivir* umfasst also das gesamte Leben, insbesondere seinen gemeinschaftlichen Aspekt. Ohne Gemeinschaft existiert es nicht. (…) Das *bien vivir* lädt dazu ein, nicht mehr zu verbrauchen, als das Ökosystem ertragen kann, die Produktion von Abfällen, die nicht unter Wahrung der Sicherheit wieder absorbiert werden können, zu vermeiden, und es spornt dazu an, all das, was wir benutzen müssen, wieder zu verwenden und wieder zu verwerten. Es zielt also auf Recycling und Genügsamkeit und wirkt der

---

[15] Thomas FATHEUER. Buen Vivir: Eine kurze Einführung in *Lateinamerikas* neue Konzepte zu den Rechten der Natur. Herausgegeben von Heinrich-Böll-Stiftung. Band 17, 2011, 23. In: https://www.boell.de/sites/default/files/Endf_Buen_Vivir.pdf. Zugang: 28.01.2014.

[16] Leonardo BOFF. Achtsamkeit: Von der Notwendigkeit, unsere Haltung zu ändern, München, 2013, 81.

Knappheit entgegen. In der Zeit der Suche nach neuen Wegen für die Menschheit bietet das *bien vivir* Elemente einer Lösung, die alle Menschen und die gesamte Gemeinschaft des Lebens umfassen muss."[17]

3. Politische Bedeutung

In Ecuador wurde das Konzept des *Buen Vivir* 2008[18] sogar in die Verfassung (Präambel und Artikel 3) als Staatsziel aufgenommen. Dort werden „Rechte des guten Lebens" grundlegend festgelegt und mit wirtschaftlichen, sozialen und kulturellen Menschenrechten verbunden. Initiator war Alberto Acosta, damals Präsident der verfassungsgebenden Versammlung und Minister für Energie und Bergbau in Ecuador. Ihm lag besonders an einer Neuorientierung des Entwicklungsmodells, und wie anderen Theoretikern des Konzeptes ging es ihm darum, sich von der okzidentalen Idee des Wohlstandes zu distanzieren. Wachstum stelle kein erfolgversprechendes Modell mehr dar, so Acosta.[19] Im Gegenteil. Die Menschheit steuere auf einen „kollektiven Selbstmord" zu, wenn sie so weitermache wie bisher. In einem Interview stellt Acosta klar, dass „Buen Vivir" in Ecuador oft von den Politikern benutzt, aber nicht in das alltägliche Leben umgesetzt wird. Er erklärt: Das Buen Vivir ist kein Rezeptbuch. Es ist nicht ein neues abstraktes Entwicklungsmodell.[20]

Bolivien folgte dem Beispiel Ecuadors[21] schon ein Jahr später und nahm das Konzept 2009 als *Suma Qamana* in die Verfassung auf. Noch im selben Jahr wurde das Bekenntnis zum guten Leben erstmals auf dem Weltsozialforum in Belem in Brasilien präsentiert und die Erklärung „Aufruf zum Guten Leben" mit dem Leitsatz verabschiedet: „Wir wollen nicht besser leben, wir

---

[17] Ebd., 81-82.
[18] Thomas FATHEUER, a.a.O.
[19] Siehe dazu: Alberto ACOSTA a.a.O., 61-82.
[20] Blanca S. FERNÁNDEZ, Liliana PARDO y Katherine SALAMANCA. Diálogo com Alberto ACOSTA. In: En busca del sumak kawsay. Íconos. Revista de Ciencias Sociales No. 48. 2014, s. 104-105. In: https://www.flacso.org.ec/portal/ publicaciones/detalle/iconos-revista-de-ciencias-sociales-no-48en-busca-del-sumak-kawsay.4063.
[21] Thomas FATHEUER. Buen Vivir: Eine kurze Einführung in *Lateinamerikas* neue Konzepte zu den Rechten der Natur. Herausgegeben von Heinrich-Böll-Stiftung. Band 17, 2011, s. 14-19. In: https://www.boell.de/sites/default/files/Endf_Buen_Vivir.

Reformation Radikal: „Buen Vivir" – ein Beitrag aus Lateinamerika 253

wollen gut leben". 2010 wurde das Konzept beim Weltsozialforum in Porto Alegre erstmals auch über die lateinamerikanischen Grenzen hinaus als Alternative zum Modell des Wirtschaftswachstums diskutiert.[22]

Daher wird *Sumak Kawsay*, *„Buen Vivir"*, das *„Gute Leben"* zum Symbol oder zur Metapher für alternative politische, ökonomische Konzepte. In diesem Sinn schreibt Boff:

> „Gegen das *bien vivir* wird eingewandt, es sei im großen Maßstab praktisch nicht umsetzbar und allzu utopisch. Vielleicht ist es zurzeit tatsächlich schwer zu verwirklichen. Das alte, kranke System stirbt nur langsam, das neue, im Entstehen begriffene wird nur unter Mühen geboren. Doch nach der großen Krise, der wir unvermeidlich entgegengehen und die die Fundamente unseres Lebens auf diesem Planeten erschüttern wird, kann die Idee des *bien vivir* in höchstem Maße inspirierend sein."[23]

Aus Lateinamerika kommen neue Töne und Bewegungen. Für viele scheinen sie utopisch zu sein, aber die Utopie *schenkt* uns Hoffnung und erweitert den Horizont, sie bewegt, neue Wege zu gehen. Im April und Mai 2014 trat Alberto Costa mit der Grupo Sal in einer Reihe von Konzertlesungen über das Thema "Buen Vivir" in verschiedenen Städten Deutschlands auf. Die Einladung dazu lautete:

> "Um die Diskussion über das 'Buen Vivir' auch im deutschsprachigen Raum anzuregen und zu befeuern, präsentiert die lateinamerikanische Musikgruppe Grupo Sal gemeinsam mit Alberto Acosta ein neues Programm, das einen informativen, aber auch künstlerischen Zugang zu der Frage nach einem Guten Zusammenleben ermöglicht. (...) 'Sumak Kawsay', auch bekannt als 'Buen Vivir', ist eine Lebensanschauung der indigenen Andenvölker, die in den letzten Jahren vermehrt internationale Aufmerksamkeit erregt. Der Grund dafür liegt in der Aufforderung lateinamerikanischer Politiker, zentrale Aspekte dieser Lebensweise auch in industrielle Gesellschaften zu integrieren. 'Buen Vivir' zielt nicht nur auf ein Leben im Einklang mit der Natur und allen Geschöpfen, es bedeutet auch konkret eine neue 'Ethik der Entwicklung', es fordert ein soziales und solidarisches Wirtschaften und eine Abkehr von

---

[22] Sumak kawsay. In: http://de.wikipedia.org/wiki/Sumak_kawsay. Zugang 02.02.2014.
[23] Leonardo BOFF. Achtsamkeit, a.a.O., 82 .

Wirtschaftswachstum als zentralem Entwicklungskriterium."[24]

4. Buen Vivir: Widerstand, Visionen, Hoffnung und Gnade Gottes

Diese Prinzipien werden heute wiederentdeckt im Licht unseres Glaubens an das Evangelium, das nach einer neuen sozialen, politischen, kulturellen und wirtschaftlichen Gesellschaftsordnung ruft. Es ist interessant zu bemerken, dass dieses Konzept und diese Praxis von den indigenen Völkern kommt. Indigene wurden in der lateinamerikanischen Geschichte gekreuzigt und getötet. Diese gekreuzigten Völker sind in einem Auferstehungsprozess. Nach Ellacuría sind die Bilder des Gekreuzigten in Lateinamerika solche, die einen Gott zeigen, der unterwegs in der Geschichte ist, d.h. unterwegs in Richtung auf Auferstehung. Es geht auch um die Auferstehung des leidenden gekreuzigten Volkes Lateinamerikas.[25] Es ist ein Gott, der sich mitten im Leid erhebt, ein Gott, der für alle Menschen ein Leben in Vollkommenheit will – für die unterschiedlichen Gruppen in ihrer Vielfalt wie auch für die ganze Schöpfung.

Buen Vivir bezeichnet eine neue Weise, den Planeten zu bewohnen und sich mit ihm in Beziehung zu setzen. Wir in Lateinamerika verstehen es so, dass dieses Konzept „buen vivir" eine Theologie der Auferstehung und eine Ethik der Beziehung mit Liebe und Gerechtigkeit entwickelt. Die Theologie des Gekreuzigten und Auferstandenen ruft uns auf, Körper zu retten, nämlich die Körper der Menschen und des Planeten Erde in aller Vielfältigkeit.

Boff spricht von der Ethik der Gerechtigkeit und ihrem männlichen Substrat, von der Ethik der Achtsamkeit und ihrem weiblichen Substrat. Gerechtigkeit und Achtsamkeit zusammen bedeuten dann eine integrale Ethik.[26] Als Teil des allgemeinen Priestertums aller Gläubigen sind wir für die Pflege/Fürsorge/Achtsamkeit gegenüber der guten Schöpfung verantwortlich.

---

[24] Buen Vivir: Neue Töne aus Lateinamerika: Das Recht auf ein gutes Leben. Eine Begegnung mit Alberto Acosta und Grupo Sal. In: http://www.grupo-sal.de/html/ buenvivir.htm. Zugang 31.03.2014.

[25] ELLACURÍA, I. El pueblo crucificado. In: Mysterium Liberationis: Conceptos fundamentales del la Teología de la Liberación. V. 2. Madrid, 1990, 189-216.

[26] Leonardo Boff. Achtsamkeit, a.a.O., 87-104.

Achtsamkeit mit Gerechtigkeit gegenüber der Natur und allen Formen von Leben muss Teil unseres alltäglichen Lebens sein.

Die Auferstehung Jesu geschah auch in einem Garten (Johannes 20,1-18). Der Garten ist Metapher für das Gute Leben. So formuliert Marcelo Barros, brasilianischer Mönch, Theologe und Schriftsteller: „Das Bild des auferstandenen Jesus ist der Ausgangspunkt dieses restaurierten Universums, zu dem alle Menschen, die das Leben und die Gerechtigkeit lieben, eingeladen sind sich anzuschließen und es zu verteidigen."[27] Die Theologie des Gekreuzigten und Auferstandenen ruft uns demnach dazu auf, in Kooperation mit Gott das Leben der Menschen und den Planeten Erde in all seiner Vielfalt zu retten. Eine andere Welt ist möglich für alle Menschen und die Natur!

Das Konzept *Buen Vivir* verweist auf die Leiden der Natur. So stellt Ivone Gebara fest:

> „Im Übrigen gibt es auch Kreuze, die wir anderen auferlegen und die uns selber nicht einmal unmittelbar bewusst sind. In analoger Weise kann man auch von dem Kreuz sprechen, das die Entwicklungsideologie verschiedenen Ökosystemen aufgebürdet hat, von dem Kreuz der Zerstörung der Ozonschicht, von dem Kreuz des Atomkriegs und des Krieges der Sterne. Birgt das nicht die Aufforderung an uns weiter zu blicken als bis zum Kreuz Jesu, um so die Notwendigkeit eines weiteren und konkreten Heils für die ganze Schöpfung in den Blick zu nehmen?"[28]

Auch die Mutter Erde (Pachamama) ist gekreuzigt und muss die Auferstehung erleben (Römer 8.18-22), und das ist sehr wichtig für unser Leben als Menschen, Tiere, Pflanzen, Luft, Wasser. Diese Weltanschauung, Teil eines von Gott zum Leben bestimmten Ganzen zu sein, wirkt sich sowohl auf das Selbstverständnis und Verhalten der Einzelnen als auch auf das überindividuelle Verhalten im politisch-gesellschaftlichen Bereich aus. Wir sind Menschen nicht weil wir konsumieren können, sondern weil wir gut leben wollen, mit der Natur verbunden und in Sorge für sie und unser Leben. Unsere ursprüngliche Bestimmung ist es, füreinander da zu sein und in Gemein-

---

[27] Marcelo BARROS. Páscoa para o mundo crucificado, 2008. In: http://www.miamsisal.cl/?p=264. Zugang. 30.05.2013.
[28] Ivone GEBARA, Die dunkle Seite Gottes. Wie Frauen das Böse erfahren, 2. Aufl. Freiburg 2000, 158.

schaft zu leben, „denn es ist nicht gut, dass der Mensch allein sei" (Gen 2,18). Menschen wollen und sollen ein Leben in Fülle haben (Joh 10,10). In diesem Sinn wollen wir Blumen, Bäume, Tiere bewundern, eine leichte Luft atmen, sauberes Wasser trinken, den Sonnenuntergang genießen, denn „die Erde ist des Herrn, und was darinnen ist, der Erdkreis und die darauf wohnen." (Psalm 24,1). Die Menschen sind nicht das Zentrum der Schöpfung. Das Ziel der Schöpfung ist der Sabbat "...und ruhte von allen seinen Werken, die Gott geschaffen und gemacht hatte" (Gen 2,2).

Nach Paulo Suess ist gutes Leben (Kawsay Sumak) eine Utopie, sehr nahe an der Utopie des Reiches Gottes, das in seiner Fülle eschatologisch ist. Die Utopie ist immer kritisch gegenüber der aktuellen Situation mit ihren Ideologien, falschen Versprechungen und Veräußerungen.[29] „Buen Viver" ist eine Utopie, die uns Kraft gibt zu kämpfen für eine Welt, wo *Gerechtigkeit und Frieden sich küssen* (Psalm 85,11). Das Konzept des Buen Vivir/Guten Lebens ist kein Rezept oder eine mechanische Applikation, sondern ein Horizont, der uns Mut macht, die Wirklichkeit neu zu erkennen und zu kämpfen für eine gerechte Verteilung der Vermögenswerte des Planeten (Erde, Wasser, Luft, etc..), für die Anerkennung und den Respekt der Anderen und für ein Leben, das sich nicht in Wettbewerbsverhältnissen, sondern in Gegenseitigkeit und Dankbarkeit vollzieht.[30]

Die Zehn Gebote werden in der Goldenen Regel zusammengefasst: "Was ihr wollt, dass euch die Leute tun sollen, das tut ihnen auch". Jesus hat die Zehn Gebote als dreifache Liebe interpretiert: zu Gott, zum Nächsten und zu sich selbst. „Buen Vivir" zeigt uns, dass auch die Liebe zur Natur[31] und allen Lebensformen fundamental sind für ein ethisches Leben. Die Ethik der Liebe

---

[29] A luta pelo território: o centro simbólico e real do Bem Viver. Entrevista especial com Paulo SUESS. In: http://www.ihu.unisinos.br/entrevistas/525351-a-luta-pelo-territorio-o-centro-simbolico-e-real-do-bem-viver-entrevista-especial-com-paulo-suess. 7. November 2013. Zugang: 31.01.2014.

[30] Jairo Denis Arce MAIRENA. Espiritualidad Jairo Denis Arce MAIRENA. Espiritualid y Ecologia: en búsqueda de la harmonía total. 1. Ed. Managua, Cieets, 2014.

[31] Eduardo GALEANO, La naturaleza no es muda. In: Semanario Brecha. 18.04.2008, Montevideo. Galeano sagt in diesem Sinn bezüglich der semitischen zehn Gebote: „Gott hat in seinen zehn Geboten vergessen, die Natur zu erwähnen (...). Der Herr hätte hinzufügen können: 'Ehre die Natur, deren Du selbst Teil bist'."

hat mit Achtsamkeit und Gerechtigkeit des gesamten Lebens für unsere Mitwelt zu tun.

Im kleinen Katechismus listet Luther alles auf, was zum Brot[32] gehört. Tägliches Brot ist ein aktuelles und ökumenisches Thema in Lateinamerika. Dazu spricht die Auslegung Martin Luthers zur vierten Bitte im Kleinen Katechismus: „Was heißt denn tägliches Brot? Alles, was Not tut für Leib und Leben, wie Essen, Trinken, Kleider, Schuhe, Haus, Hof, Acker, Vieh, Geld, Gut, fromme Eheleute, fromme Kinder, fromme Gehilfen, fromme und treue Oberherren, gute Regierung, gutes Wetter, Friede, Gesundheit, Zucht, Ehre, gute Freunde, getreue Nachbarn und desgleichen." Alles was wir brauchen für ein gutes Leben gehört zur vierten Bitte des Vaterunsers: „Unser tägliches Brot gib uns heute." Im Zusammenhang dieser Bitte erinnere ich mich an ein Gedicht des katholischen Bischofs Dom Pedro Casaldáliga (São Felix do Araguaia – Brasilien): „Alles ist relativ, außer Gott und dem Hunger."[33] In diesem Gedicht kommt zum Ausdruck, dass der Mangel an Brot das ganze Leben determiniert. Der „Hunger" dieser Welt ist der "Ort" Gottes, und Gott hört den Schrei nach Brot und einem freien Leben: „Und der Herr sprach: Ich habe gesehen das Elend meines Volkes in Ägypten und habe ihr Geschrei gehört über die, die sie drängen; ich habe ihr Leid erkannt und bin herniedergefahren, dass ich sie errette von der Ägypter Hand und sie ausführe aus diesem Lande in ein gutes und weites Land, in ein Land, darin Milch und Honig fließt..."(Exodus 3,7-8). Die Gerechtigkeit Gottes ist die fürsorgliche Erhaltung des Lebens jeden Tag, wie das Volk Israel es nach der Mannageschichte erlebt hat (Exodus 16,1-22).

Gott hört auch den Schrei nach Brot und Achtsamkeit von der Natur, Röm 8: 17-23:

---

[32] Martin LUTHER. Vater Unser: die vierte Bitte, In: Der Kleine Katechismus. In: Evangelisches Gesangbuch. Ausgabe für die Evangelische Landeskirche Anhalts, die Evangelische Kirche Berlin-Brandenburg-schlesische Oberlausitz, die Evangelische Kirche der Kirchenprovinz Sachsen, Leipzig, 2006, 806.3.

[33] CASALDALIGA, Pedro, in: SOBRINO, Jon. Epílogo, VIGIL, José Maria (org.). Descer da cruz os pobres: Cristologia da libertação (obra da Comissão Teológica Internacional da Associação Ecumênica de Teólogos/as do Terceiro Mundo; prólogo de Leonardo Boff). São Paulo: Paulinas, 2007, 345-457, hier S. 346.

„Wenn wir aber Kinder Gottes sind, dann bekommen wir auch einen Anteil von dem, was ihr gehört. Wenn wir einen Anteil am Reichtum Gottes erhalten, verbindet uns das mit dem Messias, so gewiss wir sein Schicksal teilen, auf dass auch wir zusammen mit ihm von Gottes Glanz erfüllt werden. Ich bin überzeugt, dass die Leiden, die wir jetzt! zum gegenwärtigen Zeitpunkt erfahren, ihre Macht verlieren im Schein der kommenden göttlichen Gegenwart, die sich an uns offenbart. Die gespannte Erwartung der Schöpfung richtet sich darauf, dass die Töchter und Söhne Gottes offenbar werden. Denn die Schöpfung ist der Nichtachtung ausgeliefert – nicht aus freier Entscheidung, sondern gezwungen von einer sie unterwerfenden Macht. Sie ist aber ausgerichtet auf Hoffnung. Denn auch sie, die Schöpfung, wird aus der Versklavung durch die Korruption befreit werden und wird teilhaben an der Befreiung der Kinder Gottes durch die göttliche Gegenwart. Denn wir wissen, dass die ganze Schöpfung mit uns gemeinsam schreit und mit uns zusammen an der Geburt arbeitet – bis jetzt! Denn nicht nur sie allein schreit, sondern auch wir, die wir schon die Geistkraft als ersten Anteil der Gottesgaben bekommen haben, wir schreien aus tiefstem Innern, weil wir sehnlich darauf warten, dass unsere versklavten Körper freigekauft und wir als Gotteskinder angenommen werden" (Bibel Gerechter Sprache).

Nicht alle in Lateinamerika haben das tägliche Brot, viele kämpfen für Arbeit, Land, Wasser, Gesundheit, Bildung, Nahrung, Gerechtigkeit. Viele kämpfen um das Überleben.[34] Luther sagt auch zu der vierten Bitte: „Gott gibt das tägliche Brot auch ohne unsere Bitte allen bösen Menschen, aber wir bitten in diesem Gebet, dass er's uns erkennen lasse und wir mit Danksagung

---

[34] Eine arme Frau aus Teresina/Brasilien hat einmal folgendes Gebet gesprochen: „Mein lieber Gott, danke für die Pappe, die ich zum Schlafen habe, aber hilf auch meiner Nachbarin, dass sie auch eine gute Pappe zum Schlafen hat und dass sie am morgigen Tag für ihre Kinder Essen hat." Es ist eine Bitte um Brot in der Hungersnot, in der eine arme Frau für eine andere arme Frau betet, wenn es Abend wird, an einem Tag, an dem das tägliche Brot nicht gekommen ist. Sie bittet für den nächsten Tag wegen des Hungers des heutigen Tages Aus dem Bericht von Missao Zero/IECLB – Teresina/ Piauí/Brasilien – Theologiestudent Mateus Holz Tasso. In: Claudete BEISE ULRICH/ Silfredo DALFERTH. Bibelarbeit über das „täglich" aus der Evangelischen Kirche Lutherischen Bekenntnisses in Brasilien. In:*Bibelarbeiten* aus der internationalen Ökumene zur 11. Vollversammlung des Lutherischen Weltbundes, Evangelische Lutherische in Württemberg, 2010, 35. In:http://www.dimoe.de/ fileadmin/mediapool/ einrichtungen/E_dimoe/2010-03-04_Handr_Bibelarbeiten_LWB_ vollvers.pdf. Zugriff am 12.03.2014.

empfangen unser tägliches Brot."[35] Aus diesem Denken heraus ist das christliche Ethos ein Ethos der Gnade, das tägliche Brot in all seinen Dimensionen ist die Gnade Gottes.[36] Das bedeutet, dass die Bitten um das tägliche Brot Pluralbitten sein müssen. Das Vater Unser ist ein plurales Gebet in einer multikulturellen und multireligiösen Welt. Wir bitten nicht nur für uns selbst, sondern auch für die ganze Welt, für die Natur und vor allem für die Armen.

Mit einem Gedicht von Dorothee Sölle möchte ich diese Reflexion schließen.

Zeitansage

Es kommt eine zeit
da wird man den sommer gottes kommen sehen
die waffenhändler machen bankrott
die autos füllen die schrotthalden
und wir pflanzen jede einen baum

Es kommt eine zeit
da haben alle genug zu tun
und bauen die gärten chemiefrei wieder auf
in den arbeitsämtern wirst du
ältere leute summen und pfeifen hören

Es kommt eine zeit
da werden wir viel zu lachen haben
und gott wenig zum weinen
die engel spielen klarinette
und die frösche quaken die halbe nacht

Und weil wir nicht wissen
wann sie beginnt
helfen wir jetzt schon

---

[35] Martin LUTHER. Vater Unser: die vierte Bitte, In: Der Kleine Katechismus, a.a.O.
[36] Claudete BEISE ULRICH/ Silfredo DALFERTH, a.a.O.

allen engeln und fröschen
beim lobe gottes[37]

Abstract

„Buen vivir" - Good life for the whole planet

As Christians from Latin America we are on our way, in a new learning process. We are learning from our brothers and sisters, the indigenous peoples, what it means: „buen vivir", a good life for the whole world. This learning process is not without conflict. In Brazil and in all of Latin America there are a lot of conflicts concerning the question of land. For example indigenous groups stand up against the political agenda of mining, dam-building and constitutional changes for indigenous territories: It's a matter of land! We have to keep in mind who is suffering the most from destruction of nature and climate change. They are the poorest groups of people.

„Buen vivir"/"Bem viver" breaks with all known concepts of development, highlights the relationship with nature and respects her as fundamental issue for an ethic with communion as her frame of reference. „Buen vivir" does not aim at „having more", at accumulation and growth, but at social balance. The concept of „Good life"seeks a new relationship between humans and nature and a change in civilization. *Pachamama,* „Mother earth" builds the center, she, who gives life to all creatures, retains and nourishes them. In Luther's small catechism, he names everything that belongs to bread. It's not only food, but all life…"Mother earth" as well. Everything in nature (earth, air, water, fire, plants, flowers, trees, animals, sky, etc.) given to us comes as a present by the grace of God and we have to look after it and be thankful. „How many are your works, Lord! In wisdom you made them all; the earth is full of your creatures" (Ps 104, 24). We only have this one earth – and we must learn to live with one another in the diversity and wealth of creation.

„Buen vivir"/"Bem viver" originates from the indigenous peoples, therefore from people whose ancestors have in some cases been crucified and killed in colonial times. The descendants from these „crucified peoples" are now in some

---

[37] Dorothee SÖLLE. Zeitansage. In: Loben ohne lügen. Gedichte, Berlin: Wolfgang Fietkau Verlag, Kleinmachnow: 2000, 7.

kind of process of resurrection. For this reason we understand the concept of „Buen vivir" as a „theology of resurrection". In Latin America today there are still many suppressed, beaten and crucified people, but they are in a process of uprising, in an awakening – in what we call resurrection in theology and in the gospel.

The theology of the crucified and resurrected is calling us to save bodies, that is to say the bodies of people, of planet earth, in her diversity. With this in mind the indigenous peoples – crucified in the past and now in the process of resurrection – bring a new proposal to life on earth. A new world is possible for all people and for nature! „Buen vivir" emphasizes that all people and the entire nature have a right to and need of „bread and roses". People and nature are hungry for bread and beauty/mindfulness. The assignment of theology is to fight for and to proclaim the right of good life/"buen vivir" for the entire creation.

DIE PSALMEN ALS MANTEL DES MESSIAS

Klara Butting

1. Spiritualität ist „in"

Eine regelrechte Spiritualitätsbewegung hat in Deutschland, zumindest in den alten Bundesländern Kreise gezogen. Menschen, betroffen von den gesellschaftlichen Zentrifugalkräften, suchen die Verbundenheit aller Kreatur in Stille und Natur. Pilgern oder Sitzen in der Stille, aber auch Tanz und Körpergebet sind gefragte Wege zu mystischen Gotteserfahrungen. Die Evangelische Kirche in Deutschland hat diese Nachfrage aufgegriffen. Das Wort Spiritualität hat nichts Anrüchiges mehr. Allerlei Formen der Meditation werden praktiziert. Pilgerwege wurden erstellt, Pilgerbegleiter ausgebildet. Klöster wurden zu Herbergen und Auszeitorten ausgebaut. Spiritual Consulting für Führungskräfte wird angeboten.

Durch die Konzentration auf geistliche Erfahrungen ist das politische Selbstverständnis des christlichen Glaubens in den letzten Jahren in den Hintergrund getreten ist. Wir gehen eher pilgern als demonstrieren, machen spirituelle Erfahrungen eher in der Stille als bei der Besetzung von Bohrplätzen oder der Blockade von Bauzäunen. Umso notwendiger ist die Einsicht in die Not, die sich in der Sehnsucht nach Verbundenheit zu Wort meldet. Die Individualisierung unserer Lebenswege betrifft alle Lebensbereiche. Wo jeder Mann und jede Frau eigene Wege zwischen Beruf und Familie, Arbeits- und Wohnort finden muss, wo Rente und Krankenversicherung Privatsache sind, ist auch die Gottesbeziehung betroffen. Man mag die individualisierte Suche nach „meinen" heilenden Quellen jenseits von Tradition und Gemeinde, die dem Wort „Spiritualität" anhaftet, misstrauisch beäugen, rückgängig machen lässt sie sich nicht. Denn die Zerstörung sozialstaatlicher Errungenschaften und sozialer Strukturen in Europa schreitet fort und die Träume vom geeinten Europa und der Einen Welt weichen den Angstvisionen der eigenen Verarmung. Die Suche nach Verwurzelung und spirituellen Haftpunkten ist eine notwendige Gegenbewegung. Genauso notwendig ist allerdings eine neue Verständigung über die politischen Dimensionen, die die Gottesbeziehung in unserer Glaubensüberlieferung hat. Wenn wir über die Erneuerung von Kirche und Theologie nachdenken, gehört dazu die Frage, wie Vereinzelte auf ihrer Suche nach Stille, Natur und Gotterfahrungen den Rückweg zur Gemeinschaft finden können.

2. Die Einheit Gottes

Wenn es nach der Bibel geht, ist die Einheit alles Lebendigen, die die Gottsuchenden zu erfahren hoffen, eine hoch politische Angelegenheit. Sie ist zentrales Thema der biblischen Glaubensüberlieferung. Das biblischen Glaubensbekenntnis, das *sjema jisrael*, spricht davon: „Höre Israel: Der EWIGE (JHWH) ist unser Gott, der EWIGE ist Einheit!" (5. Mose 4,5f). Der Gottesname wird genannt, die vier Konsonanten: JHWH, die Martin Luther mit „der HERR" übersetzt hat. In vielen deutschsprachigen jüdischen Übersetzungen lesen wir „der Ewige". Die Übersetzung „Bibel in gerechter Sprache"[1] bietet eine Vielfalt von Wiedergabemöglichkeiten an: z.B. die oder der EWIGE, die oder der HEILIGE, die LEBENDIGE. Die Vielfalt will gewährleisten, dass nicht eine der Bildreden zum Gottesbild erstarrt. Hinter all diesen Versuchen bleibt der Gottesname ein Geheimnis – und doch wird mit dem Namen das Wesen Gottes offenbart. Denn ein Name bedeutet Ansprechbarkeit und Unterscheidbarkeit. Wenn in Israel erzählt wird, dass Gott sich als Name zeigt, wird dieser Gott als Gegenüber bezeugt, als ein „Du", der/die identifiziert und angesprochen werden will. Mit ihrem Namen sagt die Gottheit über sich: Ich will von anderen Mächten, die in dieser Welt wirken, unterschieden werden. Der Name bedeutet: Gott ist nicht die Schicksalsmacht, die alles wirkt und alles schafft. Nicht alles, was in der Welt geschieht, ist Gottes Tat. Im Gegenteil: Israel hat den Namen Gottes in der Sklaverei als eine Gegenstimme kennen gelernt. Ein brennender Dornbusch, der nicht verbrennt – in diesem Bild haben sie diese Erfahrung überliefert (2. Mose 3). Eine der wichtigsten Erklärungen der jüdischen Überlieferung sieht in dem brennenden Dornbusch das Symbol für Israels Leiden in der Unterdrückung. Im Leiden, in der Sklaverei zeigt Gott seinen Namen. Hier zeigt er sein Wesen. In Worte gefasst heißt dieses Bild vom brennenden Dornbusch: Die Welt steht in

---

[1] Eine Bibelübersetzung, die Entwicklungen zusammengeführt, die Kirche und Theologie im letzten halben Jahrhundert im Blick auf das Thema Gerechtigkeit geprägt haben, U.Bail u.a. (Hg.), Bibel in gerechter Sprache, Gütersloh 2006.

Brand, aber mitten in dem Feuer des Leidens gibt es die Erfahrung, dass das Leiden die Liebe nicht zerstören kann. Mitten im Leiden gibt es die Stimme der Menschlichkeit, die erzählt, dass Humanität durch Gewalt nicht korrumpiert werden kann.

Diese Stimme der Humanität bekennt das *sjema jisrael* als Gott: „Der EWIGE (JHWH) ist unser Gott!" (5. Mose 4,5f). Die Stimme der Menschlichkeit, die sich ihnen in der Sklaverei gezeigt hat, ist Gott. Darum geht es in der gesamten Bibel. Das hört sich für uns zunächst nicht besonders aussagekräftig an, weil in unserem Sprachgebrauch Gott an die Stelle des Namens getreten ist. Gott ist für uns ausschließlich ein Name für den/die Eine/n, die/der sich in der Bibel offenbart. Aber in der Bibel selbst ist das nicht so. Das Wort Gott benennt den Regierungsanspruch. Gott – das ist eine Berufsbezeichnung, wie König. Gott – das ist ein Job, der getan werden muss. Auf diesen Job haben viele Anspruch erhoben. Der Pharao, der König von Ägypten, wollte als Gott verehrt werden. Später wollten die Kaiser in Rom als Gott verehrt werden. Martin Luther kannte noch den Klang dieses Wortes, wenn er im Großen Katechismus bei der Auslegung der 10 Gebote zu der Frage „Was heißt ‚einen Gott haben' bzw. was ist ‚Gott'? die Antwort gibt: „Ein ‚Gott' heißt etwas, von dem man alles Gute erhoffen und zu dem man in allen Nöten seine Zuflucht nehmen soll". Martin Luther zeichnet mit dieser Definition den Machtanspruch nach, der dem Wort „Gott" im biblischen Sprachgebrauch inhärent ist. In einem Kontext, in dem die Regierungsspitzen imperialistischer Mächte beanspruchen, Gott zu sein und die Weltgeschichte zu bestimmen, behauptet die biblische Glaubensüberlieferung, dass die Stimme der Menschlichkeit kein Hirngespinst ist, sondern unter den Menschen Raum gewinnt.

Die Existenz anderer Mächte und Gewalten wird nicht geleugnet. Und doch ist die EWIGE nicht eine Macht neben anderen Mächten. Das Bekenntnis sagt: „Die EWIGE ist die einzig Eine". Der Satz ist schwer zu übersetzen, weil das hebräische „*echad*" (einzig) sowohl für das quantitative „eins", als auch für das qualitative „einzigartig" steht. Es geht um beides. Der biblische Gott ist einzigartig. Er/sie ist anders als alles, was wir kennen. Er ist „jenseits" vom Bekannten. Er ist „transzendent", denn er/sie geht über das Bestehende hinaus, unsichtbar, unverfügbar, nicht männlich oder weiblich. Zu keinem Zeitpunkt wurde Gott verstanden nach dem Bild unseres menschlichen Personseins. Im Gegenteil. Als Bild Gottes zu leben, ist unsere Bestimmung als gesamte Menschheit (1. Mose 1,27), eine Bestimmung, die jedermann und jeder Frau ihre Berufung gibt, und doch unser individuelles Personsein übersteigt. Versöhnte Menschheit, die in ihrer Unterschiedlichkeit von männlich und weiblich Frieden findet. Vielfalt, die sich einigen und einen kann, das ist Bild Gottes. Denn die biblische Gottheit ist „eins". Die Einzigkeit Gottes besteht in seiner/ihrer Einheit. In Versöhnungsprozessen erfahren wir unsere Bestimmung. In Beziehungsreichtum unter Menschen ahnen wir Gottes Beziehungsfülle. Alle Antagonismen und Dualitäten, die unser Leben bestimmen – in Gott ist der Weg ihrer Versöhnung. Auch wenn unsere Gegenwart von Gewalt verstört ist, in Gott ist die Ganzheit des Lebens, die Verbundenheit alles Lebendigen, die Bestimmung aller zu Frieden und Einheit gegenwärtig. In diesem Sinne legt Paulus das biblische Glaubensbekenntnis angesichts der Macht des römischen Imperiums aus: „Auch wenn da vieles ist, was Gott genannt wird, sei es im Himmel, sei es auf der Erde, – es gibt ja viele Götter und viele Herren – , so gibt es für uns doch nur *einen* Gott, den Vater, von dem her alles ist und wir auf ihn hin und *einen* Herrn, Jesus Christus, durch den alles ist und wir durch ihn" (1 Korinther 8,5-6). Jedes Denken von grundlegenden Dualitäten wird verweigert. Das Böse ist keine selbstständige Gegenmacht, kein Gegengott. Es ist nur Negation des Guten, Verweigerung unserer Bestimmung. In der Einen Gottheit ist auch der Konflikt zwischen Macht und Liebe gelöst. Israel bekennt, dass es Gott gelingt, beides in sich zu vereinen: Gott wird sein Recht durchsetzen und dabei seiner Liebe treu bleiben. Die biblische Rede von Gottes Rache und seinem Zorn, der die Gewalttätigen vernichten wird, wurzelt in diesem Bekenntnis der Einheit. Wo Gewalt unsere Phantasie deformiert und Hass und Vernichtungswünsche wachsen lässt, vertrauen wir unsere entstellten Wünsche Gott an und trauen ihm die Auseinandersetzung mit den Gewalttätigen zu, die uns deformiert. Gott wird Gewalt und Willkür beenden und dabei der Barmherzigkeit zum Sieg verhelfen.

Die Worte des Glaubensbekenntnisses tauchen in der Bibel auch als Zukunftsvision auf. Im Buch des Propheten Sacharja wird vom Ende aller Gewalt geträumt: „An jenem Tag wird der EWIGE der einzig Eine (*echad*) sein" (14,9). In Hinblick auf die ganze Erde ist das Bekenntnis „der EWIGE ist der einzig Eine" Zukunftsmusik. Gott will sich mit uns einen und in seiner Schöpfung zur Ruhe kommen. Diese Sehnsucht prägt die gesamte Bibel. Wir hören davon bis zur letzten Buchseite, wenn Johannes, der Verfasser der Johannesapokalypse einen neuen Himmel und einen neue Erde sieht und hört, dass Gott unter dem Menschen zur Ruhe gekommen ist (21,3f.). Wer mit dem Gott der Bibel in Berührung kommen, wird von dieser Sehnsucht infiziert. Deshalb sind in der biblischen Glaubensüberlieferung Einheitserfahrungen Berufungserfahren (vgl. Jesaja 6). Zur mystischen Erfahrung der Einheit gehört die sperrige Auseinandersetzung mit einem Du, das uns zu Versöhnungsprozessen ruft und zu Friedensarbeit beauftragt.

3. Reformation heute – Umkehr zum Alten Testament

Die Einsicht, dass Gottes Einheit eine Geschichte der Einigung ist, an der wir Anteil haben, gehört zum christlichen Glauben. In jedem Gottesdienst werden Schöpfer, Jesus der Christus und die Heilige Geistkraft, die in der Gemeinschaft der Heiligen Gestalt gewinnt, als Ereignisweisen des Einen Gottes bekannt. Doch hinter dem so oft wiederholten Bekenntnis verborgen ist ein Konflikt, der sich in jedem Bibelgespräch offenbart, wenn es um das Schriftverständnis geht. Die Väter und Mütter der Kirche haben die Einheit Gottes in der Einen Schrift aus Erstem und Zweitem Testament bezeugt.[2] Sie haben sich gegen Marcion gestellt, der im 2. Jahrhundert n. Chr. als erster Theologe schied zwischen einem guten Gott der Liebe im Neuen Testament und dem bösen Gott des Alten Testamentes. Marcion sah in Schöpfung und Erlösung verschiedene Götter am Werk. Schöpfung, Gesetz und Gericht – dafür war der Gott des Alten Testaments verantwortlich, den er aus dem christlichen Kanon verbannen wollte. Marcion wurde zum Ketzer erklärt. Gegen ihn haben die Kirchenväter und -mütter die Einheit der zweigeteilten Schrift aus Erstem und Zweitem Testament als Zeugnis der Einheit Gottes festgehalten. Trotz dieser grundlegenden theologischen und politischen Entscheidung der alten Kirche, gehört der theologische Kampf gegen das Alte Testament und seine Biblizität zur Geschichte des Christentums. Bereits der Name „Altes Testament" unterstellt, der erste Teil unserer Bibel sei Vorge-

---

[2] Dazu Ton Veerkamp, Die Welt anders. Politische Geschichte der Großen Erzählung, Berlin 2012, 386 ff, der beschreibt, wie die altkirchlichen Bekenntnisse in der Sprache der Philosophie die Einheit der Testamente festhalten. Vgl. auch seinen Beitrag in Band 1 dieser Reihe: „Im Namen des Vaters und des Sohnes und des Heiligen Geistes. Nur noch eine Hohlformel?", in: Ulrich Duchrow/ Carsten Jochum-Bortfeld: *Befreiung zur Gerechtigkeit, Band 1 der Reihe „Die Reformation radikalisieren"*. Münster: Lit, 2015.

schichte und veraltet. Eine aufwärtsstrebende Linie wurde konstruiert, bei der das Neue Testament das Ziel des Alten ist. Eine Entwicklung im Gottesbild vom jüdischen Gott der Rache hin zu dem christlichen Gott der Liebe wurde zum Allgemeinplatz christlicher Lehre. Die letzte Konsequenz dieser Lehre wurde sichtbar in der Zeit des Nationalsozialismus, als Christen und Christinnen überall in Europa den Mord an jüdischen Menschen zumindest in Kauf genommen haben. Sie haben dem Vernichtungsversuch als im Grunde überfälliges und gerechtes Ende des Judentums hingenommen. In Reaktion auf dieses Versagen der Kirchen hat eine theologische Umkehrbewegung begonnen, die den inneren Zusammenhang zwischen der Verantwortungsbereitschaft der Kirchen im Diesseits und ihrem Schriftverständnis erkannt hat. In der Umkehr zum Alten Testament und seiner Akzeptanz als Schrift muss der christliche Glaube zur Liebe zu den Menschen und dem Einen Gott zurückfinden. Insofern liegt das Erbe der Reformation noch vor uns. Die reformatorische Hinwendung zur Bibel muss heute als Hinwendung zum Alten Testament vollzogen werden. Nur wenn wir die Einheit der Bibel ernst nehmen, werden wir angesichts unbiblischer Privatisierung oder verharmlosender Verjenseitigung einen neuen Zugang zum christlichen Glaubens finden.

Die Umkehr zum Alten Testament kristallisiert sich an dem Verhältnis zum Judentum und dem kirchlichen Versagen, doch auf dem Spiel stehen die Authentizität des christlichen Glaubens und seine politische Gestalt. Denn nur wo die Einheit der Schrift uns über die Einheit Gottes belehrt, ist Gott nicht Universalgott nach dem Bild weltlicher Monarchen, sondern Ruf, der befreit. Plötzlich spricht unser Bekenntnis „ich glaube an Gott, den Vater, den Allmächtigen, den Schöpfer des Himmels und der Erde" dem biblischen Credo nach und erzählt von der Stimme der Befreiung, die Gott ist und Einheit aller Dinge. Die Rede von Gott, dem Vater, dem Allmächtigen, erschafft in unseren Köpfen nicht mehr den allmächtigen Weltenlenker, der Gutes und Böses willkürlich austeilt. Unsere Bilder von Allmacht definieren nicht länger den Vater, und plötzlich traut auch unser Glaube auf die Eine, deren Bindung an Menschen der Vatername ausspricht. „Vater" wird zu einem Gottesnamen, der von der Beziehungsfähigkeit der Gottheit erzählt und das Geheimnis der biblischen Gottheit zum Ausdruck bringt. Unser Bekenntnis bekommt eine revolutionäre Struktur. „Vater" und „Allmächtiger" sind Kontraste, keine Komplementärbegriffe. Wir fügen Unvereinbares zusammen und sprechen aus, dass die Stimme, die uns zur Übernahme der Weltgeschäfte ruft – dafür steht das patriarchale Bild vom Vater und seinen Söhnen[3] –, sich gegen angeblich unveränderbare Gesetzmäßigkeiten, gegen Machtgier und sonstige Anwärter auf das Gottesamt durchsetzen wird. Der Vatername erzählt von einer Gottheit in Beziehungen, die in Gemeinschaft mit Menschen die Erde zu einem Wohnort macht für alle Kreatur. Ihre Macht ist nicht eine alles durchwaltende Allmacht, die bewirkt, dass alles Böse auch sein Gutes hat und der Unterschied zwischen Gut und Böse relativiert werden kann. Ich betone dies, weil es im Kontext der gegenwärtigen Spiritualitätssuche auch diese Vorstellung gibt, dass es an sich nichts Gutes und Böses gäbe, sondern dies nur in unserer Betrachtungsweise existiert; dass wir uns also allein in unserem Bewusstsein über gesellschaftliche und persönliche Probleme erheben müssten. Doch noch ist in dieser Welt nicht alles eins! Sondern alle sind von dem Einen gerufen, sich zu einigen – mit ihren Mitmenschen, Mitkreaturen und mit Gott. „Vielleicht ist der Mangel an Mystik innerhalb der protestantischen Kirchen vor allem ein Mangel an gelebter Gegenseitigkeit" hat Dorothee Sölle vermutet.[4] Wir wagen nicht zu sagen, dass Gott unsere Segenskräfte für seine Geschichte braucht. Wir wagen nicht zu glauben, dass jedermann und jede Frau gerufen ist, ein Stück von Gott in sich selbst und unter uns Menschen zu retten. Wir wollen Gott die Ehre geben und bekennen seine Allmacht. Doch die Macht, die alles Zertrennende überwindet und die Heilung und Einheit allen Lebens wahr werden lässt, ist keine Allmacht, die von außen interveniert und in einem gewaltigen Streich alles Trennende beseitigt. Die Macht, die mächtiger ist als alles andere, ereignet sich in der Beziehung, im Wort, das uns anspricht, uns aufrichtet, und uns zu Menschlichkeit und Erbarmen zurückruft. So hat es z.B. Paulus erzählt, der eine Krankheit loswerden wollte und von Gott erfährt: „Lass dir an meiner Gnade genügen, denn meine Kraft kommt in Schwachheit zur Vollendung" (2. Korinther 12,9). Er erfährt das Geheimnis der Geschichte Gottes mit den Menschen.

---

[3] Vgl. Psalm 89, 27, dazu Klara Butting, Eine Theologie der Macht Gottes, in: Junge Kirche 2/2013, 1-4, oder Röm 8,14-17, dazu Claudia Janssen, Christus und seine Geschwister (Röm 8,12-17,29f.), in: M. Crüsemann/C. Jochum-Bortfeld (Hg.), Christus und seine Geschwister. Christologie im Umfeld der Bibel in gerechter Sprache, Gütersloh 2009, 64-80.

[4] Dorothee Sölle, Mystik und Widerstand. „Du stilles Geschrei", München 2003 (5. Auflage), 144.

Zur Vollendung will Gott unter uns und mit uns kommen. Gerade wo wir mit unseren Verletzungen ringen, wo wir darum kämpfen, uns vom Negativen nicht überwältigen zu lassen, kann die Überwindung des Bösen sich in uns und unter uns ereignen und Gott zu seiner Fülle kommen. Es geht – so hat Abraham Heschel formuliert – in der Beziehung zwischen Gott und Mensch nicht um Unterwerfung unter Gottes Willen, auch nicht um „bloße Abhängigkeit von Seinem Erbarmen. Es wird nicht gefordert, Seinem Willen zu gehorchen, sondern zu tun, was Er ist".[5]

4. Das Mysterium der Einheit

In vielen christlichen Gemeinden erinnert die trinitarische Doxologie „Ehre sei dem Vater und dem Sohne und dem Heiligen Geiste" am Ende der Psalmenlesung daran, dass Christinnen und Christen das Beten der Psalmen als eine spirituelle Einheitserfahrung verstanden haben. Dietrich Bonhoeffer beginnt sein Psalmenbüchlein mit dem Staunen über dieses Geheimnis: „Es ist zunächst etwas sehr Verwunderliches, dass es in der Bibel ein Gebetbuch gibt. Die Heilige Schrift ist doch Gottes Wort an uns. Gebete aber sind Menschenworte. Wie kommen sie daher in die Bibel? Wir dürfen uns nicht irremachen lassen: die Bibel ist Gottes Wort, auch in den Psalmen. Sind also die Gebete zu Gott – Gottes eigenes Wort?"[6] Er legt dieses Wunder getreu der christlichen Auslegungstradition mit Hilfe trinitarischer Begrifflichkeit aus: Der Gottessohn Christus sei Beter der Psalmen; er bete und klage zu Gott als Mensch unter Menschen und so würden die Worte zu Gott Gottes Wort. Der Heilige Geist stünde dafür ein, dass dies ein inklusives Geschehen sei, in das wir, wenn wir die Psalmen beten, einbezogen seien.[7] Die trinitarische Begrifflichkeit, die das Psalmengebet mit christlichen Deutungskategorien interpretiert, lässt die politischen und gesellschaftlichen Herausforderungen der Einigung mit Gott und dem Messias-Christus unbenannt. So konnte es pas-

---

[5] Abraham Heschel, Gott sucht den Menschen. Eine Philosophie des Judentums, Neukirchen-Vluyn 1992, 224.

[6] Dietrich Bonhoeffer, Das Gebetbuch der Bibel, Berlin 1969, 5.

[7] Vgl. Rinse Reeling Brouwer, Beziehung als Grundkategorie im Reden von Gott und vom Menschen, in: Junge Kirche 2/2013, 11-14, der am Beispiel Augustins Psalmenlektüre als einen Schlüssel der Trinitätslehre beschreibt.

sieren, dass sich die Psalmen unter Christinnen und Christen großer Beliebtheit erfreuen und für die christliche Theologiebildung herangezogen wurden, und zugleich Jesu Messianität vom Messianismus des Alten Testaments abgegrenzt wurde. Dass Jesus *die* jüdischen Messiaserwartungen zurückgewiesen habe, ist einer der theologischen Allgemeinplätze, mit denen wir in der Kirche leben. Christologie interpretiert das Psalmengebet, nicht umgekehrt das Psalmengebet die Christologie. Die Aussagen über den Christus werden gewonnen, als würde das, was über ihn zu sagen ist, „zunächst unabhängig von der Schrift und damit logisch wie theologisch vor ihr" feststehen.[8] Doch allein der umgekehrte Weg ist möglich. Wir wissen nämlich nicht, was Christus heißt, es sei denn, dass wir aus der Hebräischen Bibel lernen, „was eigentlich der Inhalt, der Sinn und die Absicht dessen ist, was wir 'Christus' nennen"[9].

So wird der Psalter zum Übungsweg christlicher Umkehr. Hier kristallisieren sich verschiedene Herausforderungen, vor denen wir stehen. Die eine ist der notwendige Blickwechsel: Die Umkehrung der Leserichtung, die mit der Anerkennung des Alten Testaments als Schrift gegeben ist, wird zur Herausforderung für christliche Theologiebildung – auch für die Neulektüre der Reformation. Die Bilder von Christus können den Psalmen nicht länger übergestülpt werden, sondern die Psalmen müssen als Verstehensraum für den Messias gelesen werden. Die zweite ist die Gottessuche isolierter Menschen: Der Psalter bietet denen, die heute angesichts der Zerstörung der gesellschaftlichen Netze bei Gott Halt suchen, Anknüpfungspunkte, und führt sie dabei zurück zur Gemeinschaft. Er eröffnet spirituelle Erfahrung von Transzendenz und Verbundenheit, die zugleich politische Erfahrungen sind. Beim Lesen der Psalmen wird das alte Motto der Frauenbewegung neu erlernt: Das Private ist politisch! Die spirituelle Isolation, die mit gesellschaftlicher Vereinzelung einhergeht, wird überwunden.

---

[8] Frank Crüsemann, Das Alte Testament als Wahrheitsraum des Neuen. Die neue Sicht der christlichen Bibel, Gütersloh 2011, 295.

[9] Cornelis Heiko Miskotte, Wenn die Götter schweigen. Vom Sinn des Alten Testaments (aus d. Niederl. übers. v. H. Stoevesandt), München 1966, 166f.

Die Psalmen als Mantel des Messias 271

Unsere Psalmengebete als Gotteswort zu hören, ist uns nicht selbstverständlich, weil wir die Psalmen in der Regel versweise wahrnehmen oder einzelne Lieblingspsalmen rezitieren. Die Verwandlung dieser Verse und Gedichte von Menschenwort in Gotteswort geschieht mit dem Hören der Einzeltexte im Buchganzen. Für die Psalmen gilt, was für jeden anderen biblischen Text eine Selbstverständlichkeit ist, dass sie in den Zusammenhang eines Buches gehören.[10] Die Buchkomposition „Psalter" ist der Verstehensraum, in dem sich die einzelnen Psalmen als Gottes Wort und Weisung präsentieren. Die Psalmen sind ein sozialer Raum. Hier hören wir die Stimmen unserer Mütter und Vätern im Glauben; hier erstehen zentrale Figuren unserer Glaubensüberlieferung wie David oder Mose; hier lernen wir die Auseinandersetzung mit Israels Gottheit; hier ereignet sich Gottes Wort und Antwort auf unser Suchen. Dieser soziale Raum wird uns als Erfahrungsraum der Gottheit Israels gewiesen. Ein fünfteiliges Buch wird uns überliefert, gegliedert durch die Segensformel „Gesegnet die EWIGE, der Gott Israels, von der Weltzeit her und für die Weltzeit. Amen, Amen", die im Laufe des Buches in leichter Variation vier Mal wiederholt wird (Psalm 41,14; 72,18f.; 89,53: 106,48). Die Segensformel unterteilt und deutet. Gott wird gesegnet! Mit dieser Geste werden die Psalmen als Gottes Werk interpretiert. Gott handelt und spricht in den Gebeten der Menschen. Die Fünfteilung, die erreicht wird, unterstreicht diese Deutung. Sie ist im Kontext der Bibel, die mit den fünf Büchern Mose beginnt, ein Programm. Der Psalter steht als Antwort und Verarbeitung der Tora neben der Tora und will selbst als Gottes Weisung zum Leben, als Tora, verstanden werden.

Ein Weg wird beschritten aus extremer Isolation (Psalm 1,1) hin zur Verbundenheit aller, die atmen, im Gotteslob (150,6). Die Chronologie der Ge-

---

[10] Siehe dazu Klara Butting, Erbärmliche Zeiten – Zeit des Erbarmens, Theologie und Spiritualität der Psalmen, Uelzen 2013; oder die Einleitung in Frank-Lothar Hossfeld/ Erich Zenger, Psalmen I 1-50 (NEB 29), Würzburg 1993, 5-25. Einen Überblick über die Buchkomposition vermittelt auch Beat Weber, Werkbuch Psalmen III. Theologie und Spiritualität des Psalters und seiner Psalmen, Stuttgart 2010. Bei Weber geht allerdings der für die Messiaserwartung des Psalters wichtige Aspekt verloren, dass die betende Gemeinde eine messianische Rolle spielt. Er trennt die zwei zentralen Themen, Messias und Gebet der Gemeinde, indem er neben Ps 1 & 2 auch Ps 3 zur Ouvertüre des Psalters rechnet.

schichte Israels strukturiert diesen Weg. Der Psalter zeichnet in Auseinandersetzung mit der Davidfigur die Geschichte Israels nach. Am Anfang wird das Königtum eingesetzt (Psalm 2). Israels Gott stellt den Königen der Erde, die glauben die Welt beherrschen zu können, seinen König auf dem Zion entgegen. Psalmenlesend werden wir hineingestellt in eine globale Auseinandersetzung um Gottes Lebensregeln der Solidarität – und müssen uns mit ihrem Scheitern konfrontieren. Die Hoffnungen auf universale Gerechtigkeit werden am Ende des 2. Buches in Psalm 72 noch einmal formuliert. In diesem Psalm wird das Königtum an den Thronfolger Salomo übergeben und die Zeit der Nachfolger Davids eingeläutet. Doch das 3. Buch endet mit der Klage über das Scheitern des davidischen Königtums (Psalm 89). Die Psalmen 2, 72 und 89 interpretieren die Psalmen 2-89 als einen Durchgang durch die Geschichte des davidischen Königtums – seine Stiftung, seine Vererbung und sein Versagen.[11] Im 4. und 5. Buch des Psalters werden neue Lebensperspektiven nach der Katastrophe entwickelt werden. Auch hier begegnet der Name David und auch Königspsalmen tauchen an zentralen Stellen wieder auf (101; 110; 132; 144).[12] In Auseinandersetzung mit David und seinem Königtum werden aus den Trümmern der gescheiterten Geschichte Zukunftsbilder entwickelt.

Die Chronologie der Geschichte Israels als Ordnungsprinzip des Psalters betont den politischen Charakter der Gottesbeziehung. Gottsuche ist Auseinandersetzung mit Geschichte und Politik des Gemeinwesens. Zum Gebet gehört die Zeitung oder – im Fall der Psalmen – die Samuelbücher, die

---

[11] Erich Zenger nennt die Teilsammlung 2-89 deshalb den messianischen Psalter, Erich Zenger, „Es sollen sich niederwerfen vor ihm alle Könige" (Ps 72,11). Redaktionsgeschichtliche Beobachtungen zu Psalm 72 und zum Programm des messianischen Psalters Ps 2-89, in: Eckhart Otto / Erich Zenger (Hg), „Mein Sohn bist du" (Ps2,7). Studien zu den Königspsalmen (SBB 192), Stuttgart 2002, 66-93.

[12] „Königspsalmen" werden seit Anfang des 18. Jahrhunderts eine Reihe von Psalmen genannt, denen gemeinsam ist, dass sie von einem König handeln (Ps 2; 18; 20; 21; 45; 72; 89; 101; 110; 132; 144). Seit die Psalmenexegese die Buchkomposition des Psalters im Blick hat, ist deutlich geworden, dass die Königspsalmen für die Struktur und Theologie des Psalmenbuches eine zentrale Rolle spielen, siehe z.B. Georg Braulik, Christologisches Verständnis der Psalmen – schon im Alten Testament? in: Klemens Richter u.a. (Hg.), Christologie der Liturgie. Der Gottesdienst der Kirche – Christusbekenntnis und Sinaibund (Quaestiones Disputatae 159), Freiburg [Br.] 1995, 57-86, 59.

Chancen und Scheitern der Geschichte Israels im Land durchdenken. Dabei wird weder die Zeit Davids, noch die Geschichte irgendeines Königs im Psalter in ihrem ursprünglichen Verlauf erschlossen. David ist keine Figur der Vergangenheit. Sein Gedenken ist Gestaltung der Zukunft. Davids Name ist eine Chiffre für gestaltbare Gemeinschaft.[13] Er löst den Blick von Fremdherrschaft und Ohnmacht und führt zur Auseinandersetzung mit der eigenen Geschichte, ihren Fehlern und ihrem Hoffnungspotential zurück. Sein Name steht in der biblischen Glaubensüberlieferung für die kurze Zeitspanne, in der Israel als nationale Einheit im Land existent war. Davids Name hält die Hoffnung wach, dass Israel als selbstständige Größe im eigenen Land kein Hirngespinst ist, sondern dass selbstbestimmtes Zusammenleben trotz aller Konflikte in Zeit und Raum gestaltet werden kann. Ein Großteil der biblischen Glaubensüberlieferung verbindet die messianische Erwartung mit dem Namen Davids (z.B. Jeremia 33,14-18; Ezechiel 34,23). Auch im Psalter geht es um diesen neuen David. Die Überschrift „*ledawid*" (von/für David), die nahezu die Hälfte aller Psalmen mit David in Verbindung bringt,[14] lesen wir gewöhnlich als Verfasserangabe „von David" und nutzen sie zur historischen Rekonstruktion von Königsgeschichte. Doch die Überschriftennotiz *ledawid* meint eher „für David" als „von David". Die Davidfigur wird im Psalmengebet neu gestaltet.

Der Psalter interveniert mit dieser Neukonstruktion der Davidfigur in eine gesellschaftliche Konfliktsituation im nachexilischen Juda, die in der Ouvertüre des Psalmenbuches (die Psalmen 1 und 2) als Verstehenshorizont des Buches aufscheint.[15] Eine international vernetzte Elite ist an die Macht gekommen und gibt in allen Lebensbereichen den Ton an (Psalm 1,1). Der

---

[13] Matthias Millard spricht von einer „Personenchiffre", die den Bezug auf ein „lokal und sozial" geeintes Israel andeutet – „ein Israel, das – im Duktus der biblischen Geschichtsdarstellung – noch nicht in Nord- und Südreich, geschweige denn in verschiedene Diasporagruppen aufgespalten ist", Matthias Millard, Die Komposition des Psalters. Ein formgeschichtlicher Ansatz (FAT 9), Tübingen 1994, 231.

[14] Die Psalmen 3; 7; 9; 18; 34; 51; 52; 54; 56; 57; 59; 60; 63; 142 werden außerdem mit bestimmten Situationen der Davidgeschichte, die die Samuelbücher erzählen, verknüpft.

[15] Klara Butting, Erbärmliche Zeiten – Zeit des Erbarmens, Theologie und Spiritualität der Psalmen, Uelzen 2013.

Psalter benutzt den Begriff *rascha*. Die Übersetzung Martin Luthers mit „Gottlose" führt in die Irre. Nicht die Ungläubigen oder Atheisten sind gemeint, sondern Verbrecher und zwar die Verbrecher „in Anzügen". Sie bewegen sich im Zentrum der Gesellschaft. „Frevler" übersetzt Martin Buber. „Krimineller" ist die Bedeutung dieses Wortes in Neuhebräisch. In der Septuaginta steht an vielen Stellen „*anomos*" – Gesetzloser. Gedacht ist an Menschen, die sich über die Weisungen hinwegsetzen, die in Israel überliefert werden. Gleich der erste Vers des Psalters nennt dieses Wort „*rascha*", das von da an den gesamten Psalter durchzieht. 84 Mal kommen „die Frevler" im Psalmenbuch vor. Erich Zenger nennt den Psalter deshalb „die Geschichte einer dramatischen Auseinandersetzung zwischen Gerechten und Frevlern bzw. zwischen ohnmächtig Armen und übermächtig Reichen."[16] In Psalm 2 meldet sich diese Elite mit dem Freiheitsruf zu Wort, die Fesseln der Solidarität, für die Israels Gottheit einsteht, zu sprengen. Sie propagieren die Freiheit, die den Leistungsträgern unbeschränkte Möglichkeiten bietet, für sich selbst zu sorgen. Ihr Ruf spiegelt die gesellschaftliche Entwicklung im nachexilischen Juda. Überregionale Handelsbeziehungen setzen Maßstäbe, gegenüber denen die lokale Gesetzgebung rückständig erscheint. Die Tora, die Akkumulation bremsen und Solidarität judäischer Familien organisieren will, wird zur Fessel. Sabbatgesetze, die die wirtschaftliche Entwicklung zur Förderung des lokalen Zusammenlebens regulieren, sind anachronistisch. Geld vermittelt Verfügungsmacht und gewährt Lebensqualität, unabhängig von einer Solidargemeinschaft. Während Massenarmut wächst, etablieren sich mächtige Familien mit riesigem Großgrundbesitz.

Der Psalter verfolgt angesichts der gesellschaftlichen Spaltung in Gewinner/innen und Verlierer/innen das Ziel „der Identitätsbildung für Israel"[17]. Wer Psalmen liest, wird in Israels Ringen um eine gerecht gestaltete Gemeinschaft mit hinein genommen. Furchtbare Not schreit aus den Psalmen. Scheitern, Verschleppung und Versklavung, menschenverachtende Herrschaft globaler Eliten, politische Ohnmacht, massenhafte Verelendung, gesellschaftliches Abseits, Auseinandersetzung mit eigener Schuld und das zähe Ringen

---

[16] Erich Zenger, Ein Gott der Rache? Feindpsalmen verstehen, Freiburg u.a. 1998, 25.

[17] Egbert Ballhorn, Zum Telos des Psalters. Der Textzusammenhang des Vierten und Fünften Psalmenbuches (Ps 90-150) (BBB 138) Berlin, Wien 2004, 372.

um einen Neuanfang werden Teil der kollektiven Erinnerung. Wer Psalmen liest, übt angesichts himmelschreienden Elends die Beharrlichkeit und den langen Atem, die für die Suche nach Lebenswegen nötig sind, und lernt die Wege Gottes in der eigenen Gegenwart aufzuspüren und zu gehen. Für Christinnen und Christen, die aus den Völkern stammen und keine jüdischen Wurzeln haben, wird dieser Lernweg des Psalters zum Lehrhaus biblischen Glaubens. Er ist Einweisung zum Mitgehen mit Israel und seinem Gott. Wir geraten in die Bundesgeschichte Gottes mit seinem Volk hinein und lernen, als Partnerinnen und Partner dieser Geschichte zu agieren. Eine „Sprachschule für neu Hinzugekommene aus den Völkern" hat Matthias Loerbroks das Psalmenbuch genannt. „Zunächst als Gast-und Nebenhörer, als Forum, dann auch als Mitsprechende lernen sie, ihren Platz, ihre Rolle im Bund zu finden, schließlich mit Israel den Namen des Herrn anzurufen und auszurufen, ihm zu klagen, ihn anzuflehen, sein Nähe, sein Antlitz zu suchen, seine großen Taten zu preisen".[18]

5. Der Körper des Messias

Die politische Institution des „König-Messias" – so der Titel des Königs in der Hebräischen Bibel, der im Psalter immer wieder begegnet – wird im Psalmenbuch zu einer theologischen Kategorie, die zur Auseinandersetzung mit herrschenden Gewaltverhältnissen befähigt. Die Hoffnung, dass gerechtes Zusammenleben trotz Fremdherrschaft und Korruption der Eliten gestaltbar ist, wird mit der Erwartung einer messianischen Figur aus den Trümmern der Geschichte geborgen. Nicht zufällig haben die Psalmen Pate gestanden, als die Freunde und Freundinnen Jesu von seinem Leben und seiner messianischen Würde zu erzählen versuchten. Ob die Worte, die Jesus bei seiner Taufe hört oder die Worte, die er sterbend spricht – Psalmen haben diesen Erzählungen ihre Gestalt gegeben. Denn der Psalter ist ein Buch über den Messias, den Christus-König, den neuen David. Dabei verbindet das Psalmenbuch zwei Aspekte der messianischen Idee, die im Laufe ihrer Geschichte auseinandergefallen sind und im Konflikt zwischen Christentum und Judentum eine zentrale Rolle gespielt haben. Typisch für das Judentum sei – so

---

[18] Matthias Loerbroks, Weisung vom Zion. Biblisch-theologische Orientierungen für eine Kirche neben Israel (SKI 19), Berlin 2000, 130.

hat Gershom Scholem es beschrieben – ein Begriff der Erlösung, die „sich in der Öffentlichkeit vollzieht, auf dem Schauplatz der Geschichte und im Medium der Gemeinschaft, kurz, der sich entscheidend in der Welt des Sichtbaren vollzieht und ohne solche Erscheinung im Sichtbaren nicht gedacht werden kann". Erlösung im Christentum werde hingegen „als ein Vorgang im ‚geistlichen' Bereich und im Unsichtbaren" verstanden, „der sich in der Seele, in der Welt jedes einzelnen, abspielt, und der eine geheime Verwandlung bewirkt, der nichts Äußeres in der Welt entsprechen muss."[19]

Im Psalter holt die messianische Figur, die in Psalm 2 in unser Gebet Einzug hält, die Betenden auf den Schauplatz der Geschichte. Eine globale Auseinandersetzung um Gottes Lebensregeln der Solidarität wird der Horizont unseres Betens. Der Psalm zeichnet die Einführung des Königtums in Israel nach. Den „Königen der Erde", die als Repräsentanten einer globalen Unrechtsordnung genannt werden (Psalm 2,2), stellt Gott seinen König, den Gesalbten (hebräisch: Messias, griechisch: Christus), entgegen. Angesichts des Herrschaftsanspruchs einer internationalen Elite zieht Israels Gottheit sich nicht aus der Welt zurück, sondern geht in die kaputte Welt hinein. Der Messias ist Gottes Versprechen, dass Gott die Welt nicht verfehlter Politik überlässt. Politik, die von globalen Unrechtsstrukturen dominiert wird, soll Schauplatz für Gottesrecht und Menschenrechte werden.

Wenn in Psalm 3 die Gebetssammlung mit der Bemerkung beginnt: „Ein Psalm für David. Als er vor seinem Sohn Absalom floh", beginnt für die Betenden das Durchbuchstabieren von politischen Fehlentscheidungen und Abbrüchen. Sie treten an einer Stelle in die Geschichte ein, an der die Einheit Israels durch die Machtfixierung seines Regenten wieder zerfällt. David hatte im Verlauf des Absalomaufstands durch Hausmachtpolitik und Geheimverhandlungen mit der Provinz Juda ein erstes Auseinanderbrechen der Einheit Israels in Nord und Süd heraufbeschworen (2. Samuel 19). Psalm 3 zeichnet in diese Situation eine innere Wandlung ein. Der/die Betende findet aus Isolation zurück zur Gemeinschaft und bittet am Ende um Segen für das

---

[19] Gershom Scholem, Über einige Grundbegriffe des Judentums, Frankfurt am Main 1970, 121.

gesamte Volk (Psalm 3,9).[20] Der Psalm ist Midrasch,[21] so der jüdische Begriff für die Neuerzählungen biblischer Geschichte. In Psalm 3 tauchen Handlungsmöglichkeiten auf, die über Davids Worte und Taten in den Samuelerzählungen hinausgehen. Im Leben derjenigen, die im Psalter das Gespräch mit Gott suchen, wird die alte Geschichte neu geschrieben. Getreu der jüdischen Weisheit, dass „Vergessen das Exil verlängert, Erinnerung das Geheimnis der Erlösung ist", wird den Frauen und Männern, die sich Psalmen betend auf die Auseinandersetzung mit David einlassen, erlösende Kraft zuerkannt. Das Leben der Betenden wird zu einem Ort, an dem die Kämpfe und noch offenen Probleme, die in Davids Geschichte zutage treten, ausgetragen werden.

Für die vereinzelten Menschen, die in Not und Anfechtung sich selbst und Gott verstehen wollen, wird der Weg zu Gott ein Weg aus der Isolation hin zu der Erfahrung Generationen übergreifender Verbundenheit. Frauen und Männer, die nicht mehr weiter können, werden zu einer das eigene Ich transzendierenden Wirklichkeit geführt. Sie verkleiden sich in die Davidfigur und lernen sich als Menschen wahrnehmen, die die Gesellschaft gestalten. Die Erfahrung von Verbundenheit führt zurück zu der eigenen unverwechselbaren Würde und Bestimmung. Auch hier gilt: Einheitserfahrungen sind Berufungserfahrungen. Betend bekomme ich einen neuen Horizont, mich selbst und meine Situation zu verstehen. Betend vollzieht sich die Erkenntnis, dass jede und jeder einzelne mit der Verarbeitung von Leid, Verfehlung und Dankbarkeit teilhat an der großen Politik, für die der Name David steht. Jedermann und jede Frau ist auch in Isolation und Bedrängnis mitverantwortlich für die Vollendung der Geschichte der gesamten Menschheit. Dabei misst sich die uns gegebene Macht nicht an der gesellschaftlichen Stellung, der Größe des Aktionsradius oder der Menge der Gestaltungsmöglichkeiten, die wir haben. Auch wenn wir denken, dass wir nichts tun können, auch wenn unsere Handlungsspielräume auf die Bewältigung unserer eigenen Not oder Krankheit beschränkt sind oder durch die politische Situation minimiert werden, wir lernen uns Psalmen betend als Menschen kennen,

---

[20] Klara Butting, Erbärmliche Zeiten, a.a.O., 35.
[21] Brevard S. Childs nannte die Psalmen Midraschim der überlieferten Geschichte, Brevard S. Childs, Psalm Titles and Midrashic Exegesis, in: JSSt 16 /1971, 137-150.

auf die es bei Gottes Veränderung der Welt ankommt. Private Notlagen werden politisiert. Der eigene Körper wird Feld der bisher ungelösten gesellschaftlichen Einigungsprozesse. Das eigene Leben wird zu einem Ort von Gärung und Vorbereitung der kommenden Zeit.

Die auseinanderstrebenden Aspekte der messianischen Idee werden im Psalmenbuch verknüpft. Auch dort, wo Unrecht nur noch durch spirituelle Disziplin entmachtet wird, bleibt die konkrete politische Gestalt des Gemeinwesens der Horizont von Auseinandersetzung und Spiritualität. Beten mit David übt Spiritualität ein, ohne zu spiritualisieren. Der innere Weg bereitet die neue Welt Gottes vor, der spirituelle Rückweg zur Gemeinschaft ist Vorübung für gesellschaftliche Versöhnung. Die messianische Vision des Psalmenbuches finde ich in einer Definition von Messianismus wieder, die Emmanuel Lévinas im Nachdenken talmudischer Texte formuliert hat: „Der Messianismus ist also nicht die Gewissheit der Ankunft eines Menschen, der die Geschichte anhält. Er ist meine Fähigkeit, das Leid aller zu tragen. Er ist der Augenblick, in dem ich diese Fähigkeit und meine universale Verantwortung erkenne".[22] Weder eine historische Gestalt steht den Herausgeber/innen des Psalters bei ihrer Rede vom David-Messias vor Augen, noch ist der Messias eine Figur der Endzeit, die die Geschichte abbricht.[23] Sie ist Berufung aller, die Psalmen beten. Betend, um eine Lebensperspektive ringend wird jede/jeder Teil der messianischen Figur, die der Ewige denen entgegenstellt, die am Elend anderer verdienen. Auch dort wo der Weg der Einigung über Grenzen hinweg nicht denkbar ist – im Gebet wird er erprobt. In den Betenden und durch sie erstehen Wege hin zu einer neuen geeinten Menschheit. Der Körper des Messias, den wir als Bild der Gemeinde aus den neutestamentlichen Schriften kennen, ist bereits in den Psalmen ein Bild der Gemeinde. Die Psalmen sind der Mantel des Messias. Wer sie liest, kleidet sich in diesen Mantel und der Tag kommt nahe, an dem Gott nicht mehr zerteilt ist in arm und reich, sondern alles, was Atem hat, vereint ist, im Lobe Gottes.

---

[22] Emmanuel Lévinas, Schwierige Freiheit. Versuch über das Judentum, Frankfurt a. M. 1992, 95.

[23] Markus Saur, Die Königspsalmen. Studien zur Entstehung und Theologie (BZAW 340), Berlin. New York 2004.

Abstract

Klara Butting unfolds the Book of Psalms as a way of learning Christian conversion including two specific challenges: 1. the change of direction of traditional Christian reading, judging and down-grading the Old Testament from the perspective of seemingly Christian truths. By contrast the Book of Psalms is a space for understanding the New Testament speaking of the Messiah. 2. The turning away from privatized spirituality. Butting, in her liberation theological reading of the Book of Psalms, shows that the psalms open a spiritual experience of transcendence and interconnectedness, which at the same time are political experiences and which can overcome the spiritual isolation, which goes hand in hand with societal disconnectedness.

Martin Luther's Concern for the Common Person
Implications for the Process of Economic Globalization

Santhosh J. Sahayadoss

The world is rapidly changing. The process of globalization has brought about rapid transformation, making the world "a global village." Those understanding the dynamics of the global market and who are gifted with marketable knowledge and skills are rewarded economically and play an influential role in society. Unfortunately, there are many who have neither the knowledge nor the requisite skills to participate in the process of globalization. They are considered "dispensable" and are ignored by those who enjoy the benefits of globalization. These "drop-outs" are the poor, who do not have occasion to participate in the global market and are left at the mercy of the system. In the third world, these are neither supported by the government nor allowed to participate in the benefits of globalization. Economic recession affects not only the third world but also the first world. Thereby poverty has become a global issue.

The chapter asserts that poverty is a reality all over the globe, in spite of the economic prosperity of many elites around the world. Given this premise, we seek to investigate how Luther responded to the reality of the poor and how Luther was concerned about the common poor person. Luther's insights into the social and economic context of his times can direct us to rediscover their relevance for our contemporary society.

This chapter will first present the basic features of globalization, focussing on the relation between globalization and poverty, greed, and the neglect of the common person. In the latter part of this chapter we will explore Luther's response to the issues of poverty and greed that ultimately leads to the neglect of the common person. Even though the present context and Luther's context are very different given the 500 years gap in time, it remains striking to identify how key issues abide.

Luther is often criticised for maintaining the status quo, however, we will argue against this criticism. Luther was interested in bringing about change in society. Luther clearly and categorically expressed his concern for matters regarding the welfare of the common person. It is important to analyse Luther's involvement in the peasant's revolt, because Luther is often accused of neglecting the common person especially the case of the peasants. It is necessary to revisit the two kingdom concept, in order to demonstrate that he was not bent on maintaining the status quo but was for bringing in a positive change.

Because Luther was primarily a theologian, we shall investigate the theological basis of Luther's economics. Then we will examine the main ethical issues of concern to Luther: poverty, greed, and concern for the common person. This inquiry will draw forth the implications of Luther's thought for the process of economic globalization.

1. Globalization and Its Impact

1. 1. Salient Features of Globalization

Globalization is an "ambivalent phenomenon." Before studying its negative repercussions, let us consider some of the positive aspects. Globalization is a process that fosters integration of peoples and communities. In past generations people of different nations and regions lived unconnected lives. In a nation like India, people in the South hardly knew about life in the North. Through globalization people of different regions live in proximity with one another. Nations that were once closed in their attitudes toward other nations have begun to work closely with others toward economic and human development.[1] Globalization has also resulted in the dissemination of science and technology, improved health facilities, and the latest in social networking. Consequently, radical change has taken place in communication and information technologies.[2]

---

[1] Cf. Amal Raj Chellakan, Eradication of Poverty and Empowerment of the Poor: Theology of Creation and the Newest Policies of Development in the Age of Globalization (Delhi: ISPCK, 2007), xvi.

[2] Cf. Tissa Balasuriya, "Recolonization and Debt Crisis," in *Globalization: A Challenge to the Church*, ed. P. Jagadish Gandhi and George Cherian (Chennai, Nagpur: Association of Christian Institutes for Social Concern in Asia, National Council of Churches in India – Urban Rural Mission, 1998), 8.

According to Hans Küng, the process of globalization is a consequence of scientific and technological growth that was fueled by the emergence of economic prosperity during the 19th century in Europe. This movement spread from Europe to penetrate all national boundaries across the globe. Subsequently, a major transition took place from national self-interest in one's own economy to a global interest that could lead to a greater international economic prosperity. Küng ascertains that the process of globalization has become irreversible and cannot be undone.[3]

Gary J. Wells offers this observation:

"Globalization has accelerated as a result of many positive factors, the most notable of which include: the collapse of communism and the end of the Cold War; the spread of capitalism and free trade; more rapid and global capital flows and more liberal financial markets; the liberalization of communications; international academic and scientific collaboration; and faster and more efficient forms of transportation. At the core of accelerated global integration - at once its principal cause and consequence - is the information revolution, which is knocking down once-formidable barriers of physical distance, blurring national boundaries, and creating cross-border communities of all types."[4]

Researchers assert that the whole globalization process results from the desire of the developed industrial world to expand its territories and make enormous profit. Subsequently, they have made in-roads into third-world economies through the influence of policy makers and with the help of international financial institutions. The third-world countries have had to make structural adjustments to adopt this program. Now they find it difficult to leave the road of liberalization and privatization and exit the process of globalization.[5]

---

[3] Cf. Yahya Wijaya, "Economic Globalization and Asian Contextual Theology," in *Theological Studies* 69 (2008): 313. See also Hans Küng, *Global Ethics for Global Politics and Economics* (London: SCM, 1997).

[4] Gary J. Wells, "The Issue of Globalization – An Overview," accessed December 7, 2013, http://digital commons.ilr.cornell.edu/ers/6.

[5] Cf. M. Victor Louis Anthuvan, *The Dynamics and the Impact of Globalization: A Subaltern Perspective* (Madurai: Amirtham Publications, 2006), 171.

Another feature of globalization involves impacts on the environment. Environmentalists assert that trade liberalization has adverse effects on the environment; globalization promotes development at the cost of environmental protection. Without proper environmental protection policies, globalization leads to serious environmental disasters. The common people are at greater risk because of the forces of environmental racism. Globalization remains unconcerned about the dangers that it may cause to future global humanity.[6]

According to a report by the United Nations on human development:

> "Environmental damage is another indicator of global poverty and inequality. Deforestation, soil erosion, water depletion, and declining fish stocks and biodiversity detail a growing scarcity of essential resources. Efforts to address these losses through the recycling of raw materials, emission controls, and improved waste management have helped. Yet the threats remain."[7]

Poverty continues to exist today in extremely inhuman forms, especially in the third world. Essentially, there are two types of studies made on globalization. The first type asserts that globalization has resulted in the abolition of poverty, looking at the positive effects of globalization and communicating the message that globalization is good both for contemporary society and for future generations.

The second type of study, however, reveals that globalization has done more harm to humanity than good. These studies point out that poverty remains a reality and is part of the present existential predicament. No one can gloss over the reality of poverty even in the West, given the economic recession in the recent past. Suffering was evident all over the world. Those in the third world witness how the common poor person is left out to suffer on his/her own. Only a few have been able to take advantage of the process of globalization by moving from the middle class to the upper echelons of soci-

---

[6] Cf. M.A. Mohamed Salih, "Globalization, Sustainable Development, and Environment: A Balancing Act," in *Globalization and Development Studies: Challenges for the 21st Century*, ed. Frans J. Schnurman (New Delhi: Vistaar Publications, 2001), 123.

[7] June O'Connor, "Making a Case for the Common Good in a Global Economy: The United Nations Human Development Report," in *Journal of Religious Ethics* 30/1 (2002): 163.

ety. Business-minded people also have sometimes moved forward from the lower class to the middle sections of society.

Unfortunately, those at the bottom of society have been left out. The Hebrew Bible records God's preferential option for the poor. The climax of this concern is evident through the prophet Amos. Jesus was with the common poor people, who were like sheep without a shepherd. Learning from this biblical message, Luther expressed concern for the weak and ignored in society. In accord with the biblical testimony, Jesus, and Luther the reformer, we too are called to identify with the common poor person in our society.

We cannot remain oblivious to the presence of poor people in our neighborhoods. Luther's understanding can be helpful for us today in dealing with the neglect of the common person. Poverty is still a reality and good Christians are called to respond in the spirit of Christ.

1.2 Globalization and Poverty

With the whole world as a single market, the sudden withdrawal of foreign investment has disastrous effects on local firms and their economies. Studies reveal that "globalization excludes a whole lot of unskilled groups of people giving rise to further impoverishment. Due to privatization there is loss of guaranteed employment."[8] Many are uncertain about the future. Globalization also results in the growth of unemployment. Whenever small industries are unable to compete with international firms, whenever traditional arts and crafts are neglected because of modern globalized products, and whenever people leave their native environment and move to cities in search of jobs, the result has been job loss for the indigenous communities and the increase of poverty.

In a third world country like India such a predicament has led to religious conflicts, social unrest, and outburst of violence. Heiko Schrader observes: "A common argument in the globalization debate is that globalization smoothens difference and income disparities. Poor countries and poor people

---

[8] P.G. Jogoland and S.M. Michael, "Introduction," in *Globalization and Social Movements: Struggle for a Humane Society*, ed. P.G. Jogoland and S.M. Michael (New Delhi: Rawat Publications, 2006), 5.

can benefit from information that is freely available via internet. Such a view is a myth."[9] Analysts of the causes of unemployment note that safety nets were not put in place before introducing trade liberalization. Consequently, those losing their jobs struggle with poverty. Even though liberalisation of the economy promises growth and financial security, the reality is far from it. Some consider that misery and insecurity only has increased.[10]

In spite of the economic reforms that were initiated because of globalisation, better quality of life for all was not achieved. Promises were made about increasing incomes and employment opportunities, but these promises were not fulfilled. Not only is poverty a reality in Asia, but even worse is the reality of abject poverty.[11] Walter Fernandes asserts: "The basic feature of globalization is the marginalization of the majority for the profit of a few."[12] There is a growing tendency to forget the poor. This is known as the "amnesia of the poor."[13] The present trend is to neglect, exclude and forget the vulnerable groups, if they are unable to participate in the development plan.

Felix Wilfred emphasises: "The worst thing happening with globalization is that the poor are not wanted; they are a burden; they have simply become redundant."[14] Even the production needs and patterns are designed according to the desires of the powerful and the rich. The needs of the poor are constantly and consistently ignored. K.C. Abraham remarks: "The condition of the poor has deteriorated. The nature of the development is such that vast

---

[9] Heiko Schrader, "Globalization, Fragmentation and Modernity," in *Globalization and Social Movements: Struggle for a Humane Society*, 13.

[10] Cf. Joseph E. Stiglitz, *Globalization and Its Discontents* (New Delhi: Penguin Books, 2002), 17.

[11] Cf. Brojendra Nath Banerjee, *Globalization: Rough and Risky Road* (New Delhi: New Age International, 1998), 152.

[12] Walter Fernandes, "Globalization, Liberalization and the Victims of Colonialism," in *Globalization and Its Victims*, ed. Michael Amaladoss (Delhi: Vidyajyoti, Education and Welfare Society/ ISPCK, 1999), 20.

[13] Antony Kalliath, "Globalization: Colonization Perpetuation," in *Religion and Politics from Subaltern Perspective*, ed. Thomas Kadankavil (Bangalore: Dharmaram Publications, 1999), 122.

[14] Felix Wilfred, "Church's Commitment to the Poor in the Age of Globalization," in *Vidyajyoti* 62 (1989): 80.

masses of the third-world have become redundant."[15] Amal Raj Chellakan has studied the phenomenon of globalization and insists that the neglect of the poor is based on the attitude of the global market:

"Globalization as a master narrative gives ... birth to an unrestrained economy of the free market that usurps power, disintegrates peoples and nations, and excludes the poor and marginalized. Since the states have no control any longer over markets, the markets create distinctive zones called core, semi-periphery, and periphery. The universe seems to be ruled by the core which looks at its own interests, and which regards periphery as market-unworthy. ... This system pushes the vast majority to the edges of the society. ... [E]conomic globalization, when it goes to the extreme, ignores human life, human dignity, and human rights, especially when looking at these realities from the standpoint of the victims of globalization."[16]

To glorify the free market system is the basic principle of capitalism. V.M. Kurien argues that the market has taken the center stage and has become a "globalized institution."[17] Those who cannot participate in the market and find employment are forced to face poverty. Poverty is not simply a lack of means to acquire sufficient resources, rather poverty deprives a section of society from providing opportunities to earn a living.[18] Mohan Razu insists that poverty is not mere "income poverty," but a denial of choices and opportunities to live a dignified life.[19] Poverty should not be understood only as "lack of income," but as lack of education, nutrition, health, power, and voice in society. This makes the poor vulnerable and drives them to live in fear.[20]

---

[15] K.C. Abraham, "Third World Theology: Paradigm Shift and Emerging Concerns," in *Confronting Life: Theology out of the Context*, ed. M.P. Joseph (Delhi: ISPCK, 1995), 213.

[16] Amal Raj Chellakan, Eradication of Poverty and Empowerment of the Poor: Theology of Creation and the Newest Policies of Development in the Age of Globalization, xvi-xvii.

[17] V.M. Kurien, "Evolution of the Market and Its Social Implications," in *Voices from the Third World: Theology in the Context of Globalization* 21 (June, 1978): 173-178. See also Chellakan, *Eradication of Poverty and Empowerment of the Poor*, 73.

[18] Cf. I, John Mohan Razu, *Global Capitalism as Hydra* (Delhi: ISPCK/BUILD, 2006), 96.

[19] Cf. Mohan Razu, Global Capitalism as Hydra, 98.

[20] Cf. Mohan Razu, Global Capitalism as Hydra, 100.

Amartya Sen, the noted economist, reiterates that the basic drawback of globalization is the failure to share the potential gains acquired through globalization with the poor. In order that the poor also get their share in the profit, extensive institutional reforms must take place within the structure of global economy. Sen emphasises: "The central issue of contention is not globalization itself, nor is it the use of market as an institution, but the iniquity in the overall balance of institutional arrangements which produces very unequal sharing of the benefits of globalization. The question is not just whether the poor, too, gain something from globalization, but whether they get a fair share and a fair opportunity."[21]

June O' Connor reports about the global economy:

"Renewed attention to the poor in our time is not simply a one directional expression of charity. Charity of this sort is often enough received more as pity that breeds dependence than as love that generates freedom. Rather, empathy for the poor which expresses itself in neighbor-love and justice has as its goal the participation of the poor in many tasks of political participation, economic productivity, cultural creativity, and social harmony. Only if they participate will they be poised to contribute."[22]

Critics of globalization categorically affirm that globalization is a process that grants to the powerful control of the economy. Such a delegation of the power solely to the upper sections of society ultimately results not only in the neglect of the common poor persons but also harming them.[23]

India decided to enter into the globalization and liberalization process more than two decades ago. Two decades of experimenting with globalization has revealed certain facts. Felix Wilfred writes: "The experiences in our country (India) show that a formal democratic system could co-exist with capital accumulation and exploitation in spite of mass poverty and destitution all around. This is the anomaly we experience in India and South Asia at large."

---

[21] Amartya Sen, "How to Judge Globalism," *The American Prospect*, 1-14 January, 2002.

[22] June O'Connor, "Making a Case for the Common Good in a Global Economy: The United Nations Human Development Report," in *Journal of Religious Ethics* 30/1 (2002): 169.

[23] Emma Aisbett, "Why are Critics so convinced that Globalization is Bad for the Poor?" accessed on November 15, 2013, http://www.nber.org/chapetrs/c0113.

He contends that the misery of the poor remains unnoticed and ignored at the end of the process of liberalization and globalization.[25] A drastic change needs to take place wherein the basic needs of the poor are taken into consideration, relegating the significance of homogenization of culture to an insignificant position, and preventing migration of workers from villages to cities in search of jobs that do not exist.[26]

Since the onset of globalization, there has been an increase of acts of crime, drug abuse, and terrorism.[27] The negative effects of globalization need to be taken seriously, accompanied by a proactive response to prevent such harmful acts. Above all, the constant widening of the gap between the powerful, affluent sections of society and the powerless, poorer sections of society should be curbed.[28]

1.3 Globalization and Greed that Negates the Interest of the Common Person

Economic globalization has two major functions. First, it focuses on the concentration of capital, wealth, and power. Second, it strengthens the market forces. Globalization induces and promotes high competitive spirit.[29] This competitive spirit leads to greed. Greed begets more greed and the ones who pay the price are the poor. The well-being of humanity and the concern for the common person is at stake because of an economic system whose basic

---

[24] Felix Wilfred, "Current Political Economy," in *Theology of Economics in the Globalized World: Indian Approaches*, ed. Jacob Parappally and Antony Kalliath (Bangalore: ITA & ATC, 2010), 107.

[25] Cf. Felix Wilfred, *Asian Dreams and Christian Hope: At the Dawn of the Millennium* (Delhi: ISPCK, 2000), 11-12.

[26] Cf. Tissa Balasuriya, "Globalization," in *Dictionary of Third World Theologies*, ed. Virginia Fabella and R.S. Sugirtharajah (Maryknoll: Orbis Books, 2000), 92.

[27] Cf. Walter Fernandes and Anupama Dutta, *Colonialism to Globalization: Five Centuries after Vasco da Gama* (New Delhi: Indian Social Institute, 1999), 18.

[28] Cf. Kwok-Keung Yeung, "Utopian Vision, Local Alternatives: Resistance to Globalization in Developing Asia," in *Journal of Theologies and Cultures in Asia*, 2 (2003): 73-95.

[29] Cf. P.C. Jain, *Globalization and Tribal Economy* (New Delhi: Rawat Publication, 2001), 41.

principle is founded on greed.[30] Felix Wilfred points out: "The present capitalist system as the epicentre of greed is also the source of violence. Open and subtle forms of violence of all kinds have become a strategy to safe guard the unjust accumulation of resources and wealth."[31] The only way to bring peace in the world is by restraining the capitalist economy that promotes greed. Studies on globalization indicate that capitalism and peace cannot go together. Great harm is done to the common person because of the greed which is the driving force of globalization.

Globalization promises development and all nations are interested in development. However, we must clarify what is meant by development. V.J. John observes: "Development if measured in terms of the amount of goods and services produced rather than by what is produced and how it is distributed. The stress was on capital accumulation, consumerist life-style, and globalization of economy."[32] Instead of efficiently managing the resources and providing for the basic needs of the common person, the focus is solely on increasing the profit and catering to the needs of only the consumer class within society. Development that disregards the human rights of all people, especially the poor, and the environment cannot be considered as a positive development.

Sebastian Kochupurackal insists: "Real development should focus of sustainable growth for the whole creation ... the principle of sustainability means providing an acceptable quality of life for present generations without compromising that of future generations."[33] Not only is the common person neglected in the process of development but also the environment. Greed coupled with a consumerist life-style inevitably leads to environmental destruction. Samuel Ryan describes an attitude that ignores environmental concerns

---

[30] Felix Wilfred, "Current Political Economy," 98.
[31] Felix Wilfred, "Current Political Economy," 100.
[32] V.J. John, *The Ecological Vision of Jesus: Nature in the Parables of Mark* (Bangalore/Tiruvalla: CSS/BTTBPSA, 2002), 37.
[33] Sebastian Kochupurackal, *Eco-Mission: A Paradigm Shift in Missiology* (Bangalore: Asian Trading Corporation, 2007), 183.

as morally and spiritually polluting.[34] Leonardo Boff remarks that it is impossible to be faithful to the process of globalization that leads to consumerism and greed and also to prevent the breaking down of environment. One cannot give attention to both aspects. Unless we are set free from bondage to greed, we can neither save the environment nor enhance the quality of life of the common person.[35]

The native people of those countries, who are poor, highly depend on nature for their survival. As long as globalization penetrates every part of society, nature is endangered and the poor native people's life becomes precarious. Globalization is harmful for the environment. If this is not convincingly argued, the poor native people's life will be negatively affected. Wesley S. Ariarajah burlesques economic globalization for turning a blind eye to the environmental disorders that are evident in the present. He observes: "There is a genuine fear that uncontrolled quest for prosperity, unconscionable exploitation of earth's limited resources, growing poverty, and deprivation of large sections of human community, and the renewed willingness on the part of the rich and powerful nations to conduct outright wars to protect their economic self-interests are a recipe for an impending global disaster."[36]

Tissa Balasuriya warns that if the process of globalization is not redirected toward a genuine development that includes all people, especially the poor and the marginalized, the greed and selfishness of the rich will continue to treat the environment with contempt, while ignoring the common person will eventually lead to natural disaster and great misery for the native people.[37] The need of the hour is to invest time and energy to find alternative strategies

---

[34] Cf. Samuel Rayan, "Theological Perspectives on the Environmental Crisis," in *Religion and Society* 2 (June, 1990): 23. See also Santhosh J. Sahayadoss, "Reconsidering Theological Discourse on Creation, Redemption and Aspects of Globalization in order to Build an *Earth Community* that Promotes Eco-justice, in *Eco-Justice*, ed. Hubert M. Watson (Mangalore: Indian Theological Alumni of the University of Regensburg and BTESSC, 2011), 55-72.

[35] Cf. Leonardo Boff, *Cry of the Earth, Cry of the Poor* (Maryknoll: Orbis Books, 1997), 5.

[36] Wesley S. Ariarajah, "Religious Diversity and Inter Faith Relations in a Global Age," in *Negotiating Borders: Theological Explorations in a Global Era*, ed. Patrick Gnanapragasam and Elizabeth Fiorenza (Delhi: ISPCK, 2008), 334.

[37] Cf. Tissa Balasuriya, "Globalization," 93.

that consider the welfare of the common poor person and bring hope for the marginal.

The only option before us to save the environment is to combine economic globalization with environmental globalization. Prabha Panth explains:

"Economic globalization spreads a uniform pattern of development worldwide. At the same time, environmental problems are also getting globalized. To tackle this global environmental destruction, global environmental laws and regulations are established that have to be implemented across all countries. This is environmental globalization. However, the tenets, practices and policies of economic globalization clash with those of environmental globalization. In this conflict, economic globalization prevails and the same environmental destructive type of development is continuing all over the world. ... Unless economic globalization is co-ordinated with environmental globalization and they work towards a single goal, it will become very difficult to achieve sustainable development worldwide."[38]

The Marxist critique of capitalism analyzes the crisis of over production propelled by greed for more profit. As the global crisis advances unnoticed, perhaps the wise saying of an American Indian Tribal will come true: "Only after the last tree has been cut; only after the last river has been poisoned; only after the last fish has been caught; only then you will find that money cannot be eaten."[39]

Mass Media join company with the free market economy to promote consumer culture. The new generation of young people are constantly mesmerized to believe that supporting and being part of the materialist consumerist culture is a legitimate desire. In this process, violence becomes entertainment and the pursuit of pleasure becomes the ultimate goal of life.[40] We need to support a counter culture that challenges the materialist culture of globalization. In a world where people are constantly coaxed to amass wealth and mis-

---

[38] Prabha Panth, Globalization and Sustainable Development: Economic and Environmental Conflicts," in *Ecology and Human Well-being*, ed. Pushpam Kumar and B. Sudhakara Reddy (New Delhi: Sage Publication, 2007), 285.

[39] Bonn B.T Juego and Johannes D, Schmidt, "The Political Economy of the Global Crisis," accessed on December 21, 2013, http://vbn.aau.dk/files/19023517/Juego-Schmidt_APISA_4_Paper__Final_.pdf.

[40] Cf. Ariahrajah, "Religious Diversity and Inter Faith Relations in a Global Age," 335.

led to believe that wealth can lead to happiness, we need to disclose that this pursuit leads to disaster. When pursuit of wealth takes center stage, people inevitably become selfish and unconcerned about the less-fortunate. As long as profit at the cost of others is the order of the day, the common poor person will be ignored.[41] Wherever community life is replaced by individualism and wherever the welfare of the community is put at risk because of greed and selfishness, the impending doom of communities and societies has come one step closer.

2. Foundations on which Luther's Concern for Society are Built

Luther was primarilty a Professor of Biblical Studies. For quite a long time, Luther was not considered as an ethicist. Reinhard Hütter states that Luther "never lectured on theological ethics and never published a scholarly monograph on the subject matter, as did his colleague Melanchthon. Yet, if one approaches the Reformers, guided by the interest in their impact on the Christian life and on Christian ethics, Luther turns out to be by far the more interesting and controversial figure, especially among those who try to claim or blame him for the shape of later epoch."[42]

2.1 Defending Luther against Criticisms and Establishing Luther's Concern for Society

Before we demonstrate how Luther's thoughts are relevant in an age of globalization, let us examine some of the criticisms hurled at Luther. Ernst Troeltsch portrays Luther as a conservative ethicist who had the tendency to separate private and public morality.[43] Similarly, Max Stackhouse critiques Luther as mainly involved in reforming the church in spiritual matters that

---

[41] Cf. Mehbooh Francis Sada, "Globalization – An Extension of Euro-American Capitalism in the Third World," in *Globalization: A Challenge to the Church*, 84.

[42] Reinhard Hütter, "Martin Luther and Johannes Dietenberger on *Good Works*," in *Lutheran Quarterly* 6/2 (Summer, 1992): 127.

[43] Cf. Ernst Troeltsch, *The Social Teaching of the Christian Churches,* trans. Olive Wyon (New York: Harper & Row, 1960), 472-511. See also Carter Lindberg, "Reformation Initiatives for Social Welfare: Luther's Influence at Leisnig," in *The Annual of the Society of Christian Ethics* (1987): 79.

were peculiar to his times. He points out that Luther was unconcerned about the social and political movements of his time.[44] Luther's theology has been accused of focusing only on the inner spiritual aspects of life and neglecting the social-political dimensions. Carter Lindberg ascertains that even though Luther was a professional academic theologian, still his theology had a pastoral approach and included ethical concerns. Luther inculcated and established a new ethos based on Christian teachings that proved to be useful for his community and useful for us as well.[45]

2.2 Justification by Faith as Basis for Social Concern

Even though it is true that Luther did not develop a theology of social change, his understanding of justification by faith called for active participation in society.[46] Criticising Luther from the perspective of a modern understanding of development is anachronistic. As a theologian and responsible Christian citizen, Luther clearly articulated his views on important issues concerning the welfare of society. Jürgen Moltmann argues that an interpretation of spiritual and secular realms as representing 'private' and 'public' spheres of life in Luther's writings does not portray the complete picture. This interpretation leads to the perception that faith is other-worldly and this world has no faith. Faith in God becomes unreal and reality becomes godless.[47]

For Luther, the Christian who is justified by God has to respond in loving service to humanity. Therefore, the Christian has a responsibility in society. The Christian cannot consider faith as a private matter that has no consequence for public life in society. If the justified Christian is only bent on de-

---

[44] Cf. Max L. Stackhouse, *Creeds, Society and Human Rights* (Grand Rapids: Eerdmans, 1984), 173. See also Lindberg, "Reformation Initiatives for Social Welfare," 80.

[45] Cf. Carter Lindberg, "Luther on Poverty," in *Lutheran Quarterly* 15 (2001): 86-95.

[46] Cf. Paul J. Rajashekar, "Luther's Doctrine of Justification and Christian Social Responsibility in India," in *Bangalore Theological Forum* 15/3 (Sept-Dec, 1983): 209.

[47] Cf. Jürgen Moltmann, Politische Theologie – Politische Ethik (München: Chr. Kaiser Verlag, 1984), 135. See also Santhosh J. Sahayadoss, Martin Luther on Social and Political Issues: His Relevance for the Church and Society in India (Frankfurt am Main: Peter Lang, 2006), 48.

veloping a personal relationship with God that has no consequence for a life of service in society, he/she has not understood the repercussions of being justified by God. Paul J. Rajashekar insists that claiming Luther promoted such a detached Christian existence is a distorted understanding that needs correction.[48] Walter Altmann explains that Luther had a personal experience of liberation through the process of being justified by God. This new state of being justified by God through faith motivated him to change and challenge the church and society for the better.[49]

Luther perceived that the justified Christian need not lead a life of obsession with oneself but was called to realise his/her responsibility toward the community at large. Altmann observes: "Justification by grace and faith implies a radical principle of equality among human beings and of valuing each one of them before God; it implies utter opposition to all forms of discrimination against persons and to all limitations of the quality and dignity of their lives. Persons are valued for who they are, never for what they possess, produce or consume. ... The degradation of any person offends God."[50] The Christian who has been justified by God becomes aware that he/she can honor God for this favor by loving and serving people. The justified Christian not only values human life but also is motivated to work with God for the welfare of others.

Anabaptists, by contrast, often desired to distance themselves from the world. Hans Schwarz argues that Luther did not agree with Anabaptists. Rather, he called for an active engagement with the affairs of the world.[51] Christians are never complacent about being justified by God through faith. They constantly pursue that path of "faith active in love." However, the Christian does not attempt to apply the Gospel directly into the context of society. So-

---

[48] Cf. Paul J. Rajashekar, "Luther's Doctrine of Justification and Christian Social Responsibility in India," 199.

[49] Cf. Walter Altmann, *Luther and Liberation*, trans. Mary M. Solberg (Minneapolis: Fortress Press, 1992), 4.

[50] Altmann, Luther and Liberation, 5.

[51] Cf. Hans Schwarz, *True Faith in the True God: An Introduction to Luther's Life and Thought,* trans. Mark William Worthing (Minneapolis: Augsburg Fortress, 1996), 90.

ciety functions on the basis of reason.[52] The Christian uses the gift of reason in society to share God's love with everyone by serving.

Service to humanity is a natural response of the justified Christian because he/she is filled with gratitude for the grace that God has shown toward him/her.[53] Luther set an example of living a life that was set free to serve others because of God's justifying grace. Luther wrote about economic abuses, educational reforms, establishing municipal welfare systems, relief for the poor, and protest against high taxes.[54] Such writings demonstrate that he was not only concerned about the welfare of the church, but also the welfare of society. Carrie Moseman explains: "[F]aith in Christ frees one from the need to merit any righteousness and at the same time leads one to be a servant of Christ, or 'a Christ' to others. The commandments direct us to serve our neighbor, not out of duty, but because of the love we have received from God."[55]

Luther, in his *Treatise on Good Works* states: "Our own self-imposed good works led us to and into ourselves so that we just seek our own benefit. But God's commandments drive us to our neighbor's need, that by means of these commandments we may be of benefit only to others and to their salvation."[56] Thus Luther calls for a shift from self-centered works to other-centered service. Luther was confident that no amount of work can ever earn righteousness. God alone graciously imputes righteousness to the believer.

---

[52] Cf. *LW* 51: 7.

[53] Cf. Jerome King Del Pino, Luther' Theology of the Cross as Reflected in Selected Historical Contexts of Social Change from 1521-1525: A Study of Theory and Practice (London: University Microfilm International, 1980), 120.

[54] Cf. *LW* 45: 245-310 (Luther on Economic Abuses); *LW* 45: 347-348 (Luther on Educational Reform); *LW* 45: 169-194 (Luther on Establishment of Municipal welfare System); *LW* 7:158-159 (Luther on Establishment of Grain Reserve); *LW* 7: 159-160 (Luther's Protest against High Taxes). See also Robert Allen Kelly, *Free Conscience and Obedient Body: Martin Luther's Views on Authority in Church and State Analysed in the Context of His Theology of the Cross* (London: University Microfilms International, 1981), 187.

[55] Carries Moseman, "Martin Luther on 'Becoming a Christ to One's Neighbour'," in *Presbyterion* 26/2 (Fall, 2000), 96.

[56] Luther, Treatise on Good Works, The Christian in Society I, in LW 44: 71.

Therefore the call is to "become a Christ" for the sake of our neighbor. Moseman points out that Luther cautioned against a wrong motive in serving others, thinking that God needs our work. Luther emphasizes that we need to have a right motive in serving others:

> "But you might ask 'Why does God not do it all by [God' self], since [God] is able to help everyone and knows how to help everyone?' Yes, [God] can do it; but [God] does not want to do it alone. [God] wants us to work with [God' self]. [God] does the honor of wanting to effect [God's] work with us and through us. And if we are not willing to accept such honor, [God] will, after all, do the work alone, and help the poor. ... Although [God] alone is blessed, [God] does us the honor of wanting to share [God's] blessedness with us."[57]

Therefore, God's justification of the believer re-directs his/her attention from the self to others. Thus, the welfare of the neighbor becomes the central focus. Eventually, we become lords and servants. Through justification by faith and subsequent union with Christ, we become lords of all. As a response to the grace showered upon us by God, we forsake personal enjoyment and benefits and become servants of all.[58] This service of love toward others is founded on God's love shown toward us. Therefore, we can confidently say that Luther was concerned about the welfare of suffering people, because of the grace he had received from God.

2.3 Luther's Two Kingdom Concept: A Call for Involvement in Society

The foundational aspect of Luther's theology and ethics is faith in God. Luther's primary focus is to declare God's salvation of humanity by faith through grace. At the same time, God intends to work through faithful Christians for the world. Gotthold Müller explains Luther's argument: "The call to faith does not occur to free us from the world and its tasks, but it is a call to service for the world. Here Luther's Christianity and especially also his ethics received their tremendous dynamic and power."[59] Even though many ac-

---

[57] Luther, Treatise on Good Works, The Christian in Society I, in LW 44: 52.
[58] Cf. Luther, Treatise on Christian Liberty, Career of the Reformer, in LW 31: 343.
[59] Gotthold Müller, "Luther's Ethic in Present Day Crisis," in *Journal of the Evangelical Theological Society* 16/4 (Fall, 1973): 209.

cuse Luther of separating the kingdom of God from the kingdom of the world, Luther actually talked more about how these two kingdoms penetrate one another and are interconnected. In Luther's thought there is no this-worldly agenda that is not related to God and God's plans and purposes for this world.

There is no pure and separate secular realm where God has no place. Luther could not separate God from the world. Luther asserts that when God creates, God does not leave the creation to function on its own. Instead, God remains, sustains, and rules the world which God has created.[60] Luther does not agree with the Greek world view which separates matter and spirit. This kind of differentiation that leads to a complete severing of the secular realm from the spiritual realm cannot be ascribed to Luther. The battle between the kingdom of God and the kingdom of the devil is the basis from which Luther argues how the spiritual and the secular realms can work together in one accord against the forces of evil.[61]

Hans Schwarz contends that while Luther earlier followed the Augustinian distinction of the two kingdoms, he later moved away from this position. According to Augustine, humanity was divided into two groups, namely true believers who trust in Christ and unbelievers who have no faith. Christians who proclaim faith in Christ belong to the kingdom of God. The unbelievers, who are under the rule of law, belong to the kingdom of the world. The Christian is called to suffer in the world among unbelievers where sin permeates every part of society. The world was considered "the enemy of God." Schwarz reiterates that Luther discarded this Augustinian understanding and moved on to affirm that God is active in the world, working both through the spiritual realm and the secular realm. Subsequently, Luther addressed the significance of marriage, property, and vocation, which belong to the secular realm.[62]

---

[60] Cf. Luther on Zechariah 13: 9, *Lectures on the Minor Prophets III Zechariah*, in *LW* 20: 173.
[61] Müller, "Luther's Ethic in Present Day Crisis," 209.
[62] Cf. Hans Schwarz, *True Faith in the True God: an Introduction to Luther's Life and Thought,* trans. Mark William Worthing (Minneapolis: Augsburg Fortress, 1996), 82.

Martin Brecht affirms that it was challenging for Luther to distinguish the kingdom of God from the kingdom of the world while still clearly spelling out how they are related to one another. There was a constant threat to look at the two kingdom concept from one particular point of view which leads to misunderstandings.[63] One such misinterpretation emerged in the 20th century, wherein Luther was blamed for creating a gulf between the sacred and secular realms, leading the church in Germany to become indifferent toward the social and political problems of society. Schwarz maintains that some even saw a thread connecting Augustine to Luther and eventually to Adolf Hitler. This misunderstanding of Luther comes from a poor understanding of his two kingdoms concept.[64] In fact, some had a personal agenda in interpreting Luther in this fashion. They wanted to keep the secular and the sacred realms apart, using Luther for their support, so that the development of science and the problems of industrialization and colonialization would not be challenged by the religious community. It is unfortunate that Luther's ideas were used for this self-serving agenda.[65]

Ulrich Duchrow asserts that the motive behind such misinterpretations of the two kingdoms was directed toward making the secular realm so autonomous that it becomes a "law unto itself."[66] The secular realm was given autonomy to do whatever was pleasing to itself and thereby keep God out of the picture. Luther never pleaded for an unconditional submission to the secular authorities. Whenever the authorities of the secular realm go against the principles of reason, justice, and natural law, the Christian has the obligation to disobey, resist, and criticise the evil that is perpetuated by the authorities.[67]

---

[63] Cf. Martin Brecht, *Martin Luther: Shaping and Defining the Reformation 1521-1532*, trans. James L. Schaf (Minneapolis: Fortress Press, 1990), 119.

[64] Cf. Schwarz, True Faith in the True God: an Introduction to Luther's Life and Thought, 80.

[65] Cf. Thomas W. Strieter, "Two Kingdoms and Governances Thinking for Today's World," in *Currents in Theology and Mission* 16/1 (1989): 29.

[66] Cf. Ulrich Duchrow, Lutheran Churches – Salt or Mirror of Society? Case Studies on the Theory and Practice of the Two Kingdoms Doctrine (Geneva: LWF, 1977), 16-17.

[67] Cf. Luther, *To the Christian Nobility of the German Nation concerning the Reform of the Christian Estate, The Christian in Society* I, in *LW* 44:142. See Strieter, "Two King-

David C. Steinmetz argues that Luther was not indifferent to the political dilemmas of his day. Luther was optimistic about the power inherent in Christian faith and in human reason to challenge any form of evil in the secular realm.[68] Craig L. Nessan remarks that there are many instances in Luther's preaching where he addressed the abuses of political rulers in a direct way.[69]

The two realms are not in conflict with one another. Both realms complement each other. According to Luther, since even true Christians are unable to live without sin, they are in need of the law.[70] The secular realm can help the spiritual realm by forcing law and order on all, so that the gospel can be preached. In turn, the church can produce good citizens who have good intentions and a strong character.[71] The secular realm can support the spiritual realm and vice-versa. However, Luther states that "the temporal government has laws which extend no further than to life and property and external affairs on earth, for God cannot and will not permit anyone but himself to rule over the soul."[72] Moreover, when the secular realm lacks in its ethical actions and becomes indifferent to the concerns of the people, revealing its perverse motives and imposing an unacceptable way of life which reveals lack of fear of God, the Christian should not only disobey but even resist such evil authorities.

Lewis W. Spitz observes that Luther's position regarding resistance to the government has been a guiding principle both in Luther's time and for our present world. Luther did not separate the two kingdoms, leading to the no-

---

doms and Governances Thinking for Today's World," 30. See also Walter Altmann, *Luther and Liberation* (Minneapolis: Fortress Press, 1992), 70-71.

[68] Cf. David C. Steinmetz, *Luther in Context* (Bloomington: Indiana University Press, 1986), 124-125.

[69] Cf. Craig L. Nessan, "Liberation Theology's Critique of Luther's Two Kingdom Doctrine," in *Currents in Theology and Mission* 16(1989): 261. See also Altmann, *Luther and Liberation*, 78-80.

[70] Cf. Luther, Temporal Authority: To What extent it should be Obeyed, The Christian in Society II, in LW 45: 90.

[71] Cf. Luther, To the Christian Nobility of the German Nation concerning the Reform of the Christian Estate, The Christian in Society I, in LW 44:130.

[72] Cf. Luther, Temporal Authority: To What extent it should be Obeyed, The Christian in Society II, in LW 45: 105.

tion that God rules the church and the Devil rules the world. God is in control of both realms. However, human agents hold responsible positions in both the realms. The authorities in both the realms are expected to do good to the people and govern with best intentions for the welfare of humankind. If these human agents who are supposed to do good, turn out to be demonic and abuse their power, resistance to such evil agents/persons becomes unavoidable. In such a situation, the Christian has the right and duty to resist, because what is being done is not the will of God.[73]

2.4 Re-visiting Luther's Involvement in the Peasant's Revolt

We have seen that the Christian who is justified by grace is set free to serve the neighbors who are in need. The Christian has the duty to confront evil wherever he/she finds it, both in the spiritual and secular realms. Having established these two foundational principles, we can proceed to spell out his thoughts on poverty, greed, and concern for the common person. However, before we venture into addressing these issues, we need to discuss Luther's involvement in the Peasant's revolt. This is of paramount importance because Luther has been accused of wanting to maintain the *status quo*. Critics assert that if he had been for social change and for the welfare of the peasants, he would not have written *An Open Letter on the Harsh Book against the Peasants*.[74]

Luther wanted to bring about social change. He had a vision not only of what the church ought to be, but also how the society ought to function. He was constantly trying to bring about change in church and society, so that there would be peace, harmony, and right understanding of God and the world. Luther was concerned about the situation of the peasants. He was bringing change to their difficult and challenging situation. But Luther was not for bringing change through violence. When reformation broke out in the church in a violent manner, he was not for it. Therefore, it is necessary to

---

[73] Cf. Lewis W, Spitz, "The Christian in Church and State," in *Martin Luther and the Modern Mind*, ed. Manfred Hoffman (New York: The Edwin Mellen Press, 1985), 140.

[74] Cf. Luther, An Open Letter on the Harsh Book against the Peasants, The Christian in Society III, in LW: 46: 55- 84. Cf. Craig Nessan's chapter in this vol., 77ff.

reconsider the involvement of Luther in the peasant's revolt, so that this involvement does not undermine his concern for the poorer sections of society.

Luther has been criticized both in his times and in the modern period because of his involvement in the peasant's revolt. Marxist interpreters have accused Luther of being blind to the ethical consequences of his reformatory thoughts.[75] Friedrich Engels blamed Luther of encouraging the peasants at the beginning of their struggle but ditching them when their demands were unacceptable to the princes. When the princes violently suppressed the peasants, Luther not only allowed it but was for it. Socialists applaud Thomas Müntzer for giving his life for the cause of the peasants. Müntzer stood with the peasants till the end and was for their well-being. But Luther joined with the powerful. There is even a criticism of Luther that he favored two kinds of morality, one which is exercised in private and another practiced in the public. Steinmetz reports on criticism against Luther, wherein Luther seems to have urged "the peasants to live in accordance with the private morality of the Sermon on the Mount, while sanctioning the custodians of public morality, the secular princes, to re-establish order over anarchy by any violent means at their disposal."[76]

Heinz Zahrnt reminds that the demand of the peasants was not something that first emerged during Luther's times. The peasants began their agitation long before 1525. However, they had no one who was influential enough to stand with them and support them in their cause. During Luther's times, the peasant movement became stronger. It was only because Luther appeared as the friend of the common person that the peasants approached him freely with their 12 Articles. As the revolt reached its peak, the peasants thought that it would be profitable to listen to Thomas Müntzer and follow the path of violence rather than heed Luther, who was explaining the theology of the cross to them. On the one hand, the peasants merely used the name of Luther to make their position strong. On the other hand, the rulers used Luther to

---

[75] Cf. Del Pino, Luther's Theology of the Cross as Reflected in Selected Historical Contexts of Social Change from 1521-1525: A Study of Theory and Practice, 54. Cf. Craig Nessan's chapter in this vol., 75ff.

[76] Steinmetz, *Luther in Context,* 113.

justify their slaughtering of the peasants.[77] Luther was strongly criticised for turning his back on the peasants at the very end. Many gloss over the fact that the peasants were ready to murder as many princes as possible and were even thinking of capturing power.

Schwarz, explaining Luther's involvement in the peasant's revolt, writes:

"During the peasants war ... [Luther] initially took up the complaints of the peasants (who were being exploited by the nobility and upper classes) and warned the ruling class. "For rulers are not appointed to exploit their subjects for their own profit and advantage, but to be concerned about the welfare of their subjects." Yet he also warned the peasants, "the fact that the rulers are wicked and unjust does not excuse disorder and rebellion" ... He warned both sides ... However, when peasants took up arms, Luther reminded the princes of their duty."[78]

Luther was not against social change. He knew that his theology and ethics would bring change. Nevertheless, he believed in persistence in the struggle, constant appeal to the authorities, a prophetic voice against wickedness, and, above all, trust in God to bring about change. Luther would rather have the peasants suffer, persevere, and persist in their struggle in order to achieve their demands. Luther considered some of their demands to be legitimate. He warned the peasants that Thomas Müntzer was misleading them and that violence was not the right means to achieve their goal. Luther would bring social change through persistent suffering and patience rather than by "fist."[79] However, this does not lead to acceptance of evil and injustice in society.

Christians, Luther said, should resist injustice and evil done to the neighbor. He writes: "You suffer evil and injustice and yet at the same time you punish evil and injustice ... in one case you consider yourself and what is yours; in the other you consider your neighbor and what is his."[80] The Chris-

---

[77] Cf. Heinz Zahrnt, *Martin Luther – in seiner Zeit – für unsere Zeit* (München: Süddeutscher Verlag, 1983), 132-135.

[78] Schwarz, True Faith in the True God: an Introduction to Luther's Life and Thought, 90.

[79] Cf. Luther, Admonition to Peace: A Reply to the Twelve Articles of the Peasants in Swabia, The Christian in Society III, in LW 46: 31-32.

[80] Luther, Temporal Authority: To What extent it should be Obeyed, The Christian in Society II, in LW 45: 96.

tian is called to exhibit the virtues of toleration, patience, and forgiveness. This is with regard to his or her personal struggles. On the other hand, Christians cannot tolerate their neighbor's affliction. They have the duty to defend the rights of the neighbor. This is why Luther proposed to develop a common chest for the poor; admonished greed whenever he found it, particularly in trade and commerce; he protested against high taxes and was concerned about the less fortunate people, in whose language he translated the Bible.

Before exploring Luther's ideas on poverty, his criticism of greed in society, and his concern for the common person, we must be clear that Luther was not against social change and that he was not against the poor peasants. The only reason Luther turned against the peasants at the end is because he believed in following the path of the cross and therefore he could not agree with the peasants in adopting violent methods to bring about change and reformation either in the church or society. Charles R. Biggs explains this aspect of Luther:

> "For many, the beginning of the Reformation was liberating and freeing in the realization of our righteousness and peace before God because of Christ; the work of the reformation was done humbly through translation of the word of God, and through preaching. For others, the Reformation was an opportunity at radicalism and pride. This was one of the unfortunate consequences of the German Reformation. Rather than understanding that God builds up his kingdom and overthrows the devil's kingdom through preaching, some took it upon themselves to turn the reformation into revolution. In one incident during this time, twelve hundred students, workmen, and other common people attacked and demolished in a few days sixty houses belonging to Roman Catholic priests, and the priests only escaped the violence by fleeing for their lives. Dr. Luther rightly was angry at this uproarious anarchy, and knew that this would bring great shame to the gospel of Jesus Christ, and reflect poorly on the Reformation. ... Luther preached to his congregation in Wittenberg from the word of God for eight days on the importance of the Reformation being sought from within; first the reformation that must take place within a man's heart by God's sovereign Spirit, and then the reformation that must take place outwardly with peace and power through the Word, as

unbiblical practices are discarded and the Scriptural teaching upheld."[81]

3. Relevance of Luther's Theology and Ethics for the Globalized World

Luther's theology and social involvement point toward his concern for the weaker sections of society, on the one hand, and the call for the privileged to serve the needy, on the other. We will now consider two major contributions of Luther for this age of globalization. We shall pay particular attention to Luther's concern for the poor through his desire to establish a common chest for their welfare and his critique of greed that plagued trade and commerce. Luther's attack on greediness was motivated by its effects on the normal life of the common person. Here is a connection between Luther's context and ours. Luther's concern for the poor challenges us to be compassionate toward them today. Similarly, greed existed during Luther's times. But today greed has grown by leaps and bounds because of globalization. It is worthwhile to return to Luther's writings to engage his thinking about poverty and greed, so that we can let Luther speak to us today.

3.1 Luther's Concern for the Common Person Reflected in the Bible Translation Work

It is noteworthy to mention that Luther's concern for the common person was not only reflected in his writings on poverty and greed, but also in his effort to translate the Bible into the language of the common person and to write hymns in the language of the common people. Before we consider Luther's arguments for the welfare of the poor people in material terms, it is important to recall his concern about their spiritual welfare. Mark S. Krause, a scholar regarding Luther's Bible translation, remarks that Luther is usually remembered for his contributions in the areas of church history, theology, and even political history. However, Luther's greatest contribution, known as

---

[81] Charles R. Biggs, "The Reformation and the Life of Martin Luther," accessed on December 28, 2013, http://www.monergism.com/thethreshold/sdg/Reformation.Church.History.Martin.Luther.PT.2.pdf.

"Luther Bible," is often forgotten. The Luther Bible has had great historical significance. Even today it is known for its special and unique quality.[82]

Luther sought to replace the authority of the Pope with the authority of the Scripture. Thereby, Luther attempted to bring the message of the Bible to the common people. If the Bible was accessible only for the priestly elite (because of their knowledge of Hebrew, Greek, and Latin), the Bible could not speak as the Word of God to the conscience of the common person. Therefore, Luther took up the challenge to translate the Bible into the language of the common person. Krause comments: "First, Luther was well-grounded in the German spoken by the peasants of his day. He was raised alongside simple German-speaking folk and often adopted their direct, earthly, even coarse expressions. Second, Luther's university career gave him contact with the more elegant German of the bourgeois. He was not limited to simple peasant speech, but could read and write the highest German of his day."[83] Luther chose the German of the common person instead of the "high" German of the elite to translate the Bible:

> "We do not have to enquire of the literal Latin, how we are to speak German, as these asses do. Rather we must enquire about this of the mother in the home, children on the street, the common man in the market place. We must be guided by their language, the way they speak, and do our translating accordingly. That way they will understand it and recognize that we are speaking German to them."[84]

Along with efforts to translate the Bible into the language of the common people, Luther was also interested in writing hymns to teach the evangelical faith to the lay person. Luther understood that the common church-going person could understand neither the evangelical faith nor truly worship God as long as the Mass was in Latin. He even did not like the term "Mass." Instead he used the word *Gottesdienst*. Luther desired that worship be conducted in the language of the common people, facilitating the growth of their faith in God. In order to promote enthusiasm in worship, he wrote hymns that could

---

[82] Cf. Mark S. Krause, "Martin Luther's Theory of Bible Translation," in *Stone-Campbell Journal* 2 (Spring, 1999): 57.

[83] Krause, "Martin Luther's Theory of Bible Translation," 60.

[84] Luther, On Translating: An Open Letter, Word and Sacrament, in LW 35: 189.

be sung during the service in the language of the people.⁸⁵ Luther's translation and hymn-writing work offer evidence of his concern for the common person. Now we proceed to consider his views on poverty and greed.

3.2 Luther's Interest in the Welfare of the Poor

From the very beginning of his carrier, we can trace Luther's concern for the poor. It is evident already in the 95 theses. Luther's 43rd thesis states: "Christians are to be taught that he who gives to the poor or lends to the needy does a better deed than he who buys indulgences."⁸⁶ Luther went on to emphasize the significance of helping the poor in his explanation of the doctrine of justification by faith. Lindberg explains:

> "Luther's doctrine of justification cut the nerve of the medieval ideology of poverty. Since salvation is a gift of God apart from human works, both poverty and almsgiving lose saving significance. By de-spiritualizing poverty, the Reformer could recognize poverty in every form as a personal and social evil to be combated. Justification by grace alone through faith alone affected a paradigm shift in the understanding of poverty and the poor. Poverty is no longer seen as the favored status of the Christian, but rather a social ill to be ameliorated even if it cannot be ultimately cured."⁸⁷

Luther argued that the evils in society, especially poverty, should be opposed. Luther writes: "Poverty, I say, is not to be recommended, chosen or taught; for there is enough of that by itself ... just as you will have all other evils. But constant care should be taken that, since these evils are always in evidence, they are always opposed."⁸⁸ For Luther the poor are not objects of charity but they are our neighbors, who should be served with an attitude of justice and equity.

---

[85] Cf. Gracia Grindal, "The Rhetoric of Martin Luther's Hymns: Hymnody Then and Now," accessed on December 31, 2013, http://worldand-world.luthersem.edu/content/pdfs/26-2_Renewing_Worship/26-2_Grindal.pdfs.

[86] Luther, Explanations of the Ninety-five Theses or Explanations of the Disputation concerning the value of Indulgences, Career of the Reformer, in LW 31: 202.

[87] Carter Lindberg, "Luther on Poverty," in *Lutheran Quarterly* 15 (2001): 89.

[88] Luther on Deuteronomy 15: 4, in *Lectures on Deuteronomy* (*LW* 9: 148).

In order to oppose injustice that perpetuates poverty, Luther proposed structural changes that would consider the welfare of the poor. Luther saw a need to work in close cooperation with the local governments to put into effect structural changes through welfare policies. The need to establish a "common chest" was one of the primary efforts taken by Luther. Through the common chest the poor were helped and efforts were taken to prohibit begging. Interest free loans were given, orphans and widows were helped, and support for the education and vocational training of poor children were proposed. Lindberg remarks that Luther's plan for a common chest was a novel idea that transformed theology into social praxis.[89]

Luther even suggested setting aside a part of ecclesiastical property for the purpose of helping the needy. He recommended that the church devote a part of church property toward the fund of the common chest, out of which gifts and loans could be given to all the needy as an act of Christian love.[90] Albrecht Steinwachs comments: "The practice of the common chest is a shining witness to the social achievement of the Reformation, which attended not only to spirit and soul but knew that 'peace on earth' included care for people's physical well-being."[91] The Lutheran reformation did not neglect the social side of life. Luther's initiatives provide the basis for serious reflection as to how we can advocate for the poor who are neglected by the process of globalization.

By establishing a common chest, Luther also shared concern about helping those who are ill, poor, or who lack shelter, clothing, nourishment, and care.[92] In his lectures on Galatians 2:10 and Deuteronomy 15:1, Luther expressed his concern for those who are helpless in society. In his commentary on Galatians 2:10, Luther wrote:

> "Next to the proclamation of the Gospel it is the task of a good pastor to be mindful of the poor. For wherever the church is, there must be poor people.

---

[89] Lindberg, "Luther on Poverty," 89.

[90] Cf. Luther, Ordinance of a Common Chest, The Christian in Society II, in LW 45: 172.

[91] Albrecht Steinwachs, "The Common Chest as a Social Achievement of the Reformation," in *Lutheran Quarterly* 22 (2008): 194.

[92] Cf. Luther, Ordinance of a Common Chest, The Christian in Society II, in LW 45: 189.

Most of the time they are the only true disciples of the Gospel, as Christ says (Matt 11:5): 'The poor have the Gospel preached to them.' For both human beings and the devil persecute the church and bring poverty upon many, who are then forsaken and to whom no one wants to give anything. ... Everywhere true religion is in need, and Christ complains that he is hungry, thirsty, without shelter, naked, and sick (Matt 25:35). On the other hand, false religion and wickedness flourish and abound with all sorts of possessions. Therefore a true bishop must be concerned also about the poor, and Paul here admits that he was."[93]

While summarizing his thoughts on Deuteronomy 15, Luther emphasized that the poor should not be left neglected in the land. Because there will always be poor people in any society, the Christian must be ready to give to the poor from tithes or loans or from some other source.[94]

Based on Luther's concern for the poor, we need to think about how to help the poor who are victims of globalization today. Mere sympathy will not suffice. We need to build structures that can safeguard and help the poor, just like Luther implemented structural changes that would help the poor.

3.3 Luther's Ethical Concern in Trade and Commerce against Greed

Luther's times witnessed a change in socio-economic conditions, particularly the shift from feudal control over economic matters to a profit economy based on capitalism.[95] As greed was growing in a market based economy, Luther found it important to oppose the rising forces of transnational capitalism. Luther "saw the entire community endangered by the financial power of a few great economic centers. ... He saw an economic coercion immune to normal jurisdiction that would destroy the ethos of the community."[96]

Luther took responsibility to reflect on the economic developments of his day, so that justice could be done to the common person. While his proposal

---

[93] Luther on Galatians 2: 9, *Lectures on Galatians,* in *LW* 26: 105.
[94] Cf. Luther on Deuteronomy 15: 1, *Lectures on* Deuteronomy, in *LW* 9: 144.
[95] Lindberg, "Luther on Poverty," 87.
[96] Cynthia D. Moe-Lobeda, *Healing a Broken World: Globalization and God* (Minneapolis: Fortress Press, 2002), 126.

for a common chest was accepted and put into practice, his critique of greed in capitalism gained little support. Luther constantly admonished the bankers for raising the interest rates but this prophetic plea fell on deaf ears. Luther proposed that the social needs of the community should be an utmost priority and that acquiring personal gain should not be at the expense of the welfare of the community. Following Old Testament principles of the Jubilee Year, Luther recommended that the capitalists cancel the debts of the poor who were unable to pay back.[97]

From 1519 to 1540, Luther constantly wrote against usury and criticized the expanding money business that led to a credit economy, which harmed the common person. In Luther's *Large Catechism*, Luther addressed the plight of the poor in the context of the growing capitalist economy. He wrote: "Daily the poor are defrauded. New burdens and high prices are imposed. Everyone misuses the market in his own wilful, conceited, arrogant way as if it were his right and privilege to sell his goods as dearly as he pleases without a word of criticism."[98] Luther exposed the many ways that the lust for profit took shape in trade and commerce of his day.[99] He expressed his anger at the growing greed of his times by commenting that the world is one big "whore house" that is submerged in greed, where big thieves prey on little thieves and big fish eat little fish.[100]

Luther realised that many common practice of merchants was based on greed. Luther describes the merchant's attitude: "I care nothing about my neighbor; so long as I have my profit and satisfy my need, of what concern is it to me if it injures my neighbor in ten ways at once?"[101] This kind of trading represented robbing and stealing of another's property. He pointed out that

---

[97] Cf. Luther on Deuteronomy 24: 14, *Lectures on* Deuteronomy, in LW 9: 243.

[98] Luther, The Large Catechism, in The Book of Concord: The Confessions of the Evangelical Lutheran Church, ed. Theodore G. Tappert (Philadelphia: Fortress Press, 1959), 397.

[99] Cf. Luther, *Trade and* Usury, *The Christian in Society* II, in *LW* 45: 245-273.

[100] Cf. Luther on Matthew 6: 23, The Sermon on the Mount (Sermons) and the Magnificat, in LW 21: 180; Luther, Trade and Usury, The Christian in Society II, in LW 45: 272; Luther on Psalm 82: 4, Selected Psalms II, in LW 13: 60.

[101] Luther, Trade and Usury, The Christian in Society II, in LW 45: 247.

the price of the goods becomes higher in proportion to the need of the common people. This is not only unchristian but also an inhuman attitude.[102] Luther pleads with the merchants by reminding them "your selling is an act performed toward your neighbor, it should rather be so governed by law and conscience that you do it without harm and injury to him, your concern being directed more toward doing him no injury than toward gaining profit for yourself."[103]

However, Luther was not against a merchant taking the reasonable profit that is his/her due. He quotes Luke 10:7: "The laborer deserves his wages." Luther is not against merchants receiving the fair profit that is due to them. Nevertheless, he believed that the temporal authorities should appoint wise and honest men to decide on reasonable prices for all products.[104] Luther asserts: "Where the price of goods is not fixed either by law or custom, and you must fix it yourself, here one can truly give you no instructions but only lay it on your conscience to be careful not to overcharge your neighbor, and to seek a modest living, not the goals of greed."[105]

Luther was also against the credit system that developed during his time, which is so common in today's world:

> "In what has been said I have wished to give a bit of warning and instruction to everyone about this great, filthy, widespread business of trade and commerce. If we were to tolerate and accept the principle that everyone may sell his wares as dear as he can, approving the practice of borrowing and forced lending and standing surety…that would be the same as…how one could at the same time live and act in accordance with divine Scripture and contrary to divine Scripture….these are like three fountainheads from which the whole stream of abomination, injustice, low cunning, and trickery flows far and wide. To try to stem the flood without stopping up the source is a waste of effort and energy."[106]

---

[102] Cf. Luther, Trade and Usury, The Christian in Society II, in LW 45: 248.
[103] Luther, Trade and Usury, The Christian in Society II, in LW 45: 248.
[104] Cf. Luther, *Trade and* Usury, *The Christian in Society* II, in *LW* 45: 249.
[105] Luther, Trade and Usury, The Christian in Society II, in LW 45: 250.
[106] Luther, Trade and Usury, The Christian in Society II, in LW 45: 260-261.

Luther was terribly upset about the economic situation of his time. Perhaps, he was disillusioned about the situation and found no hope of bringing about transformation, which is very much applicable to our context of globalization. Luther in his desperateness says that such greedy people are not worthy to be called human beings and should not be allowed to live among human beings. They are beyond receiving any form of instruction, correction, and advice. They are open and shameless about their envy and greed. Therefore Luther proposes: "The temporal authorities would do right if they took from such fellows everything they had, and drove them out of the country."[107]

Luther also based his attack on greed from the biblical point of view. In his *Lectures on Psalms*, Luther insisted that faith, which is the true worship of God, is the opposite of greed. Greed is idolatry.[108] He opined that greed is related to impiety and unbelief. Unbelief leads to injustice and injustice is caused by greed. Even in his commentary on Ephesians 5:3-5, Luther pointed out that Paul finds a connection between idolatry and greed. In Ephesians 5:5, Paul writes, "The one who is greedy is an idolater." The holiness of Christians demands that they overcome the desires of greed and attempt to live a holy life without greed.[109]

Luther considered the person who kept money and goods for one's own interests and pleasures to be a greedy person. On the other hand, a true Christian would use them to help the poor and support churches and schools.[110] When a person is unconcerned about the suffering of the poor and keeps everything for oneself, thinking that it is rational and necessary, he/she deserves God's wrath. Luther remarked that the wicked grasp and take hold of everything. They are not satisfied, and they even take from the poor.[111] Luther believed that God's wrath against greed was manifested in his times in shortag-

---

[107] Luther, Trade and Usury, The Christian in Society II, in LW 45: 265.

[108] Cf. Luther on Psalm 111: 10, *Selected Psalms II*, in *LW* 13: 391.

[109] CF. Luther on 1 Timothy 6: 17, Commentaries on 1 Corinthians 7, 1 Corinthians 15, Lectures on 1 Timothy, in LW 28: 378.

[110] Cf. Luther on Genesis 28:22, *Lectures on Genesis: Chapters 26-30*, in *LW* 5: 260.

[111] Cf. Luther on Psalm 112:9, *Selected Psalms II*, in *LW* 13:418.

es, plague, war, and blood shedding. Whenever generosity is replaced by greed, we are provoking God's wrath.

In his commentary on Matthew 6:24, Luther criticizes people who accumulate goods for themselves and do not even use them for their own subsistence. Such people live under the influence of greed and do not understand anything about God's word and God's kingdom.[112] Similarly, in his interpretation of Isaiah 5:8, Luther compares greed with idolatry and does not consider it as a lesser form of evil.[113] Luther, perhaps, saw no way out of this struggle to overcome greed:

> "Many a person thinks he has God and everything he needs when he has money and property; in them he trusts and of them he boasts so stubbornly and securely that he cares for no one else. Surely such a man also has a god – mammon by name, that is, money and possessions – on which he fixes his whole heart. It is the most common idol on earth. He who has money and property feels secure, happy, fearless, as if he were sitting in the midst of paradise. On the other hand, he who has nothing doubts and despairs as if he never heard of God. Very few there are who are cheerful, who do not fret and complain, if they do not have mammon. This desire for wealth clings and cleaves to our nature all the way to the grave."[114]

Whatever is dear to a person, Luther says, is one's god. It is to this that one's heart is attached; one thinks about it day and night. Whoever considers money as important and keeps it for himself, in order to satisfy his own desires, will not be concerned about his or her neighbor.[115] Therefore, greed in individuals and society is a stumbling block in building God's kingdom and establishing a humane just world.

Preaching on Luke 16:19-31, the parable of the rich man and Lazarus, Luther reminds that the human tendency towards greed has been addressed by

---

[112] Cf. Luther on Matthew 6: 24, The Sermon on the Mount (Sermons) and the Magnificat, in LW 21: 189.

[113] Cf. Luther on Isaiah 5:8, Lectures on Isaiah 1-39, in LW 16: 61.

[114] Luther, The Large Catechism, in The Book of Concord: The Confessions of the Evangelical Lutheran Church, ed. Theodore G. Tappert (Philadelphia: Fortress Press, 1959), 365.

[115] Cf. Luther on Matthew 6: 21, The Sermon on the Mount (Sermons) and the Magnificat, in LW 21: 175.

Jesus himself.[116] Greed is sometimes understood by society as talented, smart, and careful stewardship. Such an understanding is contrary to the Christian perception of wealth as a tool and a channel to communicate God's grace to the less fortunate.[117] Wealth itself may not be evil according to biblical teaching, but greediness is sin. Not all the rich are portrayed negatively in the Bible, but only those for whom wealth is the primary concern.[118]

Luther was aware of the deep corruption of human nature. He understood the difficulties involved in establishing the kingdom of God in the economic spheres of life. Ricardo Willy Rieth summarizes Luther's critique of greed that was prevalent in trade and commerce:

> "Luther was convinced that greed can be opposed only by faith. Therefore, he charges believers within the church of Jesus Christ with the responsibility of assuming the gospel's exhortations in relation to the progressive establishment of the kingdom of God and the practice of justice, not transforming them into a kind of moralism or a reason to withdraw from the world, but observing them seriously as orientation and instruction to promote positive changes in the economic sphere."[119]

We can conclude from Luther's views on poverty and greed that just as he proposed structural changes, in order to cater to the need of the poor, we need structural changes in this age of globalization to keep concern for the poor alive. As did Luther, we need to condemn greed in every sphere of life, particularly greed that is promoted by globalization. Even though human nature is corrupt with money and wealth as the order of the day, we need to constantly challenge the attachment to the material things and the abuse of the common person. We need the spirit of Luther to accomplish this task.

In exploring globalization, especially its neglect of the poor and the growth of greed, and in juxtaposing Luther's awareness of these issues, we have learned that a prophetic condemnation of greed is of utmost importance cou-

---

[116] Cf. Luther on Genesis 30: 30, *Lectures on Genesis 26-30*, in *LW* 5: 371.

[117] Kathryn D'Arcy Blanchard, "'If you do not do this you are not now a Christian': Martin Luther's Pastoral Teachings on Money," in *Word & World* 26/3 (Summer, 2006): 303.

[118] Cf. Ibid. 304.

[119] Richard Willy Rieth, "Luther on Greed," in *Lutheran Quarterly* 15 (2001): 249.

pled with structural changes that help and support the poor. Such a spirit is based on faith active in love toward the neighbor, what Luther calls the true service of God (*Gottesdienst*). Luther ascertained that there is no greater service of God than helping and serving the needy.[120] People of all faiths are summoned to join together to love and serve the God of the poor by checking the power of greed and helping the neighbor in true spirit, which is the acceptable worship of God.

Luther understood "service to God" not merely to be based on liturgical worship but rather as service that manifests faith in all spheres of life. The economic sphere needs special attention in the contemporary globalized world. May the triune God – Father, Son, and Spirit – challenge us in the spirit of Luther, to become a community that cares for those who are less fortunate by overcoming the greed within!

Abstract

Das Projekt der imperialen Globalisierung durchdringt jeden Aspekt menschlichen Lebens auf Erden, und wir können seine Wirkung nicht ignorieren. Die Effekte dieses Prozesses sind in der ganzen Welt sichtbar. Besonders in Asien waren sie sehr negativ. Wirtschaftliche Rezession führt zu dem Verlust von Arbeitsplätzen, höheren Preisen, verstärkter Inflation, und die Vernachlässigung der einfachen Menschen bestimmt die Tagesordnung. Einige gewinnen reichlich im Prozess der Globalisierung. Aber die Mehrheit verliert. Die Eliten, Mächtige und Reiche, empfangen viel durch die Globalisierung. Einfache Menschen sind auf sich selbst gestellt. Die Prozentzahl derer, die unter diese Kategorie fallen, insbesondere derer, die ums Überleben kämpfen, ist in Asien größer als im Westen. Politiker, die die Wirtschaftspolitik bestimmen, interessieren sich immer weniger für die Wohlfahrt der einfachen Menschen.

Luther, der vor 500 Jahren in einem verschiedenen Kontext lebte, sorgte sich um die einfachen Menschen, die vom reichen Teil der Gesellschaft seiner Zeit vernachlässigt wurden. Luther schrieb über die Hilfe für die Armen, trat für fairen Handel und die Bildung der einfachen Menschen ein. Selbst seine Beteiligung am Kampf der Bauern, obwohl oft missverstanden, belegt seine Sorge für

---

[120] Cf. Luther, Preface – Ordinance of a Common Chest (1523), The Christian in Society II, in LW 45: 172.

die einfachen Menschen, nämlich die Bauern. Dieses Kapitel untersucht die Schriften Luthers, um Luthers Sorge für die einfachen Menschen zu erkunden und zu interpretieren. Manche meinen aufgrund von Luthers Bibelübersetzung, dass seine Anstrengung sich vor allem darauf richtete, die Schrift in der Sprache der einfachen Menschen zur Verfügung zu stellen. Unsere Analyse seiner Schriften zeigen aber, dass sein Einsatz für sie weit darüber hinausging. Diese Einsichten werden dann mit dem gegenwärtigen Prozess der Globalisierung in Verbindung gebracht und gezeigt, wie dieser die einfachen Menschen vernachlässigt. Am Schluss werden die Implikationen von Luthers Denken für die globalisierte Welt heute aufgezeigt.

Martin Luther and Reformation Theology: an East Asian Perspective

Paul S. Chung

A contextual and constructive interpretation of Martin Luther and Reformation theology in East Asian perspective is necessary in order to radicalize his insight into God's solidarity with those living poverty-stricken lives and to recognize the gifts of religious cultural diversity. Three distinctive interests remain undercurrents in Asian theological construction when it comes to political-economic responsibility, cultural reality of religious pluralism, and the web of life in fullness. These characterize emancipation, inculturation (or contextualization), and integrity of life as central for Asian theological imagination. Asian contextual theologies take issue with the Western hegemonic model of self-interested individualism and dominion embedded within the interplay between knowledge, power, and discourse. To what extent does a theological epistemology emerging from Martin Luther claim the triune God as the source of life in support of emancipation, inculturation, and fullness of life? Such a reading strategy challenges the structural reality of violence, injustice, and dominion in society, culture, and religion, which is perpetuated against humanity and the web of life in creation.

This chapter aims to hermeneutically and practically retrieve the prophetic potential of Reformation theology to set forth on radical, new, and alternative possibilities of liberation, life for all creation in fullness, and recognition of people of other cultures and faiths. Given this agenda, the chapter critically examines a Japanese colonial interpretation of Luther's theology of the cross (Kazoh Kitamori), as seen through the angle of *minjung* theology. A critical analysis of the Japanese colonial theology of God's pain helps us to understand to what extent the project of inculturation is undertaken in terms of a critique of ideology and is driven by solidarity with the life of the victims.

Furthermore, we shall investigate Luther's reflection of the triune God as the source of life and emancipation, exploring his hermeneutical-prophetic direction on behalf of emancipation, inculturation, and integrity of life in creation. This perspective, framed within a postcolonial orientation, provides new terrain in advancing the study of the future of Martin Luther and Reformation theology in East Asia. This process transcends Western modernist-neo-colonial epistemology, which is reproduced in the historical and political-economic realm in the context of increasing forces of economic globalization in Asia (for example, in Japan). The generalizing term "Asian" was embedded within the Japanese colonial context, which offered a counter force to Western imperialism in the late nineteenth and early twentieth centuries. The colonial character of "Asian" continued to shape the Japanese imperial understanding of God's pain with reference to Reformation theology.

1. Luther and God's Pain in Japanese Colonial Context

In a study of *Christian Theology in Asia*,[1] we observe that the churches in Asia have attempted to maintain their identity and integrity by articulating their own theologies. The terms "Asian," "Asian sense," or "Asian method" highlight the context, relevance, characteristics, and orientation of Asian theological works. A genealogical and archeological study of the unifying term "Asian" reveals its political and colonial usage within the context of Japan's nationalism and colonialism.

The Japanese colonial discourse of "Asian" might be traced to Japanese imperial theology and its reference to Japanese life in the Post-Hiroshima context. The first attempt to read Luther in this imperial direction was undertaken in the Japanese cultural context. Hence, I critically examine Kitamori's seminal book, *The Theology of the Pain of God*.[2]

In the wake of World War II, Kitamori (1916-98) explored the suffering of God in terms of a traditional Japanese *Kabuki* drama. The traditional and imperial *Kabuki* drama is rather shunned by those who wanted to break away from Japan's reprehensible colonial past. However, Kitamori utilizes Japanese cultural terms such as *tsurasa* (vicarious suffering), in order to propose a theology of the cross. Given Luther's metaphor of "death against death" on the cross, Kitamori unfolds his theology in terms of "pain against pain." A

---

[1] *Christian Theology in Asia*, ed. Sebastian C.H. Kim (Cambridge: Cambridge University Press. 2008), xi-xii.
[2] Kazoh Kitamori, *The Theology of the Pain of God* (Eugene: Wipf & Stock, 2005, Reprint).

notion of "God in pain" comes to the foreground in the sense that God embraces those who do not deserve to be embraced.[3]

Kitamori's theology of the cross operates by way of analogy in relation to pain, that is, *analogia doloris*,[4] incorporating the Japanese word *tsurasa* into the wounded heart of God.[5] Silence in God's mystery and *tsurasa* are the guiding metaphors for underscoring Kitamori's theological project, featuring God as the One who loves the unlovable through the sacrifice of Christ. Commenting on Kitamori's theology, Kosuke Koyama has shown that "embracing and enduring *tsurasa* becomes an intercultural correspondence to Luther's concept of 'God fighting with God'."[6] Kitamori utilizes *tsurasa*, re-rooting the Christian narrative of a theology of the cross in the Japanese cultural matrix.[7]

Certainly, Kitamori takes *deus absconditus* in Luther's thought as the theological epistemology for understanding God's pain, because the hidden God is the fundamental principle of Luther's theology, from which all the rest of Luther's thought emerges.[8] Emphasizing the hidden God enmeshed in pain, Kitamori maintains that God's eternal decision to deliver the Son to the world becomes the hermeneutical bedrock for proposing the analogy of pain, which contrasts to the Roman Catholic (and Barthian) teaching on the analogy of being and analogy of faith.

Kitamori transforms Luther's teaching on justification imbued with justice into a mysticism of God's pain and silence in the fashion of the hidden God. In so doing, unfortunately, he expunges the social-critical and prophetic dimensions of the grace of justification in matters pertaining to Japanese colonialism, its historical responsibility, and guilt. Kitamori sidesteps the human capacity to love and respect the righteousness and justice of *deus absconditus* only through *deus revelatus* (the revealed God) in his *resignatio ad infernum*

---

[3] *Ibid.*, 27.
[4] *Ibid.*, 56.
[5] *Ibid.*, 138.
[6] Kosuke Koyama, *Waterbuffalo Theology* (Maryknoll: Orbis, 1974), 120.
[7] *Ibid.*, 115.
[8] Kitamori, The Theology of the Pain of God, 107.

(descent into hell), thereby the vicarious representative of those innocent victims. For Luther, Jesus Christ as a mirror of the Father's heart is also the first born among many brothers and sisters. Jesus Christ as the exemplary prototype stands with the tormented, because he is the one who suffers injustice among victims of violence, the forsaken among the forsaken.

Actually, Kitamori's book was completed at the very height of the war. Written during the war, Kitamori idealizes and even fetishizes the tragic suffering of the Japanese people, through which one perceives and comprehends the pain of God, while completely ignoring the innocent victims who suffered under Japan in other Asian countries. Kitamori completely eradicates the real victims of WW II, those suffering and murdered during the period of Japanese colonization. For instance, Japanese troops committed a series of atrocities in Nanjing during the Japanese War of Aggression against China. The brutal slaughter of innocent people, together with the rape and destruction of that ancient and beautiful city occurred over a period of six weeks between December 1937 and January 1938. A God identified with the pain of Japanese people remains questionable and even dangerous, because this God is mute and elusive about the outcry of all the real victims during the brutality of WW II.

2. God's Suffering in Solidarity with Minjung

The Japanese colonial reading of God's pain has faced a radical challenge from *minjung* theology, which refines the theology of the cross according to Jesus' socio-biography in deep solidarity with those who are marginalized, suppressed, and outcast. *Minjung* theology entails a strong critique of Japanese ideology, which emulated Western civilization in terms of colonialism, scholarship, and hegemony. A *minjung* theological reading of God's pain emphasizes Jesus' life connection with the *ochlos-minjung*, in which the gospel of the kingdom of God reinvigorates *minjung*-subaltern as the subject of history. Here Bonhoeffer's insight into a theological epistemology from below remains crucial to the radical horizon of the gospel. That is, "from the perspective of the outcast, the suspects, the maltreated, the powerless, the oppressed, the reviled—in short, from the perspective of those who suffer."[9]

Minjung theology is a postcolonial-liberative project in relation to the *minjung*-subaltern, which seeks to discover the globalization of cultures and histories within the structural violence of Western modernity in the aftermath of colonialism. It articulates the lingering effects of the colonial aftermath, while archeologically reading the previous history of the innocent victim, in order to remember the forgotten for our neo-colonial present. A project of inculturation in this regard endeavors to appreciate the distinctive character of culture for a thick description of the gospel narrative in the context of world Christianity. It debunks legitimatization of a racist, paternalistic, and neo-colonial system embedded within the civilization of the West. Thus inculturation as the critical and creative process aims at discovering and advancing Christian values that are already inherent in culture. It also entails a potential of emancipation from Western-centrism, archeologically discovering God's ongoing work in Christ and Spirit in a different culture. It enhances God's presence within the people, their culture, and history.

Challenging Kitamori's Japanese cultural-imperial reading of Luther, I have presented an interreligious hermeneutic for radicalizing Luther's theological insights in encounter with the Asian reality of *minjung* and Buddhist compassion through social engagement.[10] Faith, gratitude, and universal compassion in the Buddhist tradition do not stand in contradiction to Christian teaching. Rather, such a perspective needs to be appreciated and applied in any translation of the Reformation teaching of justification into East Asian language, culture, and religion. In a hermeneutical circle, the meaning of the living voice of the gospel is contextualized, while at the same time keeping a critical distance from the past colonial limitations and the current neo-colonial errors. Life together with the Other, grounded in faithfulness to the living and emancipatory Word of God, has priority over an individualist ontology in this prophetic project of interpretation and discipleship for ethical

---

[9] Dietrich Bonhoeffer, *Letters & Papers from Prison*, ed. E. Bethge (New York: Macmillan, 1971), 17.

[10] Paul S. Chung, *Martin Luther and Buddhism: Aesthetics of Suffering*. 2nd ed. (Eugene: Pickwick, 2008).

solidarity with the Other.[11] This theological project is grounded in an anamnestic reasoning and the subversive memory of Jesus, whose socio-biology for the gospel of the kingdom of God embraces his people – the *massa perditionis* (public sinners and tax collectors, thereby *ochlos-minjung*).

Driven by this postcolonial imagination, next we radicalize Luther's theological insights to make them more amenable to ecclesiology and theology in East Asia on behalf of emancipation, inculturation, and fullness of life in creation.

3. Martin Luther: The Triune God and the Church

For Luther, God is eternally a glowing oven full of love, who is fully revealed in Jesus Christ, "a mirror of the Father's heart." Jesus opens to us "the most profound depths of his fatherly heart and his pure, unutterable love."[12] The triune God, revealed as the fountain of love, speaks in terms of God's strange work, law, and the gospel.

In contrast to the Greek *logos*, the "word" in Christian tradition is pure event, because the Word became flesh. Creation once took place through the word of God, such that the miracle of language is explained in the non-Greek notion of the creation. In his exposition of John's Prologue, Luther argues that God is the Word speaking in, with, and to God's self. God speaks because God is the Word – a force of communication – enabling communication within God's self and for the world. Luther conceived of God as the subject of divine speaking in promise, dialogue, and relation.[13]

This perspective characterizes God as the source of life, communication, and redemption, such that Trinity means a living, relational, and emancipatory God. God as the speaking subject upholds Luther's notion of gospel in the sense of the living voice of God. God is living, effective, life-giving, prophetic, and redemptive in gospel, since God's Trinitarian being is framed in

---

[11] Emmanuel Levinas, *Otherwise Than Being or Beyond Essence*, trans. Alphonso Lingis (Pittsburgh: Duquesne University Press, 2004), 37-38.

[12] Martin Luther, "Large Catechism," in Robert Kolb and Timothy J. Wengert, eds., *Book of Concord: The Confessions of the Evangelical Lutheran Church* (=BC) (Minneapolis: Fortress, 2000), 439-440.

[13] LW 52:45-46.

the internal structure of the speech-event in loving communion, that is, promise, dialogue, and participation.

The Word of God mediates God *in self* with God *for us* in the sense of *verbum relationis* (the word of relation), which comprehends faith and life of the world as linguistic, creational, and emancipatory. The Triune God comes to us in historical time: God the Creator, God the Redeemer, God the Sanctifier in God's salvific-missional drama, because "the Father gives us all creation, Christ all his work, the Holy Spirit all his gifts."[14]

God's act of speech to the church and the world is inseparably connected with the power of the Holy Spirit, who was actually poured out upon all flesh at Pentecost. With the gift of speech, people of every nation can understand each other. God's self-bringing to speech captures language, that is, the essence of language. This language is rooted in God's word-in-deed, that is, the Greek translation of the Hebrew notion of *dabar* into the *logos*.

The church is sent into the world and exists for the sake of the world, because the church as the assembly of saints, is created through the Word and the sacraments in the presence of the Holy Spirit. The Holy Spirit "[a]ffects faith where and when it pleases God in those who hear the gospel...not on account of our own merits but on account of Christ."[15] Luther characterizes the motherly character of the church, because it is "the mother that begets and bears every Christian through the Word of God" through the Holy Spirit. The Spirit illuminates and inflames our hearts.[16]

4. Hermeneutic of the Gospel and Interpretation

For Luther, Holy Spirit plays a normative role in the interpretation of the Scripture. There exists a dialectical and dialogical relationship between the character of the *verbum dei* (as spoken word) and the character of "writtenness" in the presence of the Holy Spirit. Insofar as gospel, as the living voice of God, is sung and proclaimed as an oral cry, it is a voice resounding in all the world, shouted and heard in all places through the proclamation of the

---

[14] "The Large Catechism," BC 440.
[15] "Augsburg Confession," art. 5, BC 41.
[16] "Large Catechism," BC 436.

Word of God. Luther's cardinal metaphor of "what promotes Christ" offers a hermeneutical principle in establishing dialogue with the world of the entire Scripture as well as the realm of creation. This is also the criterion for judging all scriptures regarding whether they are in agreement with what drives Christ.[17] Thus the concept of *viva vox evangelii* implies the priority of the spoken word (God's Saying; *dabar* in Hebrew) over the written word (the Scripture).

A scientific-critical investigation of Scripture retains its validity in qualifying Reformation theology as hermeneutical, critical theology for effectively communicating the meaning of the biblical narrative to people in the world. In his "Introduction to the Psalter" (1531) Luther further states that "there [in the whole Bible] you see into the heart of all the saints."[18] The humanity of the biblical authors and their limitations are not concealed, but actually uncovered and exposed to our exegetical investigation. The authors' historicity and sociopolitical situation in Scripture were shaped and influenced by their lives and voices, which were embedded within the socioeconomic and historical circumstances. This perspective helps us to comprehend that historically conditioned traditions and social connections remain influential factors in exploring and interpreting Scripture in a decisively political, prophetic, and socio-critical manner. Understanding assumes social and political agency in the interpretation of the effective involvement of God's Word in the life of world.

In light of God's communicative action, it is worth noting that Luther in the "Smalcald Articles" proposes that the "mutual colloquium and consolation of brothers and sisters"[19] is the fifth form of the gospel in relation to preaching, the sacraments, and the ecclesial office. Luther's understanding of the Word of God is more rich and profound than Karl Barth in his threefold sense of the Word of God.

---

[17] "Preface to the Epistles of St. James and St. Jude," in John Dillenberger, ed. *Martin Luther: Selections from His Writings* (Garden City, NY: Anchor, 1961), 36.

[18] Helmut Gollwitzer, *An Introduction to Protestant Theology,* trans. David Cairns (Philadelphia: Westminster, 1978), 58.

[19] "Smalcald Articles," BC 319.

God's Word, understood interpersonally, retains an authority which is located in *mutual colloquium*. Luther adds the *consolation of brothers and sisters*, explaining this as a supplementary characteristic of God's Word. Thus Luther grounds his concept of the fifth form of the gospel in Matthew 18:20. "For where two or three are gathered in my name, I am there among them." God is understood as the one who is involved in the public and communicative life: "The Lord is witness between you and me forever…The Lord shall be between me and you, and between my descendants and your descendants, forever" (1 Sam 23:42). Luther therefore articulates the presence of God in the midst of God's people – Israel and the nations together (Zech 2:10-11; Ez 43:7; Joel 2:27).

Accordingly, Luther's hermeneutical theology in critical and prophetic relief is in accordance with Hebrews 1:1: "God spoke to our ancestors in many and various ways by the prophets." The word of God in Jesus Christ is indispensably connected with God's act of speech, which was undertaken throughout all the ages in their plural horizons of effect. The Hebrew way of expression remains in force, because God's word is related to a real thing or action, transcending the question of ontology. God's being is in God's word-in-deed, namely, speaking is doing, so that the word is the deed.[20] Luther is convinced of the necessity of interpretation, because Scripture is not merely the written word belonging to the past. Rather it is the *living* voice of God, which encounters us in our midst, here and now (Heb 4:12-13, 1 Cor 1:18, Is 55:10-11). Luther's creative engagement with the living and prophetic word of God can be undertaken over and against all normative and authoritative interpretation when previously established and placed over Scripture.

A notion of critical, contextual theology in this regard becomes indispensable, because the living word of God is not mechanically conveying or repeating certain words or statements from the Scripture to people in different times and places. Considering human life, language, and culture in the translation of the biblical narrative, we observe that even the same word can be said differently in another context. Luther offers clear inspiration for advanc-

---

[20] F. W. Marquardt, *Das christliche Bekenntnis zu Jesus dem Juden: Eine Christologie 1* (Munich: Chr. Kaiser, 1990), 141-145.

ing the relationship between God's word and interpretation through a contextual-constructive translation (or inculturation) of the biblical narrative, which remains central to the theological project of World Christianity today.[21] This perspective becomes arbiter in radicalizing Luther's insights, when it comes to political economic responsibility, integrity of life in creation, and recognition of the people of other cultures and faiths.

5. Gospel in the Midst of Political Witness

Luther's view of the gospel in the midst of political witness entails critical and prophetic potentials in critiquing and renewing the problems of social structure. As Luther argues against corruption by the powerful, "the princes" and "big shots" find it quite tolerable that the whole world should be criticized if only they themselves are exempted from this criticism. But they must certainly be criticized too, and anyone entrusted with the office of preaching owes it to them to point out where they act unjustly and do wrong, even if they protest that such criticism of rulers will lead to rebellion."[22]

Accordingly, the political realm belongs to political *diakonia* in faithfulness to God in terms of *parrhesia* (telling the truth in an audacious manner). For the sake of the freedom of the gospel, Luther spoke out against those who sought ideologically to misuse his theology of justification for a theology of revolution.[23] However, for Luther, the justified becomes a collaborator with God, because faith alone justifies. Once justified, we enter the active life of loving our neighbors.[24] Faith is active in love, seeking justice and prophetic *diakonia* in the public realm, because grace becomes, indeed, impulse and motivation for praxis and transforming activity.

---

[21] Lamin Sanneh, Whose Religion Is Christianity? The Gospel beyond the West (Grand Rapids: Eerdmans, 2003).

[22] Cited in Ulrich Duchrow, *Global Economy: A Confessional Issue for the Churches?* trans. David Lewis (Geneva: WCC, 1987), 7.

[23] Although his discourse – "suffering, suffering, cross, cross is the Christian right, no other" – was attacked during the Peasants' War (1524), Luther's radical critique of the state's violence must not be forgotten.

[24] Gollwitzer, Krummes Holz – aufrechter Gang: Zur Frage nach dem Sinn des Lebens (Munich: Kaiser, 1985), 313.

The grace of justification, which entails the living Christ in union with us in Word and sacrament, makes the grace of justification and faith dynamically related to the service of the needy in the public sphere. Luther prophetically expresses Eucharistic theology in connection with anamnestic reason standing in solidarity with people who suffer: "Here your heart must go out in love and learn that this is a sacrament of love. As love and support are given you, you in turn must render love and support to Christ in his needy ones. You must feel with sorrow all the dishonor done to Christ in his holy Word, all the misery of Christendom, all the unjust suffering of the innocent, with which the world is everywhere filled to overflowing. You must fight [resist], work, pray, and – if you cannot do more – have heartfelt sympathy."[25]

The grace of justification, which is grounded in the sacramental dimension of God's promise and righteousness, underpins the church's responsibility in coping with the unjust suffering of the innocent by means of resistance, labor, prayer, and heartfelt sympathy. The celebration of the Eucharist reinvigorates the church's participation in God's mission, standing in solidarity with the unjust suffering of the innocent, in whom the risen Christ is present. A critical, emancipatory theology finds validity in witness to the God of justice in connection with the dangerous and subversive memory of Jesus, who is in deep solidarity with *ochlos-minjung* (Luke 4:18-19).[26]

As articulated in Luther's *Commentary on the Magnificat* (1520-1521), Mary actually became impoverished and was completely wrapped up in poverty. Without any human help, God alone may do the work.[27] Mary, as an example of the grace of justification, shapes and underscores the church in terms of preferential service of the subaltern-*minjung*. She addresses the challenge of God's initiative against the patriarchal culture of the powerful, their hierarchical system, and institutionalized dominance. Luther, in a letter to Friedrich (March 7, 1522), expressed his new discovery of political theology with a theological turn: "The spiritual tyranny has become weak. That is

---

[25] "The Blessed Sacrament of the Holy and True Body and Blood of Christ, and the Brotherhoods " (1519), in *Martin Luther's Basic Theological Writings*, ed. Timothy F. Lull (Minneapolis: Fortress, 1989), 247.

[26] Craig L. Nessan, *The Vitality of Liberation Theology* (Eugene: Pickwick, 2013), 65-76.

[27] LW 21:328-29.

only what I regard with my writings. Now, I see that God drives further, insofar as God works in Jerusalem and two regiments. I have learned newly that not merely spiritual, but also worldly power must obey the Gospel...It shows itself clearly in the story of the Bible."[28]

6. God and Economic Justice

Luther's view of the economic realm marks a promising field, as seen in his critique of the system and practice of early capitalism. Until the beginning of 1525 Luther was preoccupied with economic issues on the question of usury. Luther regards mammon as the chief example in opposition to God, fighting for the sake of the poor and needy against the "devouring capital" system, which dominated the social reality of the early capitalism at his time. For Luther, those who have everything needed (money and property) – without care for anyone else – have a mammon-god. They set their whole hearts on money and property: "This is the most common idol on earth."[29]

In the Old Testament, God's grace summons us to corresponding action, because faith in the God of Torah is active and effective in love and service of our fellow humans as well as in care for other creatures. Economy (*oikonomia*) is the law or the management of the household, which compounds *oikos* (household) and *nomos* (law or management). Since our relationship to God is influenced by economic realities, unjust economic conditions have the power to ruin the true worship of God, because worship of God is replaced by worship of mammon.

Luther's understanding of the Torah becomes a catalyst for appreciating the correlation between law and gospel for the sake of economic justice. His deliberation of the unity of the Word of God maintains that word and deed are one in God and the Hebrew word *dabar* is expressed as *verbum facere* ("to do" the Word). Torah in the Latin term *institutio* and *doctrina* (denoting

---

[28] WA Br 2,461.61.
[29] "Large Catechism," BC 387.

command and promise) must be comprehended in the Jewish sense of the Bible as "divine instruction" rather than its translation as "law."[30]

Torah contains law/gospel, command/promise, judgment/grace, identifying the unity of the Word of God in such correlations. Luther comprehends faith in accordance with the First Commandment, which implies *Deum justificare* (giving God justice). When we act on faith in God's promise and accept God's forgiveness, we give God justice, the justification of God.[31] The Torah is more comprehensive than the accusing law, since the word of the covenant and the promise of salvation are the same as revealed in Jesus Christ.[32]

In faithfulness to *dabar* as God's effective word, Luther's discovery of the Torah can facilitate our understanding of the law-gospel hermeneutic in a more dynamic, living, and prophetic manner, especially in matters of the church's public responsibility and economic justice. For Luther, the Old Testament entails "certain promises and words of grace, by which the holy fathers and prophets under the law were kept, like us, in the faith of Christ."[33] Luther notices "the promises and pledges of God about Christ"[34] as the best thing in Moses, in whom there is a fine order, a joy about the gospel of Christ. Moses is a well of all wisdom and understanding.[35] Here is evangelical freedom or delight in appreciating and undertaking the gospel dimension

---

[30] Pinchas E. Lapide, "Stimmen jüdischer Zeitgenossen zu Martin Luther" in *Die Juden and Martin Luther – Martin Luther und die Juden: Geschichte, Wirkungsgeschichte, Herausforderung,* ed. Heinz Kremers, et al (Neukirchen-Vluyn: Neukirchener, 1985), 172.

[31] H. J. Iwand, *The Righteousness of Faith According to Luther,* ed. Virgil F. Thompson, trans. Randi H. Lundell (Eugene: Wipf and Stock, 2008), 21.

[32] In his *Table Talk,* Luther said: "The Hebrew drinks from the spring source, but the Greek from water that flows from the source. The Latin drinks from the puddles." WA Tr 525.

[33] "Preface to the Old Testament (1523, revised 1545)," in Timothy F. Lull and William R. Russell, eds. *Martin Luther's Basic Theological Writings* (Minneapolis: Fortress, 2005, 2nd edition), 114.

[34] Luther, "How Christians Should Regard Moses," in *ibid.,* 129.

[35] *Ibid.,* 121. During his stay in Coburg, Luther wrote his letter to Justus Jonas (June 30, 1530), stating that the Decalogue is the dialectic of the Gospel and the Gospel is the rhetoric of the Decalogue. Therefore we have, in Christ, all of Moses, but in Moses, not all of Christ. Luther became a new student of the Decalogue. WA Br 5,409, 26-29.

of the law (*paranesis*), that is, an evangelically conceptualized notion of the law.[36]

Given this, Luther takes seriously the most internal core of the Torah, the Decalogue, for Christian faith. Luther's theological axiom of God versus mammon is elaborated in his critical analysis of economic issues in the context of the seventh Commandment of the Decalogue ("You are not to steal") as discussed in his *Large Catechism* (1529). Luther remains a prophetic voice for God's *oikonomia* versus the political reality of mammon. The economic reality, which is stamped by misusing the market in an arbitrary, defiant, and arrogant way, causes the poor to be defrauded every day, as new burdens and higher prices are imposed upon their life.[37]

Ulrich Duchrow makes a substantial contribution by maintaining that the economic arena is no longer simply an ethical problem for Luther, but has become a confessional problem. Confession to God and resistance against mammon is grounded in the confessional notion of *status confessionis*.[38] Luther takes issue with mammon as a system of totality, in which people want to be god of the whole world through mammon and to have themselves worshipped as such.[39] The concept of greed acts as a critical arbiter in Luther's theological thought, because greed contradicts truth and faith in God's promise. Luther's sharp critique of the devouring system of capital accumulation expresses a prophetic voice against the Christian character of early capitalism in reference to colonialism in America.[40] In the practice of usury, speculation, and hoarding, Luther was keenly aware of the irrational and dangerous aspects of early capitalism, demonstrated by his ability to see clearly the political-economic alliance between the Catholic Church, Charles V, and the Fug-

---

[36] H. J. Iwand, *Luthers Theologie, Nachgelassene Werke*, eds. H. Gollwitzer et al. (Munich: Chr. Kaiser, 1983), 203-204. For Luther, the original root of all good lies in taking delight in the Law of the Lord (Psalm 1).

[37] "Large Catechism," BC 417-418.

[38] "Formula of Concord," BC 516.

[39] Duchrow, *Global Economy*, 176.

[40] Karl Marx, *Capital, 1: A Critique of Political Economy*, trans. Ben Fowkes (London: Penguin, 1990), 649-650. Luther stands in line with the prophetic stance of Bartolomé de Las Casas (1484-1566) against Spanish mission and colonialism.

gers. This perspective became inspiration for the church in East Asia to challenge the principalities and powers generated under the colonization of economic globalization and its tenet of possessive individualism today.

In this light, it is important to critically review Max Weber's evaluation of Luther's theology regarding economic justice. For Weber, Luther's concept of vocation has been interpreted as indifference to the spirit of capitalism, because the society is regarded as already produced and sanctioned by the divine order of creation. Accordingly, Luther's attack upon the great merchants of his time was neither biblically nor prophetically grounded. Rather Weber contended that Luther's critique of economic injustice was ironically claimed as a part of the spirit of capitalism, an expression of economic traditionalism. Thus Weber continued to argue that Luther lacked ethical rationalism, because he was not capable of maintaining the fundamental relationship between worldly activity and religious principle.[41]

Against Weber's misunderstanding, however, Luther himself considered the importance of economic life and justice in his theological deliberation of God and Torah, when it came to the connection between the first commandment and the seventh commandment. Luther's prophetic stance against the structures of mammon, which is grounded in God's justice and economic righteousness in the Old Testament, forms a substantial impulse for the church's responsibility for economic justice. Luther's stance for God versus mammon is biblically inspired, prophetically driven, and deeply embedded within the endeavor of creating fair and just life arrangements.[42]

7. God's Universal Reign and Creatio Continua

Luther's teaching of justification can be seen in connection with God's universal reign, which acknowledges the dignity of people outside the walls of Christianity. God the Creator works all in all. God's ongoing act in the new creation (*creatio continua*) implicates divine power itself in preserving the creation and being present in creation's innermost and outermost aspects.

---

[41] Weber, *The Protestant Ethic and the Spirit of Capitalism*, trans. Talcott Parsons (Mineola, NY: Dover, 2003), 85.

[42] Paul S. Chung, Church and Ethical Responsibility in the Midst of World Economy: Greed, Dominion, and Justice (Eugene: Cascade, 2013), 38-40.

God's on-going act of new creation in the world points to Luther's insightful concept of God, notably emphasizing the first function of law in reference to the gospel (and also sharpening our identity as created collaborators with God, as St. Paul teaches to in 1 Corinthians 3:9). St. Paul, in front of the Areopagus, bore witness to *solus Christus*, expressing his conviction that everyone lives, moves, and has his/her being in the universal reign of God (Acts 17:22, 27-28).

For Luther, God is wholly incomprehensible and inaccessible, as St Paul witnessed (Rom 11:33).[43] Divine majesty is reserved for God's self alone, since "God must therefore be left to himself in his own majesty."[44] This means that God works life, death, and all in all, keeping Godself free over all things. The hidden God, coupled with God's universal reign, works in the world through irregular grace. God is the Provider of all life arrangements, enhancing the integrity of life in creation in terms of political responsibility, economic justice, and recognition of the Other.

Theology of the cross, seen in connection with a theology of creation, finds its validity in upholding a theology of life in solidarity with those who are fragile, victimized, and vulnerable. This perspective characterizes theology of the cross as a theology in the flesh, which embraces fullness of life for creation and humanity in a holistic manner.

For Luther, a lively faith goes hand in hand with praise of God's beauty and glory in creation. All creatures are tools in the service of God's work, even behind "masks" (*larva Dei*), under which God hides God's activity. God remains free in the ceaseless activity with which God works all in all. The article of creation is one of faith. Faith in God's creation is faith in the triune God. Faith and justification correlate with ecological or environmental stewardship, which is indispensable for shaping and directing theology in a linguistic, creational, and emancipatory manner, transcending the limitations of Western modernity.

---

[43] *Luther and Erasmus: Free Will and Salvation,* eds. E. Gordon Rupp and Philip S. Watson (Philadelphia: Westminster, 1969), 330.
[44] *Ibid.*, 201.

Luther's marvelous sense of the aesthetic dimension in creation is striking, because "the wonderful and most lovely music [comes] from the harmony of the motions that are in the celestial spheres."[45] This is a beautiful text for church and theology in East Asia, which is committed to keeping the aesthetic sense of creation intact for ecological stewardship and eco-justice. We are encouraged to listen attentively to the beautiful music of God coming from creation, because creation is conceived of as a linguistic and salvific phenomenon. God's work takes place in faithfulness, also in the realm of creation. Creation is the sphere of dialogue and communication occurring between God and the creatures. Given that creation is the communicative sphere, the world is to be understood as a text which is readable and decipherable, through which God may speak to us in a completely different manner than heard in the ecclesial sphere. This perspective finds validity in the East Asian sense of the web of life and of nature in a harmonious and holistic manner, which is crucial in Buddhist, Confucian, and Daoist visions of human life fully interconnected with other creatures and nature as a living organism.

8. Mission: Invitation and Dialogue

Luther's recognition of Others invites them to the gospel, while acknowledging that the non-Christian leads a morally mature life on the basis of the commands written upon all human hearts. Furthermore, Luther acknowledges in Abraham's faith journey that God becomes an advocate for Hagar and Ishmael. Luther's remark about Ishmael is striking at this point: "For the expulsion does not mean that Ishmael should be utterly excluded from the kingdom of God…The descendants of Ishmael also joined the church of Abraham and became heirs of the promise, not by reason of a right, but because of irregular grace."[46] Luther's Christological idea of grace does not stand in competition with God's embrace of the Other through irregular grace.

---

[45] LW 1:126.
[46] LW 4:42-44.

Bonhoeffer incorporates Luther's radical understanding of the gospel into his theology of the cross from below: "the curses of the godless sometimes sound better in God's ear than the alleluias of the pious."[47] The biblical radicalism of Luther's teaching of justification takes seriously such blasphemies more than many conventional hymns of praise.

Luther provides a hermeneutical way of speaking about God with all-embracing and inclusive force, while retaining a radical and particular direction. The dialectic between the exclusive tendency and an all-inclusive comprehensiveness enables Luther's language about *sola* (alone) to be closely associated with the term *simul* (at the same time). *Sola*, in the sense of biblical uniqueness, cannot be comprehended adequately without connection to God's universal *simul* in biblical openness toward the world. Thus gospel in the sense of *viva vox evangelii*, (more than proclamation) offers a living dynamism in underlying communication and translation of the biblical narrative through dialogue with the world.

Luther's teaching of justification, when seen in light of God's universal reign and irregular grace, has an inclusive dimension, which becomes obvious particularly in his commentary on 1 Timothy 2:4. Here the exclusive proposition is expressed in universal terms, because God causes all people to be saved.[48] Accordingly, Luther boldly appreciates pagan authority as a model to show the responsibility of secular authority. Luther was not reluctant to praise the Turkish state and exercise a critique of Christian authorities with unprecedented frankness.[49] As a gentle and rich Lord, God grants a great measure of gold, silver, riches, dominion, reason, wisdom, languages, and kingdoms to those outside Christian religion.

Luther warns against misleading people of other religions through a forced conversion to Christianity by means of colonialism and domination.[50] In-

---

[47] Bonhoeffer, *Act and Being*, ed. Wayne W. Floyd, Jr., trans. H. Martin Rumscheidt (Minneapolis: Fortress, 1996), 160.

[48] LW 28:260. His reflection on Jesus' descent into hell also runs in this direction.

[49] Gerhard Ebeling, *Luther: An Introduction to His Thought* (Minneapolis: Fortress, 2007), 189.

[50] Volker Stolle, *Luther Texts on Mission: The Church Comes from All Nations*, trans. Klaus D. Schultz and Daniel Thies (Saint Louis: Concordia, 2003), 104-105.

stead, mission can only be effective when it is performed with the continual renewal of the church and Christian existence, excluding the human purposes of dominion, cultural imperialism, and confessional rivalry. As Luther states: "it is not said, therefore, that God desires to convert everyone. St. Paul only declares of the Gospel that it is a cry, which he causes to go out over everyone. It is supposed to be pure blessing."[51]

This perspective supports mission as prophetic dialogue and inculturation, which is historically embodied in the case of Karl L. Reichelt (1877-1952) in his dialogue and collaboration with people of other faiths.[52] Luther's theology of conversion becomes arbiter in postcolonial formation of God's mission in recognition of the others. Our mission is to invite people to the mystery, love, and promise of God in the gospel of Jesus Christ for all, communicating its universal message and translating and interpreting it anew in different times and places. Luther's linguistic renovation and its dialectic of particular-universal becomes a driving force for upholding our public witness as prophetic dialogue within a pluralistic world of many religions, in support of interreligious solidarity for justice, peace, and integrity of creation.

9. Conclusion

In this study of Martin Luther and Reformation theology in East Asian perspective, we have sought to radicalize his insight into God as the Source of Life in solidarity with those who are fragile, vulnerable, and victimized. In so doing, we deepen Luther's recognition of the Other in a contextual and constructive framework to undergird inclturation, emancipation, and integrity of creation. I conclude the East Asian interpretation of Luther by summarizing arguments for the future of Reformation theology as articulated in this chapter.

First, the Christian confession of Jesus Christ in the tradition of Reformation theology emphasizes the Son of God as the eternal and incarnate Word, who stands at the borderline between Israel and all nations, identifying

---

[51] *Ibid.*, 29. Lutheran confessional theology states that "Conversion to God is the work of God the Holy Spirit alone." "Formula of Concord," BC 561.

[52] See Reichelt's legacy in connection with Tao Fong Shan Christian Centre, Hong Kong, China.

himself with the lowest of the low among his brothers and sisters (Mt 25:31). This is characteristic of our understanding of the triune God as the Source of life and of God's emancipation in solidarity with and recognition of the subalterized – massa perditionis – for the kingdom of God has come in Jesus Christ.

Second, Luther's theology of justification needs to be extended and renewed in different times and places, especially in light of Luther's congenial notion of the gospel as the living voice of God. God as the Subject of speaking encourages us to acknowledge and respect the world of creation in which God continues to work and address. The Reformation teaching of justification should break through its encapsulation within Western possessive individualism under the colonization of the Empire; instead it should be reclaimed as way of expressing God's deep compassion in the death of Jesus Christ for all, reinforcing interreligious dialogue.

Third, a postcolonial reading of Reformation theology in East Asian context advances a project of inculturation, in order to undergird interreligious dialogue, adopting a new departure in the critique of an imperial version of Reformation theology or misuse of its scholarship in the service of the powerful in the ecclesial context of East Asia. In dialogue with Reformation theology, a theological project of inculturation entails prophetic-hermeneutical reasoning in revealing and clarifying the emancipatory and constructive values inherent in Asian religions and cultures. It archeologically focuses on what has been subjugated and foreclosed in the study of cultures and religions regarding the irregular side of history, society, and church. It is undertaken in terms of anamnestic reasoning in dangerous and subversive remembrance of Jesus's socio-biography with his people.

Fourth, theology of the cross, seen in light of a theology of creation, can overcome the previously tainted imagery between the cross and crusade in colonial age. This refers to a refurbishing of the theology of the cross for a theology of life (resurrection) seen in light of God's solidarity with the minjung and economic justice for all (theology in the flesh). This claims a postcolonial formation of theologia crucis as a radical critique of any cultural compromise with colonial or imperial directions. Through the Reformation notion of irregular grace, the goodness of creation is fulfilled and restored in God's grace of justification through divine reconciliation and solidarity with the innocent victim and wholeness (shalom) for all creation.

Fifth, the Lutheran insight into the living and emancipatory Word entails self-criticism and self-renewal for the project of inculturation, emancipation, and integrity of life, in order to deepen its prophetic-contextual horizon for political responsibility, economic justice, integrity of creation, and recognition of the Other. Law-gospel hermeneutics should be comprehended in a Torah-Gospel correlation, in which there is evangelical delight in doing Torah through prophetic words and economic justice for the world. This teaching can serve as a hermeneutical bedrock for articulating God's universal reign by sharpening the theologia crucis in terms of dialogue, recognition, and collaboration with people in the world. This reinvigorates interreligious dialogue in a practical direction for emancipation, inculturation, and ecological sustainability. For instance, universal compassion, social engagement, economic justice, and ecological sustainability in the Buddhist tradition needs to be appreciated in any contextualization of the Reformation teaching of justification, together with political-economic responsibility and social-ecological engagement, especially in the critical project related to a second Axial Age for "interreligious solidarity for just relations."[53] Through the process of interreligious dialogue, a fusion of horizons in a critical-emancipatory framework generates new meaning for the gospel of justification by faith, which is active in love and which seeks understanding and justice in the public realm across the globe.

Abstract

Asiatische „irreguläre Theologie" (repräsentiert durch die zweite Generation der Minjung-TheologInnen in Nordamerika) setzt sich mit Luthers Erbe (wie es durch Bonhoeffer neu interpretiert wurde) in der Perspektive des ostasiatischen Kontextes in Dialog mit asiatischen Religionen auseinander. Die asiatische irreguläre Theologie folgt einer postkolonialen Lektürestrategie, die auf gleichsam archäologische Weise Themen wieder hervorholt, die in westlichen Studien zu Luther und Bonhoeffer vermieden oder verdeckt werden. Weiterhin präsentiert sie die irreguläre Seite der Theologie als ein Sprachereignis (Gottes Sprachakt

---

[53] For this pioneering direction in interreligious dialogue based on a critical-emancipatory framework, see Ulrich Duchrow and Franz J. Hinkelammert, *Transcending Greedy Money: Interreligious Solidarity for Just Relations* (New York: Palgrave Macmillan,, 2012).

durch Kirche und Welt), das von den Verwundbaren, den Verletzlichen und den zu Opfern Gemachten artikuliert wird – dem subalternen Minjung (dem einfachen Volk). In diesem Projekt wird Gott als die trinitarische Quelle des Lebens interpretiert als Antwort auf die strukturelle, kulturelle und religiöse Gewalt gegen Menschen und Schöpfung. Diese Lesart von Luther und Bonhoeffer zielt darauf, die westliche Art herauszufordern, die eigene beschränkte Position anderen aufzudrängen. Dabei interpretiert und kontextualisiert sie Einsichten der lutherischen Tradition neu für die multireligiösen Gesellschaften Asiens durch besondere Hervorhebung und Wertschätzung bestimmter Motive, durch kritische Dekonstruktion und kreative Rekonstruktion.

EINE KRITISCHE WEITERFÜHRUNG REFORMATORISCHER IMPULSE
DIETRICH BONHOEFFER UND DOROTHEE SÖLLE

Renate Wind

1. Luthers Rechtfertigungslehre im Licht der Bergpredigt. Dietrich Bonhoeffers Kritik an der „billigen Gnade" in der „Nachfolge"

Dietrich Bonhoeffers theologisches Denken kreist um zwei Fragen: Wer ist Christus für uns heute und: Wie wird Kirche zu einer Gemeinschaft von Glaubenden, in der das Evangelium eine neue soziale Gestalt erhält. Die Frage, was Kirche in spiritueller und sozialer Hinsicht zu Kirche macht, stand am Anfang seines theologischen Denkens, und sie hat ihn seitdem nicht mehr losgelassen. Die 1927 fertig gestellte Doktorarbeit trägt den Titel „Sanctorum Communio" – eine dogmatische Untersuchung zur Soziologie der Kirche.[1] Auf der Suche nach einer tragfähigen Gemeinschaft und einer überzeugenden Glaubenspraxis für sich selbst, getrieben von der Notwendigkeit, eine glaubhafte Identität als Theologe und zugleich als ein dem Erbe der Aufklärung verpflichteter Wissenschaftler zu finden, definiert Bonhoeffer hier die Kirche als „Gemeinschaft der Heiligen" und diese Gemeinschaft mit der Formel „Christus als Gemeinde existierend". Obwohl diese Formel zunächst noch ziemlich abstrakt bleibt, wird in ihr doch deutlich, dass Bonhoeffer von nun an die Frage, was Kirche zur Kirche macht, mit der Frage verbindet, die zu seinem zentralen Lebensthema wird: „Wer ist Christus für uns heute?" Wann und wie ist die christliche Gemeinde wirklich Christus? Wie und an welchem konkreten Ort ist Christus wirklich existent? Bonhoeffer hat diese Fragen, einmal aufgeworfen und zusammengebunden, in den weiteren Abschnitten seines theologischen Denkens nach und nach zu konkretisieren versucht. Diese Konkretionen sind jedoch nicht abstrakte theoretische Denk-

---

[1] Veröffentlicht in: BONHOEFFER, Dietrich: Sanctorum Communio. Eine dogmatische Untersuchung zur Soziologie der Kirche, Dietrich Bonhoeffer Werke (DBW) 1. München: Kaiser, (1927) 1986.

schritte gewesen, sondern „Theologie im Vollzug", ständige Reflexion von neuen, existentiellen Erfahrungen, von im Glauben reflektierter politischer und kirchlicher Praxis. Bereits in „Sanctorum Communio" stellt Bonhoeffer die These auf, dass die Kirche, die „Christus" ist, eine neue soziale Gestalt entwickeln müsse. In kritischer Abgrenzung gegen eine deutsche evangelische Kirche, die politisch immer noch der Verbindung von „Thron und Altar" und soziologisch einer bestimmten bürgerlichen Schicht verhaftet war, stellt er fest: „Die kommende Kirche wird nicht bürgerlich sein."[2] Dem bürgerlichen Erbauungsverein, der sich Kirche nennt, hält der Vikar Dietrich Bonhoeffer 1928 in einem Gemeindevortrag entgegen, dass für eine solche Kirche Christus nicht ans Kreuz gegangen sei. Hier wird eine erste Konkretion deutlich, die bei Bonhoeffer immer mehr in das Zentrum der Lehre von Christus und der Kirche rückt: An Christus, dem *Gekreuzigten*, hängt das Selbstverständnis und die Praxis der „Gemeinschaft der Heiligen".

Die Zeit von 1930 bis 1931 verbringt der inzwischen promovierte und habilitierte Pfarrer und Wissenschaftler am Union Theological Seminary in New York. Die Erfahrungen und Begegnungen, mit denen er dort konfrontiert wird, werden ihn von Grund auf verändern. In den Basisgemeinden des „anderen Amerika" kommt er der Kirche, die er sucht, auf die Spur. In den Ladenkirchen und Selbsthilfezentren von Harlem, in der ökumenischen und kosmopolitischen Atmosphäre des Seminars, den Anfängen der amerikanischen Bürgerrechtsbewegung und in der Begegnung mit den Vertretern des „social gospel", die die Gebote Christi in soziale und politische Kategorien umzusetzen versuchen, findet Bonhoeffer einen neuen Ansatz von weltlich gelebtem Christentum. Lebensentscheidend aber wird die Begegnung mit Jean Lasserre, einem jungen Pfarrer aus Frankreich.[3] Auf ihn projiziert Bonhoeffer erst einmal alle antifranzösischen Ressentiments des vaterländisch gesinnten deutschen Bürgertums – und stößt damit ins Leere. Jean Lasserre ist Pazifist und hält ihm entgegen: Man kann nicht Christ und Nationalist in einem sein. Glauben wir an die heilige, allgemeine Kirche, die Gemeinschaft der Heiligen? Schlagartig wird ihm im Dialog mit dem „Erbfeind" klar, dass die „Sanctorum Communio" auch Franzosen umfasst, und dass der Gedanke an die Kirche, die „Christus" ist, die Spaltung der Gemeinde Christi in Nati-

---

[2] Ebd., 292.
[3] Zu seiner Begegnung mit Lasserre äußert sich Bonhoeffer in *Widerstand und Ergebung (DBW Bd. 8)*. Gütersloh: Kaiser, 1998, 541f.

onen, Rassen und Klassen verbietet. Bonhoeffer wird sich von nun an diese Haltung zu eigen machen und mit der Bergpredigt begründen, mit der Lehre Jesu von der „besseren Gerechtigkeit", die die Friedensstifter selig preist und die Liebe zum „Feind", zum Anderen, zum Fremden fordert. Damit steigt er aus einer lutherischen Tradition aus, die die Bergpredigt nicht als Anweisung zur Umgestaltung der Welt sieht, sondern als Hinweis auf deren Erlösungsbedürftigkeit, die die Kirche im Evangelium von der Gnade Gottes verkündigt. Diese Trennung von Glauben an das persönliche Heil einerseits und der Eigengesetzlichkeit der Welt in ihrer politischen und sozialen Realität andererseits, die der Lutheraner Bonhoeffer zuvor noch in Gemeindevorträgen und Vorlesungen vertreten hat, wird er nun nicht mehr mit vollziehen. Später wird er in einem Brief an den Bruder Karl-Friedrich Bonhoeffer schreiben:

> "Ich glaube zu wissen, dass ich eigentlich erst innerlich klar und aufrichtig sein würde, wenn ich mit der Bergpredigt wirklich anfinge, Ernst zu machen... Es gibt doch nun einmal Dinge, für die es sich lohnt, kompromisslos einzutreten. Und mir scheint, der Friede und die soziale Gerechtigkeit, oder eigentlich Christus, sei so etwas."[4]

Mit diesem neuen Bewusstsein kehrt er im Juni 1931 nach Deutschland zurück. Dort hatte gerade die NSDAP nach einem erdrutschartigen Wahlsieg 107 Sitze im Reichstag gewonnen, und ein Ende der wirtschaftlichen und politischen Krise der Weimarer Republik war nicht abzusehen. Dietrich Bonhoeffer, der in seinen Studienjahren ein eher unpolitischer Mensch gewesen war, wird sich nun aktiv in die gesellschaftlichen Auseinandersetzungen einmischen und Position beziehen. An der Theologischen Fakultät der Berliner Universität, an der er als Privatdozent Vorlesungen hält, ist er bald als Pazifist und Sozialist verschrien. Neue Formen sozialen Lernens, am Union erprobt, ziehen an sozialen Fragen interessierte Theologiestudenten und besonders auch die damals noch vereinzelten Theologiestudentinnen an. Der studentische „Bonhoefferkreis" engagiert sich an sozialen Brennpunkten, Bonhoeffer selbst übernimmt eine Konfirmandengruppe im Arbeiterviertel Prenzlauer Berg. Er zieht aus der Grunewaldvilla aus und mietet sich nördlich vom Alexanderplatz ein. Die Konfirmanden lernen die Bibel kennen, aber auch Schachspielen und Englisch. Der Pfarrer macht mit ihnen Ausflüge und imponiert als Fußballer. Der Konfirmationsgottesdienst wird gemeinsam vorbereitet, und die Predigt enthält Bilder aus den roten Arbeiterliedern:

---

[4] DBW 13, 272f.

Eine kritische Weiterführung reformatorischer Impulse 341

„Keiner soll euch je den Glauben nehmen, dass Gott auch für euch einen Tag und eine Sonne und eine Morgenröte bereitet hat, und dass er uns das gelobte Land sehen lassen will, in dem Gerechtigkeit und Liebe und Frieden herrscht, weil Christus herrscht."[5]

Gleichzeitig wird Bonhoeffer in der ökumenischen Bewegung aktiv. In Cambridge wird er 1931 auf der Jahrestagung des Weltbundes für Freundschaftsarbeit der Kirchen zu einem der europäischen Jugendsekretäre gewählt. Auf einer der folgenden ökumenischen Konferenzen wird er die alte Formel „Christus als Gemeinde existierend" neu konkretisieren:

„Dem Christen ist jeglicher Kriegsdienst, jede Vorbereitung zum Krieg verboten. Die Liebe kann unmöglich das Schwert gegen einen Christen richten, weil sie es mit ihm auf Christus richtet."[6]

Zu dieser Zeit hat Dietrich Bonhoeffer die nationale Grenze des Gemeindegedankens ebenso gesprengt wie die soziale. Und er hat die Trennung von der Verkündigung des Evangeliums und der Notwendigkeit politischen Handelns endgültig hinter sich gelassen:

„Trachtet nach dem, was auf Erden ist! Daran entscheidet sich heute viel, ob wir Christen Kraft genug haben, der Welt zu bezeugen, dass wir keine Träumer und Wolkenwandler sind. Dass wir nicht die Dinge kommen und gehen lassen, wie sie sind. Dass unser Glaube wirklich nicht das Opium ist, das uns zufrieden sein lässt inmitten einer ungerechten Welt. Sondern dass wir, gerade weil wir trachten nach dem, was droben ist, nur umso hartnäckiger und zielbewusster protestieren auf dieser Erde."[7]

Als 1933 ein solcher Protest gefordert ist, bleibt Bonhoeffer ein einsamer Rufer in der Wüste. Der bald nach Hitlers Machtergreifung einsetzende nationalsozialistische Terror richtet sich zunächst fast ausschließlich gegen links – und wird von den Kirchenführern beider großen Kirchen ausdrücklich begrüßt. Otto Dibelius, zu der Zeit Generalsuperintendent in Berlin, predigt am 21. März 1933 über alle Rundfunkstationen: „Wenn der Staat seines Amtes waltet gegen die, die die Grundlagen der staatlichen Ordnung untergraben, gegen die vor allem, die mit ätzendem und gemeinem Wort die Ehe zerstö-

---

[5] BETHGE, Eberhard: Dietrich Bonhoeffer, Eine Biographie, 6. Aufl., München: Kaiser, 1986, 275.

[6] GREMMELS, Christian/Pfeifer, Hans: Theologie und Biographie, Zum Beispiel Dietrich Bonhoeffer. München: Kaiser, 1983, 43.

[7] Predigt zu Kol 3,1-4, in : DBW 11, 445.

ren, den Glauben verächtlich machen, den Tod für das Vaterland begeifern – dann walte er seines Amtes in Gottes Namen. Wir haben von Dr. Martin Luther gelernt, dass die Kirche der staatlichen Gewalt nicht in den Arm fallen darf, wenn sie tut, wozu sie berufen ist, auch wenn sie hart und rücksichtslos schaltet."[8] Drei Wochen später hält Dietrich Bonhoeffer einen Vortrag vor einem Kreis von Berliner Pfarrern. Mit seinen Ausführungen über „Die Kirche vor der Judenfrage"[9] nimmt er Stellung zu dem Anfang April 1933 erlassenen "Gesetz zur Wiederherstellung des Berufsbeamtentums", mit dem jüdische und kommunistische Beamte aus dem Dienst entlassen werden. Dies und die offen terroristischen Übergriffe auf Juden und Andersdenkende ist für Bonhoeffer Grund genug, nicht nur uneingeschränkte Solidarität mit den Opfern zu fordern, sondern auch die Bereitschaft, „dem Rad in die Speichen zu fallen". Der von Dibelius vertretenen konservativen Interpretation der lutherischen Zwei-Reiche-Lehre setzt er eine andere Deutung entgegen: Gerade weil der Staat, das „Regiment Gottes zur Linken" Recht und Ordnung schaffen soll, muss er dann, wenn er es nicht tut, mit Nachdruck daran erinnert, im äußersten Fall auch dazu gezwungen werden. Doch mit dieser Forderung, dem NS-Regime mit politischem Widerstand zu begegnen, bleibt er in seiner Kirche allein.

Am 23. Juli 1933 finden in der deutschen evangelischen Kirche Kirchenwahlen statt. Zum ersten Mal kandidiert die 1932 gegründete Gruppe der „Deutschen Christen", die für die Deutschen ein „artgemäßes Christentum" fordert, das „deutschem Luthergeist und heldischer Frömmigkeit" entspricht. Dieses so genannte Christentum enthält alle Elemente der Nazi-Ideologie und ein Programm zur Gleichschaltung der deutschen evangelischen Kirche im Sinne des NS-Staates. Obwohl es eine Gegenliste „Evangelium und Kirche" gibt, erhalten die „Deutschen Christen" über 70% der Wählerstimmen und besetzen damit fast alle kirchlichen Schlüsselpositionen. Der Predigt, die Bonhoeffer daraufhin hält, ist die Erregung dieser Tage deutlich anzumerken. Der sonst eher spröde Prediger ruft der Gemeinde zu:

„Es heißt Entscheidung, es heißt Scheidung der Geister... Kommt, ihr... Alleingelassenen, die ihr die Kirche verloren habt, wir wollen wieder zurück

---

[8] Zitiert in: PROLINGHEUER, Hans: *Kleine politische Kirchengeschichte.* Köln: 1984, 53.

[9] BONHOEFFER, Dietrich: Die Kirche vor der Judenfrage (1933). *DBW 12.* München : Kaiser, 1997, S. 349-58

zur Heiligen Schrift, wir wollen zusammen die Kirche suchen gehen... Kirche bleibe Kirche!... Bekenne, bekenne, bekenne!"[10]

Unter dem Motto „Bekenntnis" werden sich bald immer mehr evangelische Christinnen und Christen zusammen finden, die sich nun doch gegen den Reichsbischof von Hitlers Gnaden und die Gleichschaltung der Kirche zu wehren beginnen. Als erst die preußische und dann auch die Nationalsynode der evangelischen Kirche die Einführung des Arierparagraphen und damit die Ausgrenzung getaufter Juden aus der Kirche beschließen, entwickelt sich aus einer ersten Protestbewegung, dem von Martin Niemöller gegründeten „Pfarrernotbund", die „Bekennende Kirche", die auf ihrer Bekenntnissynode in Wuppertal-Barmen im Mai 1934 mit der „Barmer Theologischen Erklärung"[11] ein deutliches Wort des Widerstandes gegen die Irrlehren der „Deutschen Christen" und die rigiden Gleichschaltungsmaßnahmen des NS-Staates formuliert. Jedoch auch das „Barmer Bekenntnis" enthält kein einziges Wort des Protestes gegen die Menschenrechtsverletzungen im nationalsozialistischen Deutschland. Stattdessen betonen die Vertreter der „Bekennenden Kirche" immer wieder ihre politische Loyalität: es gehe im Kampf der Bekennenden Kirche allein um die Verteidigung und Erhaltung der Kirche und des Evangeliums. Dietrich Bonhoeffer ist tief enttäuscht über diese Haltung: „Es muss endlich mit der theologisch begründeten Zurückhaltung gegenüber dem Tun des Staates gebrochen werden," schreibt er an einen Freund aus der Ökumene, „es ist ja doch alles nur Angst. ‚Tu deinen Mund auf für die Stummen' – wer weiß denn das heute noch in unserer Kirche, dass dies die mindeste Forderung der Bibel in diesen Zeiten ist."[12] Und zehn Jahre später wird er in einem Entwurf für ein kirchliches Schuldbekenntnis schreiben:

„Die Kirche... war stumm, wo sie hätte schreien müssen. Die Kirche bekennt, die willkürliche Anwendung brutaler Gewalt, das leibliche und seelische Leiden unzähliger Unschuldiger, Unterdrückung, Hass und Mord gesehen zu haben, ohne ihre Stimme für sie zu erheben, ohne Wege gefunden zu haben, ihnen zur Hilfe zu eilen. Sie ist schuldig geworden am Leben der

---

[10] Bethge, a.a.O., 348.
[11] BARMER THEOLOGISCHE ERKLÄRUNG, hg.v. A. Burgsmüller und R. Weth: Neukirchen: Neukirchener Verlag, (1982) 1983 2. Aufl.
[12] BETHGE, Eberhard/Bethge, Renate/Gremmels, Christian: *Dietrich Bonhoeffer. Sein Leben in Bildern und Texten.* München: Kaiser, (1986) 1989 4. Aufl., 127.

Schwächsten und Wehrlosesten Brüder (und Schwestern) Jesu Christi."[13]

Im Laufe des Jahres 1933 muss Bonhoeffer erkennen, dass er mit seiner Forderung nach politischem Widerstand auch in der Bekennenden Kirche zunächst völlig isoliert bleibt. Die einzigen, die ihm beigepflichtet hätten, die religiösen Sozialisten, gehören selbst schon zu den Verfolgten. In dieser Situation beschließt er, wie er an Karl Barth schreibt, „für einige Zeit in die Wüste zu gehen" und ein Auslandspfarramt in London zu übernehmen. Anfang Oktober 1933 verabschiedet er sich von seinen Berliner Studentinnen und Studenten mit den Worten. „Es gilt nun, in der Stille auszuhalten und an allen Ecken des deutsch-christlichen Prunkhauses den Feuerbrand der Wahrheit anzulegen, damit eines Tages der ganze Bau zusammenkracht."[14]

Als Bonhoeffer Anfang 1935 von der „Bekennenden Kirche" nach Deutschland zurück gerufen wird, haben sich dort auch die Fronten im Kirchenkampf geklärt. Auf einer zweiten Bekenntnissynode in Berlin-Dahlem ist die Einrichtung eines Notkirchenregiments und damit der organisatorische Aufbau einer Oppositionskirche beschlossen worden. Sie wird in den kommenden Jahren den harten Kern, die „bekennende" Bekennende Kirche bilden, im Gegensatz zu dem größeren kompromissbereiten Flügel, der sich auf ein „Befriedungskonzept" der Reichsregierung einlässt und mit gemäßigten „Deutschen Christen" in „Reichskirchenausschüssen" zusammenarbeitet. Dieser Widerstandskirche steht der „Bruderrat" vor, der mit der Einrichtung eigener Predigerseminare beginnt. Die Leitung des Predigerseminars in Finkenwalde wird Dietrich Bonhoeffer übernehmen, der damit zu einer zentralen und umstrittenen Gestalt im Kirchenkampf wird. In dieser Zeit fängt für ihn zugleich eine Lebensphase an, in der er den Versuch macht, so etwas wie ein heiliges Leben zu führen. Neu ist dieser Gedanke nicht; die „Gemeinschaft der Heiligen" muss nun aber neu definiert und konkretisiert werden. Denn die herkömmliche Existenzform der Gemeinde, die Kirche, ist dort, wo er lebt, zerschlagen, und er soll helfen, neue Formen zu finden und aufzubauen. Wie aber soll das gehen, ohne dass die, die diese neue Kirche wollen, sie selbst verkörpern, sie mit ihrer ganzen menschlichen Existenz sichtbar machen? In dieser Zeit entsteht Bonhoeffers bekanntestes Buch, „Nachfolge", eine Aktualisierung der Bergpredigt: *„Christus hat sein Leben auf dieser Erde noch nicht zu Ende gebracht. Er lebt es weiter im Leben seiner (Nach-*

---

[13] BONHOEFFER, Dietrich: *Ethik (DBW Bd. 6)*. München: Kaiser, 1992, 129f.
[14] Bethge, a.a.O., 377.

folgerinnen und) Nachfolger." In dieser Nachfolge fordert Bonhoeffer kompromissloses Eintreten für Frieden und Gerechtigkeit. Entsprechend beginnt das erste Kapitel mit einer radikalen Absage an eine lutherische Position, die der Kirche die Verkündigung des „reinen Evangeliums" von der Gnade Gottes verordnet und die Welt ihrer „Eigengesetzlichkeit" überlässt:

> "Billige Gnade ist der Todfeind unserer Kirche... In dieser Kirche findet die Welt billige Bedeckung ihrer Sünden, die sie nicht bereut und von denen frei zu werden sie erst recht nicht wünscht... Man kann die Tat Luthers nicht verhängnisvoller missverstehen als mit der Meinung, Luther habe mit der Entdeckung des Evangeliums der reinen Gnade einen Dispens für den Gehorsam gegen das Gebot Jesu in der Welt proklamiert."[15]

Leben nach der Bergpredigt, Nachfolge Jesu und „Gemeinschaft der Heiligen" bedeutet also nicht Rückzug in eine private Frömmigkeit, sondern Grundsatzprogramm einer Kirche, die der Welt nicht erlaubt, zu tun was sie will. An dieser Stelle beginnt der Konflikt, den Bonhoeffer immer bewusster aufnehmen und austragen wird, auch gegen die politische Enthaltsamkeit der Mehrheitsfraktion in der Bekennenden Kirche.

Bonhoeffer wird sich am Ende dem konspirativen Widerstand gegen das Naziregime anschließen und die beiden letzten Jahre seines Lebens im Gefängnis verbringen. In den Monaten vorübergehender Hafterleichterung wird ein freundlicher Wachmann Briefe an der Zensur vorbei aus dem Gefängnis schmuggeln. In ihnen wird Bonhoeffer noch einmal neu fragen, wo Christus ist in einer Welt, die sich mehr und mehr von den traditionellen religiösen Institutionen emanzipiert. Seine Antwort lautet: Christus ruft nicht zu einer neuen Religion auf, sondern zum Leben, und dieser Ruf gilt allen Menschen in einer Welt, in der wir nur noch gemeinsam leben und überleben können. Doch wo Leben bedroht und gefährdet ist, da ist Christus, der Gekreuzigte, solidarisch mit den Leidenden. Der Ort, an dem Christus am Ende für Bonhoeffer ist, ist die politische Konspiration, die ungesicherte Glaubenspraxis in der freiwilligen Schuldübernahme, die Begegnung mit den von aller Welt verlassenen Mitmenschen im Tegeler Gefängnis und in der Hölle des Konzentrations- und Vernichtungslagers. Hier entsteht die letzte und tiefste „Gemeinschaft der Heiligen". In dem Gedicht „Nächtliche Stimmen in Tegel" beschreibt Bonhoeffer die Ängste und Hoffnungen einer Nacht, die damit endet, dass der Mitgefangene aus der Nachbarzelle in den frühen Morgen-

---

[15] BONHOEFFER, Dietrich: *Nachfolge (1937)*. München: Kaiser, 1989, 30f.

stunden zur Hinrichtung abgeführt wird: „Ich gehe mit dir, Bruder, an jenen Ort, und ich höre dein letztes Wort: 'Bruder, wenn mir die Sonne verblich, lebe du für mich.'"[16] Der Bruder, von dem hier die Rede ist, ist nicht mehr allein der christliche Bruder, sondern der Bruder in gemeinsamen Leiden und gemeinsamer Hoffnung, der atheistische, sozialistische, jüdische Bruder. Am Ende seines Lebens ist Bonhoeffers Verständnis von Christusnachfolge weltlich, religionslos, solidarisch. Der Glaubensakt wird ein Lebensakt im „Beten und Tun des Gerechten unter den Menschen"[17].

Am 21.Juli 1944 schreibt Dietrich Bonhoeffer an Eberhard Bethge einen Brief, der so etwas wie ein Vermächtnis ist. In der Erwartung, früher oder später in den Untergang der Widerstandsbewegung mit hinein gezogen zu werden, legt er Rechenschaft ab über seinen Weg:

„Ich habe in den letzten Jahren mehr und mehr die tiefe Diesseitigkeit des Christentums kennen und verstehen gelernt. Nicht ein homo religiosus, sondern ein Mensch schlechthin ist der Christ, wie Jesus... Mensch war... Ich dachte, ich könnte glauben lernen, indem ich so etwas wie ein heiliges Leben zu führen versuchte... Später erfuhr ich, und ich erfahre es bis zur Stunde, dass man erst in der vollen Diesseitigkeit des Lebens glauben lernt."[18]

2. Die Forderung nach einer neuen Reformation.
Dorothee Sölles befreiungstheologische Aktualisierung

Die Wahrheit wollte sie wissen, deshalb studierte sie Theologie. Am Anfang war es ein intellektuelles Abenteuer, doch es wurde der Beginn einer abenteuerlichen Lebensreise, eine große Suche nach Heimat und Identität, nach Gerechtigkeit und Frieden, nach Gott und seinem Reich des Schalom. Auf dieser Reise wurde Dorothee Sölle irgendwann klar, dass sich Wahrheit nicht abstrakt definieren, sondern nur konkret erleben lässt. Diese Erkenntnis hat in eine radikale Lebenspraxis geführt, in das unbedingte Engagement für Gerechtigkeit und von da aus zu neuen Perspektiven über Gott und seine Wahrheit.

---

[16] Widerstand und Ergebung, DBW 8, 523.
[17] Ebd., 435: "unser Christsein wird heute nur in zweierlei bestehen: im Beten und im Tun des Gerechten unter den Menschen".
[18] Ebd., 541ff.

Dorothee Sölle hat sich in ihrem Denken von vielen Männern und Frauen der christlichen Tradition inspirieren lassen; einen lebenslangen Dialog hat sie jedoch mit Dietrich Bonhoeffer geführt, dessen fragmentarische Gedanken zu einem weltlich gelebten Christentum in ihrem Reden und Schreiben weiter gedacht und konkretisiert wurden. Dazu gehört nicht zuletzt der von Bonhoeffer geforderte Perspektivenwechsel, nämlich in der Nachfolge Jesu die großen Ereignisse der Weltgeschichte aus der Perspektive von unten, aus der Sicht der Leidenden sehen zu lernen. Eng damit verbunden ist die Aufforderung, in diesem Kontext eine neue Sprache für das alte Evangelium zu finden. Bonhoeffer wies darauf hin, dass dies nur möglich ist, wenn die Kirche ein anderes Selbstverständnis und eine neue Praxis entwickelt:

> „Unsere Kirche, die in diesen Jahren nur um ihre Selbsterhaltung gekämpft hat, als wäre sie ein Selbstzweck, ist unfähig, Träger des versöhnenden und erlösenden Wortes für die Menschen und die Welt zu sein. Darum müssen die früheren Worte kraftlos werden und verstummen, und unser Christsein wird heute nur in zweierlei bestehen: im Beten und im Tun des Gerechten unter den Menschen. Alles Denken, Reden und Organisieren in den Dingen des Christentums muss neugeboren werden aus diesem Beten und aus diesem Tun... Es ist nicht unsere Sache, den Tag vorauszusagen – aber der Tag wird kommen – an dem wieder Menschen berufen werden, das Wort Gottes so auszusprechen, dass sich die Welt darunter verändert und erneuert. Es wird eine neue Sprache sein, vielleicht ganz unreligiös, aber befreiend und erlösend, die Sprache einer neuen Gerechtigkeit und Wahrheit, die Sprache, die den Frieden Gottes mit den Menschen und das Nahen seines Reiches verkündigt."[19]

Dorothee Sölle gehörte zu den Menschen, die das Wort Gottes in einer neuen Sprache zu verkündigen verstanden. Zeit ihres Lebens ist sie freischaffende „Theologiearbeiterin" – so hat sie sich selbst genannt – gewesen, für die es in unserem Land und unserer Kirche kein Predigt- und Lehramt gab, die sich aber einen unübersehbaren LeserInnen und HörerInnenkreis zunächst außerhalb der Institutionen von Kirche und Universität geschaffen hat. Viele Menschen, die sich von der traditionellen Kirche, ihrer Erscheinung und Sprache abgewandt haben, finden in ihren Texten und Reden ebenso neue Hoffnung und Erkenntnis wie diejenigen Christinnen und Christen, die ihrer Kirche ein offenes, der Welt und den Menschen zugewandtes Gesicht geben wollen. In Verbindung mit ihrem Interesse für Kunst und Literatur und mit

---

[19] Ebd. 435f.

ihrer eigenen literarischen Begabung hat sie eine Sprachform geschaffen, mit der die Rede von Gott in eine säkularisierte Gesellschaft hinein neu gestaltet werden konnte. In ihren 1971 verfassten

„Thesen über die Kriterien des theologischen Interesses an Literatur" heißt es:

„Die Theologie findet in der Sprache der Kunst eine nicht-religiöse Interpretation der theologischen Begriffe.

Theologische Begriffe sind solche, die den Menschen in seiner Totalität aussprechen und die ihn auf sein ewiges, d.h. authentisches Leben beziehen, z.B. Sünde, Gnade, Sterben, Auferstehen, Gerechtigkeit, Frieden.

Das Entdecken der nicht-religiösen Interpretation, das die Theologie leisten soll, ist nicht mit der Reduktion auf eine theologische Nomenklatur abgegolten oder mit der vagen Parallelisierung dichterischer und theologischer Darstellungen. Entdeckt will gerade der Gehalt der in der religiösen Nomenklatur erstarrten Begriffe werden, gefunden ihre gegenwärtige Konkretion. ‚Sünde' oder ‚Gnade' sind theologische Leerformeln, deren einziger Wert darin liegt, dass sie uns zu einer Fragestellung verhelfen, auf die erst nicht-religiöse, weltliche Konkretion antwortet. Erst die Prädikate sagen, was das Subjekt sei.

Theologisch relevant ist, was uns öffnet, was ‚ein neues Organ in uns aufschließt' (Goethe), was uns aus der Versicherung des Gewussten herausnimmt, was uns mit den eigenen Klischees konfrontiert, was uns entlarvt, was unser Verhältnis zur Welt und damit uns selber ändert."[20]

Dass Dorothee Sölle glaubhaft von Gott reden konnte in einer Welt der Gewalt, hat mit dieser Bereitschaft, das Verhältnis zur Welt und damit sich selbst zu ändern, zu tun, damit, dass dieses Reden dem Protest gegen die Welt der Gewalt entsprungen und mit dem Tun des Gerechten unter den Menschen verbunden war.

Sie selbst hat immer wieder darauf hingewiesen, dass erst aus einer neuen persönlichen und politischen Praxis neue Worte für das alte Evangelium gefunden werden. Der Vorrang der Orthopraxie vor der Orthodoxie, den die Theologie der Befreiung betont, hat in ihrem Denken und Handeln Gestalt angenommen, in dem Wissen darum, dass die Praxis selbst immer wieder

---

[20] SÖLLE, Dorothee: Thesen über die Kriterien des theologischen Interesses an Literatur. *Almanach 4 für Literatur und Theologie.* Wuppertal: 1970, 206f.

zum Ort der Erkenntnis wird. Der von dem lateinamerikanischen Befreiungstheologen Gustavo Guiterrez formulierte erste und zweite Akt der Auslegung des Evangeliums wird so zum Charakteristikum theologischer Existenz heute: erst im bewussten Leben für die und mit den anderen, in Parteilichkeit und Solidarität wird sich in einem zweiten Akt der Auslegung der Sinn der Schrift, des Evangeliums, neu erschließen, und es werden sich neue Wege und Worte der Verkündigung einstellen. Auf dieses Experiment hat sich Dorothee Sölle in wachsender Konsequenz und mit ihrer ganzen Existenz eingelassen. Das hat ihr Reden von Gott glaubwürdig gemacht.

Glaubwürdig war dieses Reden von Gott auch deshalb, weil Sölles theologischer Ansatz gerade darin bestand, dieses Reden von Gott in Frage zu stellen: Wie kann man nach Auschwitz von einem Gott reden, „der alles so herrlich regieret"? Für sie bleibt zunächst die „Erfahrung vom Ende einer objektiven, allgemeinen, oder auch subjektiven, privaten, jedenfalls aber unmittelbaren Gewissheit", theologisch gesprochen: es bleibt die Erfahrung vom „Tode Gottes".[21] Diese Erfahrung kann nur dadurch aufgehoben werden, dass Christus diese Leerstelle besetzt: als Stellvertreter Gottes vor den Menschen und als Stellvertreter der Menschen vor Gott. In dieser Beziehung der Gegenseitigkeit, wird aber Gott in Christus auch in seiner Ohnmacht erlebt, der die Hilfe von Menschen braucht, um erkennbar zu werden. „Christen stehen bei Gott in seinem Leiden – das unterscheidet Christen von Heiden" hatte bereits Bonhoeffer in einem Brief aus dem Gefängnis geschrieben.[22] In einem späteren Kommentar zu diesem ersten „Kapitel Theologie nach dem ‚Tode Gottes'" schreibt Sölle:

> „Die Antworten, die hier gesucht werden, hängen mit Jesus von Nazareth zusammen, dem ‚Menschen-für-andere', wie Bonhoeffer ihn genannt hat. Nicht mehr kann Gott als Gewissheit des Herzens, als sozial repräsentiert in der Kirche vorausgesetzt werden. Wir fangen vielmehr am gottlosen Nullpunkt, den die entwickelte bürgerliche Gesellschaft darstellt, an, und nehmen wahr, dass Einer, der uns in vielen Brüdern und Schwestern begegnet, anders lebte als wir: Jesus, der mir verständliche und doch entfernte Bruder, mit dem ich mich ohne eine unvermittelte Gottesnaivität auf den Weg machen kann. Wenn es für mich eine theologisch-politische Kontinuität gibt, dann liegt

---

[21] SÖLLE, Dorothee: Stellvertretung. Ein Kapitel nach dem Tode Gottes. Stuttgart: Kreuz, 1965, 11.
[22] A.a.O., DBW 8, 515f.

sie in diesem Anfang bei dem Machtlosen, dem Leidenden und dem Hiesigen. Es ist klar, dass aus diesem Ansatz nicht gerade eine Siegerchristologie entstehen kann. Nicht: er hat's geschafft, darum auch wir, sondern: er wird gekreuzigt, jeden Tag. Mit ihm sein, sein Bild im Herzen tragen, ihm folgen heißt, sich eine Lebensperspektive zu eigen zu machen, die im wesentlichen, unüberbrückbaren Konflikt zur Gesellschaft, in der wir leben, steht."[23]

In dem von Dorothee Sölle 1968 für das erste politische Nachtgebet verfassten „Credo" heißt es:

Ich glaube an Jesus Christus
der Recht hatte, als er,
„ein einzelner, der nichts machen kann"
genau wie wir
an der Veränderung aller Zustände
arbeitete und darüber zugrunde ging
an ihm messend erkenne ich,
wie unsere Intelligenz verkrüppelt
unsere Phantasie erstickt
unsere Anstrengung vertan ist
weil wir nicht leben wie er lebte
jeden Tag habe ich Angst
dass er umsonst gestorben ist
weil er in unseren Kirchen verscharrt ist
weil wir seine Revolution verraten haben
..."[24]

So hätte es der Reformator Martin Luther vor 500 Jahren nicht gesagt. Trotzdem sind viele reformatorische Impulse, die von ihm ausgegangen sind, bei Dorothee Sölle wieder zu erkennen. Am Reformationstag des Jahres 1968 provozierte Dorothee Sölle in einer Fernsehsendung mit dem Thema "Brauchen wir eine neue Reformation"? mit folgenden Sätzen:

„Die Zustände in der evangelischen Kirche heute haben große Ähnlichkeit mit denen in der katholischen Kirche vor der Reformation. Damals wie heute stellen Menschen Fragen, auf die die Kirche keine Antwort weiß, weil sie sich mit der bestehenden wirtschaftlichen, sozialen und politischen Ordnung ohne

---

[23] Sölle, Stellvertretung, a.a.O., 11.

[24] SÖLLE, Dorothee/Steffensky, Fulbert (Hg.): *Politisches Nachtgebet in Köln*. Stuttgart/Mainz: Kreuz/Matthias Grünewald, 1970, 27.

Eine kritische Weiterführung reformatorischer Impulse 351

Vorbehalt identifiziert hat. Die wirklichen religiösen Fragen unserer Zeit werden von den unruhigen Christen gestellt, die Gerechtigkeit und Frieden für alle verlangen, die sich mit den bestehenden Zuständen nicht abfinden können, die die Humanisierung der Welt als die Sache Christi ansehen."[25]

Ausgehend von der These, dass sich die Reformation Martin Luthers deshalb ausbreitete, weil die Menschen fromm sein wollten, sieht Dorothee Sölle auch in der heutigen Gesellschaft bei vielen Menschen diesen Wunsch, fürchtet aber, dass ihr guter Wille an den Kirchen scheitert, denn auf ihre „theologisch-politischen Fragen antwortet die Kirche nicht oder nur ganz allgemein", sie verschanzt sich hinter einem „dogmatischen Lehrsystem" und einer „hierarchisch aufgebauten Verwaltung". Programmatisch erklärt Sölle:

„Für die Reformation, die wir brauchen, stelle ich drei Thesen auf:
Christus hat die Leidenden formuliert, die Kirche formuliert sich.
Christus lebte mit den Armen, die Kirche gehört zur reichen, satten Welt.
Christus hat Partei ergriffen, die Kirche verhält sich neutral."[26]

Mit dieser Kritik knüpfte Dorothee Sölle nicht nur an Martin Luther, sondern auch an Dietrich Bonhoeffer an, der 1944 im Gefängnis schrieb: „Kirche ist nur Kirche, wenn sie für andere da ist." Dazu sagte Sölle:

"Unsere Kirche hat sich nie klar dafür entschieden, diesen Satz ernst zu nehmen – sie ist immer und vor allem Kirche für sich selbst geblieben. Sie spricht sich nicht für die Stummgewordenen aus (…) Sobald sie das täte, käme sie in Konflikte mit unserer Gesellschaft, die so viele Menschen zum Verstummen und zur Resignation zwingt. Ängstlich bemüht, Konflikte zu vermeiden und jedes Element von Protest aus dem Protestantismus heraus zu halten, lässt sie sich auf eine verharmloste entpolitisierte, individuell-religiöse Verkündigung beschränken."[27]

Ausgehend von diesen Positionen hat Dorothee Sölle das Element des Protestes im Protestantismus neu zu beleben versucht. Sie war Avantgarde und Fanal, Symbol- und Identifikationsfigur, sie war eine aufgeklärte und darum politische und kämpferische Frau. Sie hat für das Politische Nachtgebet ebenso gestanden wie für die Blockadeaktionen vor Militärstützpunkten. Sie hat Wegzeichen der Hoffnung gesetzt für alle, die aufbrechen wollten in das

---

[25] Fernsehmanuskript, von F.S. freundlich zur Verfügung gestellt.
[26] Ebd.
[27] Ebd.

gelobte Land der Freiheit, Gleichheit und Geschwisterlichkeit und die sich dabei oft genug in der Wüste wiederfanden. Sie hat die Befreiungsversuche und Emanzipationsprozesse einer unruhigen Generation im Aufbruch in ihrer Widersprüchlichkeit begleitet und dem Widerstand gegen die Strukturen der Gewalt eine spirituelle Dimension verliehen, die über die Erfolge und Niederlagen des Tages hinausreicht. Sie hat in einer Sprache geredet und geschrieben, die die biblischen Texte als Zeugnisse der Befreiung erkennbar werden ließ.

Das politische Nachtgebet, das 1968 zum ersten Mal stattfand, öffnete die Kirche wieder für Menschen, die sich einbringen wollten in die politischen und sozialen Fragen ihrer Zeit, die eine neue öffentliche Diskussion und Kultur forderten, die gegen die vielfachen Erfahrungen von Gewalt eine Vision von Frieden und Gerechtigkeit entwickeln wollten. Die etablierten Kirchenleitungen verschlossen ihnen damals die Türen, doch die neue reformatorische Bewegung ließ sich nicht aufhalten. Denn diesmal ging es nicht um eine konfessionelle Auseinandersetzung, sondern um eine ökumenische Basisbewegung einer Kirche von unten gegen die Kirche von oben in beiden Konfessionen. So sagt es Dorothee Sölle am Ende ihres Reformationsvortrags programmatisch:

„Eine Kirche der Armut, eine Kirche des politischen Engagements – das ist ein Leitbild, das die konfessionellen Gremien hinter sich lässt (…) Die Hierarchien sind sich weithin einig gegen diese antiautoritäre Bewegung der Christen in beiden Lagern."[28]

Dass sich die kirchliche Basis gegen die Hierarchie stellen darf und muss, wenn sie nur so das Evangelium von Christus wieder zur Geltung bringen kann, ist gutes reformatorisches Erbe. Dass sie allerdings auch politisches Engagement im Sinne einer befreiungstheologischen Perspektive wahrnehmen sollte, geht über die traditionelle lutherische Zwei-Reiche-Lehre deutlich hinaus. Dass die reformatorische Freiheit auch Freiheit von Gewalt und Ausbeutung bedeuten sollte, wurde allzu bald und allzu lange zugunsten einer individualistisch gedeuteten Rechtfertigungslehre vergessen.

Deutlich wird dies für Dorothee Sölle an der Entpolitisierung der Gestalt Jesu und seines Todes. Mit Luther stellt sie die das Kreuz Jesu in den Mittelpunkt des Glaubens, will die Passion Jesu aber nicht trennen von seinem Le-

---

[28] Ebd.

ben und Wirken. Für Sölle ist das Leiden Jesu die Konsequenz seiner herrschaftskritischen Praxis, nicht das von Gott gewollte Sühneopfer.[29] Jesus ist nicht der alleinige Erlöser, sondern ist umgeben von Brüdern und Schwestern, sein Tod ist nicht das blutige Sühneopfer, mit dem die Vergebung der Sünden erkauft wird. Dorothee Sölle erteilt der Sühneopfertheologie eine deutliche Absage. Diese degradiert die Menschen zu passiven Empfängern, die sich nicht verändern müssen. Sie ist überzeugt, dass dies nicht das Interesse Jesu gewesen sei. Jesus rufe vielmehr dazu auf, ihn geschwisterlich auf seinem Weg zu begleiten.[30] Ihm auf diesem Weg zu folgen heißt, die Perspektive der Opfer einzunehmen, in den Opfern der Gewaltgeschichte den Gekreuzigten selber wahrzunehmen: „Jesus wird in der Todesqual sein bis zum Ende der Welt", sagt sie mit Blaise Pascal. *„Die radikale Passion für die Gerechtigkeit, die Parteinahme für die Enterbten, führt in die Passion des Leidensweges"*[31] – wer Jesus auf diesem Weg folgen will, wird selbst in den Widerstand geführt, der Leidenschaft und Leidensbereitschaft voraussetzt.

Hier geht Dorothee Sölle kritisch über die von Martin Luther angestoßenen reformatorischen Impulse hinaus, um die vielfältigen, in der Geschichte oftmals unterdrückten Traditionen des „linken Flügels" der Reformation wieder aufzunehmen: die sozialrevolutionäre Praxis Thomas Müntzers, die radikale Friedensethik der Quäker, den konfessionsübergreifenden mystischen Protest, das „Nein zur Welt wie sie jetzt ist". In oft provozierender und radikaler Weise hat Dorothee Sölle den Versuch unternommen, alle diese Strömungen in die Spiritualität und Praxis einer „neuen Reformation" einzubringen, die sich nicht mehr an Konfessionen festmachen lässt, sondern an einem gemeinsamen, ökumenischen Engagement für Gerechtigkeit, Frieden und Bewahrung der Schöpfung. So wird sie am Ende ihres Reformationsvortrags sagen: *„Eine Reformation, die nicht von allen Christen gemeinsam getragen wird, ist undenkbar."*

---

[29] Dazu s. den Beitrag von Franz Hinkelammert in Band 1 dieser Reihe.
[30] Vgl. SÖLLE, Dorothee: Der Erstgeborene aus dem Tod. Dekonstruktion und Rekonstruktion von Christologie. In: CRÜSEMANN, Marlene u.a. (Hrsg.): *Christus und seine Geschwister*. Gütersloh : Gütersloher Verlagshaus, 2011, 180.
[31] Ebd., 184.

Abstract

One of the most compelling and relevant contributions of Bonhoeffer was his radical criticism of "cheap grace" and the disastrous consequences of the two kingdoms teaching. Bonhoeffer called for consequential discipleship, not only for the institutional church but for the life of the world.

Soelle renewed this challenge by calling in the late 1960s for a "new reformation", in order for the church to serve as a genuine counterculture representing the authentic body of Christ. The heritage of Bonhoeffer was preserved and extended in an exceptional way and contributes to the ongoing challenge of radicalizing the reformation in light of our contemporary global crisis.

AUTHORS/AUTORINNEN UND AUTOREN

Charles Amjad-Ali, Ph.D., Th.D., The Martin Luther King, Jr. Professor of Justice and Christian Community (Emeritus) and Director of the Islamic Studies Program (Emeritus) at Luther Seminary, St. Paul, MN/USA; The Desmond Tutu Prof. of Ecumenical Theology and Social Transformation in Africa, University of Western Cape, Cape Town/South Africa.

Claudete Beise Ulrich, Dr. theol., Professorin an der Faculdade Unida em Vitória/Espírito Santo/Brasilien. Z. Zt. Missionsakademie an der Universität Hamburg zum Schreiben eines Buches über „Frauen und Reformation".

- Professor at Faculdade Unida em Vitória/Espírito Santo/Brazil. Presently at Mission Academy, University of Hamburg/Germany, writing a book on „Women and Reformation".

Klara Butting, Dr. theol., apl. Professorin für Altes Testament an der Universität Bochum, Leiterin des Zentrums für biblische Spiritualität und gesellschaftliche Verantwortung an der Woltersburger Mühle/Ülzen, Autorin und Herausgeberin der Jungen Kirche.

- Professor of Old Testament at the University of Bochum, Director of the Center for Biblical Spirituality and Social Responsibility at Woltersburger Muehle, Uelzen/Germany, Author and Editor of the journal Junge Kirche.

Paul Chung, Th.D., ehemaliger Assistenzprofessor am Luther Seminary, St. Paul, MN/USA. Jetzt lehrt er Reformationstheologie und -geschichte am Graduate Theological Union und Pacific Lutheran Theological Seminary und ist Pastor der Holy Shepherd Lutheran Church, California, U.S.A.

- Has served as Associate professor at Luther Seminary. Currently he teaches Reformation history and theology at the Graduate Theological Union and Pacific Lutheran Theological Seminary, while serving as pastor at Holy Shepherd Lutheran Church, California, U.S.A.

Ulrich Duchrow, Dr. theol., apl. Professor für Systematische Theologie, Universität Heidelberg.

- Professor of Systematic Theology, University of Heidelberg.

Antonio Gonzáles Fernández, Dr. theol., Direktor für Studien und Publikationen an der Xavier Zubiri Stiftung in Madrid und Theologieprofessor am Centro Teológico Koinonía in Madrid, Spanien. Autor mehrerer Bücher, darunter „God's Reign and the End of Empires" und „The Gospel of Faith and Justice".

- Director of Studies and Publications at the Xavier Zubiri Foundation (Madrid) and Theology Professor at Centro Teológico Koinonía in Madrid, Spain. He is the author of several books, including God's Reign and the End of Empires and The Gospel of Faith and Justice.

Karl Koop, Ph.D., Professor für Geschichte und Theologie, Direktor des Graduiertenkollegs für Theologie und Diakonie, Kanadische Mennonitische Universität, Winnipeg/Kanada. Seine Forschungsschwerpunkte sind Täuferstudien, Ökumene und Ekklesiologie.

- Professor of History and Theology, Director, Graduate School of Theology and Ministry, Canadian Mennonite University, Winnipeg/Canada. His research interests include Anabaptist studies, ecumenism, and issues related to ecclesiology.

Craig L. Nessan, Th.D., Professor für kontextuelle Theologie und Dekan am Wartburg Theologischen Seminar. Seine Forschungsinteressen sind Befreiungstheologie, Ethik, Mission und Kirchenführung.

- Academic Dean and Professor of Contextual Theology, Wartburg Theological Seminary, Dubuque, Iowa/USA. His research interests include liberation theology, ethics, mission, and church leadership.

Jaime Adrián Prieto Valladares, Dr. theol. an der Universität Hamburg/Deutschland (1992); derzeit Post-Doc-Studien zu dem Gebiet der Geschichte, Kultur, Religion und der Afro-Brasilianischen Literatur an der Fakultät der Künste und Humanwissenschaften, Unigranrio, Rio de Janeiro/Brasilien. Autor des Buches "Mission und Migration", Mitglied der Mennonitischen Kirche Costa Rica.

- Ph.D. at University of Hamburg (1992), presently Post-Doc-Studies on history, culture and African-Brasilian literature at the Faculty of Art and Humanities, Unigranrio, Rio de Janeiro/Brazil. Author of the Book "Mission und Migration", Mitglied der Mennonitischen Kirche Costa Rica

Santhosh J. Sahayadoss, Th.D., Professor in der Abteilung Christian Theology am New Theological College, Dehradun, Indien. Autor von "Martin Luther on Political and Social Issues: His Relevance for Church and Society in India."

- Associate Professor in the department of Christian Theology at New Theological College, Dehradun, India. He is the author of Martin Luther on Political and Social Issues: His Relevance for Church and Society in India.

Renate Wind, Dr. theol., Professorin für Altes und Neues Testament an der Evangelischen Hochschule für angewandte Wissenschaften in Nürnberg und Pfarrerin. Viele Veröffentlichungen, darunter Biographien über Dietrich Bonhoeffer, Camilo Torres und Dorothee Sölle.

- Professor for Old and New Testament and Church History at the Lutheran University of Applied Sciences in Nürnberg and a Protestant Pastor. She is widely published and the author of biographies of Dietrich Bonhoeffer, Camilo Torres, and Dorothee Sölle.

Website des Projekts / Website of the project

www.reformation-radical.com/www.radicalizing-reformation.com

Darin ist der Fortgang des Projekts zu verfolgen. Außerdem sind hier die Abstracts der in den 5 Bänden veröffentlichten Kapitel in der jeweils nicht gedruckten Sprache zu finden, ebenso wie deren Übersetzungen, soweit vorhanden.

Here you find information about the follow-up of the project, the abstracts of the chapters, and the translations of these, if available.